# RADIO
## WARFARE

# RADIO WARFARE

## OSS and CIA Subversive Propaganda

### LAWRENCE C. SOLEY

PRAEGER

New York
Westport, Connecticut
London

7/9/90

49

**Library of Congress Cataloging-in-Publication Data**

Soley, Lawrence C.
    Radio warfare : OSS and CIA subversive propaganda / Lawrence C.
Soley.
      p.    cm.
    Bibliography: p.
    Includes index.
    ISBN 0–275–93051–3
    1. World War, 1939–1945—Propaganda.  2. Propaganda, American.
3. Radio broadcasting—United States.  4. United States. Central
Intelligence Agency.  5. United States. Office of Strategic
Services.  I. Title.
D810.P7U53   1989
940.54′886′73—dc19         88–25187

Library of Congress Catalog Card Number: 88–25187
ISBN: 0–275–93051–3

First published in 1989

Praeger Publishers, One Madison Avenue, New York, NY   10010
A division of Greenwood Press, Inc.

Printed in the United States of America

The paper used in this book complies with the Permanent
Paper Standard issued by the National Information Standards
Organization (Z39.48—1984).

10  9  8  7  6  5  4  3  2  1

# CONTENTS

# PREFACE

Although literacy is more widespread today than during any previous period, world illiteracy remains high. In the early 1970s, an estimated 780 million people over the age of 15 were illiterate; by 1980, the number reached 820 million. In Africa, about three-fifths of the population is illiterate, and in Asia, approximately one-half. It is therefore no surprise that ideological wars are primarily fought with radio, not the pen or sword. The illiterate masses of the world can understand the messages that they listen to on their radio receivers but cannot read printed messages. *Clandestine Radio Broadcasting* (Praeger, 1987) discussed the radio wars that have been fought in Europe, Asia, Latin America, and Africa during the last three decades. I was senior author of that book. *Radio Warfare*, by contrast, discusses how the strategy and tactics of radio warfare evolved.

*Radio Warfare* examines the propaganda strategy of Hitler's Germany, British responses to this strategy, and the effect of British actions on U.S. psychwar techniques. The book's emphasis is U.S. subversive warfare during World War II, for studies of British and German psychological warfare strategy during this conflict have been described elsewhere. Sefton Delmer's *Black Boomerang* (1962), Charles Cruickshank's *The Fourth Arm* (1977), and Ellic Howe's *The Black Game* (1982) are studies of British subversive warfare techniques. J. A. Cole's *Lord Haw-Haw and William Joyce* (1965) and Willi Boelke's *Die Macht des Radios* (1977) examine German subversive propaganda. *Radio Warfare* is the first study of the United States' radio warfare methods.

An understanding of World War II subversive propaganda operations is essential to an understanding of current U.S. tactics, because the

Central Intelligence Agency (CIA), the principal subversive warfare agency, evolved from the wartime Office of Strategic Services (OSS). Many directors of the CIA were in OSS or had knowledge of OSS psychwar operations. How the CIA is similar to and different from its wartime predecessor is one of the focuses of *Radio Warfare*. Although all conclusions in the book concerning the OSS and CIA are mine, I must thank Gordon Auchincloss, Joseph Matovich, William Morwood, Abraham Polonsky, James Withrow, and John Zuckerman for their assistance and willingness to discuss their experiences with me. They were responsible for the creation and execution of many of the psychwar stations described in *Radio Warfare*. Their help was essential to my understanding of OSS and its subversive radio operations.

# ABBREVIATIONS

| | |
|---|---|
| ABSIE | American Broadcasting Station in Europe |
| ACLU | American Civil Liberties Union |
| AGFRTS | Air and Ground Forces Resources and Technical Staff |
| BBC | British Broadcasting Corporation |
| CBS | Columbia Broadcasting System |
| CIA | Central Intelligence Agency |
| CIAA | Coordinator of Inter-American Affairs |
| CIG | Central Intelligence Group |
| COI | Coordinator of Information |
| DCI | Director of Central Intelligence |
| DNB | Deutsche Nachrichten Büro (German news service) |
| EH | Electra House (British Department of Propaganda in Enemy Countries) |
| ETO | European Theater of Operations |
| FBI | Federal Bureau of Investigation |
| FBIS | Foreign Broadcast Intelligence Service of FCC |
| FCC | Federal Communications Commission |
| FIS | Foreign Information Service of COI/OWI |
| G–2 | U.S. Army Military Intelligence |
| GS(R) | British War Office General Staff |
| HUAC | House Un-American Activities Committee |
| IRIS | Interim Research and Intelligence Service |

| | |
|---|---|
| JCS | U.S. Joint Chiefs of Staff |
| KPD | German Communist Party |
| MBS | Mutual Broadcasting System |
| MI(R) | British Military Intelligence (Research) |
| MO | Morale Operations branch of OSS |
| NBC | National Broadcasting Company |
| ND | Neues Deutschland (U.S.-created) |
| NID | British Naval Intelligence Division |
| NSDAP | German National Socialist (Nazi) Party |
| NSC | National Security Council |
| OFF | Office of Facts and Figures |
| OGR | Office of Government Reports |
| OKW | Oberkommando der Wehrmacht (German High Command) |
| ONI | Office of Naval Intelligence |
| OPC | Office of Policy Coordination of CIA |
| OSO | Office of Special Operations of CIA |
| OSS | Office of Strategic Services |
| OWI | Office of War Information |
| POW | Prisoner of War |
| PWB/AFHQ | Psychological Warfare Branch/Allied Force Headquarters |
| PWB/12th AG | Psychological Warfare Branch/12th Army Group |
| PWD | Psychological Warfare Division |
| PWE | British Political Warfare Executive |
| PWS | Psychological Warfare Service |
| RCA | Radio Corporation of America |
| SACO | Sino-American Cooperation Organization |
| SHAEF | Supreme Headquarters Allied Expeditionary Force |
| SI | Special Intelligence branch of OSS |
| SIS | Special Intelligence Service |
| SO | Special Operations branch of OSS |
| SOE | British Special Operations Executive |
| SO1 | British Special Operations 1 |
| UNITA | National Union for the Total Independence of Angola |
| UPI | United Press International |

# RADIO
## WARFARE

# 1

## SUBVERSIVE RADIO BROADCASTING

Just after 2 a.m. every night, "Radio 1212" signed on with its signature tune of "Twelve twelve calling... twelve twelve calling... twelve twelve calling." Twelve twelve was the wavelength on which the station operated—1212 meters, or 247 kilohertz. Its broadcasts provided nightly news about Gen. Dwight Eisenhower's march toward Germany. The radio station claimed to be German-based and -operated, but unlike other Third Reich stations, gave exact news about happenings on the western and eastern fronts.

A decade after "Radio 1212" operated, Guatemalans heard broadcasts from a station called "Voice of Liberation," which called on democratically elected President Jacobo Arbenz to resign. Arbenz, the station claimed, was attempting to make Guatemala a Communist dictatorship. On June 27, 1954, the station announced that two columns of rebel soldiers were converging on the capital city. Shortly thereafter, President Arbenz resigned and fled the country. Rebel military leader Col. Castillo Armas assumed the Guatemalan presidency. He was the first in a series of military dictators to rule Guatemala. In late 1960, a hitherto unknown station, "Radio Swan," made similar demands of Fidel Castro, whom the station referred to as a "Communist dictator." Unlike Arbenz, Castro refused to resign. In the early morning of April 17, 1961, Radio Swan began broadcasting cryptic messages such as "Look at the rainbow... the fish will rise soon." That morning the Bay of Pigs invasion was launched.

Ten years later, a radio station purportedly operated by backers of deposed Prince Sihanouk called upon Cambodian girls to assist Sihanouk in his bid to return to power by sleeping with North Vietnamese soldiers.

The broadcasts of this "Voice of the National United Front of Kampuchea" insulted traditional Cambodian morality, was a discredit to Prince Sihanouk's moral stature, and admitted that North Vietnamese troops were in Cambodia, something that Sihanouk and North Vietnam had long denied.

A station calling itself the "Free Voice of Iran" was first heard during 1980, claiming to broadcast from liberated territory within Iran. The radio station reported that Ayatollah Khomeini had usurped power from the legal president, Shahpur Bakhtiar. Like its predecessors, the Free Voice of Iran demanded that Khomeini resign or face civil war. At the same time, but half-way around the world, another clandestine station, "Radio Quince de Septiembre," was first heard. It claimed to broadcast from Nicaragua and demanded that the recently installed Sandinista government abdicate power. Having betrayed the revolution, the station said, the Sandinistas were unfit to lead the nation.

Although broadcasting forty years apart, to different continents, and under different political and military circumstances, Radio 1212 and Radio Quince de Septiembre, as well as the other stations, have one thing in common—they are United States-sponsored clandestine stations. Clandestine stations are illegal political stations that advocate civil war, revolution, or rebellion. Clandestine stations provide misleading information as to their sponsorship, transmitter location, or raison d'être. Radio 1212 claimed to be located in Germany and operated by a group of loyal Rhinelanders critical of Nazi censorship, but was actually operated by the Psychological Warfare Branch of the 12th Army Group. The station broadcast from Luxemburg. Radio 1212 misrepresented its source, station location, and raison d'être. The station mixed verifiable news information with rumors and falsifications. The rumors and falsifications were designed to undermine German war morale. Later, Radio 1212 attempted to start an anti-Nazi revolution by reporting that uprisings had already occurred in several cities.

Voice of Liberation claimed to be located in Guatemala, but its transmitters were actually located in Nicaragua and on Swan Island, Honduras. The station was operated by CIA agents and several Guatemalans trained at a CIA base in Miami. Most of what the station broadcast was falsified: the station didn't broadcast under dangerous physical circumstances; Castillo Armas had few troops—300, not the 5,000 that the station claimed; and two rebel columns never marched on Guatemala City. Radio Swan contended that it was a commercial radio station owned by the Gibraltar Steamship Company. The Gibraltar Steamship Company was a CIA cover headed by Thomas Dudley Cabot, a former director of the State Department Office of International Security Affairs. Like Voice of Liberation, this station was located on Swan Island. The station was designed for one purpose—to undermine Castro, not sell commercials.[1]

The Voice of the National United Front of Kampuchea that exhorted Cambodian girls to sleep with North Vietnamese soldiers was neither based in Cambodia, as claimed, nor operated by backers of Prince Sihanouk. The station broadcast from a CIA complex in Laos. The Voice was one of a number of clandestine stations emanating from the complex; other stations broadcast to North Vietnam, South Vietnam, Thailand, and Laos. The CIA-operated Voice of the National United Front of Kampuchea imitated Prince Sihanouk's high-pitched, distinctive voice. This "Sihanouk" frequently declared his allegiance to "Mao Tse-tung thought," admitted that North Vietnamese troops mistreated Cambodians, and joyfully recalled how he and the Kampuchean Communist Party (or Khmer Rouge) frequently clashed during the 1960s. The Khmer Rouge was the largest and most powerful faction in the National United Front. The purpose of the clandestine station was to discredit Sihanouk, who had been deposed in an unpopular 1970 coup led by Gen. Lon Nol, a friend and ally of the United States. The National United Front opposed Lon Nol and the massive U.S. military presence in Indochina.[2]

Shortly after the Free Voice of Iran signed on in 1980, U.S. newspapers reported that the station was operated by Gholam Oveissi, a general under deposed Shah Mohammad Reza Pahlavi.[3] Oveissi, in exile from Iran, was a strong supporter of U.S.-Iranian military ties during the Shah's rule. One newspaper, the now-defunct *Cleveland Press*, reported in a front-page story that the radio's operation signaled the end of Ayatollah Khomeini's rule.[4] A week later, the CIA admitted that it was behind the Free Voice of Iran.[5] The station's transmitters were located in Egypt, not Iran as claimed. Egyptian president Anwar Sadat, a friend of the deposed Shah, gave the CIA permission to use its transmitters in exchange for radar equipment.

Radio Quince de Septiembre was the secret broadcasting station of the Nicaraguan Democratic Force, a counterrevolutionary (or contra) guerrilla army composed of former members of dictator Anastasio Somoza's National Guard. The FDN was based in Honduras, from where it broadcast to Nicaragua. The contras were backed and financed by the United States. Until February 1986, funding for the station was covertly provided by the Reagan administration from the CIA's general fund, over which President Reagan and then-CIA director William Casey had wide discretionary power. Covert funding was necessary because Congress prohibited the administration and U.S. government agencies from giving military assistance to the rebels when it appropriated $27 million for nonlethal contra aid in 1984. In fact, the bill appropriating the $27 million expressly prohibited the CIA from distributing the money because Congress feared that CIA personnel might allow the contras to buy military or paramilitary equipment rather than food and clothing, something that Congress did not want to happen. Congress's fears were based on previous CIA activities in Nicaragua, which included the distribution of a manual to the contras that recommended, among other things, assassinating Nicaraguan officials.[6]

During the 1940s and early 1950s, clandestine radio operations were defined as a tactic of "psychological warfare." The 1950 U.S. Army field manual entitled *Psychological Warfare Operations* contains a section on clandestine station operations. During the late 1950s and 1960s, acknowledging that the United States was not at war but that tactics like clandestine broadcasting could nonetheless still be used, the term "psychological operations" replaced the term "psychological warfare" in government and military vocabularies. The U.S. army even renamed its manual *Psychological Operations*.[7] During the 1970s, the term "secret wars" was used to refer to the same tactics and strategies that had previously been defined as "psychological warfare."

Under President Nixon, U.S.-sponsored secret wars were managed by the "40 Committee," comprised of Henry Kissinger, representing the National Security Council; Attorney General John Mitchell; and representatives of the State and Defense departments and the Joint Chiefs of Staff.[8] Clandestine stations operated by the CIA broadcast to countries such as Cambodia and Laos where the United States was conducting its secret wars. The term "secret wars," with its implication of potentially greater military involvement, was replaced by "covert action" in the early 1980s. "Covert action" is a more publicly palatable term than secret wars, but involves essentially the same activities. Like Nixon, President Reagan developed a committee, sometimes referred to as the "208 Committee" because it met in room 208 of the Old Executive Office Building, that directed the "covert actions." Covert actions were conducted by the United States in Afghanistan, Angola, Cambodia, Ethiopia, Libya, Nicaragua, Poland, and Surinam.[9] Clandestine stations broadcast to all of these countries, although the United States was probably not involved in the operation of all of the stations.

The Afghan mujahedin, who oppose the Marxist government in Kabul, operate several clandestine stations with foreign help. The stations broadcast from within Afghanistan and from abroad. At least one of the stations, "Voice of the Islamic Revolution in Afghanistan," broadcasts from Iran. The United States sponsors an aboveground radio program entitled "Radio Free Afghanistan" that is transmitted over Radio Free Europe-Radio Liberty facilities. The National Union for the Total Independence of Angola (UNITA) operates a clandestine station called "Voice of Resistance of the Black Cockerel." UNITA is the guerrilla army headed by Jonas Savimbi that opposes the pro-Soviet government headquartered in Luanda. The clandestine station claims to broadcast from UNITA-controlled territory in Angola, but is probably located in South Africa. Several clandestine stations broadcast to Cambodia: Voice of Democratic

Kampuchea, Voice of the National Army of Democratic Kampuchea, Voice of the Khmers, and Voice of the Joint Resistance. All of the clandestine stations are operated by guerrilla armies that oppose the Vietnamese-backed government of Heng Samrin. The Ethiopian government of Mengistu Haile Mariam is bombarded by clandestine broadcasts sponsored by the Eritrean People's Liberation Front (EPLF), a secessionist guerrilla army with Marxist leanings; the Tigre People's Liberation Front, which is allied with the EPLF; and the West Somali and Abo Liberation Fronts, which are supported by the Somali government. A clandestine station called "Voice of the Libyan People" broadcasts against Libyan leader Muhammar Qadhaffi. It is believed that this station, like the Free Voice of Iran, transmits from Egypt. Clandestine stations operated by the outlawed Solidarity labor union broadcast sporadically from within Poland. Solidarity has even managed to clandestinely break into television newscasts with its messages. The clandestine "Radio Free Surinam" appeared in late 1983 and broadcasts against the government there.[10]

Two things distinguish the secret wars conducted by the Reagan administration in Afghanistan, Angola, Nicaragua, and elsewhere from those of previous administrations: one, the wars were overt rather than covert, despite being referred to as "covert actions"; and two, they were waged with the assistance of private organizations that received funds from the U.S. government. The openness of U.S. assistance to rebel groups was the result of laws enacted following Nixon's presidency and the Reagan administration's belief that the Soviet Union constituted an expansionist empire that respected only one thing—force. Following public disclosures of Nixon's secret wars, Congress limited presidential prerogatives in conducting secret and not-so-secret wars. Congress passed the War Powers Act in 1973; the amendment to the Foreign Assistance Act in 1974, which required that presidentially approved CIA ventures be described to the appropriate committees of Congress; and the Clark Amendment in 1976. The Clark Amendment prohibited direct or indirect military involvement in Angola, where the CIA had been covertly aiding UNITA and an even weaker guerrilla faction, the National Front for the Liberation of Angola. The effect of such legislation was that secret wars became increasing public.

The Reagan administration viewed pro-Soviet governments in Angola, Ethiopia, and Nicaragua as Soviet puppets rather than indigenous governments. It followed that rebels who opposed these governments were fighting Soviet Communist expansion. To limit Soviet expansion, the Reagan administration adopted a policy of arming anticommunist "freedom fighters." The *Washington Post* reported that tales of heroic freedom fighters, battling against vastly superior weapons, "captured the imagination of President Reagan."[11] The policy of arming rebel groups was, of course, pursued for reasons other than that it captured the president's imagination: the policy was believed to be a method that could slowly "bleed" the USSR at minimal cost to the United States; provided the United States with additional bargaining chips in negotiations with the Soviet Union; and had major domestic political benefits for the president. President Reagan, as a result of his public support for freedom fighters, appeared as a strong rather than "wimpish" president who did more than his predecessors to combat Soviet expansionism. The policy was also very popular with immigrants who entered the United States from Cuba, Vietnam, Cambodia, and other countries where Communist governments had come to power. Because of the president's policies, they gave the Republican party substantial monetary and political support.[12]

In fall 1985, President Reagan belatedly adopted UNITA's cause as his own and lobbied for the repeal of the Clark Amendment. The repeal of the amendment led to a two-step policy of arming the Angolan rebels: providing them first with intelligence and communications and afterward supplying them with arms. In Afghanistan, U.S. financing of the mujahedin reached $500 million annually, but there were consistent reports that much of the aid, which was shipped through Pakistan, never reached the rebels. An estimated $12 million was given annually to Cambodian anti-communist rebels. In 1986, Congress appropriated $4 million specifically for guerrillas supporting Prince Sihanouk. The aid was used for buying medicine and food and for upgrading the transmitter of their clandestine station, Voice of the Khmers, so that it could reach all of Cambodia. Under intense pressure from the White House, Congress approved a $100 million aid package for the contras in June 1986. The contras obtained additional financing at the end of 1986 to construct a new clandestine station called Radio Liberation. The station was not only built with U.S. assistance, but plans for it were unveiled at a press conference held by Elliot Abrams, the assistant secretary of state for inter-american affairs. In Ethiopia, Libya, and Surinam, the Reagan administration financed opposition political factions rather than guerrilla movements.[13]

Large-scale assistance was also provided to opposition organizations and guerrillas through private channels. The National Endowment for Democracy, a private anti-communist organization established in 1983, received $53.7 million in U.S. government funds to conduct propaganda abroad. The National Endowment gave the Solidarity labor union in Poland money to print underground periodicals. Some of the money was undoubtedly used for clandestine broadcasting. The board of directors of the National Endowment included Frank Fahrenkopf, chairman of the Republican National Committee; former secretary of state Henry Kissinger; and Charles Manatt, former chairman of the Democratic National Committee. The endowment's chairman, John Richardson, was president of Radio Free Europe during the 1960s when the station was covertly funded by the CIA. Richardson was assistant secretary of state for education and cultural affairs under presidents Nixon and Ford and later worked with National Endowment president Carl Gershman at the Freedom House, another private anti-communist organization. During the early 1980s, the Freedom House collected money to buy transmitters for making clandestine broadcasts to Afghanistan. The National Endowment also provided funding for the Nicaraguan opposition newspaper, *La Prensa*. Other private organizations that provided anti-Sandinista Nicaraguans with aid during the last decade were CAUSA International, the Latin American political organization of Reverend Sun Myung Moon's Unification Church; anti-Castro groups headquartered in Miami; retired Air Force Maj. Gen. Richard Secord's Stanford Trading company; and the World Anti-Communist League, headed by retired general John K. Singlaub. The latter group raised money for the contras to conduct "psychological operations" against the Sandinista government.[14]

The United States has directly or indirectly sponsored numerous clandestine stations over the past four decades, but it is not alone in this. The Soviet Union and its Eastern European allies have also been frequent sponsors of clandestine broadcasts. During the 1980s, the "Voice of the Turkish Communist Party" and "Our Radio" broadcast to Turkey from East Germany and Romania. Our Radio first appeared in 1958 and has broadcast continuously since. The "National Voice of Iran" broadcasts to Iran from the Soviet Union, and another station, "Voice of Iranian Toilers," broadcasts against Ayatollah Khomeini from a transmitter in Afghanistan. The National Voice signed on in 1959. During the 1970s, several clandestine stations broadcast from the Eastern bloc: "Radio Independent Spain," "Radio Free Portugal," "Voice of Truth" and "Voice of the Emigrant." Radio Independent Spain was the voice of the outlawed Spanish Communist Party. It broadcast anti-Franco material to Spain between 1941 and 1977. Radio Free Portugal broadcast against the Salazar and Caetano dictatorships for twelve years before being silenced in 1974. Like Radio Independent Spain, Radio Free Portugal broadcast from transmitters in Romania and Hungary. The Voice of Truth broadcast to Greece from Romania and East Germany until 1975. The station operated for thirty years. It first appeared in 1944 as "Free Greece Radio." Voice of the Emigrant originated in East Germany and broadcast to Italian emigrant workers in West Germany for a brief period during the late 1960s and early 1970s.[15]

During the 1950s and 1960s, the Eastern bloc sponsored broadcasts from "Radio Iran Courier," "Oggi in Italia," "Ce Soir en France," and "German Freedom Station 904." All of these stations were the official voices of the Communist parties for the countries to which the stations broadcast. During the late 1940s, the Soviet Union sponsored broadcasts of the Yugoslav Revolutionary Émigré Radio and the Azerbaijan Democratic Station. The Yugoslav station broadcast against Marshall Tito after the outbreak of the Stalin-Tito feud. The Azerbaijan Democratic

Station broadcast against the Shah of Iran. The station appeared shortly after the shah signed a military agreement with the United States.

During World War II the Soviet Union, like the United States, was engaged in psychwar radio operations. But unlike the United States, Soviet involvement in clandestine radio broadcasting preceded the war. Early Soviet involvement in clandestine broadcasting was through the Comintern or Third International, which was headquartered in Moscow. Comintern-sponsored clandestine stations broadcast in Czechoslovakia, Hungary, Germany, and Italy a decade before the outbreak of World War II. During March 1931, Czechoslovak authorities searched for a "secret Communist radio station" that had been issuing proclamations in the Czech, Hungarian, and German languages.[16] A month later, a Communist station was heard in Hungary giving clear and coded instructions from the Comintern on the 1300-meter band.[17] In December 1932, three Communist party members were arrested in Germany for operating a radio station that drowned out regular broadcasting programs with Communist propaganda. The station urged poor workers to seize unoccupied housing and urged rent strikes. The station was reportedly audible throughout Berlin.[18] In 1937, a Communist-sponsored station called "Libertad" addressed the workers of Milan, Italy. The broadcasts consisted of left-wing news, "propagandistic speeches," and denunciations of fascism.[19] A similar station broadcast to Germany around the same time. German leaders claimed the anti-Nazi station originated in the Soviet Union, not Germany as claimed. This and the Italian clandestine station actually transmitted from Spain, not the Soviet Union, but were operated under Soviet encouragement and direction. By 1933, the Communist parties of Europe were under complete Soviet control and rarely implemented a strategy that lacked Soviet or Comintern approval.[20]

The Soviet Union also broadcast revolutionary messages to Europe from aboveground Soviet transmitters between its founding in 1917 and the adoption of the popular front strategy in the 1930s. The popular front was devised to halt the spread of fascism in Europe by building multiparty and multinational anti-fascist alliances that included Communist parties. The popular front paralleled Stalin's domestic campaign of building "socialism in one country." Socialism in one country emphasized national industrial expansion at the expense of international revolution. The Comintern's adoption of the popular front strategy and Stalin's preoccupation with internal development led to Radio Moscow's dropping of revolutionary broadcasts.

Immediately following the revolution, however, the Bolsheviks used wireless telegraphy to issue calls for worldwide revolution. The broadcasts were addressed "To all, all, all!" who were listening. During the Polish war of 1920 and the Soviet civil war, the Bolshevik party used radio to issue appeals to the international working class to mobilize in its behalf.[21] Broadcasts were made to many countries of the world, calling upon the working class to arise against capitalism. Bolshevik calls were so strident that Great Britain insisted that antipropaganda provisions be included in the Anglo-Russian Trade Agreement of 1921. Included in the Anglo-Russian Trade Agreement were the following passages:

The present treaty is conditioned upon the fulfillment of the following: Both sides will refrain from hostile acts or measures against the other party as well as from introducing into its territory any official, direct or indirect propaganda against the institutions of the British Empire or the Russian Soviet Republic ... [The Soviet Government pledges that] it will refrain from any attempt or incitement through military, diplomatic, or any other ways of any Asiatic nation to British interests or those of the British Empire.[22]

The agreement failed to stop the Soviets from conducting propaganda against the British government. A few years after the agreement was signed, Radio Moscow was addressing revolutionary messages to Asia and the British working class. In 1923, the Curzon ultimatum, which protested Soviet propagandizing and revolutionary activity in Asia, was issued by Great Britain. The British threatened to cancel the 1921 trade agreement if the Soviets continued.[23] Although the Soviet Union toned down its activities, it did not stop.[24] Revolutionary broadcasts from above-ground Soviet transmitters continued until the 1930s, when the popular front strategy was adopted. With the adoption of the popular front strategy, Soviet radio attacks on democratic countries stopped and attacks on Italy and Germany increased. Following the signing of the Hitler-Stalin Nonaggression Pact in 1939, this policy was reversed. Attacks on Germany ended and attacks on the democratic powers started.[25]

The Soviet Union was not alone in sponsoring subversive radio propaganda. Italy, Great Britain, Germany, and France also sponsored international radio propaganda prior to and immediately following the outbreak of World War II in 1939. When Great Britain opposed the Italian military campaign in Ethiopia, Italy launched a massive radio attack on Britain. Much of the Italian radio propaganda was directed at the Middle East, where Great Britain claimed a sphere of influence. The sphere of influence included Iraq, Yemen, Palestine, Jordan, and Egypt. The Italian-sponsored Arabic language radio programs consisted of music and traditional stories interspersed with political attacks on Britain. The attacks accused the British of exploiting Arabs while favoring Jews. To assure that their stations generated a large audience, radio receivers that were locked on the Italian-used frequencies were given free to Arabs by the Italians. The radio receivers were given to Arab café owners and shopkeepers so that a large number of Arabs could listen to the broadcasts from the same receiver.[26] After the outbreak of the war, Italy sponsored similar attacks from a clandestine station called the "Voice of the Arab Nation." This clandestine station claimed to be of Arab rather than Italian origin.[27]

Italy also directed propaganda attacks on France, whose North-African and island colonies were coveted by Italian premier Benito Mussolini. The attacks on France originated on aboveground transmitters, but Italy also conducted anti-French propaganda from a clandestine transmitter called "Radio Corse Libre." The station claimed to be operated by secessionist Corsicans who belonged to the Party of Corsican Independence. This "independence" party was created by Italy, from where the clandestine station broadcast. Corsica was one of the French possessions that Mussolini wanted to annex. Mussolini claimed that Corsica historically belong to Italy; that Corsicans were Italians, as demonstrated by their language; and that France had used Corsica, Tunisia, and its other colonies to "imprison" Italy.[28]

Radio Corse Libre was not Italy's first try at clandestine broadcasting. During the Spanish civil war, a station called "Radio Verdad" broadcast in Spanish and Catalan against the republican government. The station claimed to be Spanish-based and -operated, but transmitted from Italy. The station referred to itself as the mouthpiece of nationalist Spain.[29] Italy supported General Francisco Franco's rebels with military assistance in addition to the radio broadcasts.

Great Britain's entry into international radio broadcasting was in response to the Italian broadcasts to the Middle East. In autumn 1937 the British-owned Palestine broadcasting station began regular broadcasts in Arabic. On January 3, 1938, the British Broadcasting Corporation (BBC) inaugurated the Arabic Service, its first foreign-language service. Among speakers who appeared on the first day of the BBC's service was a son of the king of Yemen. The daily Arabic service consisted of forty-five minutes of music and talks followed by fifteen minutes of news. The talks focused on Islam and were given by pro-British Arab leaders. The news was presented objectively, without the vituperation characteristic of the Italian broadcasts. In March 1938, the BBC started Spanish and Portuguese language broadcasts. The transmissions were directed at Latin America, where Germany directed much of its anti-British radio propaganda. All of the radio propaganda originating from Great Britain until just prior to Germany's invasion of France was from aboveground transmitters.[30]

The first British-sponsored clandestine broadcast was from an experimental station called the "German Revolution Station" ("Sender der Deutscher Revolution"), which appeared on April 17, 1940 on the shortwave band. In a recorded broadcast, the station said: "The Nazis are shouting that we must march against England, but are they marching against England? No. It is the German youth who perishes. Hitler and his criminals are sending German youths to their deaths." The German Revolution Station repeated this announcement on April 19, reappeared on May 7, and then disappeared again. The sporadic operation of the station was due to an absence of trained staff that could produce more than a few amateurish scripts. The station reappeared on October 7 as "Sender der Europäischen Revolution" after a staff of German leftists was assembled that could produce a continuous supply of programs.[31]

The first long-lived British-sponsored clandestine station was merely a continuation of a clandestine station that broadcast to Germany from France between autumn 1939 and May 1940. The France-based station was commonly referred to as the "German Freedom Station" ("Deutscher Freiheitssender"), which was the name given to several other illegal anti-Nazi stations that broadcast to Germany beginning in 1932. The first Britain-based broadcast of the German Freedom Station occurred on May 26, 1940. Its announcer was Carl Speiker, who had worked on the French-sponsored station before fleeing to Great Britain. The station continued to broadcast until March 15, 1941, when Mr. Speiker left Britain for the United States.[32]

France sponsored a second anti-Nazi clandestine station that broadcast until the German invasion. The station was called "Radio Liberty." It broadcast to Austria from Fécamp, Normandy, but claimed to be a mobile transmitter located in Austria.[33] The station was similar in operation and content to its German counterpart and so became known as the "Austrian Freedom Station."

Prior to the Munich crisis, France conducted no international propaganda broadcasts. Following Munich, domestic mediumwave stations and one international shortwave station carried programs in Italian, English, Spanish, and Arabic that were directed at foreign audiences. German language programs on mediumwave were ostensibly directed at the German-speaking populace of French Alsace, but could be received by listeners in the Reich. The broadcasts often contained news censored from the German media. Popular with listeners in Germany, the German-language broadcasts from France were jammed by the Nazi government.

"Radio Paris Mondial" was the only shortwave broadcasting station in prewar France. It inaugurated broadcasts in 1937. Until September 1939, when the station was placed under government control, Radio Paris Mondial was operated as a private enterprise. The controlling interest in the station was in the hands of Albert Sarraut, a former minister of the interior and minister of education. Although broadcasting in a multiplicity of languages before Munich—Russian, Italian, Spanish, Portuguese, and German—its programs were neither popular nor propaganda. Broadcasts consisted of literati reading their works, classical comedies and dramas, and news bulletins presented in an objective manner but having the unfortunate habit of not being up-to-date and of having been written by Frenchmen with less-than-perfect foreign-language skills. For example, when Radio Paris Mondial reported on Howard Hughes's acclaimed Paris to Moscow flight, it broadcast that Hughes was preparing to take off, when in fact he had left France an hour and a half earlier. The personnel of radio stations in other countries were never so poorly informed. The staff and writers for the foreign language news broadcasts were also poorly trained. Although the on-air announcers were nationals of the countries to which the station broadcast, the writing for the programs was done by Frenchmen who sometimes produced comically inept translations.[34]

Poorly trained personnel were employed at Radio Mondial because the salaries paid by the station were very low, discouraging the best domestic talent. According to Charles Rolo and other anti-Fascists, the low salaries, while discouraging the employment of those with talent, attracted "fifth columnists" to the station, who worked to undermine France's resistance against the Germany enemy. These agents for the Third Reich "did not confine themselves to turning out suspiciously mild broadcasts with subtle overtures of defeatism, but energetically intrigued to sabotage" all attempts to make the station an effective propaganda arm.[35] Rolo, like many other writers of 1940, believed that a Nazi fifth column undermined France's ability to fight and led to the rapid defeat of the French army during the brief May-June 1940 war.[36]

One propagator of the fifth-column "theory" of France's collapse was Edmond Taylor, who became a United States Office of Strategic Services (OSS) psychological warfare strategist during World War II. Taylor was a journalist in France during the period of phony war, who observed and recorded the activities of purported fifth columnists in a book, *The Strategy of Terror*. Taylor's book became a widely cited work among psychological warfare theorists, as it supposedly described how rumors, sabotage, and aboveground and clandestine broadcasts worked together to bring about the French defeat.[37] While with the OSS, Taylor emphasized the need to fight Germany using fifth-column techniques—fighting fire with fire. He recommended that the United States employ rumor campaigns, clandestine broadcasts, secret agents, and sabotage in fighting the war.[38] He was not alone in this advocacy. Great Britain believed it necessary to fight and defeat Germany using fifth-column techniques and Gen. "Wild Bill" Donovan, the head of the OSS, also believed in the effectiveness of this strategy. After World War II ended, Taylor continued to advocate the use of fifth-column, psychological warfare techniques. Taylor recommended that the United States step up its propaganda attack on the Soviet Union, train Eastern European exiles as guerrillas, and drop them back into Eastern Europe, where they would conduct a campaign of sabotage and terror against the Communist regimes. The propaganda and terror campaigns would lead to an erosion of support for the Communist governments and eventually lead to their collapse.[39] This is what Taylor believed Germany did to bring about the collapse of France during World War II. Taylor's recommendations on how to "heat up" the cold war, needless to say, brought an outpouring of criticism from the left and congratulations from the far right.[40]

According to Taylor, Germany conducted a "word war" against France between 1937 and 1940. The German attack was skillfully designed to "demoralize the enemy, to destroy the cohesion, discipline, and collective morale [of France] . . . to break the enemy's will-to-win or simply his will-to-resist." Radio broadcasts supplemented and reinforced a word-of-mouth campaign conducted within France by "German and Italian agents, of whom there were hundreds in France, some in key positions."[41] The agents were not German by birth, but Frenchmen who had been swayed by Nazi propaganda. The French Nazis conducted a campaign of treachery that led to the collapse of the state.

Fifth columnists not only operated within France, but were located in Germany and broadcast to France. Two of the better known agents who broadcast to France were Paul Ferdonnet and André Obrecht, better known as the "Traitors of Stuttgart." Ferdonnet was a right-wing journalist, who, before defecting to Germany, had considerable stature. Ferdonnet and his assistants broadcast to France several times a night from "Radio Stuttgart," seeking to pit citizens against the government, workers against the bosses, hawks against doves, and the French against the British. Ferdonnet continuously reported that the conflict with Germany was caused by France's alliance with Great Britain. Great Britain, the leading imperialist nation of the world, was out to plunder and colonialize France and Germany, the broadcasts claimed. British soldiers were better paid, better fed, better dressed and always trying to buy French women wherever they were stationed in France, the broadcasts said. The British were well off because they milked the world and were slowly doing the same to France. The British wanted the French to fight their war, Ferdonnet repeated. To emphasize this point, the broadcasts always used the slogan, "England means to fight this war to the last Frenchman."[42]

The "traitors of Stuttgart" were said to work with fifth columnists in France, who cabled secret information to Germany that was then broadcast back to France. The fifth columnists, in high positions, had access to information that was not available to the public or enlisted men. When troops were transferred, many soliders reported that they first heard of the transfers from Radio Stuttgart, not their commanding officers. When an officers' meeting was held in Arras, Ferdonnet managed to obtain the name of the well-known restaurant where the officers had lunch. Ferdonnet also broadcast what he claimed was the lunch menu and the wines that accompanied each course. Enlistees, eating their rations, believed the broadcasts to be true. When several English officers stationed in France had an argument with Frenchmen at the Café Triomphe, Ferdonnet "broke" the story, giving an exact description of the incident and the names of the British officers. Such broadcasts created an aura of omniscience for Ferdonnet, even though much of what he said was fabricated or obtained from the French media.[43]

There is evidence that there was widespread listenership to the Radio Stuttgart broadcasts.[44] The French public listened because they distrusted what their government and the French media said. The distrust originated because of the government's vacillating policies, past deceptions, and failure to clearly explain why it was at war with Germany over Poland. The alliance with Great Britain also resurrected the long-lingering Anglophobia in France, particularly among the military. Civilian socialists, who had previously been in the anti-fascist movement, were also distrustful of the government. A major factor in the distrust was that the Communist party had shifted from vociferous opposition to quiescent acceptance of Hitler while simultaneously attacking the French bourgeoisie. The Communist party, under orders from the Comintern, switched its attacks from nazism to the French government following the signing of the German-Soviet Nonaggression Pact. This resulted in the government arresting and interning French Communist party leaders. Many rank-and-file Communists and Socialists viewed the suppression of the Communist party as an attack on the working class by a capitalist government. Because of this, many leftists fell prey to Ferdonnet's arguments that the war against Germany was being waged by "wealthy plutocrats in alliance with British imperialism."

The stance of the Communist parties after the Nazi-Soviet Pact led many, particularly in the United States, to see Communists as "red Nazis." As such, they were viewed as part of the fifth column that was working to undermine the democracies.[45] In the United States, the Communist turnabout alienated even their former allies and led to investigations by the House Un-American Activities Committee. Even the American Civil Liberties Union (ACLU), a long-time defender of minority speech, turned against the Communist party. In 1940, Communist leader Elizabeth Gurley Flynn, a charter member of the ACLU, was tried by the civil liberties union board for being opposed to democratic government and expelled.[46] The Dies or House Un-American Activities Committee, a bastion of anticommunism to begin with, used the Communists' newfound defeatist positions as grounds for pursuing an investigation of their activities. Finally President Roosevelt, who was known as prolabor and tolerant of Communists, attacked them as fifth columnists, saying that "strikes and slowdowns are in many cases instigated by Communists and other subversive elements acting in the interest of foreign enemies."[47] The attacks on the Communist party continued until June 1941, when Hitler's invasion of the Soviet Union forced a new about-face on the

Communists. The Communists then called for United States support for the allies and intervention against the Axis. As a result of their support for the allies, investigations of Communist activities were halted during the war, only to be resumed afterward.

German minister for propaganda, Joseph Goebbels, exploited the French Communist party's hostility toward the French government and tacit acceptance of nazism by starting a clandestine radio station, "Radio Humanité," that claimed to be the underground voice of the French Communist party, which had been declared illegal on September 26, 1939. The purpose of the station was to sow defeatism and supplement the German aboveground broadcasts directed at France. The clandestine station promoted pacifism, called for demonstrations in support of peace, opposed overtime work at military factories, and renounced military conscription. Although Communists today assert that the clandestine station "was intended to discredit the Communist Party among sections of the population,"[48] its real purpose was to use actual Communist positions to achieve German objectives. The station didn't need to falsify Communist defeatism; it was a fact. The French Communist party itself issued propaganda that sounded very much as though it had been written by Nazi fifth columnists: "By all appropriate methods, using all your resources of intelligence and all your technical knowledge, prevent, delay, or make unusable what is manufactured for war."[49] Acts of sabotage committed by French Communist workers did occur. Three aircraft engines at a factory at Boulogne-Billancourt were blown up. Six workers were arrested for the explosions and three, who confessed to membership in the Young Communist organization, were executed. Such activities, not to mention the operation of Radio Humanité, solidified the view of French statesmen that the Communist party was functioning as a fifth column for Germany.

Plans for Radio Humanité were laid in late 1939, when Goebbels assigned Alfred Ingomar Berndt, the head of the propaganda mininstry's broadcasting division, the task of coordinating plans for the station with the German High Command (OKW) and the Ministry of Foreign Affairs.[50] At the same time, plans were made for providing a clandestine transmitter to the Irish Republican Army, which, like Germany, viewed Great Britain as the enemy. While discussions of Radio Humanité began in October 1939, the station did not appear until December 16, 1939.[51]

During its initial period of operation, the scripts of Radio Humanité were written by a staff of French Communist intellectuals, who either refused to or were unable "to appeal to the primitive mass instincts," which Goebbels considered a necessity for good propaganda. Instead, the scriptwriters produced programs that were dull and doctrinaire. As a result, Goebbels solicited Ernst Torgler and his intimate friend, Maria Reese, to write the scripts in early June 1940, as the German army advanced toward Paris. Torgler and Reese were former German Communist party members who became Nazi sympathizers. Torgler had been a defendant with Georgi Dimitrov at the famous Reichstag fire trial, where Maria Reese was a witness. Torgler was excluded from a deal made between Hitler and Stalin that freed Dimitrov and two other Bulgarian defendants. After being abandoned by Stalin and the German Communist party, Torgler and Reese turned on the Communists.[52]

Torgler denied that Maria Reese wrote scripts for Radio Humanité but said that he and Wilhelm Kasper, a friend and former Communist who was brought out of a concentration camp, were forced to "supply a few draft appeals to the French workers" by Goebbels. The appeals called on workers to stop resisting the German army and "avoid unnecessary bloodshed." Torgler and Kasper were joined by Karl Albrecht, another former Communist who later oversaw the operation of a clandestine station that broadcast to the Soviet Union.[53]

Radio Humanité was not the only German-sponsored clandestine station that broadcast to France prior to the May-June 1940 war. There were two others: "Poste du Réveil de la France" and "Voix de la Paix." Réveil de la France, also known as "Radio Revolution," began operating on the shortwave band on December 27, 1939.[54] The station's signal was initially weak and it claimed to be broadcasting from within France. The announcers' French was good, but their presentation of materials was amateurish rather than professional.[55] This gave the desired impression that the station was actually operated by ordinary Frenchmen who opposed the government's war policy. Radio Réveil, like broadcasts coming from Radio Stuttgart, asked Frenchmen why they were at war with Germany. Answering its own question, Radio Réveil said that England feared Germany, "whom they consider as a rival, whereas rightly or wrongly, we are considered too weak to hinder them in their domination of half the globe."[56] The station, throughout the early months of 1940, repeated the same theme: France was weak, the Germans were strong, and Great Britain was using France to fight its imperial war. As broadcasts continued, Radio Réveil increasingly addressed a Nazi fifth column that was supposedly composed of opponents to Prime Minister Paul Reynaud, who replaced Édouard Daladier in March. The attacks on Reynaud from Radio Réveil paralleled attacks on the prime minister from Radio Humanité, as well as the real, but underground, French Communist party press.

When Germany attacked France in May, Goebbels ordered Radio Réveil to create a mood of panic in France.[57] The station began broadcasting on longwave in addition to shortwave to expand its listenership, while employing three techniques to encite panic: one, it called on fifth columnists to mobilize; two, it carried hysterical appeals to capitulate or face a bloodbath; and three, it exaggerated the ferocity of the German military advance. Fifth columnists were called upon to conduct a "national revolution" against Reynaud, who was said to be conducting a "Jewish war." The station later called on its supporters to "prevent the present members of the Government [from] fleeing the country." Prior to France's capitulation, Radio Réveil demanded Reynaud's death. The station appealed to France to capitulate because to do otherwise would "cause tremendous bloodshed not only among soldiers, but still more among civilians." As German troops marched toward Paris, the clandestine station shrieked:

It is criminal and senseless to defend Paris and have it destroyed. Paris must be declared an "open city." The National Revolution will save Paris as Belgians saved Brussels—in spite of the murderer Reynaud.[58]

The broadcasts of Radio Réveil were calm and restrained compared to the broadcasts of Voix de la Paix. Like Radio Réveil, Voix de la Paix signed on in the shortwave spectrum before the attack on France. Immediately after the invasion, it also appeared on mediumwave.[59] The station claimed to be located in France and operated by a fifth-column peace organization with a large following. Voix de la Paix said that the peace organization included French officers, who were given instructions:

The officers who have received our instructions personally and in whom we have complete confidence must observe their instructions to the letter . . . Anyone pretending to act for our movement but unable to produce our official identification card should be handed over to the chief of the group. All chiefs have constantly to be on the alert and ready to execute Order No. 202d as soon as instructions are given.[60]

There was, however, no fifth column in the French army, no peace organization, no membership cards or Order 202d, as the station claimed. To incite panic, the station went to great extremes. On June 3, Radio Paris, the official government station, announced that "German aircraft attempted to bomb Paris and the surrounding region . . . our fighters quickly responded to the attack." To this, Voix de la Paix retorted:

In the German air attack on Paris, which was very much more serious than was at first reported, many thousands of bombs were launched on the city and suburbs. It may have been only military objectives that were bombed, but, nevertheless, besides the killing of civilians in the city, 13 fires broke out in the centre of town and 48 in the suburbs, while many factories were very badly damaged. According to press reports from neutral countries 1200 persons are said to have been killed and over 6000 wounded.[61]

The station also appealed to make Paris "an open city." If bombing was not enough to frighten the citizens of Paris, the following broadcast should have:

All Paris is threatened with poisoning because Fifth Columnists have succeeded in poisoning several reservoirs of drinking water. . . . Is Paris to be another Warsaw . . . [with] the blood of our women and children flowing along the pavement?[62]

As France collapsed, Voix de la Paix, like Radio Réveil, called for the death of Reynaud. Reynaud resigned on June 16, was arrested, but not executed. He remained in captivity during the war. Marshal Philippe Pétain, a World War I hero and vice-premier in Reynaud's cabinet, became the new prime minister. He obtained an armistice from the Germans and, believing it to be the only way to maintain what was left of French independence, began cooperating with them.

When the collapse of France appeared imminent, "Radio Corse Libre," the Italian-sponsored clandestine station that had broadcast during 1939, returned to the air. It reappeared on June 1. The Italians waited until French resistance had crumbled before starting their clandestine station or making a declaration of war. Italy declared war on France on June 10, four days before the German army entered Paris. The Italian-sponsored station, like Radio Réveil and Voix de la Paix, claimed that the retreat of the French army threatened civilians with annihilation. "France cannot defend us," the station announced. "We are already suffering from lack of food, and a tightening of the blockade would starve us out." The station called for the overthrow of the French government as the means of "liberation."[63]

In addition to Voix de la Paix, Radio Réveil and Radio Humanité, two other German-sponsored clandestine stations began broadcasting to France in June, shortly before the capitulation: "Camarade du Nord" (Friend of the North) and "Voix de la Bretagne" (Voice of Brittany). Both stations claimed to be operated by indigenous opponents of Reynaud who were seeking peace with Germany. Voix de la Bretagne claimed to be operated by separatist Britons seeking help from Germany to achieve independence.

## THE FIFTH-COLUMN FEAR IN GREAT BRITAIN

The method and suddenness of the French collapse profoundly affected British thinking. It was now feared that a fifth column might exist within Great Britain that could undermine resistance, as was believed to have occurred in France. The fear of a fifth column was intensified because of Hitler's plan to invade the island nation (Operation Sealion). Britain was aware of the plan because British security forces had broken the secret ciphers used in German military and government communications. The invasion threat meant that Great Britain would have to fight an attack launched from abroad and one launched from within by fifth columnists. The defeat of France and the retreat at Dunkirk also made it clear that Great Britain could not defeat Germany using conventional military tactics or without the assistance of the United States.

The specter of a fifth column in Great Britain was driven home by the activities of several pro-Nazi British émigrés, who broadcast to Great Britain from Germany, as Ferdonnet and Obrecht had to France. The English-language broadcasters became collectively known as "Lord Haw-Haw." Lord Haw-Haw first appeared on German radio on April 10, 1939.[64] The early broadcasts were probably made by Norman Baille-Stewart, a British citizen who was court-martialed for violating the Official Secrets Act in 1933, sentenced to five years imprisonment and released in 1937, after which he moved to the continent. Little attention was paid to the early Lord Haw-Haw broadcasts by the British public or government, which still believed that Hitler could be appeased and peace secured. It wasn't until the outbreak of war on September 3 that the English-language broadcasts were noticed by either the British public or media. And it wasn't until September 6 that William Joyce, who appropriated the title of Lord Haw-Haw, made his first broadcast.

Joyce was born in Brooklyn, New York in 1906, the son of an immigrant Irish father and English mother. In 1909, his parents uprooted and returned to Ireland, where William Joyce was raised and educated. In Ireland, he was taught fealty to the British crown rather than Irish nationalism by his parents. This loyalty to the crown made Joyce and his parents outcasts in Ireland, so they moved to England. There his fealty evolved into extreme right-wing conservatism. In 1923 William Joyce joined his first political organization, British Fascists Ltd., which opposed the "internationalism" of the Labour Party. He joined Oswald Mosley's Union of British Fascists in 1933 and in July of that year acquired a British passport, despite being an American citizen, so that he could travel to Germany to see Hitler. Some years after returning from Germany, Joyce broke with Mosley and started his own organization, the National Socialist League. Joyce remained a leader of the organization until war between Germany and Great Britain appeared imminent. To avoid having to fight on the side of the British "plutocracy" against Nazi Germany, he defected. In Germany, Joyce became short of money and fearful that he might be interned as an illegal resident. Despondent but still dedicated to the Nazi cause, Joyce applied for and received a job from the Reichsrundfunk. His job was that of an English-language commentator for the external broadcasting service.[65]

The title of "Lord Haw-Haw" was bestowed on one of the English-speaking German radio announcers by Jonah Barrington, a writer for the

*Daily Express* whose newspaper columns were based on monitored foreign radio broadcasts. The title was given to the speaker with an exaggerated aristocratic accent, who Barrington imagined had "a receding chin, a questing nose, thin, yellow hair brushed back, a monocle, a vacant eye, a gardenia in his button-hole."[66] The columnist was probably describing Baille-Stewart rather than Joyce, although neither was identified by name in their broadcasts. Joyce spoke with a sarcastic but nasal monotone, not an affected accent. Barrington had assigned humorous names to other announcers, such as "Winnie the Whopper," "Uncle Boo-hoo" and "Sinister Sam," but only the name of "Lord Haw-Haw" entered into English vernacular. It was soon applied to all male announcers who broadcast to Great Britain over Zeesen, Bremen, Cologne, and Hamburg radio transmitters.

German radio, realizing that the name "Lord Haw-Haw" received widespread recognition in Great Britain, began announcing the commentaries of William Joyce as those of Lord Haw-Haw. It was not until April 3, 1941 that Joyce identified himself in the broadcasts by his real name. After the disclosure of April 6, his broadcasts henceforth opened with the announcement: "William Joyce, otherwise known as Lord Haw-Haw." By that time, listenership to his broadcasts in Great Britain had substantially declined. Listenership to Lord Haw-Haw's broadcasts peaked during the winter of 1939–40, when over half of all British citizens reported having listened to his broadcasts. His audience declined thereafter as the novelty of the broadcasts wore off and fears of a fifth column increased.[67]

During the 1939–40 period of phony war, Lord Haw-Haw directed his attacks at the British government, which he described as Jewish and imperialist. The war, Joyce said, was caused by the plutocratic rulers of Great Britain, not Germany. What Joyce claimed was almost identical to that mouthed by the "traitors of Stuttgart." Attacks on communism would probably have been more effective than harangues against British rulers, but the Hitler-Stalin pact imposed restraints on Joyce's invective. The Soviet Union and communism, which he hated almost as intensely as he hated Jews, remained a topic about which Joyce was forced to remain silent. Joyce could not say what he really thought: that Great Britain was fighting the wrong enemy; that Great Britain should be allied with Germany in a war against Russia.

When the phony war ended in May 1940, Joyce began a series of broadcasts designed to frighten the British citizenry. Lord Haw-Haw warned that Germany would launch reprisals against British attacks on "noncombatants" in Germany cities and that the British would pay tenfold for every German injured. His strategy was to panic British citizens into opposing their government's air war on Germany. Another threat that Joyce repeated in his broadcasts was that a German invasion of the island was imminent. Hitler made similar threats. After the invasion, there would be retribution against those that supported and promoted the war, Joyce warned.

Joyce also uttered vague threats against British targets that had been singled out for air attack by Germany. The threats contained descriptions of factories, warehouses, and buildings that would soon be bombed. What Joyce said in these broadcasts suggested to many that he had an uncanny and intimate knowledge of what was happening in cities and factories across Great Britain. "Don't trouble to finish the new paint shed, you won't need it," Joyce remarked. His threat was interpreted by employees at a Midland munitions factory that they would soon be bombed, as the description given by Joyce seemed to be that of their workplace. The threat led to a drop in production at the plant. Workers at another munitions factory at Ipswich heard "accurate" descriptions of their daily activities and the plant. Such broadcasts led to speculation that a fifth column was feeding Lord Haw-Haw information about Great Britain. The speculations fueled rumors, which intensified fear of the fifth column.[68]

Lord Haw-Haw's aboveground broadcasts were accompanied by broadcasts from a German-sponsored clandestine station that claimed to be operated by members of an indigenous peace organization. The station was named the "New British Broadcasting Station." It first appeared on February 25, 1940 and was introduced by a medley of songs including "Loch Lomond," "Coming through the Rye," and "When Irish Eyes are Smiling." In its opening broadcast, the station attempted to allay fears of British listeners that it was operated by fifth columnists, saying that it was "entirely run by British people who put our country above our own interests." The station, nonetheless, attempted to instill panic in listeners by reporting that "the fifth column in England is working day and night, and among the 64,000 persons of German and Austrian nationality . . . on our soil there is a powerful nucleus for the kind of work undertaken by the fifth column."[69] Despite the assertion that others, not it, comprised a fifth column, the New British Broadcasting Station was nonetheless seen as the work of German agents operating in Great Britain. Even though the British press reported that the station originated "on the continent," the public and some members of the government initially believed that the broadcasts originated on British not German soil and some government ministers believed that the station's purpose was to communicate with agents inside of Great Britain.[70]

The station was seen for what it was—an enemy-sponsored enterprise—because it sounded very much like the enemy-sponsored broadcasts of Lord Haw-Haw: It accused the British government of having started the war; asserted that it was the "patriotic duty" of British citizens to oppose their government's war policies; and advocated a negotiated peace with Germany.[71] The clandestine station sounded very much like the broadcasts of Lord Haw-Haw because its scripts were written by William Joyce. Because the voice of Joyce was well known in Great Britain, he never worked as an announcer on the clandestine station. To have done so would have revealed the station's German location, as Joyce was known to reside there. With the collapse of France, the New British Broadcasting Station reported that an invasion of Great Britain by Germany was imminent; that aerial bombing would destroy London; and that defeat was inevitable, all positions taken by Lord Haw-Haw. It also addressed what were described as members of a large peace organization existing in England. On occasion, instructions were relayed to members of the organization.

On July 25, 1940, Goebbels assigned the clandestine station the task of spreading "alarm and fear among the British people." His instructions called for broadcasts that would cause civilians "to be seized by horror."[72] The New British Broadcasting Station implemented Goebbels's orders by reporting that civilian militiamen in the Local Defense Volunteers were too poorly trained to avoid being slaughtered when Germany invaded and that Great Britain was unprepared for the invasion. When Germany invaded, there would be chaos, the station warned. On August 14, it announced that German parachutists in British uniforms and civilian clothes had been dropped near Birmingham, Glasgow, and Manchester.[73] The parachutists had not been located by searchers in the area, the station said, because fifth columnists were hiding them. The broadcasts preyed on rumors that had circulated in Great Britain that the invasion of the Netherlands was preceded by a landing of German parachutists dressed as nuns, nurses, policemen, and postmen.[74] The announcement of the New British Broadcasting Station and the rumors concerning the Netherlands were both false.

Although the station often spoke of and addressed members of a British peace organization, there is no evidence that it or any other fifth-column group existed in Great Britain.[75] In May, British authorities had rounded up and interned potential fifth columnists—aliens and British fascists—even though most had not demonstrated any willingness to aid Germany. The potential for fifth-column activities was therefore very small. What evidence there was of a fifth column was based largely on rumors and a few isolated occurrences: leaflets distributed in early May outside factories in North London advertised the New British Broadcasting Station's frequency; transcriptions of its broadcasts were left in a few cinemas; and a man was arrested for placing a sticker on a telephone booth that contained an announcement for the clandestine station.[76] Despite the absence of a fifth column, rumors persisted that the New British Broadcasting Station's chief purpose was to instruct enemy agents.[77] The rumors were reinforced by the mass media. In one motion picture, "The Voice of Terror," Basil Rathbone played Victorian sleuth Sherlock

Holmes, who inexplicably turned up in World War II England. Holmes was asked by a stymied British war council, which included a Winston Churchill look-alike, to track down and apprehend a clandestine broadcaster and his gang of Nazi fifth columnists. In the film, as in rumors that circulated in Britain, the Nazi radio propagandist terrorized British listeners by telling of disasters—the derailing of a troop train, the bombing of an airfield, the explosion of a munitions dump, and the burning of the East End piers—before they occurred. With violin and logic, Sherlock Holmes and his simple-minded companion Dr. Watson, played by Nigel Bruce, caught the saboteurs and saved England from a fifth-column takeover.[78]

Although the fears of a fifth column receded as the war progressed, the early fear of and belief in the effectiveness of fifth columnists greatly influenced British wartime strategy. The British, in turn, influenced the direction of U.S. strategy.

## THE ORIGINS OF BRITISH PSYCHWAR

On September 24, 1938, six days before Prime Minister Neville Chamberlain brought "peace in our time" by signing the Munich Agreement, the prime minister invited Sir Campbell Stuart to his office. Chamberlain, who feared that his policy of appeasement was unraveling in the face of Hitler's continuing demands—this time for secession of the Sudetenland— asked Sir Campbell Stuart to create a secret propaganda agency like the one that existed during World War I. Stuart had been assistant director of the WWI agency known as Crewe House.[79] Between the wars he was the director of the *Times* of London. Stuart was asked to keep the new agency's plans and operations a secret, and to report to Sir Stephen Tallents. Tallents was the Director General-Designate of the Ministry of Information, which in late 1938 existed only on paper.

Sir Stephen Tallents, who developed a reputation for empire-building while head of the Empire Marketing Board and the Post Office's public relations department, clashed with Sir Campbell Stuart even before Stuart's appointment was official. Although Tallents had no experience with war propaganda, he wanted all wartime communications directly under his control. Tallents didn't want Campbell Stuart to operate a department over which the Director General-Designate did not exercise complete control. Tallents saw his role as that of information tsar rather than that of minister of information. For his attitude, Tallents was asked to resign in January 1939, one month after Campbell Stuart was officially appointed chairman of the Imperial Communication Advisory Committee.[80] The jousting of the two knights was the first of many clashes that plagued British psychwar organizations.

Sir Campbell Stuart's headquarters was located in Room 207, Electra

House, Victoria Embankment. Because of the address, Stuart's organization was known as Electra House or EH, rather than by its official, but secret, name: the Department of Propaganda in Enemy Countries. Recruited to help run Electra House were Lt.-Col. Reginald Alexander Dallas Brooks, Valentine Williams, and Ralph Murray. Dallas Brooks, a military officer with elite connections, was named head of EH's military wing.[81] Brooks served as the chief staff officer and liaison with other departments. Valentine Williams, an acquaintance of Campbell Stuart's from Fleet Street and author of numerous suspense novels, was named chief assistant to the director.[82] Ralph Murray was a language specialist who previously worked for the BBC. Sir Robert Bruce Lockhart of the Foreign Office, while technically not a member of the EH, functioned as one by attending planning meetings and serving as its expert on Czechoslovakia. Lockhart was the British consul-general to tsarist Russia until 1917. He was arrested by the Bolsheviks and traded for Russian revolutionary leader Maxim Litvinov in 1918.[83]

Electra House was given responsibility for producing propaganda directed at potential enemy countries. Since Great Britain was not officially at war during the first nine months of Electra House's existence, EH produced practice leaflets and made covert contact with other government agencies. One of the agencies with which EH made contact was the Air Ministry. Sir Campbell Stuart believed that in the event of war, the Air Ministry would be responsible for distributing propaganda leaflets, as it had been during World War I. Electra House also established contact with the Secret Intelligence Service (SIS), which had a number of intelligence-gathering agents stationed abroad. SIS had its own shortwave wireless stations that it used for maintaining contact with the agents, and a branch known as Section D that specialized in sabotage and subversion. SIS's wireless communications section (Section VII) was headed by Col. Richard Gambier-Parry. The communications section had transmitters in Buckinghamshire, not far from Bedfordshire, where EH eventually established its secret headquarters. Section D had the responsibility "of attacking potential enemies by means other than the operations of military force."[84] A second organization, similar to Section D, existed under the War Office. It was the research section of the War Office General Staff or GS(R). GS(R) specialized in the study of guerrilla warfare tactics that could be used in conjunction with military operations. After the German occupation of Prague, GS(R) was given a new name, Military Intelligence (Research) or MI(R), and assigned an instructor known for his expertise in guerrilla warfare. The instructor was Colin Gubbins, the author of several manuals on "ungentlemanly warfare," including *The Art of Guerrilla Warfare* and *How to Use High Explosives*. The unstated purpose of EH, Section D, and MI(R) were virtually the same—to encourage a continental pro-British fifth column that could undermine Germany's ability to wage war. British leaders hoped this strategy would succeed if war did occur, because the appeasement policy, which was pursued for several years, had rendered Great Britain incapable of defeating Germany using conventional military tactics.

While the Department of Propaganda to Enemy Countries' mandate gave it jurisdiction over propaganda to enemy countries, it could perform no legal operations during most of 1939, as Great Britain was at peace. This gave the British Broadcasting Corporation, not EH, responsibility for broadcasts directed at the Axis Pact nations. Because Great Britain was at peace and had no intention of provoking Hitler, Electra House operated in secret. Electra House's covert operations, as distinguished from the BBC's overt operations, gave rise to a terminology that continued to be used after the outbreak of war, and continues to be used today. Electra House employed the term "white propaganda" to refer to activities of the BBC. It used the term "black propaganda" to refer to its secret activities. After war was declared, the term "white propaganda" described propaganda that was clearly identified as originating in Great Britain, such as broadcasts of BBC's overseas services. "Black propaganda" refered to British-originated propaganda that claimed to originate within Axis countries, rather than being identified as British-sponsored. "Gray propaganda" was propaganda that had no clearly identified source. The term "black propaganda" has since been attached to all communications where the source is disguised, while "white propaganda" is used to describe propaganda where the true source is identified. According to British psychwar terminology, the German-sponsored broadcasts of Lord Haw-Haw that were carried by Radio Hamburg were "white," while the broadcasts of the New British Broadcasting Station were black.[85]

Electra House, in addition to establishing working relations with other agencies, made arrangements for its staff and equipment to be housed outside of London, as it was assumed that the Luftwaffe would bomb the capital city in the event of war. To protect Britain's defense forces, they were moved from London. Accommodations for Electra House were found at Woburn Abbey in Bedfordshire. Woburn Abbey was about forty miles from London, which made commuting easy, while sufficiently far to keep EH safe and secret. Woburn Abbey was part of the estate of the Duke of Bedfordshire, who allowed Electra House to occupy the stable wing of the abbey's riding school. The new propaganda agency grew very rapidly and soon the whole abbey was taken over by the agency, which by mid–1941 had 458 employees. When it grew even larger, new facilities were built at Milton Bryant. The Milton Bryant complex was specifically constructed for recording clandestine broadcasts. The facilities had professionally built recording studios, editing facilities, and security devices, including voice scramblers.

In August 1939, a few weeks before Germany's attack on Poland, Electra House was told to report to the Foreign Office rather than the Minister of Information. This arrangement gave EH closer contact with British subversive organizations like SIS, and kept activities of Electra House secret from the Minister of Information. In early 1940, after the outbreak of war, when Germany stepped up its black and white propaganda attacks on Great Britain, this arrangement allowed EH to ask SIS for limited use of one of its three 7.5-kilowatt shortwave transmitters for making clandestine broadcasts to Germany. SIS acceded to EH's request. On April 17, 1940, Electra House made the first of several clandestine broadcasts from the "German Revolution Station." The broadcasts were monitored and reported by the BBC's monitoring service, which was unaware that the broadcasts originated in England. The minister of information was never informed about this or a second series of clandestine broadcasts until June, when Electra House was again placed under the Minister of Information's jurisdiction. Upon hearing that EH was operating a series of secret stations without notifying him, the minister became furious.[86]

Before EH was returned to the Ministry of Information from the Foreign Office, Campbell Stuart decided to seek additional broadcasting facilities outside of Great Britain. Stuart was looking for other transmitters because the time limit that SIS set for EH's broadcasts had already been reached, despite plans for putting other "freedom stations" on the air. Stuart also believed that the political environment might make such broadcasts from Britain impossible. He feared that influential government leaders might oppose his tactic of using German-developed techniques to defeat Germany. He was apparently unaware that the cabinet and British military leaders were about to adopt fifth-column activities and ungentlemanly warfare as their major strategy for defeating Germany.[87]

On June 24, 1940, Sir Campbell Stuart left for North America to investigate the possibility of using facilities in Canada or the United States. If he were unable to find facilities that EH could control, Stuart was willing to create "an anonymous association of Germans" that would buy time from U.S. commercial shortwave stations using laundered British money. The association would make defeatist broadcasts at Germany over the U.S. transmitters. On July 5, Stuart arrived in Ottawa, where he stayed with "an intimate friend," prime minister William Mackenzie King. Stuart received permission from the prime minister to operate in Canada but found that Canada lacked the equipment needed for making psychwar broadcasts to Europe. Stuart then went to the United States. There he met David Sarnoff, chairman of the Radio Corporation of America (RCA). Sarnoff informed Stuart that RCA had a 600-kilowatt mediumwave transmitter in storage that was capable of reaching Europe from Newfoundland. The transmitter, built for but never used by a religious broadcasting group in the United States, was for sale for between £80,000 and £100,000, Sarnoff said. The RCA chairman didn't tell Stuart that the price did not include a directional antenna or other equipment that was needed to effectively operate the transmitter, for which RCA wanted more money than the equipment was worth. Stuart, upon learning of the existence of the transmitter, notified Minister of Information Duff Cooper about it on August 16.[88]

What Campbell Stuart did not realize was that by August 16, Duff Cooper was no longer his superior. Electra House was transferred from the Ministry of Information to the Ministry of Economic Warfare on July 22. The Minister of Economic Warfare was Labour leader Hugh Dalton. EH, along with Section D and MI(R), were transferred to Dalton, who was given the responsibility of merging the organizations into a single, subversive warfare unit that would "set Europe ablaze." The new organization was part of a British strategy for undermining Germany, rather than defeating her on the battlefield. The subversive warfare unit that was created was named the Special Operations Executive (SOE).

Hugh Dalton was an ideal selection for creating a subversive warfare unit. He was not just tactically but also ideologically committed to setting Europe ablaze. As a socialist, Dalton believed that the enslaved populations of Europe, together with the German working class, would eventually rebel against the Nazi system. The rebellion would begin when the Nazi economic system created privation. Great Britain could create the depressing economic conditions by keeping resources from German hands through a blockade, Dalton believed. As the blockade succeeded, conditions in Europe would worsen. The working class, responding to the hardships and clandestine calls for revolution, would rise against Hitler and end the war. As Dalton explained it:

We must organize movements in every occupied territory comparable to the Sinn Fein movement in Ireland, to the Chinese guerrillas now operating against Japan ... to the organizations which the Nazis themselves developed so remarkably in almost every country of the world. We must use many different methods, including industrial and military sabotage, labour agitation and strikes, continuous propaganda, terrorist acts against traitors and German leaders, boycotts and riots.[89]

Dalton's theory laid the groundwork for the expansion of Electra House, but not for the ultimate defeat of Germany. Hitler's grip over Europe was stronger than Dalton believed. The Nazis had ruthlessly wiped out all internal opposition, and used mass murder as retribution against anti-Nazi activities in occupied Europe. This ruthlessness created a well-deserved fear among members of the underground that militant actions of the type that Dalton hoped for would do more harm than good to the occupied nations.

Dalton's new organization, which was created from the three previously separate subversive warfare units, consisted of two branches: a psychological warfare branch code-named "Special Operations 1" (SO1), and a sabotage and guerrilla warfare branch called "Special Operations 2" (SO2). SO1 was created from Electra House but was soon staffed by experts selected by Dalton. One of the first promotions was given to Richard Crossman, a fellow socialist known as an expert on Germany.[90] Crossman was appointed head of psychwar radio operations directed at Germany. Like Dalton, Crossman was disliked by conservative members of SO1, who far outnumbered the socialists in the organization.[91] Conservatives in SO1 included Sir Robert Bruce Lockhart and Reginald (Rex) Leeper. Leeper, who was a former diplomat and head of the Foreign Office News Department before being recruited into EH, was appointed Director of SO1. He replaced Campbell Stuart as head of British subversive propaganda. Several political scientists, including Denis William Brogan and Robert W. Seton-Watson, were also recruited into the new organization. Cambridge University professor Denis William Brogan was an expert on French politics and history. He had written *Proudhon* (1934), *The Development of Modern France* (1940), and several other books on French and U.S. history.[92] Professor Seton-Watson was an expert on Hungary and the Balkans; his works included *German, Slav, and Magyar* (1916), *The Rise of Nationality in the Balkans* (1917), and *History of the Romanians* (1934). During World War I, Professor Seton-Watson was co-director of the Austro-Hungarian section of Crewe House.[93] Brogan and Seton-Watson were appointed heads of SO1's France and Balkans regional departments. George Martelli, a British naval officer of Italian descent, was appointed chief of the Italian regional department. In late 1942, he and Richard Crossman resigned as heads of their regional departments and joined General Dwight Eisenhower's Psychological Warfare Branch (PWB) in North Africa.[94] Thomas Barman was a journalist who was "intimately acquainted" with the languages and geography of Scandinavia.[95] He authored Cook's *Handbook to Norway, Sweden, Denmark, Finland and Iceland* (1936). Barman was appointed head of the Scandinavia regional department of SO1.

The first meeting of SO1's planning board was held on August 31, 1940. At the meeting, which was attended by Rex Leeper, Ralph Murray, Valentine Williams, Richard Crossman, and other regional heads, the planning board decided to start several new black stations, in addition to the one inherited from EH that broadcast to Germany. The plans included starting an Italian, French, and Romanian station, and another aimed at Germany. It was decided that the personnel needed to operate the stations would be located in different houses scattered around Bedfordshire, so that the groups would not know of the others' existence. The houses in Bedfordshire were soon used as code-names to identify the newly created clandestine stations. "DE" was the code-name for the new German station. DE stood for "Dawn Edge," a house at Aspley Guise where the German radio staff lived. "BH" was short for "Banhoff," where the staff of the EH's original German freedom station lived. "'TM" was short for Toddington Manor, where the French radio team was housed. "LF" was the code-name for Larchfield, where the staff of a third German clandestine station lived; "QC" was the code-name for the Italian station; and "DH" the code-name for the Rumanian station. As this method of referring to clandestine stations soon became very cumbersome, the code-names were changed. The code "G1" was given to the first German station, "G2" to the second German station on the air, "R1" to the first Romanian station to take to the airwaves, and "F1" to the French clandestine station, "Radio Inconnue" (Unknown Radio). This procedure made it easier to covertly identify each station.[96]

The staff of DE (or G2) consisted of members of the New Beginning, an organization of exiled anti-Stalin Marxists. Their station was called the "Sender de Europäischen Revolution" (Radio of the European Revolution). The station was supervised by Richard Crossman, but the German exiles were given tremendous freedom in writing scripts. Crossman's guidance and criticisms were usually limited to such comments as the broadcasts were "too academic" or "lacked fire." The operators were given this freedom because they were ideological kin to Crossman, and because they had already proven their dedication to overthrowing Hitler. The Sender made its first broadcast on October 7, 1940. It signed off on June 22, 1942, a year after the Soviet Union entered the war. Conflicts within the New Beginning group, created by Stalin's alliance with Great Britain, led to the silencing of the station.[97]

The second clandestine station that SO1 put on the air was "Frats Roman" (Brother Rumanians). It appeared on November 10, 1941 and spoke "For country, king and people." The third station to broadcast was Radio Inconnue. Purporting to broadcast from a hidden transmitter in Paris, the station addressed shopkeepers, artisans, and other members of the middle class. It appeared on November 15. The following day, "Radio Italia" signed on, accusing Mussolini of being Hitler's stooge. Its slogan was "Don't believe, don't obey, don't fight." On November 17, "Radio Travail" (Worker's Radio) broadcast the first of 551 programs to France.

Two days following the appearance of Radio Travail, a meeting at Woburn Abbey was held to review clandestine propaganda directed at France. Dalton, Leeper, and Gladwyn Jebb, the head of SO2, attended the meeting. Jebb suggested that agents be dropped in France with instructions to organize the industrial proletariat for action against the pro-Fascist Pétain regime. This form of subversion, Jebb suggested, was consistent with the type of propaganda originating from SO1's clandestine stations. Dalton voiced his support for Jebb's proposal. Rex Leeper, a conservative not a socialist, spoke against the proposal. Leeper said "the policy of encouraging a Left Revolution came into conflict with the declared intention of HMG to arrive at a modus vivendi with the Pétain government."[98] Leeper won the argument, not at the meeting, but through subsequent discussions with his former colleagues at the Foreign Office. The Foreign Office, backed by Churchill, ordered SOE to restrict its subversive activities to the German-occupied zones of France. Not until Germany occupied Vichy France did Churchill alter this policy.

Between January 1941 and February 1942, when Hugh Dalton resigned as head of the Ministry of Economic Warfare, the staff at Woburn Abbey created fourteen additional clandestine stations. They included a station operated by de Gaulle's Free French forces, a short-lived Italian socialist station, and a Marxist-oriented station called "Rotes Wien" that broadcast to Austria. All of the stations broadcast from transmitters controlled by SIS. One transmitter, under the supervision of Colonel Gambier-Parry, was built for the specific purpose of making clandestine radio broadcasts.[99]

Responsibilities in Dalton's subversive warfare organization were divided, with SO1 having responsibility for producing subversive messages, and SO2 having responsibility for distributing them. Adhesive labels announcing the times and frequencies of the black radio stations, leaflets, and newspapers produced by SO1 were given to SO2 for covert distribution. SO2 was also assigned the task of organizing a British fifth column in German-occupied countries. Although the division of labor existed on paper, in practice it was a different story. Being grossly understaffed, SO1 initially neglected some areas like the Balkans, so SO2 decided to produce its own propaganda for the region. Such activities created heated jurisdictional arguments between SO1 and SO2 leaders. In Cairo, the dispute became so intense that the regional branch heads were dismissed and replaced by a new man, Terrence Maxwell. Maxwell was appointed director of both branches.[100]

SO2 developed its own propaganda arm in other areas where SO1 was weak, as in Palestine. SO2 started a series of clandestine stations broadcasting from there to countries of the Mediterranean. These broadcasts were not coordinated with those of SO1. SO1 strategists, upon learning of the SO2 operations, bitterly complained that the broadcasts were made "without relation to our propaganda policy and ... without any clear direction."[101] Despite the complaints, the SO2 operations continued because SO1 lacked the personnel to take them over. When SO1 and SO2 were divided at the end of 1941, with SO1 becoming part of the Political Warfare Executive (PWE) and SO2 becoming the Special Operations Executive (SOE), SOE continued to operate the Palestine-based clandestine stations. The SOE-operated stations included "Free Voice of Greece," "Yugoslav National Radio," "Hungarian People's Station," "Radio Matteotti," and "Chetnik Radio Karadjordje."

SO1 was dependent upon SIS for beaming their black radio messages to occupied Europe. When SO1 developed a plan code-named "Intruder," it looked elsewhere for a transmitter to implement the plan, as the maximum output of SIS transmitters was 7.5 kilowatts. Intruder consisted of breaking into broadcasts of domestic German radio stations with defeatist messages using a powerful transmitter, so that large numbers of German citizens could be reached. Few Germans had shortwave receivers capable of receiving British white or black broadcasts, so Intruder was developed to overcome this handicap. The plan was first discussed in 1940, though its details were not worked out until spring 1941, when the plan was formally proposed to Hugh Dalton. Dalton approved the plan and forwarded it to Churchill on May 16, 1941. The following day, the prime minister gave it his blessing.

In order to implement the Intruder plan, SO1 decided to purchase the 600-kilowatt transmitter that RCA had in storage in the United States. Harold Robbin, an electrical engineer for Philco before the war, was sent to New York to work out the details of the purchase. Once in New York, Robbin discovered that RCA was attempting to gouge Britain for auxillary equipment needed to operate the transmitter. RCA wanted to sell the equipment at a price over which it would be the sole arbitrator. While Harold Robbin succeeded in getting the auxillary equipment at a lower price than RCA initially asked, the final price of the transmitter and auxillary equipment was over four times what David Sarnoff had told Campbell Stuart it would be. Although purchased with SO1 funds, technical control of the transmitter was given to Section VIII head, Colonel Gambier-Parry. The colonel's job was not only to house the transmitter, but operate it for SO1, the Air Ministry, the BBC, and other agencies that were in occasional need of its power. The BBC, for example, used the transmitter to increase the power of BBC broadcasts during critical events, such as the invasions of North Africa and Sicily. Soon after reaching Great Britain, the huge transmitter was given the nickname "Aspidistra." The name Aspidistra came from the lyrics of a popular song, which went: "The biggest aspidistra in the world."[102]

The Intruder plan, while approved in 1941, was not implemented until 1945 for fear that it would trigger reprisals from Germany. The BBC adamantly opposed the plan, arguing that it would lead to German interference with BBC broadcasts. Although buried because of BBC protests against it, the plan was resurrected in 1943 on the eve of the invasion of Sicily by General Eisenhower, who wanted Aspidistra to broadcast a report on German and Italian frequencies stating that Italy had capitulated to the Allies. Eisenhower hoped that the fake broadcasts would be believed by Italian military officers, who would then withdraw from combat, giving the Allies an easy victory. Churchill personally vetoed Eisenhower's proposal because he believed that it would diminish the integrity of the United Nations. Broadcasting a lie, Churchill believed, was not the best way to maintain the Allies' reputation for telling the truth.[103]

In 1945, two years after the invasion of Sicily and four years after the Intruder plan was first proposed, it was finally implemented. As Allied troops marched toward Germany following their successful landing in Europe, Eisenhower asked permission of the Combined Chiefs to have Aspidistra broadcast false information about the Allied advance on German radio frequencies. It was Eisenhower's idea to use Aspidistra to panic the German population into a massive, disorganized evacuation. If civilians with wheelbarrows, pushcarts, and other vehicles jammed the roads, the Wehrmacht's ability to retreat and retrench would be hampered. Although the Combined Chiefs were initially reluctant to approve the project, it was nonetheless approved. At the end of March, Aspidistra broadcast on Radio Frankfurt's frequency for several hours each day when the real station was silenced because of air raids. The fake Frankfurt broadcasts urged civilians to evacuate as soon as possible or face death at the hands of the rapidly advancing Allied war machine. The broadcasts succeeded in spreading panic among the German citizenry but did little to hasten the Allied victory.[104]

Between 1943 and 1945, the Aspidistra transmitter was used by a British-orginated mediumwave clandestine station called "Soldatensender Calais" (Soldiers' Station from Calais). Programs for this station were produced at the specially built communications complex at Milton Bryant. The Soldatensender claimed to be a German-operated armed forces radio station, directing news and entertainment to front-line troops. Because of the station's enormous power, it was able to reach most of occupied Europe and Germany, not just troops on the western front to whom it claimed to speak. The station's power and signal clarity produced a substantial listenership within Germany, particularly in the closing months of the war when German citizens were starved for information. German radio stations fed their listeners a diet of music rather than news. A survey conducted among German citizens immediately after the war found that 23 percent of respondents who had turned to a nondomestic German station had tuned to the Soldatensender.[105]

Although it claimed to be German-sponsored, many listeners who tuned to the Soldatensender were aware that it was an Allied operation, for it provided news that was unavailable over real German stations, and regularly spread rumors and gossip that portrayed German political and military leaders in a bad light. Because it was an obvious Allied operation, although claiming to be otherwise, the station was considered a gray, rather than black, station by it operators. The Soldatensender was listened to by a large number of Germans because it was safer to listen to than other Allied stations, like the BBC, Voice of the Supreme Headquarters Allied Expeditionary Force (SHAEF), or Voice of America.

Listening to Allied stations was forbidden in Germany, and those caught violating the law were often given the death sentence. Because Soldatensender Calais claimed to be German rather than British, many Germans felt safer listening to it than to overtly enemy stations. German leaders did little to counter the Soldatensender's claim that it was German-originated, for fear of drawing attention and listeners to the station. Their silence contributed to the station's popularity.

The Soldatensender was the brainchild of Sefton Delmer, a reporter for the London *Daily Express* who joined SO1 in 1941. Delmer replaced Richard Crossman as head of clandestine broadcasts directed at Germany, after Crossman went to North Africa with General Eisenhower's expedition. Delmer created another station that was similar to the Soldatensender in May 1941. The station was called "Gustav Siegfried Eins." Gustav Siegfried Eins has become one of the best-known clandestine stations of the war period, in large part due to Delmer's in-depth description of it in his autobiographical book, *Black Boomerang*.[106] Gustav Siegfried Eins, unlike the Soldatensender, did not claim to be an official German armed forces station, but an unofficial one. The station's chief spokesman was a noncommissioned officer called "Der Chef" (The Chief). Der Chef broadcast what superficially appeared to be pro-Hitler messages. While the broadcasts contained numerous attacks on Nazi party leaders, whom the station claimed were profiting from the war at the expense of the German military and populace, Der Chef defended Hitler, claiming that the Fuehrer was unaware of the Nazi profiteering. The purpose of the station was to turn the military against Nazi party leaders, and to turn Nazi leaders against each other with broadcasts such as this one:

If it should be a question of choosing between Goering or Himmler, then, by God and all the saints, let us have 30,000 hundred-weight of Hermann, rather than one milligram of this scheming political out-house flower, of this anemic inflated windbag, Heinrich Himmler. . . . [107]

Sefton Delmer joined SO1 in May 1941, a month in which a long-simmering jurisdictional feud between Hugh Dalton and Minister of Information Duff Cooper boiled over. The turf battle began long before either Dalton or Cooper were heads of their respective ministries. It began the day EH was established. EH was given responsibility for propaganda to enemy and enemy-occupied countries, while the BBC, over which the minister of information exercised nominal control, was assigned responsibility for other foreign broadcasts. According to this division, responsibilities switched from the BBC to EH when a country was occupied by Germany. In the first half of 1940, the European services of the BBC were supposed to transfer to EH, after German troops occupied Norway, the low countries, and France. Although jurisdiction for propaganda to these countries theoretically passed to EH, there was no accompanying transfer of staff or facilities. The existence of the same staff, and EH's being headquartered in Bedfordshire rather than London, where the BBC offices were, allowed the BBC to continue broadcasting to Western Europe, as it previously had.[108]

When Hugh Dalton became head of SOE, he did not immediately attempt to take control of BBC broadcasts to occupied Europe, as his hands were full with the merger of EH, Section D and MI(R) into a single organization. After the three organizations were successfully merged at the end of 1941, he expressed his interest in controlling white, in addition to black, propaganda directed at enemy states. Minister of Information Duff Cooper, like his predecessor Sir Stephen Tallents, maintained that broadcasts of the BBC were his responsibility. Cooper opposed every attempt by Dalton to preempt his authority. Between December 1940 and May 1941, each contestant appealed to other ministers in support of their view. This brought the conflict to the attention of the prime minister.

Churchill ordered Sir John Anderson to discuss the conflict with the feuding ministers and to come up with a solution. The solution that Anderson reached was the following: a common policy was needed for both covert and overt propaganda, but that overt and covert propaganda should be under separate heads. In effect, the "Anderson Award" perpetuated the status quo, and the conflict. When the conflict continued, Churchill attempted to resolve it by replacing Duff Cooper with a trusted friend, Brendan Bracken.[109]

Brendan Bracken was the exact opposite of Hugh Dalton: He was a conservative of humble origins. Bracken had worked his way up the British political ladder by skillfully making friends and exploiting opportunities. He was also a disciplined political chessplayer, who was good at anticipating his opponent's next move. He was particularly good at anticipating Dalton's moves, and was therefore able to skillfully outmanuever the Minister of Economic Warfare. His political skills allowed him to pry SO1 from Dalton's grasp. Bracken did this by focusing on Sir John Anderson's suggestion that a policy committee be established that would oversee the direction of covert and overt propaganda directed at enemy-controled countries. This policy committee, called the Political Warfare Executive (PWE), would function as a general staff and be responsible to Foreign Minister Anthony Eden, Minister of Economic Warfare Hugh Dalton, and the Minister of Information. Eden supported Bracken's proposal to create the PWE and his suggestions for appointees to head PWE. The appointees Bracken suggested were Robert Bruce Lockhart, Rex Leeper, and Dallas Brooks. Robert Bruce Lockhart was to head PWE, Leeper to be in charge of operations at Woburn Abbey, and Brooks the liaison with the military.

Lockhart, Leeper, and Brooks were politically masterful choices on the part of Bracken, for all were in some way associated with Dalton. Leeper was head of SO1. Brooks was also in SO1. Lockhart was technically in the Foreign Office, but served as an adviser on Czechoslovakia for EH, SO1's predecessor. Although associated with SO1, Leeper and Lockhart disliked the labor leader for personal and political reasons, and Dalton was aware of this. Dalton therefore voiced his opposition to their running the PWE without firm ministerial supervision. However, Dalton could not adamantly argue against their appointment without bringing his leadership of SOE into question. Leeper, after all, was Dalton's number one man in SO1. Eden supported Bracken's suggestions. Realizing that he was outvoted two-to-one, Dalton agreed to the formation of the PWE, thereby ceding control of SO1 to the PWE.[110] This was the first in a series of steps that eventually stripped Dalton of all jurisdiction over external propaganda. When Dalton attempted to exercise some control over PWE policy, Lockhart complained that Dalton was violating his agreement with the other ministers. Bracken consistently agreed with Lockhart, weakening Dalton's influence. A few months later, a disappointed Hugh Dalton was removed as head of the Ministry of Economic Warfare.

From Dalton's departure until the war's end, the PWE established policy for the psychwar stations beaming propaganda to occupied Europe. Although many of the black stations created while Dalton was head of SOE continued to broadcast after Dalton was moved to the Board of Trade on February 21, 1942, the 26 clandestine stations started after his departure were qualitatively different from those that took to the air in the earlier era. Although several clandestine socialist stations were started under Lockhart's leadership (e.g., the Belgian "Sambre et Meuse" and the German "Worker's Station"), more nonideological than ideological stations were created. The nonideological stations included "Astrologie und Okkultismus," "Wehrmachtsender Nord," "Blauwvoet" and the "Marshall's Order." "Astrologie und Okkultismus" was a station purportedly operated by a spiritualist, who broadcast messages from dead German troops to their families. "Wehrmachtsender Nord" claimed to be Wehrmacht-operated station broadcasting from Norway. It painted a gloomy and defeatist picture of soldiers' lives in occupied countries. "Blauwvoet" claimed to be operated by a group of Flemish collaborators. The purpose of the station was to stimulate rivalries among various collaborationist groups. The "Marshall's Order" claimed to be operated by pro-German Rumanians, who "inadvertently" made comments that would arouse anti-German sentiments among the listening audience. These stations did little to "set Europe ablaze."

## NOTES

1. For a discussion of Voice of Liberation and Radio Swan broadcasts, see Lawrence Soley and John Nichols, *Clandestine Radio Broadcasting* (New York:

Praeger, 1987); David A. Phillips, *The Night Watch* (New York: Atheneum, 1977); and Victor Marchetti and John Marks, *The CIA and the Cult of Intelligence* (New York: Alfred Knopf, 1974).

2. Details on this and other Indochinese clandestine stations can be found in Soley and Nichols, *Clandestine Radio Broadcasting*.

3. For example, see "Shah's Army Leader Says Iran Is Weary of Khomeini," *New York Times*, June 12, 1980, p. A7.

4. "Dissension Splitting Iran," *Cleveland Press*, June 12, 1980, p. 1A.

5. "US Concedes it is Behind Anti-Khomeini Broadcasts," *New York Times*, June 29, 1980, p. A1.

6. The CIA also engineered and carried out the mining of Nicaragua's harbors ("CIA Funnels 'Political' Aid to Contras, Sources Say," Associated Press Wire Report, April 13, 1986, AM Cycle). The proscription on CIA involvement in the disbursement of monies was dropped when Congress approved $100 million more in contra aid during June 1986. See "CIA is Assigned Role of Running Contra Activities," *New York Times*, July 12, 1986, p. A1.

7. *Psychological Warfare Operations* was a restricted classification publication with classification number ST 33–20–1. *Psychological Operations* was manual FM 33–5 (Washington, D.C.: Department of the Army, December 1962).

8. For a discussion of the "40 Committee," see John Ranelagh, *The Agency* (New York: Simon and Schuster, 1986).

9. "Behind 'Reagan Doctrine,' Covert Action," *Washington Post*, March 9, 1986, p. 1; "Overseeing of C.I.A. by Congress Has Produced Decade of Support," *New York Times*, July 7, 1986, p. 1A.

10. These stations are discussed in greater detail in Soley and Nichols, *Clandestine Radio Broadcasting;* and Gerry Dexter, *Clandestine Confidential* (Columbus, Ohio: Universal Electronics, 1984).

11. "Behind 'Reagan Doctrine,' Covert Action."

12. A *New York Times*/CBS poll, for example, found that the predominantly Cuban Hispanic population in Florida voted overwhelmingly Republican in the 1984 presidential election, giving President Reagan 73 percent and Walter Mondale 27 percent. See "Poll Studies Hispanic Party Loyalties," *New York Times*, July 18, 1986, p. A7.

13. "U.S. Plans to Seek Open Afghan Aid," *New York Times*, May 9, 1985, p. A9; "Sihanouk's Son Joins Father's Fight," *New York Times*, January 3, 1987, p. 4; "Contras' AM Radio Station Begins Operating," *Los Angles Times*, January 19, 1987, p. 7; "U.S. Backs New Clandestine Contra Station," *Newsday* (New York edition), January 24, 1987, p. 19; "Retired Air Force General Named as Central Figure in Secret Talks," *New York Times*, December 9, 1986, pp. 1, 16.

14. "Missionaries for Democracy: U.S. Aid for Global Pluralism," *New York Times*, June 1, 1986, p. 1. The National Endowment's projects were supplemented with additional covert actions run through the National Security Council ("Iran Sales Linked to Wide Programs of Covert Policies," *New York Times*, February 15, 1987, pp. 1, 8). A solicitation for funds by the Freedom House for the Afghan clandestine stations is contained in William McGurn, "Radio Free Kabul," *The American Spectator*, March 1983, p. 44.

A very secret, possibly illegal, program that paralleled the National Endowment's activities was headed by National Security Council member Lt. Col. Oliver

North. Using monies diverted from U.S. arms sold to Iran, North and retired Gen. Richard Secord purchased a ship for $300,000 that was to house a transmitter for broadcasting clandestine radio programs to Libya. Another $100,000 was spent on "radiotelephone equipment," as part of a plan for clandestinely broadcasting to Cuba. See "Iran Sales Linked to Wide Program of Covert Policies," *New York Times*, February 15, 1987, pp. 1, 8; "The Trail So Far," *New York Times*, May 8, 1987, p. 8; "Where the Money Went: The Secord Testimony," *New York Times*, May 6, 1987, p. 9.

15. For a discussion of these stations, see Lawrence E. Magne, "Clandestine Radio Broadcasting 1975," *World Radio and Television Handbook 1976* (New York: Billboard Publications, 1976), pp. 55–70; and Soley and Nichols, *Clandestine Radio Broadcasting*.

16. "Reds' Secret Radio Station Is Hunted in Czechoslovakia," *New York Times*, March 19, 1931, p. 11.

17. " 'Red' Radio Mystifies," *New York Times*, April 26, 1931, p. 3E.

18. "Illegal Radio Station of Reds Seized by the Berlin Police," *New York Times*, December 9, 1932, p. 28.

19. "Red Station Broadcasts to Europe 'From Milan,' " *New York Times*, April 15, 1937, p. 9.

20. "Red Radio Station Heard in Germany," *New York Times*, March 21, 1937, p. 11; "Nazis Finally Drown Out Red Broadcaster Who Appealed to Reich Nightly for 2 Weeks," *New York Times*, March 30, 1937, p. 6; Allan Merson, *Communist Resistance in Nazi Germany* (London: Lawrence and Wisehart, 1985), pp. 121, 196.

21. Harwood L. Childs and John B. Whitton, eds., *Propaganda by Shortwave* (Princeton, N.J.: Princeton University Press, 1942), p. 4; Thomas Grandin, *The Political Uses of Radio* (New York: Arno Press Reprint, 1971, c. 1939), pp. 24–25, 45–6. While Russia was the first country to use radio for disseminating propaganda, Germany was the first to use it tactically. During the last months of World War I, Germany "sent out daily bulletins in German, French and English, giving highly colored reports of German successes and minimizing their losses," but the broadcasts were received by few if any listeners, according to O. W. Reigel, *Mobilizing for Chaos* (New York: Yale University Press, 1934), pp. 87–88.

22. Cited in Adam B. Ulam, *Expansion and Coexistence* (New York: Praeger, 1968), p. 130.

23. For a description of how Lord Curzon presented British complaints to Soviet foreign minister George Chicherin, see Harold Nicolson, *Curzon: the Last Phase* (London: Constable and Co., 1934).

24. Broadcasts continued to be directed at the British working class, as well. See "Moscow Reds Now Use Radio to Address British Miners," *New York Times*, October 21, 1926, p. 1. British Parliament members were very upset with these broadcasts until they learned that "only the costliest, most aristocratic British receivers" could pick up the broadcasts, according to Heber Blankenhorn, "The Battle of Radio Armaments," *Harper's*, December 1931, pp. 83–91.

25. The Communist parties around the world followed the new Soviet policy of attacking the democratic countries, which were said to be looking to start a new imperialist war.

26. Grandin, *The Political Uses of Radio*, p. 54; Childs and Whitton, (eds.), *Propaganda by Shortwave*, p. 28.

27. *Foreign Broadcast Intelligence Service (FBIS)*, July 1, 1942, p. R2.

28. Denis Mack Smith, *Mussolini's Roman Empire* (New York: Viking Press, 1976); Grandin, *The Political Uses of Radio;* "Free Corsica," *Times* (of London), January 24, 1939, 3d ed., p. 11. The 3d edition of the *Times* is not available in most libraries, including those in Great Britain.

29. Charles Rolo, *Radio Goes to War* (New York: G. P. Putnam's Sons, 1942), p. 50. Another pro-Franco clandestine station may have originated in Germany.

30. H. Schuyler, Jr., "The Official Propaganda of Great Britain," *Public Opinion Quarterly* 3 (April) 1939, pp. 263–71.

31. No information is available in the British Public Records Office files on the operation of the "German Revolution Station." The transcript is from the *British Broadcasting Corporation (BBC)*, Monitoring Service Report, April 17, 1940, p. 1E (2). Other transcriptions are found in *BBC*, April 19, 1940, p. 1E (2) and May 7, 1940, p. 1E (b). The transcriptions leave no doubt, however, that the broadcasts originated in Great Britain. Information on the "Sender of der Europäischen Revolution" is available in Sefton Delmer, *Black Boomerang* (London: Secker and Warburg, 1962), p. 37–38; Ellic Howe, *The Black Game* (London: Michael Joseph, 1982), pp. 84–85; and "EH and SO1: Organization, Policy and Aims," *PRO*, F0898/4.

32. "Minutes of Meeting of German Regional Section on 18th March 1941," EH and SO1, *PRO*, F0898/4, p. 28.

33. *Columbia Broadcasting System* (CBS) Monitoring Report, January 15, 1940, p. 7; Rolo, *Radio Goes to War*.

34. Grandin, *The Political Uses of Radio*, p. 56; Rolo, *Radio Goes to War*, p. 83.

35. Rolo, *Radio Goes to War*, p. 84.

36. For examples of reports on fifth column activities, see Henry Torres, *Campaign of Treachery* (New York, 1942); William J. Donovan and Edgar Ansel Mowrer, *Fifth Column Lessons for America* (Washington, D.C.: American Council on Public Affairs, 1941); and Edmond Taylor, Edgar Snow, and Eliot Janeway, *Smash Hitler's International* (New York: Greystone Press, 1941). For "exposés" of fifth column activities in the United States, see John Roy Carlson, *Undercover* (New York: E. P. Dutton & Company, 1943) and Michael Sayers and Albert Kahn, *Sabotage! The Secret War against America* (New York: Harper & Brothers, 1942).

37. The book is cited in such psychological warfare "classics" as Paul Linebarger, *Psychological Warfare* (Washington, D.C.: Infantry Journal Press, 1948) and Daniel Lerner, *Sykewar: Psychological Warfare Against Nazi Germany* (Cambridge: The M.I.T. Press, 1971).

38. "Memorandum from: Edmond L. Taylor on Proposed Functions of OSS Committee," July 27, 1942, *Donovan*, box 99B, vol. 1 (unbound), tab. A.

39. Edmond Taylor, "Political Warfare: A Sword We Must Unsheath," *The Reporter*, September 14, 1961, pp. 27–31.

40. "Correspondence," *The Reporter*, October 26, 1961, pp. 9–10.

41. Edmond Taylor, *The Strategy of Terror* (Boston: Houghton Mifflin Company, 1940), p. 71 and p. 37.

42. Taylor, *The Strategy of Terror*, p. 37; Charles Rolo, "The Strategy of War by Radio," *Harper's*, November 1940, pp. 640–49; Allan M. Michie, "War as Fought by Radio," *Reader's Digest*, June 1940, pp. 17–21; and Charles Roetter, *The Act of Psychological Warfare* (New York: Stein & Day, 1974), pp. 102–6. Roetter reports that Ferdonnet's broadcasts originated from a clandestine, not an aboveground, transmitter.

43. E. Tangye Lean, *Voices in the Darkness* (London: Secker and Warburg, 1943), pp. 104–9; Rolo, *Radio Goes to War*, p. 85–87. Ferdonnet's omniscience did not help him escape from Allied troops after the defeat of Germany. He was arrested, tried, and executed by firing squad, according to " 'Stuttgart Traitor' Executed," *New York Times*, August 5, 1945, p. 19.

44. Lean, *Voices in the Darkness*, p. 105–6.

45. Although anticommunism existed before the Hitler-Stalin pact, it mushroomed afterward. See Les K. Adler and Thomas J. Paterson, "Red Fascism: The Merger of Nazi Germany and Soviet Russia in the American Image of Totalitarianism, 1930's–1950's," *American Historical Review* 75 (April) 1970, pp. 1046–64.

46. This episode is discussed in Jerold Auerbach, "The Depression Decade," in Alan Reitman, ed., *The Pulse of Freedom* (New York: W. W. Norton and Company, 1975), pp. 65–104; and Corlis Lamont, ed., *The Trial of Elizabeth Gurley Flynn by the American Civil Liberties Union* (New York: Horizon Press, 1968).

47. Cited in Richard Polenberg, "Franklin Roosevelt and Civil Liberties: The Case of the Dies Committee," *The Historian* 30 (February) 1968, p. 177.

48. A. Panfilov, *Broadcasting Pirates* (Moscow: Progress Publishers, 1981), p. 55.

49. Cited in Edward Mortimer, *The Rise of the French Communist Party 1920–1947* (Boston: Faber & Faber, 1984), p. 289.

50. Louis Lochner, ed., *The Goebbels Diaries* (New York: Award Books, 1971), p. 251.

51. Willi Boelke, ed., *The Secret Conferences of Dr. Goebbels* (New York: E. P. Dutton, 1970), p. 3; Fred Taylor, ed., *The Goebbels Diaries 1939–1941* (New York: G. P. Putnam's Sons, 1983), p. 65. Taylor, *Strategy of Terror*, p. 194, incorrectly reports that Radio Humanité began in February 1940, while Howe, *The Black Game*, p. 64, says the station appeared in April 1940. By January 1940, Goebbels was gloating because the French believed that Radio Humanité was located in Russia (see Fred Taylor, ed., *The Goebbels Diaries 1939–1941*, p. 99).

52. Fischer, *Stalin and German Communism* (Cambridge: Harvard University Press, 1948).

53. Taylor, ed. *The Goebbels Diaries 1939–1941*, p. 444; Boelke, ed., *The Secret Conferences of Dr. Goebbels*, 48.

54. Howe, *The Black Game*, reports that Radio Réveil and Voix de la Paix were actually one station called "Le Réveil de la Paix." This contradicts the transcriptions of the *BBC* and other sources reported herein.

55. *British Broadcasting Corporation (BBC)*, December 27, 1939, p. 30.

56. *BBC*, January 1, 1940, p. 3C.

57. Michael Balfour, *Propaganda in War and Peace 1939–1945* (Boston: Routledge & Kegan Paul, 1979), p. 181.

58. Broadcast of June 12 reported in Lean, *Voices in the Darkness*, p. 134.

59. The mediumwave signal of Voix de la Paix and the longwave signal of Radio Réveil probably originated from Cologne and Leipzig transmitters. See Boelke, ed. *The Secret Conferences of Dr. Goebbels*, p. 47.

60. Broadcast of May 20, 1940 reported in Lean, *Voices in the Darkness*, p. 121.

61. *BBC*, June 5, 1940, p. 2D(i).

62. *BBC*, June 12, 1940, p. 1C(v).

63. *BBC*, June 7, 1940, p. 2C (ii).

64. Princeton Listening Center, *Study of Political Broadcasting*, Report Number 10 (September 3) 1940, p. 1.

65. J. A. Cole, *Lord Haw-Haw & William Joyce* (New York: Farrar, Straus & Giroux, 1965); Harold Ettlinger, *The Axis on the Air* (New York: Bobbs-Merrill Company, 1943), pp. 39–43.

66. Jonah Barrington, "Warsaw Winnie Finds a Friend," *London Daily Express*, September 18, 1939, p. 35; also in Cole, *Lord Haw-Haw & William Joyce*, p. 115.

67. B. Henry and Ruth Durant, "Lord Haw-Haw of Hamburg: 2. His British Audience," *Public Opinion Quarterly* 4 (September) 1940, pp. 443–50.

68. Cole, *Lord Haw-Haw and William Joyce*, p. 155.

69. *BBC*, February 25, 1940, p. 26; *BBC*, June 1, 1940, p. 1B(xv); Lean, *Voices in the Darkness*, p. 126.

70. "Mystery of Anti-British Radio Station," *Times* (of London), February 27, 1940, p. 4; "Mystery of Bogus Radio Station," (London) *Daily Telegraph*, February 27, 1940, p. 1; "Billingsgate on the Air," *Times* (of London), August 21, 1940, p. 4; Letter from Valentine Williams to Colonel Brooks (July 7, 1940), *PRO*, FO 898/6.

71. In one of its earliest analyses of the station, the Foreign Broadcast Information Service concluded that the New British Broadcasting Station "follows, more or less, the lines of Lord Haw-Haw. These talks are ineffective" (*FBIS*, January 15, 1942, p. D6).

72. Boelke, ed., *The Secret Conference of Dr. Goebbels*, p. 71.

73. *BBC*, August 15, 1940, p. 1B(ii); August 16, 1940, p. 1B(i); August 17, 1940, p. 1B(i).

74. Louis de Jong, *The German Fifth Column in the Second World War* (New York: Howard Fertig, 1973 [reprint], p. 88. The assertion that the Netherlands collapsed because of fifth columnists also circulated in the United States. For example, see Joseph Bornstein and Paul R. Milton, *Action against the Enemy's Mind* (New York: Bobbs-Merrill, 1942), pp. 120–35.

75. Bradley Smith, *The Shadow Warriors* (New York: Basic Books, 1983), pp. 3–30; de Jong, *The German Fifth Column in the Second World War*.

76. Balfour, *Propaganda in War*, p. 140; Cole, *Lord Haw-Haw & William Joyce*, p. 168.

77. Balfour, *Propaganda in War*, p. 139.

78. "The Screen: Holmes Up-to-Date," *New York Times*, September 19, 1942, p. 9; "Sherlock Holmes Back again to Mastermind War," *New York Daily News*, September 19, 1942, p. 22; " 'The Voice of Terror' Speaks at the Rialto Theater," *New York Post*, September 19, 1942, p. 10; "Sherlock Holmes and the Voice of Terror," *Variety*, September 9, 1942, p. 14. In the film, the broadcasts are clan-

destinely recorded in Great Britain and then sneaked to Germany, from where they transmit back to England. Holmes discovers that the head of Germany's fifth column in England is actually a member of the British cabinet!

79. Sir Campbell Stuart wrote a history of the British World War I propaganda agency entitled *Secrets of Crewe House: The Story of a Famous Campaign* (New York: Hodder and Stoughton, 1920). Crewe House is also discussed in Stuart's autobiography, *Opportunity Knocks Once* (London: Collins, 1952).

80. Balfour, *Propaganda in War*, p. 56.

81. Brooks was eventually promoted to general, knighted, and in 1949 appointed Governor of Victoria, Australia.

82. *The Adventures of an Ensign* (London: W. Blackwood & Sons, 1919), *The Man with the Clubfoot* (New York: McBride & Company, 1918), *Okewood of the Secret Service* (New York: McBride & Company, 1919), *The Key Man* (New York: Houghton Mifflin Company, 1926), *The Knife Behind the Curtain* (New York: Houghton Mifflin Company, 1930), *Death Answers the Bell* (New York: Houghton Mifflin Company, 1932), and *The Clue of the Rising Moon* (New York: Houghton Mifflin Company, 1935) are some of the novels written by Valentine Williams.

83. Robert Bruce Lockhart's writings include *Retreat from Glory* (New York: G.P. Putnam's Sons, 1934), *Return to Malaya* (New York: G.P. Putnam's, 1936), *Guns or Butter: War Countries and Peace Countries of Europe Revisited* (London: Putnam, 1938), *Comes the Reckoning* (London: Putnam, 1947), *My Europe* (London: Putnam, 1952), and *Giants Cast Long Shadows* (London: Putnam, 1960).

84. Christopher Andrew, *Her Majesty's Secret Service* (New York: Penguin Books, 1987), p. 471.

85. This terminology is now used by Soviet and U.S. propagandists. See Vitaly Petrusenko, *A Dangerous Game: CIA and the Mass Media* (Prague: Interpress, 1978); Panfilov, *Broadcasting Pirates*; and Alfred H. Pollack, Jr., *U.S. Army Special Warfare* (Washington, D.C.: U.S. Government Printing Office, 1982).

86. Howe, *The Black Game*, pp. 74–5; *BBC*, April 17, 1940, p. 1E(2).

87. "Memo to Sir Campbell Stuart from Mr. Murray" (June 18, 1940), EH & SO1: Mr. Leeper's Meetings, 1940–1941, *PRO*, FO 898/9.

88. "Report to Rt. Hon. A. Duff Cooper, Minister of Information, by Sir Campbell Stuart" (August 16, 1940), pp. 14–21, *PRO*, FO 898/9.

89. Quoted in David Stafford, *Britain and European Resistance* (Toronto: University of Toronto Press, 1980), p. 25.

90. Crossman was editor of *New Statesman and Nation* prior to joining SO1, and author of *Friedrich Engels* (New York: Knopf, 1936), *Plato Today* (London: Allen & Unwin, 1937), and *Government and the Governed* (London: Christophers, 1939).

91. The animosity toward Crossman is particularly evident in Howe's *The Black Game*. Chapter 5 of that book consists of nothing but unkind reminiscences of Crossman. One should contrast the unfavorable comments about Crossman with Howe's favorable, but inaccurate, descriptions of Otto Strasser.

92. Other works by Professor Brogan include *The American Political System* (London: H. Hamilton, 1933), *Government of the People* (New York: Harper and Brothers, 1933), *French Personalities and Problems* (New York: Knopf, 1947), and *France Under the Republic* (New York: Harper & Brothers, 1947).

93. Stuart, *Secrets of Crewe House*, p. 11.

94. George Martelli also wrote several books, including *Italy Against the World* (London: Chatto & Windus, 1937), *Whose Sea? A Mediterranean Journey* (London: Chatto & Windus, 1938), *Agent Extraordinary* (London: Collins, 1960), and *Experiments in World Government* (London: Johnson, 1966).

95. Cook's *Traveller's Handbook to Norway, Sweden, Denmark, Finland and Iceland* (London: Simpkin Marshall, 1936), p. 5.

96. "Notes on Discussions with Regional Heads" (June 16, 1941), pp. 26–27, EH & SO1: Mr. Leeper's Meetings, 1940–41, *PRO*, FO 898/9; "Minutes of Meetings" of July 15, July 22, July 31, 1941, pp. 28, 30, 31, EH & SO1: Organization Policy and Aims, *PRO*, FO 898/4; "PID Research Units: Underground Broadcasting Stations, Part II," *PRO*, FO 898/52.

97. Delmer, *Black Boomerang*, p. 37; "Eighth Meeting on October 19, 1940," pp. 238–40, EH & SO1: Mr. Leeper's Meetings, 1940–1941, *PRO*, FO 898/9. For a discussion of the politics of and conflicts within the New Beginning group, see Lewis J. Edinger, *German Exile Politics* (Berkeley: University of California Press, 1956).

98. "Policy to France" (November 7, 1940), *PRO*, FO 898/9; Stafford, *Britain and European Resistance*, p. 39.

99. "3rd Meeting of a Committee Held by RAL" (September 14, 1940), pp. 220–21, EH & SO1: Mr. Leeper's Meeting, 1940–41, *PRO*, FO 898/9; "PID Research Units: Underground Broadcasting Stations, Part II," *PRO*, FO 898/52.

100. Bickham Sweet-Escott, *Baker Street Irregular* (London: Methuen & Co., 1965), pp. 76–78.

101. "Executive Committee Report" (February 25, 1942), "Memo from Mr. Murray to Mr. Bruce Lockhart" (February 27, 1942), "The Transmissions of the 'Free Voice of Greece' (3d Report)" (February 8–14, 1942), *PRO*, FO 898/54; Sweet-Escott, *Baker Street Irregular*, p. 79.

102. "Letter to Ralph Murray" (July 9, 1941), "Report to the PWE on the Progress of a Project Originally Undertaken by SO1" (November 23, 1941), "Notes on the 7980 Project" (January 26, 1942), "PWE German Section: Proposed Scheme for Control of 7980" (July 6, 1942), Aspidistra History, *PRO*, FO 898/43; "Draft—Aspidistra" (January 30, 1942), "Meeting in the Director of Signals' Office" (April 24, 1942), *PRO*, FO 898/349.

103. "Operation 'Husky'—False Armistice Rumours" (p. 173, handwritten), "Incoming Message from Algiers to Etousa, Agwar for action, signed Eisenhower" (June 29, 1943), "Letter to Sir Robert Bruce Lockhart from Office of War Cabinet" (July 3, 1943), *PRO*, FO 898/349.

104. The Psychological Warfare Division Supreme Headquarters Allied Expeditionary Force, *An Account of its Operation in the Western European Campaign 1944–1945* (Bad Homburg, Germany: SHAEF, October 1945), p. 55; "Use of Aspidistra to Break Down German Resistance" (January 19, 1945), JCS 1218/1, *JCS*, P. 1: 1942–45, The European Theater, reel 11, nos. 469–506; Delmer, *Black Boomerang*, pp. 195–200; Charles Cruickshank, *The Fourth Arm* (London: Davis Poynter, 1977), pp. 153–58.

105. "SHAEF, PWD: Intelligence Section—Listening to Allied Radio Broadcasts by German Civilians Under the Nazis" (June 5, 1945), *Lerner*, box 87, file 7.

106. Delmer's discussions of Gustav Siegfried Eins are reported almost ver-

batim in Ronald Seth, *The Truth Benders* (London: Leslie Frewin, 1969), pp. 60–8; Roetter, *The Art of Psychological Warfare*, pp. 171–76; and David Owen, *Battle of Wits* (London: Leo Cooper, 1978), pp. 76–81.

107. *FBIS*, April 20, 1943, p. Y3.
108. Lockhart, *Comes the Reckoning*, p. 96.
109. Cruickshank, *The Fourth Arm*, pp. 23–24.
110. Ben Pimlott, ed., *The Second World War Diary of Hugh Dalton 1940–1945* (London: Jonathan Cape, 1986), pp. 259–82; Ben Pimlott, *Hugh Dalton* (London: Jonathon Cape, 1985), pp. 329–35.

# 2

## IMITATING ENGLAND: ORIGINS OF U.S. PSYCHWAR AGENCIES

Representative Martin Dies's House Committee on Un-American Activities was born in May 1938.[1] Its birth was supported by New Dealers and liberals who hoped that the committee would expose Nazi subversion in the United States. Liberals soon had doubts about the committee after congressmen J. Parnell Thomas, Noah Mason, Karl Mundt, John Rankin, and numerous haters of "Communist Jewry" expressed support for the committee. Committee chairman Dies was a conservative Dixiecrat who was rumored to be a member of the Ku Klux Klan. Among those he considered to be purveyors of socialism and class conflict were Harry Hopkins, former secretary of commerce and Works Progress Administration head, Secretary of the Interior Harold Ickes, and Michigan governor Frank Murphy, who in 1939 was appointed U.S. Attorney General. For his views, Dies earned the dubious distinction of having received "as many favorable references in Axis propaganda . . . as any living American public figure. His opinions were quoted by the Axis without criticism at any time," according to Federal Communications Commission (FCC) monitors.[2]

J. Parnell Thomas was a Republican from New Jersey who believed the New Deal was "no different from the socialism of Hitler . . . and the communism of Stalin."[3] In 1939, he voted against improving Guam harbor and lifting the arms embargo to allow aid to be given to Great Britain. Although he voted for Lend-Lease in 1941, he voted against the War Securities bill in 1943 that stiffened espionage penalties. Noah Mason was a Republican from Illinois who opposed the New Deal, lend-lease, and civil rights legislation.[4] Representatives Thomas and Mason were members of Dies's Committee from its beginning in 1938. Karl Mundt was an isolationist who in 1940 led a congressional delegation to the Republican convention that opposed the nomination of "interventionist" Wendell Willkie. Mundt's delegation had the backing and possibly the financial support of the German Embassy. In 1940 and 1941, Mundt voted against the selective service act, opposed Lend-Lease, and urged a mediated peace between Germany and Great Britain.[5] He was a strong supporter of the Dies committee from the beginning and finally joined it in 1943. Rankin was Congress's most outspoken anti-Semite. He unabashedly blamed the war in Europe on "international Jewish bankers," not Hitler, and claimed that "Wall Steet and a little group of international Jewish bankers are . . . plunging us into a European war." Rankin hated blacks almost as much as he hated Jews. When the Red Cross suggested eliminating labels on blood that reported whether it was from blacks or whites, Rankin claimed it was a plot by "crackpots, the Communists and parlor pinks" who wanted "to mongrelize this nation." Rankin asserted that antidiscrimination orders and laws were "revolutionary, illegal and destructive." In 1945, he wrote the congressional amendment that permanently established the House Committee on Un-American Activities.[6]

As the Dies Committee started taking testimony, it became clear that Communist rather than Nazi activities were the subject of its investigations. According to Dies and those who testified, nazism and communism were identical, so that testimony that exposed Communist activities also exposed Nazi subversion. In the first volume of testimony taken by the committee, only four witnesses spoke on German-sponsored activities: John and James Metcalfe, Peter Gissibl, and Frank Davin. John Metcalfe was the Dies Committee's official investigator. The four testified about the German-American Bund. The remaining 22 witnesses testified about the Communist menace. The witnesses included H. L. Chaillaux of the American Legion, Margaret Kerr of the Better American Federation, Walter Steele of the American Coalition Committee on National Security, and others with equally dubious expertise on Marxism. Steele was the copublisher of a 1933 anti-Communist book that began with a quotation from "Chancellor Adolph Hitler." He was also publisher of the extreme right-wing *National Republic* and a colleague of notorious anti-Semite Father Charles Coughlin.[7] In the first volume of testimony before the Dies Committee, ninety pages concerned the German-American Bund, while 889 pages were devoted to Communist "propaganda activities."[8] The testimony was given in 1938, before the signing of the Ribbentrop-Molotov Nonaggression Pact, when Communist party members were ardent supporters of Roosevelt. Because of this, many New Dealers believed the Dies committee's major purpose was to damage Roosevelt's administration.

While Dies and his colleagues were chasing Communists, the media, courts, and U.S. counterintelligence agencies were chasing Nazis. A Nazi spy ring headed by Guenther Rumrich that attempted to obtain U.S. aircraft-carrier specifications, coastal defense information, and other vital defense secrets was uncovered and brought to trial in 1938. The cracking of the spy ring, when combined with the reportage of the anschluss in March and Germany's seizure of the Sudetenland from Czechoslovakia in September, kept the "newspaper-reading, newsreel-viewing and radio-listening public" filled with tales about Nazi espionage and intrigue throughout 1938.[9] As it turned out, the tales of Nazi subversion in the United States were greatly exaggerated, while Hitler's inevitable march toward war was grossly understated. The trial of Rumrich's colleagues showed that German agents were woefully unskilled and incompetent. The only data that Rumrich succeeded in obtaining was a report on the incidence of venereal disease at Fort Hamilton, Brooklyn.

If the Rumrich spy case showed that Hitler's agents were woefully unskilled at obtaining vital U.S. secrets, it also showed that U.S. agencies were equally unskilled at counterespionage. The Rumrich spy ring was investigated by the Federal Bureau of Investigation (FBI), the Office of Naval Intelligence (ONI), the Army's Military Intelligence Division (G–2), State Department security officers, the New York police, and other agencies. Despite a large number of investigating agents and agencies, fourteen of the eighteen indicted suspects managed to escape. So bad was the bungling and coordination that the judge in the espionage trial castigated the FBI, army, and navy for their extreme carelessness. While the trial exposed the need of the United States for a system of central intelligence coordination, it also brought to the attention of the public some of Germany's attempts at espionage and subversion, so much so that the FBI handled 634 cases of reported espionage in 1938, whereas in preceding years the number averaged 35. Even such simple organizations as the German student-exchange program was accused of being a den of subversion.[10]

Reports on Nazi espionage finally forced the Dies Committee to take a deeper look at Nazi subversion, even though it would have preferred to remain focused on Communist activities. In 1940, hysteria about Nazi subversive activities reached a peak following the rapid defeat of France by the Germany army. In the United States, as in England, the French defeat was blamed on a fifth column of Nazi agents and saboteurs. President Roosevelt gave these exaggerated and inaccurate reports credibility when he reported in a fireside chat of May 26, 1940, that France's defeat was attributable to the fifth column and that the United States was also the object of "The Trojan Horse. The Fifth Column that betrays a nation unprepared for treachery." He claimed that "spies, saboteurs and traitors are the actors in this new strategy. With all of these we must deal vigorously." The president added that a small group of fifth columnists in the United States was attempting to undermine the national policy through confusion, rumor, emotional appeals, and false slogans.[11] His accusations were primarily for the purpose of assuring the success of his political agenda and only secondarily for making the American public aware of a national security threat. A few months later, the Dies Committee issued its 415-page "White Paper" on German-sponsored activities in the United States. It contained no new revelations about Nazi subversion. Dies also released his own book on fifth-column activities, *The Trojan Horse in America*, which contained only 41 pages about Fascist, and 303 pages on Communist, activities. Dies also kept his name in the public eye with alarming reports about 6 million U.S. residents who he alleged were foreign agents.[12]

## ENTER COLONEL WILLIAM J. "WILD BILL" DONOVAN, ESQUIRE

Following the French collapse and in the midst of the fifth-column panic, President Roosevelt summoned Wall Street attorney William J. "Wild Bill" Donovan to the White House for a special meeting. Donovan was a prominent New Yorker who had served in the "Fighting 69th" detachment during World War I. Donovan achieved the rank of colonel in that war and relished his title of colonel as much as any southern gentleman. He liked being addressed as "Colonel Donovan." The colonel was the Republican candidate for New York attorney general in 1922 and governor in 1932, when he campaigned with Herbert Hoover. He was defeated in both elections. Between these bids for elective office, Colonel Donovan was assistant attorney general for the United States. In 1935, as a private citizen, the colonel visited Rome, where he met Premier Benito Mussolini. The meeting with Mussolini was arranged by Italian ambassador Augusto Rossi, a frequent dinner guest at the Donovan household. Colonel Donovan flew from Rome to Ethiopia, where he visited Marshal Pietro Badoglio, and to Libya, where he met Italo Balbo. Donovan then flew to London, where he briefed Foreign Minister Anthony Eden's aides on the situation in North Africa.[13]

In 1937, again as a private citizen, Donovan toured Spain, where a civil war between Republican loyalists and Italian- and German-backed rebels of General Francisco Franco was being fought. The tour earned Donovan a reputation for being well-informed on military matters, but also as a man who was "not happy if there is no war on the face of the earth."[14] Donovan also traveled to Germany to watch the Wehrmacht conduct maneuvers. The following year, he traveled to Czechoslovakia to examine the defenses of the Sudetenland. On September 29 of that year, the Sudetenland was ceded to Germany by the appeasement policies of British Prime Minister Neville Chamberlain and French Premier Édouard Daladier. The action marked the undeclared beginning of World War II. Six months later, German troops occupied Bohemia and Moravia. Slovakia was established as an independent clerico-fascist state headed by Roman Catholic priest Josef Tiso. In August, Germany and the Soviet Union signed their Non-Aggression Pact. On September 1, Germany invaded Poland, precipitating declarations of war on Germany by Great Britain and France. On September 17, the USSR invaded Poland from the east.

In December 1939, President Roosevelt asked Bill Donovan's close friend, Frank Knox, the owner of the *Chicago Daily News* and unsuccessful Republican vice-presidential candidate in 1936, to join his cabinet as secretary of the navy. Because of the war in Europe, Roosevelt wanted a bipartisan cabinet that could counter isolationist Republican claims that the Democrats wanted the United States to enter the war. Knox, reluctant to be the only Republican in an otherwise Democratic cabinet, suggested that Roosevelt add a second Republican—"Wild Bill" Donovan— to his cabinet as secretary of war. Roosevelt, acting on Knox's suggestion, invited former President Hoover's secretary of state, Henry Stimson, to be secretary of war. Although Roosevelt recognized Donovan as a civilian authority on military affairs, he did not want a secretary of war who was "not happy if there is no war." Knox and Stimson accepted the appointments and joined the Roosevelt cabinet in July 1940.

The White House meeting to which Donovan was invited during the first week in July was attended by Secretary of State Hull, Roosevelt, Knox, and Stimson. At the meeting, the situation in Europe was discussed. Contradictory information on Britain's ability to fight Germany had been consistently given to the White House and Congress by State Department officials and military leaders. Ambassador Joseph Kennedy predicted the quick collapse of England, but his attachés drew a more optimistic picture. Rear Admiral Walter Anderson presented a completely confused report to the Senate Naval Affairs committee. Donovan was asked by Roosevelt and Knox to go to England to assess the situation. He was an ideal choice for the assignment because of his reputation as a expert on military affairs; his good relations with members of the armed services, both as a colonel during World War I and as a reserve officer; his pro-England sentiments that seemingly contrasted with his background as an Irish-American Catholic; and his impeccable Republican credentials. Wild Bill accepted the commission and left for London on a Pan American clipper on July 14, stopping first in Lisbon. Donovan arrived in London on July 17.[15]

To disguise the purpose of the trip, Donovan met Edgar Ansel Mowrer in London. Mowrer was the Paris correspondent of the *Chicago Daily News*. Secretary Knox publicly stated that Donovan and Mowrer were traveling to Europe as private citizens to study fifth-column tactics. Rumors were planted that the tab for Donovan's trip was being picked up by the *Daily News*. Donovan arrived in London bearing letters of introduction from Knox, Roosevelt's administrative assistant James Forrestal, and Secretary of State Cordell Hull. These letters to British leaders said that Colonel Donovan was in England representing the U.S. government. The letters were carried by Donovan because Ambassador Kennedy was not informed in advance about the colonel's trip. Kennedy was kept in the dark so that he would not obstruct Donovan's fact-finding mission. The letters of introduction, as it turned out, were unnecessary, because British officials were eagerly awaiting Donovan's arrival. The day following Donovan's departure for London from New York, William Stephenson, ostensibly the British Passport Control Officer in New York but really the head of the British Secret Intelligence Service (SIS) and the newly-formed Special Operations Executive (SOE) in the United States, cabled London about Wild Bill's trip. He wired SIS head Sir Stuart Menzies that "Colonel William J. Donovan personally representing President left yesterday . . . United States Embassy not repeat not being informed." To King George VI, Stephenson cabled:

The American government is debating two alternative courses of action. One would keep Britain in the war with supplies now desperately needed. Other is to give Britain up for lost. Donovan is President's most trusted personal advisor despite political differences and I urge you to bare your breast to him.[16]

While the cable exaggerated Donovan's influence with President Roosevelt, it got the attention of British officials. Within hours of his arrival, Donovan was invited to Buckingham Palace to meet the king. After their introduction, King George VI handed the colonel a decoded message sent from Adolph Hitler to his field commanders. The message in part read: "Since England, in spite of her hopeless situation, shows no sign of being ready to come to an understanding, I have decided to prepare a landing operation against England." The message was one of many decoded by the top-secret Ultra project. While Donovan was not directly informed of Ultra, the message intimated Britain's ability to penetrate the communications of their enemy and provided the king an opportunity to emphasize Great Britain's will to repel any attempted invasion.[17]

Donovan met with Sir Stuart Menzies, head of the Secret Intelligence Service. Menzies stressed Britain's abilities to resist and outlined some of his plans to Donovan. Wild Bill was introduced to Colin Gubbins, head of section MI(R). Section MI(R) was the part of the Special Operations Executive (SOE) that researched and taught guerrilla warfare tactics. Gubbins believed and two years before wrote a pamphlet that argued that the war with Germany would be fought with guerrilla tactics. He was training guerrillas to fight the planned German invasion and to return to the continent to "set Europe ablaze."[18] Donovan was introduced to another form of irregular warfare at Electra House, which was nominally part of the Foreign Office until being merged with MI(R) and Section D of the Secret Intelligence Service to become the Special Operations Executive. Within SOE, black propaganda was conducted by Electra House, which was known by the code-name SO1. SO1 operated two clandestine radio stations that broadcast to Germany. This was Wild Bill's first introduction to black radio propaganda.[19]

Donovan consulted with Admiral John Godfrey, director of Naval Intelligence, who emphasized to Donovan the role played by intelligence in the war against Germany. The Colonel was also shown British radar equipment; the newest Spitfire planes; and coastal defenses. Before leaving England, Donovan was introduced to J. B. S. Haldane and George Orwell. Haldane was a Marxist professor who was experimenting with floating mines that detonated when water dissolved their retaining rings. Orwell, the noted leftist author, was fascinated by German black broadcasting techniques, about which he had studied and written.[20]

Donovan left England and returned to New York on August 4. The following day, he went to Washington to discuss his findings with Roosevelt, Knox, and other administration officials. He informed the officials that Britain's morale was high and preparations superb, but that England badly needed assistance in the form of ships, planes, and other equipment. Donovan urged "the immediate transfer of over-age destroyers to Britain" to assist her in keeping the sea lanes open.[21] Roosevelt informed Donovan that Attorney General Robert Jackson had concluded that the president lacked legal power to transfer weapons to England without congressional approval. When Wild Bill returned to his law firm in New York, he assigned James R. Withrow, a bright, young attorney who later became a morale operations officer in the Office of Strategic Services (OSS), the job of finding legal precedents that would allow Roosevelt to transfer the destroyers to Great Britain. Withrow immediately went to Washington to conduct the research. In a few days, he determined that legal precedents for the transfers existed. Based on Withrow's research, Donovan wrote a report stressing the legality of the transfers to President Roosevelt. After Attorney General Jackson confirmed the legal precedents cited by Donovan, Roosevelt traded the battleships to Great Britain in exchange for leases to British bases that could assist in the defense of the United States.[22]

Edgar Ansel Mowrer, who toured England with Donovan, wrote a series of newspaper articles about fifth-column subversion in Europe, based on information provided by the British. As a result of Knox's and Roosevelt's insistence, Donovan became coauthor of the articles. Frank Knox wrote an introduction to the reports, which were syndicated in newspapers across the United States.[23] The articles were reissued as a pamphlet bearing the title *Fifth Column Lessons for America*. The articles concluded that:

The place of artillery will in the future be taken over by revolutionary propaganda, to break down the enemy psychologically before the armies begin to function at all. The enemy people must be demoralized and ready to capitulate before military action can even be thought of... The propaganda machine for creating and sustaining a fifth column—again according to Herr Hitler's confessed theory—is of a double nature. On the one side it aims at influencing the masses. For this purpose, Herr Hitler in the present war utilizes his radio traitors, Lord Hawhaw for the English, Paul Ferdonnet for the French, and to some extent, particularly in the last two years, Communist agitators whom he tricked or corrupted into serving him. [His other aim is] the systematic corruption of the possessing and governing classes.[24]

The collapse of France came about through the implementation of this strategy:

[Hitler] troubled the entire population by his radio propaganda that insisted that France was being betrayed by Britain and the French "war-mongers." He spread horrible rumors through villages, issued fearsome reports by wireless, and then, when the population had congested the roads in their flight, machine-gunned them to heighten their panic. Meanwhile his agents within France, presumably by clandestine wireless senders, kept him perfectly informed about what was going on....[25]

Donovan's success in getting the battleships for Great Britain and the widely disseminated articles on the fifth column attracted the attention of William Stephenson, the SIS chief in the United States. Although Stephenson contacted Donovan shortly after arriving in the United States on June 21, 1940, his contacts with the colonel increased after the latter's return from England. During fall 1940, Stephenson and Donovan spent many hours together. Stephenson repeatedly told Donovan that the United States badly needed a centralized intelligence agency that could wage psychological and guerrilla warfare, in addition to collecting and distributing intelligence. Stephenson hoped that his message would reach Roosevelt through Donovan. The United States, Stephenson told Donovan, had no central agency with which Britain could share its strategic intelligence. Instead, the United States had a multiplicity of uncoordinated agencies—the same agencies that bungled the Rumrich spy case. Donovan passed Stephenson's recommendations on to the president.

In December, Stephenson suggested that Donovan and he travel to Bermuda to examine the British intelligence-gathering unit in Hamilton, and then to London for another look at British shadow warfare units there. Secretary Knox endorsed the proposed trip and suggested it be expanded to include an examination of installations in the Middle East. President Roosevelt also approved the tour and wanted Donovan to collect intelligence concerning the safety of shipping in the Mediterranean, an issue of strategic importance to the United States. After Roosevelt's endorsement was obtained, Stephenson cabled Sir Stuart Menzies about

Donovan's scheduled stop in London, reporting that "Donovan exercises controlling influence over Knox, strong influence over Stimson, friendly advisory influence over President and Hull. . . . There is no doubt that we can achieve infinitely more through Donovan than through any other individual. He is very receptive and should be made fully aware of our requirements and deficiencies."[26]

In Bermuda, the first stop of the tour, Stephenson showed Donovan the British intelligence center that intercepted and surreptitiously examined thousands of pieces of German mail destined for Latin America. Donovan was shown evidence that Germany was building a fifth column to operate in South America. From Bermuda, Stephenson and Donovan went to Lisbon, then to London. On December 18, Donovan met Prime Minister Winston Churchill, who stressed the need for U.S.-British cooperation. Menzies again saw Donovan. This time Menzies told Donovan that his intelligence service had cracked the secret German code and was intercepting secret cables. Menzies explained that the Ultra project, as it was called, was one of Britain's most important secrets.

Stephenson remained in London when Donovan left for the next leg of his tour on December 26. A few days after Donovan's departure, Stephenson returned to the United States. Wild Bill flew to Gibraltar accompanied by other SIS agents. From there, he and his escorts went to Malta, Egypt, Libya, and several countries in the Balkans. After an extended tour of the Mediterranean region, Donovan returned to London on March 3.

In England, Donovan met Winston Churchill and the king, was briefed on subversive warfare operations, and given a tour of SOE bases, including the expanded SO1 propaganda operations at Woburn Abbey.[27] Between Bill Donovan's previous tour in July 1940 and March 1941, SO1 had started seven new clandestine stations that broadcast to Romania, France, Italy, Norway, and Denmark. The Rumanian station was called "Brother Rumanians," the French stations were "Radio Inconnue" and "Radio Travail," and the Italian stations were named "Radio Italia" and "Radio Libertà."[28] It is unlikely that Donovan was informed of the stations that broadcast to occupied France, Norway, or Denmark. Great Britain attempted to keep these operations secret and refused to divulge their existence, except when absolutely necessary, to the London governments-in-exile of these countries. That Donovan was not informed about "Radio Inconnue" is supported by a memorandum in Donovan's papers that described the station as "one of the more plausibly genuine of European stations broadcasting within occupied Europe." An evaluation of the station's programming suggested that it was not pro-British.[29]

Following the tour of SOE facilities, Donovan was introduced to Hugh Dalton, the minister of economic warfare and head of SOE. Dalton, a member of the Labour party who shared the views of many European leftists, told Donovan that a British victory would be achieved because it had innumerable allies in Europe. Dalton's theory was that the British blockade would weaken the economic base within occupied Europe. The ensuing economic difficulties would stimulate proletarian unrest, which would be fomented by SOE propaganda and directed by SOE agents. The agents were being trained by Colin Gubbins for eventual dropping behind Axis lines. As in classical socialist theory, the proletariat would rise and defeat their oppressor, which in this instance was Germany.[30]

While Donovan understood the tactics described by Dalton, he failed to understand the political theory that led to their development. Donovan never comprehended what Dalton and other leftists meant by the relationship between the economic base and the political superstructure, although he would use the terminology a few months later in a memo to President Roosevelt that recommended the establishment of a centralized U.S. intelligence agency with subversive warfare functions.[31] Donovan was a Republican without great political sophistication. After listening to Dalton's explanation for SOE's development, Donovan suggested that some of his old cronies, all Republicans, might assist Dalton's forces in North Africa. Realizing that Donovan had not understood the crux of his explanation, Dalton became "horrified that Donovan would consider 'Hooverites' for such work."[32] As a result of their discussion, Dalton "lost faith" in Donovan's ability to oversee a U.S. subversive warfare organization, even though Stephenson and others from Great Britain were grooming him for that job.[33]

Donovan returned to the United States on March 18, full of exuberance concerning shadow warfare techniques. The day following his return, Donovan met with Knox and Roosevelt. He also conducted several press conferences. In private and public, Wild Bill stressed that Axis control of the Mediterranean was against the strategic interests of the United States. He predicted that the United States would soon be drawn into the conflict. "Because England is not beaten ... America is not yet threatened," Donovan warned.[34] To the president and other administration officials, Donovan stressed the need for an organization to collect intelligence for use in psychological warfare. This need was emphasized in several reports sent to Roosevelt by Donovan. Some of the reports were probably written by Bill Stephenson.[35] Roosevelt was also directly told of the need for such an agency by William Stephenson and Admiral John Godfrey, head of British naval intelligence, who arrived in the United States for an official visit in May. This "movement" to establish a single agency immediately spawned objections by the heads of the existing intelligence agencies, who felt threatened by the recommendations for a new agency. Brigadier General Sherman Miles, head of the army's Military Intelligence Division (G–2), worriedly observed:

... there is a movement on foot, fostered by Col. Donovan to establish a super agency controlling all intelligence... From the point of view of the War Department, such a move would appear to be very disadvantageous, if not calamitous.[36]

To head off the establishment of the super-agency, General Miles, FBI director Hoover and Captain Alan Kirk, chief of Naval Intelligence, started holding weekly meetings to coordinate their activities. Although the three organizations met on previous occasions under the auspices of the "Special Intelligence Service" (SIS), which was formed in June 1940 to assist in the coordination of counterintelligence activities, the contacts created more conflicts than resolutions. The SIS, rather than solving problems, exacerbated them. It gave Hoover the opportunity to castigate the other intelligence chiefs for encroaching on his ever-enlarging turf. Hoover accused Miles of repeatedly conducting investigations that were clearly the responsibility of his organization. The conflicts continued into March 1941, when rumors started to circulate in Washington that Roosevelt was planning to create a superintelligence agency. The rumors forced the three existing intelligence agencies to more closely cooperate. Not only did the three intelligence heads meet weekly, but their subordinates met daily for discussions about intelligence in all spheres. After two months of such contact, the intelligence chiefs sent a memo to Roosevelt reporting that the three agencies were in "constant liaison." The heads finally agreed on something, and so informed Roosevelt—an intelligence coordinator was no longer needed, except in such cases where jurisdictional conflicts arose between the three agencies. If a coordinator were appointed, the agency heads suggested, the coordinator's job should merely be that of a jurisdiction referee. The coordinator would be used only when requested by one or more of the agencies. The agreement by the agency heads and the recommendations had only one purpose: to stop the creation of a super-agency.[37]

While the intelligence chiefs attempted to kill the new agency before it was even created, the movement in Washington to establish the service picked up steam. Secretary of War Stimson, who was constantly drawn into the conflict between the FBI and G–2, supported the creation of a new agency. Secretary of the Navy Knox, Donovan's trusted friend, backed the proposal. The new ambassador to Great Britain, John Winant, also voiced his support, as did the British intelligence contingent in the United States. On May 31, Donovan sent to the president a formal recommendation for the establishment of a superintelligence agency. On June 10, Donovan sent an expanded version of the "Memorandum of Establishment of Service of Strategic Information" to Knox, Stimson, and Roosevelt for consideration. The memorandum reported that, while "modern warfare depends upon the economic base," strategic information is vital to "anticipate enemy intention(s)." The current "mechanism of collecting information is inadequate," Donovan concluded. Because of this, a new superintelligence agency is needed. Beyond intelligence, the memo reported, "there is another element in modern warfare . . . radio," which needs to be studied and used by the United States. Repeating what appeared in his and Mowrer's newspaper reports concerning fifth-column activities in Europe, Donovan wrote: "the use of radio as a weapon, though effectively used by Germany, is still to be perfected. But this perfection can be realized only by planning, and planning is dependent upon accurate information."[38] Donovan suggested that any Service of Strategic Information that was established needed the authority to conduct psychological warfare using the mass media as weapons. Why the two functions—intelligence and propaganda—belonged in a single organization, Donovan never explained. The explanation was missing because Donovan failed to understand the theory that underlay the development of the SOE in Great Britain, which had both intelligence and propaganda functions.

After discussions about the memorandum with his cabinet, Roosevelt decided to create the superintelligence agency that Donovan suggested. On June 18, Roosevelt asked Wild Bill to become the United States's "coordinator of strategic information." Donovan readily accepted the appointment. He immediately called Bill Stephenson to inform him of the creation of the new agency. Stephenson cabled London that day to report that his "three months of battle" had been successful. The British now had an official intelligence contact in Washington over whom they exercised great influence. Three days later, Germany attacked the USSR. The surprise attack gave Great Britain another ally in its fight with Hitler—the Soviet Union.

## THE COORDINATOR OF INFORMATION

Between June 18 when Donovan was asked to head the new superagency and July 11 when Roosevelt signed an official order establishing the "Office of Coordinator of Information" (COI), Secretary of War Stimson had a change of heart concerning the organization. In late June, General Miles's opposition to the new intelligence organization was finally brought to Stimson's attention. After consulting with other army chiefs, the secretary of war concluded that the proposed functions of Donovan's organization directly conflicted with those of military intelligence. According to Donovan's own proposal, the coordinator of strategic information would collect intelligence for defense and warfare purposes. This clearly was the function of G-2 and ONI.[39]

Stimson explained his newly formed opposition to the creation of a coordinator of strategic information to Roosevelt. FDR and the secretary agreed that the new organization's charter should be civilian rather than military in character, with all references to "military," "warfare," and "defense" deleted from its charter. Consequently, President Roosevelt's order of July 11 created a civilian coordinator of information whose duties were to collect intelligence affecting "national security" rather than national defense. All allusions to strategic, military, and defense were deleted from the order, except to state that the COI shall not "in any way interfere with or impair the duties and responsibilities of the regular military and naval advisors of the President as Commander in Chief of the Army and Navy."[40]

Nowhere in the order was Donovan given authority over propaganda, psychological warfare, morale operations, or international radio broadcasting. The only phrase in the founding order that could in any way be construed to grant the COI powers in this area read that the COI was to "carry out, when requested by the President, such supplementary activities as may facilitate the securing of information important for national security not now available to the government." Even a very elastic interpretation of this clause did not suggest that Donovan was given the responsibility of conducting international propaganda. The only indication that FDR had a propaganda function in mind when he established the COI was a request that Budget Director Harold Smith get Donovan and New York City Mayor Fiorello LaGuardia, head of the Office of Civilian Defense, together for a meeting to discuss the coordination of radio broadcasting activities.[41] The Office of Civilian Defense's responsibilities were the promotion of domestic "morale" and civil defense. LaGuardia was primarily interested in civil defense and did little to promote domestic morale, despite his mandate from FDR. Donovan saw his responsibility as Axis "morale subversion." He took this responsibility seriously.

Even before the presidential order establishing the COI was issued, Donovan recruited personnel for his new agency. His first recruit was Robert Sherwood, a renowned playwright and friend of FDR.[42] Like Donovan, Sherwood was a pro-British interventionist. He published articles, gave speeches, and wrote a play, *There Shall Be No Night*, that advocated stopping Hitler.[43] Sherwood was appointed head of the COI's Foreign Information Service (FIS). FIS had two principal responsibilities: the monitoring of Axis radio broadcasts and the countering of Axis radio propaganda abroad. It was through FIS that Donovan planned to beat the Germans at their own game. Wild Bill intended to demoralize the yet-undeclared German enemy using the same tactics that he believed the Nazis used against France—a fifth column. To Donovan, foreign propaganda functioned as an attack weapon "identified with strategic movements" that "condition[s] and prepare[s] the people and the territory in which invasion is contemplated."[44] With morale subverted, the enemy is unable to fight back. The difference between Donovan's conception and that of his counterpart in Great Britain was that the COI had no idea who would form his fifth column. Wall Street attorney Donovan differed greatly from Labourite Hugh Dalton. Donovan had no idea how to foment a proletarian revolution and, even if he did, would not want to.

Sherwood informed Donovan that an able propaganda team could be formed by hiring journalists and writers like Edmond Taylor and Douglas Miller. Taylor wrote *The Strategy of Terror*, which described Nazi fifth-column subversion in France during 1939–40. The book was consistent with Donovan's interpretation of the French collapse. Taylor believed that the only way to fight nazism was to use the same tactics that it used, which is what Donovan also believed. Miller was the author of the antiappeasement best-seller, *You Can't Do Business With Hitler*. Sherwood also suggested that Edgar Ansel Mowrer, William Shirer, John Gunther, and other journalists, who had first-hand experiences with Germany and its fifth column, be courted for recruitment. FIS's monitoring service, Sherwood believed, could most easily get off the ground by initially relying on the existing monitoring services of CBS and NBC.[45] After discussing the organization of the CBS monitoring service with William Paley, the network's chief executive, Sherwood decided to hire Edd Johnson. Johnson was the director of CBS's listening posts. He had the experience needed to establish similar facilities for COI.[46]

While Robert Sherwood was busy recruiting personnel for FIS, Donovan was seeking the assistance of poet Archibald MacLeish, head of the Library of Congress, whom Donovan hoped would help build the COI's Research and Analysis (R & A) branch. Donovan wanted R & A to be capable of collecting, analyzing, and synthesizing intelligence. Donovan hoped that R & A's output would be research reports on subjects requested by administration officials or other intelligence organizations. MacLeish suggested that Donovan hire a distinguished academic who could recruit other experts to the branch. Academics, MacLeish argued, had the training and skills to tap the vast resources available in libraries, which provided a wealth of materials that other intelligence services were failing to adequately utilize. Experts in various disciplines could most easily be recruited, MacLeish advised Donovan, if a renowned scholar were appointed head of R & A. MacLeish did not want to head the branch because he was too busy, he said.

Although too busy to accept an appointment in Donovan's organization, MacLeish managed to find time to head a domestic propaganda agency created in October 1941 by FDR. The new agency, the Office of Facts and Figures (OFF), was originally to be part of Fiorello LaGuardia's Office of Civilian Defense. Because LaGuardia did little to implement a domestic information program, the president decided to establish a separate agency for this purpose. The mandate of the Office of Facts and Figures was to centralize press information flowing to and from government agencies. Federal agencies wishing to release information to the public were to do so through OFF. Agencies wishing to obtain time from radio stations for broadcasting to the public were likewise to go through OFF. Although an excellent idea for centralizing information originating in Washington, it failed in practice to do what it was mandated to do. Most federal agencies avoided using OFF, as did the president. They continued to function as they had done before OFF's creation.[47]

The Office of Facts and Figures and the COI were not the only government information agencies that FDR created. In July 1939, the president created a clearinghouse for government studies called the Office of Government Reports. Headed by Roosevelt aide Lowell Mellett, the agency also had the responsibility of publicizing government mobilizations and making documentaries about U.S. defense efforts. In August 1940, Roosevelt created the office of the Coordinator of Inter-American Affairs (CIAA). The CIAA was headed by Nelson Rockefeller, who had urged its establishment. The objectives of CIAA were to promote North-South goodwill, to counter Axis propaganda in Latin America, and to promote dialogue between the nations of the western hemisphere. To accomplish these objectives, the CIAA distributed U.S. government information in South America and information about Latin American nations in the United States.

Acting on the advice of the Librarian of Congress, Donovan selected James P. Baxter III, the president of Williams College, to head COI's research arm.[48] Donovan correctly believed that Baxter, as both a scholar and administrator, would be capable of recruiting and supervising the R & A branch. Baxter recruited a staff of well-known and respected scholars, including French historian Donald C. McKay,[49] English historian Conyers Read,[50] Asian historian and political scientist Joseph Ralston Hayden,[51] and geographer Preston James.[52] After he got R & A started, Baxter's health quickly deteriorated. He resigned from the COI and was replaced by Harvard historian William Langer.[53]

To coordinate the activities of COI's branches, Donovan hired a troika composed of James R. Murphy, Otto C. Doering, and G. Edward Buxton. Murphy was Donovan's law clerk when the colonel was assistant attorney general. When recruited to COI by Donovan, Murphy was practicing law in Washington. Doering was an attorney in Donovan's law office in New York. Buxton was a prominent New England businessman who graduated from Harvard Law School. His claim to fame was having been the commanding officer of pacifist World War I hero, Sergeant Alvin York. The troika hired additional attorneys to serve as their assistants. Like Donovan, they felt more comfortable surrounded by other corporate attorneys than shiny-pants professors or prodding journalists. Soon, David K. Bruce, Turner McBaine, Charles Bane, Edwin Putzell, and a host of other lawyers swelled COI's ranks. Exactly what this battery of corporate attorneys was to do in COI, no one knew.

Donovan also recruited personnel from some of the most prominent and wealthy families in the United States. His Who's Who in America eventually included James and Kermit Roosevelt, Paul Mellon, Junius and Henry Morgan, William Vanderbilt, and Alfred DuPont. Corporate executives also filled leadership positions in Donovan's organization. Executives came from investment, banking, railway, and steel corporations. These captains of industry gave the organization an aura of respectability that muted some of COI's opponents. Donovan chose these recruits primarily to be administrators of his organization. Without realizing it, Donovan's selection of conservative Republican businessmen to head COI posts contradicted the organization's goal of starting a revolt in Europe.[54]

While attorneys and corporate chieftains quickly multiplied within COI, their number did not increase as rapidly as that of the journalists. Sherwood hired Edmond Taylor, former International News Service writer and CBS commentator Percy Winner, Nelson Poynter of the *St. Petersburg Times*, political writer James Warburg and *New York Herald Tribune* foreign editor Joseph Barnes. Hollywood film producer Merian Cooper and director John Ford were recruited for COI's Field Photography branch. Edmond Taylor, FIS's first recruit, was sent to England to study the methods of black radio broadcasting employed at Woburn Abbey. He was the first of many COI personnel that were trained in Great Britain. Upon his return, Taylor recommended that COI reorganize along the lines of the British Political Warfare Executive, giving greater emphasis to black propaganda. Lt. Col. Robert Solberg was sent to England to study SOE's underground organizations before organizing COI's Special Operations (SO) branch.[55] This branch conducted sabotage and worked with underground movements in occupied countries. The Special Intelligence (SI) branch of COI was also set up with British assistance. Before SI was created, British intelligence officers were COI's primary source of strategic intelligence. Other COI personnel were sent to Canada for training at an SOE school, which gave the training of U.S. personnel a high priority, thanks to Bill Stephenson.

Robert Sherwood moved the FIS branch to New York, where it could more easily recruit personnel and interface with media institutions. Its location at 270 Madison Avenue was especially helpful in recruiting personnel from advertising agencies, which lined both sides of the avenue. FIS established its monitoring and news bureaus at that address. The monitoring division started by analyzing and writing weekly reports based on monitoring done by CBS, NBC, and the Federal Communications Commission.[56] FIS later established its own monitoring service. The news bureau supplied radio stations with news and background information that reflected U.S. policy.[57] Joe Barnes screened wire service reports for stories of interest; he would select some and then send them to FIS writers, who would embellish them. The embellished reports were sent to stations as news releases. The releases at first consisted of background information to supplement news reports originating in Europe. When CBS, for example, monitored "news of bread rationing in France, FIS would supplement that report [with a]... statement pointing out that France was a self-sufficient country, and that rationing was the fruit of the German occupation."[58] The releases were primarily sent to the eleven U.S. commercial stations that broadcast internationally on shortwave. These stations broadcast an average 14 hours per day in five languages. This system of sending news releases proved to be ineffectual because FIS had no power to insure that the information broadcast by the stations correctly communicated U.S. policy. In some instances, FIS-prepared materials were aired along with Axis communiqués, giving listeners a very confused picture of U.S. policy. Despite such not-too-infrequent occurrences, commercial broadcasters were unwilling to relinquish any of their programming powers to FIS.[59]

In May 1941, Roosevelt raised the specter of government intervention in shortwave broadcasting when he ordered stations to increase their broadcasting power and to use directional antenna to target areas of the world. To head off any government intervention, the broadcasters hired a coordinator of international broadcasting, Stanley P. Richardson.[60] Richardson was a former Associated Press correspondent who had been secretary to Joseph E. Davies, ambassador to the Soviet Union. Richardson's job was to serve as a liaison between the government and broadcasters. If the government felt the broadcasters negligent in an area, Richardson would quickly communicate this to the stations' owners. He also coordinated programming, so that stations would not be broadcasting in the same language at the same time. Richardson drew up schedules for the participating stations that rotated the languages and times of broadcasts, so that when one station finished its French language broadcasts, for example, another station would only then begin its broadcasts in that language. Before Richardson's coordination, the stations frequently broadcast in the same language at the same time, reducing the audience of each station.[61]

Soon after FIS was established, Richardson took on the job of screening FIS materials and then recommending or not recommending them for broadcast. To facilitate this screening, he opened an office next to that of FIS on Madison Avenue. Richardson soon established rules that he demanded FIS follow. One of his rules was that all sources of information be disclosed, even if the source wanted to remain anonymous. When the State Department wanted FIS to relay secretly obtained information to the broadcasters saying that Hungary was "about to place seventeen divisions under German command," Richardson demanded that FIS disclose the source of the report.[62] The State Department, however, did not want to be associated with the story for fear of harming its relations with

Hungary, with which the U.S. was at peace. Communiqués sent from FIS to Richardson and then to the stations by teletype were exemplified by the following:

The following from the Coordinator of Information is for your use if desired—

A War Department statement announcing today that nearly 2,000,000 woolen blankets of the highest quality are to be purchased from American manufacturers for use of American draftees caused Washington observers to comment on the contrast between this action and recent news of the seizure by German authorities of blankets from Norway's civilian population to help protect Nazi soldiers from the Russian winter.[63]

Richardson not only screened FIS material, but soon assumed the responsibility of making sure that FIS materials were consistent with State Department policies. He would contact State representatives and ask whether a given communique accurately reflected State viewpoints. By doing so, Richardson established himself as the censor of FIS.

Donovan's international propaganda activities immediately brought him into conflict with the Coordinator of Inter-American Affairs. The day following FDR's order establishing COI, Mrs. Anna Rosenberg, an advisor to Rockefeller's CIAA and a friend of the president, called Donovan to suggest that Nelson Rockefeller and he meet to discuss areas where the two organizations might cooperate. On July 16, Donovan and Rockefeller met, discussed the situation, and parted amicably. As the COI was not yet distributing propaganda or conducting any activities in Latin America, there was little area for disagreement. The following month, Rockefeller learned that Donovan developed a multipage plan of COI activities for South America. The two agency chiefs met soon after this, again discussed potential areas of cooperation, and politely parted. Although their two meetings ended without acrimony, Donovan believed that his organization was given the responsibility for conducting propaganda abroad—and this included Latin America.

In October, alarmed by FIS's rapid growth, Rockefeller decided to challenge the Donovan organization. The CIAA announced that it was starting a competing FIS that would cover all news broadcasts to or about Latin America. The announcement brought the competing chiefs together again at the beginning of October. At the meeting, Donovan told Rockefeller that the president's July 1941 order that created COI superseded the August 1940 order that established the CIAA. The COI, not the CIAA, therefore had responsibility for broadcasts to Latin America. Rockefeller replied that COI was authorized "to collect and analyze" intelligence, not to broadcast to Latin America. The meeting ended with boiling tempers instead of a resolution. Through intermediaries, Donovan and Roosevelt appealed to FDR for a decision in their behalf. Donovan sent James Roosevelt, the president's son, to appear in his place. Rockefeller dispatched Mrs. Anna Rosenberg, the more persuasive of the two intermediaries. On October 15, Roosevelt issued an order stripping Donovan of all responsibility for informational activities in Latin America. Rockefeller won. It was Donovan's first in a series of defeats. A month later, Roosevelt ordered Donovan to refrain from all activities in Latin America. J. Edgar Hoover's FBI was given jurisdiction for intelligence-gathering in the region. This was the second of several skirmishes that Donovan lost. The next defeat stripped the coordinator of information of all propaganda and broadcasting responsibilities.

## THE U.S. BROADCASTS

The entrance of the United States into the war following Japan's attack on Pearl Harbor increased Donovan's power vis-à-vis Richardson and the commercial broadcasters. Roosevelt approved Donovan's request for $2 million to build transmitters for COI stations in Ireland, Iceland, or the Philippines, and an additional $1.5 million for the production and distribution of FIS programs.[64] To produce the programs, Sherwood hired a staff to write scripts in Czech, German, French, Italian, Spanish, Portuguese, Swedish, Danish, Norwegian, Finnish, Greek, Turkish, Dutch, Malay, Polish, Mandarin, and Cantonese. By writing its own scripts rather than just providing analyses, COI was able to control what it wanted said. The scripts were first sent to stations over teletype on a "take-it-or-leave-it" basis.[65] Stations were free to select or refuse them. Because the scripts were written in seventeen languages, while the average station broadcast in only five, most went unused. The National Broadcasting Company's two shortwave stations, for example, reported using about 40 to 50 percent of the materials FIS sent them.[66]

To assure that FIS scripts were aired as written, COI leased fifteen-minute time-blocks from several commercial shortwave stations beginning in late 1941. The leasing of time allowed COI to circumvent Richardson's censorship. The production of programs forced FIS to acquire additional space on 57th Street, which eventually housed its production studios. By the end of the year, FIS was feeding its programs to a half-dozen stations through the facilities of the CBS network. In addition to leasing time on commercial stations, COI received free time from the British Broadcasting Corporation (BBC) for airing its programs.

On February 5, 1942, FIS officially unveiled its new radio program, Voice of America. The first broadcasts of Voice of America were in German, but within three weeks, French, Spanish, and Italian programs were started.[67] Late in February, Donovan submitted and Roosevelt approved a proposal that COI and CIAA lease and operate the nine shortwave stations run by CBS, NBC, Crosley, Westinghouse, and General Electric. The proposal called for Donovan's organization to operate the stations from midnight to 4 p.m. daily and for Rockefeller's agency to broadcast to Latin America from 4 p.m. to midnight.[68] Because the international shortwave stations were operated as commercial ventures but generated little income for their owners, Donovan believed that the broadcasting companies would be happy to have the government step in to lease them. In this regard, Donovan was wrong. The broadcasters opposed government intervention in international broadcasting, fearing it would create a precedent for government intervention in domestic broadcasting.[69] Donovan's proposal was tabled until October 1942, when it was eventually put into force by Roosevelt. By October, however, COI no longer existed and FIS was part of the Office of War Information (OWI).

During the early months of 1942, FIS rapidly expanded its program output. By the middle of 1942, it was broadcasting 24 hours daily in 27 languages and dialects. The rapid expansion kept the COI branch preoccupied with administrative matters and daily routines rather than preparations for psychological warfare. FIS personnel wrote and interpreted news, hired translators and announcers for the ever-increasing number of foreign language radio programs, and made sure that output reflected the policies of the government. These activities contradicted Donovan's plans for FIS. He wanted it to become a psychological warfare, not information, agency.

Because Robert Sherwood was satisfied with what his branch was doing, Donovan and he came into conflict. Sherwood wanted FIS to be a vehicle for spreading President Roosevelt's views to the world. Donovan and the Wall Street attorneys that he hired had no intention of spreading New Deal philosophy. If they had their way, New Dealers would not even be in power in the United States.[70] Donovan not only opposed spreading New Deal philosophy but was adamantly against using radio as a purely information-disseminating medium. Donovan wanted to use radio "as an instrument of war—a judicious mixture of rumor and deception, with truth as bait, to foster disunity and confusion in support of military operations."[71] Donovan wanted to use radio in this manner even before the United States engaged in any military battles. He had FIS broadcast that Germany asked Italy to provide a million more troops in order to weaken its ally. The broadcast suggested that Germany intended to betray and attack Italy.[72] Sherwood opposed broadcasts like this one that mixed fact and rumor. He believed in maintaining a "strategy of truth" that sharply contrasted with Goebbels's use of the "big lie."

On January 24, 1942 Donovan proposed that FIS begin a psychological warfare campaign directed at French naval officers. Donovan wanted FIS radio broadcasts to cultivate a French naval audience using entertainment talks, music, news, and programs about naval developments and tactics.

The long-run objective of Donovan's proposed station was to stimulate a rebellion by the navy if Germany attempted to seize the French fleet. The station was to somehow hide that it was addressing French naval officers so as not to impair French-U.S. relations. The United States established diplomatic relations with Marshal Pétain's Vichy government after the defeat of the French Republic in 1940. How the station was to hide its purpose Donovan never made clear, but it would undoubtedly be difficult. The station was to broadcast in French rather than English and its programming was to focus on naval affairs. Given these facts, who else could the station be addressing except the French Navy? It is likely that Donovan had a clandestine radio operation in mind when he submitted this plan to the president.[73]

Donovan's ideas for radio were eagerly endorsed by Edmond Taylor, who returned from England in 1941 after studying black radio techniques at Woburn Abbey. Taylor, like Donovan, wanted FIS to engage in subversive warfare, regardless of where or how it was conducted. He disdained Sherwood's "liberals, for whom psychological warfare apparently meant radio sermons on President Roosevelt's recently proclaimed Four Freedoms."[74] Taylor had his own proposals for subversive warfare. He suggested that FIS establish an amateur-sounding, pro-Nazi radio station in Canada that would beam programs to the United States. The station was to address U.S. isolationists, pacifists, and appeasers in an attempt to discredit them. Statements, writings, and editorials of appeasement and isolationist leaders were to air alongside speeches supporting Hitler and Mussolini. Taylor hoped that the station would thereby discredit isolationists and lead to the "stern repression of the whole Nazi fifth column in America, along with its accomplices and sympathizers."[75] The problem with Taylor's proposal, in addition to its obvious illegality, was that it was based on the false premise that a German-sponsored fifth column had riddled the fabric of the United States. Taylor's proposal "horrified" his New Deal colleagues who were told of it. Robert Sherwood, in an apparent attempt to appease COI militants like Taylor, endorsed the proposal. Nonetheless, it was never implemented.

The ideological and tactical differences between Sherwood and Donovan intensified throughout the early months of 1942. In February, they stopped talking to each other. After that, Sherwood wrote President Roosevelt a letter complaining that COI was infiltrated with "rabid anti-New Dealers" and "Roosevelt haters" who did not belong in an agency "which must be the expression of the President's own philosophy."[76] On March 19, Sherwood sent FDR a "personal and confidential" letter that urged the complete dissolution of COI. The playwright recommended that COI's branches be dispersed, with SO going to the Military Intelligence Division (G–2), R & A to the Joint Board, and FIS into a "consolidated information agency." Sherwood's letter falsely asserted that

Donovan felt the same as he. Two weeks later, the COI chief in London, William Whitney, resigned, citing disagreements with Donovan over strategy.[77]

Donovan not only found himself in quarrels with his own men but with heads of other government agencies, including the CIAA, FBI, State Department, Budget Bureau, and Joint Chiefs of Staff. Around April 10, 1942, CIAA head Rockefeller, FBI king Hoover, and Undersecretary of State Sumner Welles complained to FDR that Donovan's organization was still active in Latin America, despite the order to stay out of the region. Rockefeller, Hoover, and Welles alleged that 90 COI agents were sent to Mexico after the president issued his directive. The complainants provided Roosevelt with documents that showed COI agent Donald Downes was in Mexico, as was a four-man team headed by Wallace Phillips. No documentation concerning the remaining 85 or so alleged COI agents was sent to the president, because the agents didn't exist.[78]

Donovan replied to the charges in a lengthy letter to Roosevelt. Downes, Donovan confessed, was in Mexico, but only to pick up a list of Spanish Republican activists. The list concerned COI activities in Europe, not Latin America, as Donovan's opponents were aware. Downes traveled to Mexico with the FBI's consent and returned immediately after acquiring the names, Donovan wrote. The four agents under Wallace Phillips were placed in Mexico by ONI, not COI, despite reports asserting the contrary. Rockefeller, Hoover, and Welles were aware of Phillips's ONI connections because Donovan explained the facts to Welles two weeks earlier. Donovan described the complaints as:

[a] well worn lie . . . I have no representatives in that section of the world and never have had, and all those concerned must know that to be true. I know you will recognize my anger is justified at such deliberate and continued falsehoods.[79]

While FDR accepted this explanation, this didn't end the challenges to Donovan's organization. Budget direct Harold Smith, who had long complained that Donovan's spending was out-of-control, suggested that all government information agencies be consolidated. Smith found the large number of agencies—COI, OFF, CIAA, and OGR—to be expensive, confusing, and politically damaging. The largely Republican press ridiculed the "alphabet soup" of information agencies.[80] MacLeish's Office of Facts and Figures was dubbed the "Office of Fun and Frolic" or "Office of Fuss and Feathers." Mellett's Office of Government Reports was called "Mellett's Madhouse." Smith emphasized that the agencies provided too much duplication of services. The only solution was to create a single, unified U.S. information agency. On March 7, Smith submitted a plan for the "Reorganization of the War Information Services." The plan suggested consolidating FIS with the other information agencies and dismembering

COI. The proposal, Smith assured the president, was supported by MacLeish, Mellett, and Sherwood, who secretly met to discuss and endorse the budget director's plan. Neither Donovan nor Rockefeller was present at the discussions.[81]

The Joint Chiefs of Staff (JCS) also put pressure on Donovan's organization. After meeting with the British high command in late December 1941 and early January 1942, the Joint Chiefs were convinced that they should oversee, if not control, psychological warfare. At their March 2 meeting, the Joint Chiefs discussed how they could use "the Office of the Coordinator of Information . . . to advance the war effort." They "pointed out the [COI] has available to it some superior talent which is not now being utilized in the most efficient manner. It was emphasized that if these facilities were to be best employed, they should be under military control." The Joint Chiefs appointed Navy Captain F. C. Denebrink to study and report "on how the facilities of the Office of the Coordinator of Information might best be utilized by the military services."[82]

Captain Denebrink submitted his report to the JCS on March 8. The report concluded that COI should be dismembered and its branches taken over by other government agencies. The S. I. branch could be absorbed by the State Department, ONI or G–2, Denebrink suggested. The S.O. branch could be transferred to the Marines. The foreign nationalities branch could be transferred to the State Department. R & A, which Denebrink praised as "a school of advanced research of the highest caliber," should be retained as an entity and placed under the administration of the Joint Chiefs of Staff. The administration of R & A, Denebrink concluded, required "little or no work as it is self-administering." FIS could be placed under a regular branch of the military service or Harold Smith's proposed Office of War Information.[83] The captain's proposals were tentatively approved by the JCS, which recommended that the issue be discussed with the president at their next meeting.

Realizing that his organization faced imminent destruction, Donovan took the offensive. He talked with President Roosevelt and JCS secretariat member Gen. Walter Bedell Smith. Donovan told General Smith that the COI should be placed under the control of the Joint Chiefs rather than continue as a civilian agency. Smith endorsed the suggestion because it gave the military another voice with the president through the person of Donovan, gave the military control of COI's assets, and precluded another agency from arising that might take COI's place. Donovan followed up his conversation with General Smith with a letter, emphasizing that COI could serve the JCS in the conduct of psychological warfare, something that the military now wanted to engage in. Wild Bill followed up this letter with a suggested order making COI subject to the JCS. The order was modified by General Smith, approved by the Joint Chiefs, and forwarded to the president. Donovan sent a letter to FDR on March 30, urging him to issue the order making COI a supporting agency of the JCS. Two weeks later, Donovan again urged the president to sign the order. Wild Bill favored the order not just to keep his organization intact, but because it would make COI a combat, rather than civilian information, agency. Combat, after all, was what interested Donovan most.[84]

## MORE INTERNECINE WARFARE OVER PSYCHOLOGICAL WARFARE

After numerous debates and reversals, FDR decided that FIS was to be moved intact into Smith's proposed Office of War Information (OWI). On June 13, Roosevelt issued Executive Order 9182, which consolidated FIS, OFF, OGR, and the Division of Information of the Office of Emergency Management into a single agency, OWI. OWI was given responsibility to conduct domestic and foreign informational programs through the "press, radio, motion picture and other facilities." The CIAA's information functions were not handed over to OWI out of deference to Nelson Rockefeller. In an emotionally charged presentation before the president, Rockefeller argued that CIAA's informational, educational and cultural programs were inseparable. If CIAA were stripped of its information functions, it could no longer perform any duties, Rockefeller said. Roosevelt agreed and made CIAA, not OWI, responsible for all U.S. information programs in Latin America.

The president chose Elmer Davis to head OWI. Davis was a veteran journalist who worked for the *New York Times* during World War I, had a successful freelance career during the 1920s, and joined CBS as an announcer in the 1930s. As an establishment journalist, Davis was more acceptable to the press than were New Deal activists like MacLeish and Sherwood.[85] *Time* magazine endorsed Davis's appointment, describing him as "clear-headed, sensible . . . one of the best newsmen in the business." *Business Week* praised FDR's choice, calling Davis "a solidly-grounded newspaper man . . . the esteem in which he is held by the president is shared by many." Other media followed *Time* and *Business Week*'s lead, praising Davis as an outstanding choice.[86] The new OWI chief picked Milton Eisenhower, General Dwight Eisenhower's younger brother, as associate director; Archibald MacLeish as assistant director for policy development; and Robert Sherwood as head of the Overseas Branch. The Overseas Branch was OWI's name for what had previously been FIS. Sherwood kept Joe Barnes, Edd Johnson, Percy Winner, and James Warburg, who helped establish FIS, as leaders of his branch.

On June 13, Roosevelt also issued an order creating the Office of Strategic Services (OSS) from what remained of COI. The order placed OSS under the Joint Chiefs. The duties of OSS, according to the order, were to collect and analyze strategic information and "plan and operate such special activities as may be directed by the Joint Chiefs of Staff." Donovan interpreted the latter to give OSS responsibility for clandestine broadcasting, something in which Sherwood had no interest. Less than a week before the order creating OSS was issued, Donovan wrote FDR a memo explaining the difference between information, over which OWI would have responsibility, and psychological warfare, over which OSS would have responsibility. They "use the same mediums," Donovan wrote, but their "purpose and the method would be entirely different." OSS and OWI might use radio, but in very different ways. OWI used radio as an aboveground information medium, while OSS used radio exclusively for subversion. Davis and Sherwood were aware of Donovan's claim over subversive broadcasting but refused to acknowledge this as his responsibility. They feared that Donovan, who developed a well-deserved reputation in Washington as an empire-builder, would use his asserted responsibility over subversive propaganda to acquire responsibility over all U.S. government information programs. Although Davis and Sherwood denied OSS's right to distribute any propaganda, no quarrel arose from Donovan's assertion because OSS had neither a branch nor the technical ability to implement the claim. In mid–1942, OSS had no transmitters or budget with which to buy any. Even if given a budget, transmitters were hard to obtain. OWI had already requisitioned or purchased most available broadcasting transmitters in the United States.[87]

On December 23, 1942 the JCS issued a directive giving OSS responsibility for "propaganda and warfare phases of psychological warfare," even though the Joint Chiefs were uncertain as to what psychological warfare entailed.[88] Using this directive as a guide, Donovan created the Morale Operations (MO) branch of OSS on January 3, 1943. MO was created "to incite and spread dissension, confusion and disorder within enemy countries" using secret propaganda from radio, leaflets, pamphlets, and word-of-mouth. Donovan selected Fred Oechsner, the former Berlin office chief of United Press, to head the branch.[89]

The JCS directive and subsequent creation of MO ignited Davis and Sherwood. Sherwood threatened to resign from OWI if Donovan became head of U.S. government propaganda. Davis met with FDR on January 5 and protested Donovan's new responsibility for propaganda. The president told Davis that the directive giving OWI full responsibility over U.S. information remained in effect. Roosevelt said he would discuss the issue with the JCS but instead left Washington for the Casablanca Conference on January 9. In the president's absence, Davis took his complaint to the press. Newspapers responded with headlines exposing the controversy, but the stories were less pro-OWI than Davis expected.[90] The press viewed the controversy as just one of many in which OWI was embroiled during its short life. Davis involved himself in a controversy with the military over "what should be kept secret," with General Eisenhower and the State Department over recognition of Admiral François Darlan as leader of French North Africa, and with Republican members of Congress over the publication of domestic pamphlets that allegedly promoted the Neal Deal.[91] The OWI even became the object of Dies committee criticism for hiring the Almanac Singers, a musical group with "Communist sympathies," and for employing "500 to 600 persons" who were "identified with 'subversive' organizations."[92] Fortunately for Donovan, his organization had not come under attack from the Dies committee for employing Communists, something of which OSS was "guilty." Donovan believed Communists to be among his most dedicated workers, a view he would later recant. Marxists Paul Sweezy,[93] Maurice Halperin,[94] Herbert Marcuse,[95] and Cora Dubois[96] were members of R & A. Scriptwriter Abraham Polonsky, who was blacklisted until 1968 following accusations of Communist sympathies during the postwar investigations of subversion in Hollywood, was a member of the MO branch.[97] He worked on several OSS-sponsored clandestine stations. When informed by Congressman John Rankin that an OSS agent was on the honor roll of the Young Communist League, Donovan replied that the same young man was "on the honor roll of OSS."[98]

When Roosevelt returned from Casablanca on January 31, 1943 he again met with Davis, who reiterated his complaint about the JCS directive. FDR reassured Davis but did nothing to solve the controversy. The president, as he had done in other administration conflicts, remained silent and hoped the participants would arrive at a solution without his intervention. This did not happen. Instead, Davis and Donovan dragged others into their quarrel. Davis obtained the backing of budget director Harold Smith and long-time Donovan foe, General George Strong, the G–2. Smith and Strong advised the president to strip OSS of most of its functions, not just its JCS-granted responsibility for psychological warfare. Donovan received the backing of the Joint Chiefs after they learned the conflict had become "highly explosive." At the JCS meeting on February 23, the OSS-OWI controversy was discussed. Admiral Horne concluded that the whole problem was created by OWI, which unlike all other government agencies, refused to accept the directive. Of all government agencies, Horne added, OWI gave the War and Navy departments the least help. Admiral Leahy also spoke against OWI. He questioned whether a civilian agency like OWI should be involved in any phase of "warfare." Admiral Edwards called OWI a "nuisance to theater commanders, particularly in the Pacific area." On the other hand, he believed that OSS produced "valuable results." Based on the discussion, the Joint Chiefs reaffirmed their directive, asserting that "foreign propaganda in areas of actual or projected military operations" be subject to the JCS and theater commanders. Their message was sent to the president.[99]

Before receiving the statement of the Joint Chiefs, FDR had sided completely with Davis and planned to remove OSS from under the JCS and place it under the War Department. The JCS statement, however, changed his mind. On March 12, Roosevelt issued Executive Order 9312, which gave OWI a hollow victory. In reality, it gave the Joint Chiefs responsibility for psychological warfare. The order reaffirmed OWI's responsibility to "plan, develop and execute all phases of the federal program of radio, press, publication and related foreign propaganda activities," but stipulated that "foreign propaganda in areas of actual or projected military operations... shall be subject to the approval of the Joint Chiefs of Staff. Parts of the foreign propaganda program which are to be executed in a theater of military operations will be subject to the control of theater commanders."[100] The latter phrase reaffirmed what Donovan always claimed: that propaganda and psychological warfare were distinguishable. OWI controlled propaganda, but the Joint Chiefs controlled "psychwar."

Donovan interpreted the new executive order as a victory for his organization. Although the JCS had not yet defined psychological warfare, Wild Bill had. His definition included clandestine radio broadcasting. At a lunch meeting with Davis three days after the issuance of Executive Order 9312, Davis conceded that Donovan's men were better equipped to handle black propaganda than were his, but he did not admit that clandestine broadcasting or related deceptions were OSS responsibilities. Davis agreed to "delegate" to Donovan the responsibility for operating clandestine stations but would not relinquish his jurisdictional claim.

Whether OSS was delegated, authorized, or only claimed the right to operate clandestine radio stations became irrelevent, as the agency assumed the right to do so. By the end of 1943, its claim was almost undisputed.[101] On October 27, the Joint Chiefs issued directive 144/11/D that instructed OSS to execute all forms of morale subversion, including "false rumors, 'freedom stations,' false leaflets and false documents, the organization and support of fifth column activities... for the purpose of creating confusion, division and undermining the morale of the enemy."[102] Later that year, OSS issued its Morale Operations manual that included instructions on operating clandestine radio stations. Despite this mandate, OSS-MO did not operate any subversive broadcasting stations until Colonel K. D. Mann was appointed head of MO in May 1944. He became MO chief after two previous heads, both of whom were attorneys and lacked media and administrative experience, were removed for doing little to implement MO's mandate. Colonel Mann ordered his area operations chiefs to develop black radio operations that were coordinated with other plans in their theaters of operation.[103]

OSS may have received recognition as the agency responsible for clandestine radio operations, but it was not the first or only agency that conducted such psychwar broadcasts. The first U.S.-sponsored clandestine station was operated by OWI not OSS personnel, although OSS did give the operation some support. The station broadcast under the direction of the Psychological Warfare Branch/Allied Force Headquarters (PWB/AFHQ). PWB/AFHQ was created for North Africa by General Eisenhower before the Allied "Torch" landing. Within PWB/AFHQ and elsewhere, OWI and OSS personnel closely cooperated. Only in Washington did jurisdictional conflicts erupt. "Radio 1212," a clandestine station that broadcast to the Rhineland in 1944–45 was operated by OSS and OWI personnel without any problems. On Saipan, Lt. John Zuckerman of the OSS operated the clandestine "Voice of the People" that broadcast nightly to Japan, but on Saturday nights worked as a disk jockey for the OWI's aboveground propaganda station. Cooperation like this was the rule in the field, not the exception.

## NOTES

1. Representative Hamilton Fish of New York frequently bragged that he, not Dies, headed the first committee that investigated Communist activities in the United States. Fish investigated Communist "penetration" of the schools before he was investigated himself by a Washington grand jury. The jury investigated Fish's well-publicized Nazi affiliations.

2. "Fly Reports Axis Favorable to Dies," *New York Times* February 10, 1942, p. 10; "Congress: Dies and Duty," *Time*, November 7, 1938, pp. 7–8; David Caute, *The Great Fear* (New York: Simon & Schuster, 1978), pp. 88–89.

3. "J. Parnell Thomas," *Current Biography*, September 1947, pp. 631–32; "Thomas, Impeacher," *Newsweek*, February 6, 1939, p. 17.

4. "Noah Mason," *Current Biography*, November 1957, pp. 357–58.

5. Ladislas Farago, *The Game of the Foxes* (New York: David McKay, 1971), p. 380; "Karl Mundt," *Current Biography*, July 1948, pp. 463–65; "U.S. Asks Recall of Italian Attache in Ship Sabotage," *New York Times*, April 4, 1941, p. 1. Mundt is best known for coauthoring the Nixon-Mundt Bill, which required the registration of Communist party members and "front organizations."

6. John Roy Carlson, *Undercover* (New York: E. P. Dutton, 1943), pp. 233–34; "Edelstein Dies After House Talk," *New York Times*, June 5, 1941, p. 24; "John Rankin," *Current Biography*, February 1944, pp. 555–58.

7. Carlson, *Undercover*, pp. 220–21.

8. U.S. Congressional House Committee on Un-American Activities, *Investigation of Un-American Propaganda Activities in the United States*, vol. 1 (Washington, D.C.: U.S. Government Printing Office, 1938).

9. "Spy Trial," *Newsweek*, October 31, 1938, p. 12.

10. "Prison Sentences Given 3 Spies Here," *New York Times*, December 3, 1938, p. 12; "Spy Trial"; Thomas Troy, *Donovan and the CIA* (Frederick, Md.: University Publications of America, 1981), p. 11; "New Propaganda by Reich Seen Here," *New York Times*, December 3, 1938, pp. 1, 8.

11. "Text of Roosevelt's 'Fireside Chat' Revealing Nation's Defenses," *Washington Post*, May 27, 1940, p. 4; "Text of Roosevelt's Radio Talk on the State of

Our Defenses," *New York Times*, May 27, 1940, p. 12. The panic following Roosevelt's speech was so great that New Jersey governor A. Harry Moore planned "a home defense army" to guard against the fifth column. In New York, the National Legion of the Mothers of America offered to teach rifle training to 10 million mothers "to combat any parachutist invasion." In Los Angeles, the police were mobilized to combat the fifth column attack. See *Washington Post*, May 27, 1940, p. 3.

12. "Dies Sensation," *Newsweek*, December 2, 1940, pp. 15–16; Martin Dies, *The Trojan Horse* (New York: Dodd Mead, 1940).

13. In 1943, Badoglio became the target of black radio broadcasts by the United States Psychological Warfare Branch of the Allied Field Headquarters. Balbo died in a 1940 plane crash. In 1943, Donovan's men helped operate a clandestine station that claimed to be operated by the deceased aviator.

14. Corey Ford, *Donovan of OSS* (Boston: Little, Brown & Company, 1970), p. 83.

15. Anthony Cave Brown, ed. *The Secret War Report of the OSS* (New York: Berkley Publishing, 1976), pp. 42–43; Anthony Cave Brown, *Wild Bill Donovan, The Last Hero* (New York: Times Books, 1982), pp. 149–50; Richard Dunlop, *Donovan—America's Master Spy* (New York: Rand McNally & Company, 1982), pp. 203–5.

16. William Stephenson, *A Man Called Intrepid* (New York: Harcourt Brace Jovanovich, 1976), pp. 113–14.

17. Stephenson, *A Man Called Intrepid*, pp. 113–14; Dunlop, *Donovan—America's Master Spy*, p. 209.

18. David Stafford, "Britain Looks at Europe, 1940: Some Origins of the SOE," *Canadian Journal of History* 10 (August) 1975, pp. 231–48; Stephenson, *A Man Called Intrepid*, pp. 43, 116.

19. The "Free German Station" was operating at the time of Donovan's arrival. The "German Revolution Station" might already have ceased broadcasting. It operated only briefly, having first appeared on April 17 (*BBC*, April 17, 1940, p. 1E[2]). Stephenson, *A Man Called Intrepid*, p. 117–18, reports that Donovan observed the operation of "Gustav Siegfried Eins" during this trip to London. Stephenson even recreates a discussion between Donovan and Paul Sanders, the station's chief announcer. According to Stephenson, Sanders told Donovan: "By constantly changing transmission times and frequencies, we hope to keep a good part of the Gestapo busy chasing shadows." The meeting and discussion are purely fictitious. Gustav Siegfried Eins did not start broadcasting until May 23, 1941, almost a year after the supposed meeting between Sanders and Donovan took place.

Contrary to all other reports, Nigel West, *MI6* (New York: Random House, 1983), p. 207, wrote that Donovan visited Woburn Abbey for the first time in June, 1942. West provides no references or documentation to substantiate this assertion.

20. Asa Briggs, *The War of Words* (London: Oxford University Press, 1970), p. 159, reports that Orwell was "fascinated" by German black stations. Whether he discussed the stations with Donovan is not known.

21. Dunlop, *Donovan—America's Master Spy*, p. 221.

22. Cave Brown, *Wild Bill Donovan, The Last Hero*, pp. 151–52.

23. See "U.S. Survey of Hitler Conquest Reveals '5th Column' Spearhead,"

*New York Times*, August 20, 1940, p. 6; "Donovan Says Democracies Easiest for Nazis' 'Fifth Column,' " *New York Times*, August 21, 1940, p. 9; "French Debacle Held Masterpiece of Fifth Columnists Under Hitler," *New York Times*, August 22, 1940, p. 6; "Germans Said to Spend Vast Sums Abroad to Pave Way for Conquest," *New York Times*, August 23, 1940, p. 5.

24. William J. Donovan and Edgar Mowrer, "Donovan Says Democracies Prove Easiest for Nazis' 'Fifth Column,' " *New York Times*, August 21, 1940, p. 9.

25. William J. Donovan and Edgar Mowrer, *Fifth Column Lessons for America* (Washington, D.C.: American Council on Public Affairs, 1941), p. 8.

26. Ford, *Donovan of OSS*, p. 99; Dunlop, *Donovan—America's Master Spy*, p. 231.

27. Dunlop, *Donovan—America's Master Spy*, p. 282; "Colonel Donovan's War," *Time*, March 31, 1941, pp. 19–20.

28. "PID Research Units: Underground Broadcasting Stations, Part II," *PRO*, FO898/52; Ellic Howe, *The Black Game* (London: Michael Joseph, 1982), p. 267.

29. Charles Cruickshank, *The Fourth Arm* (London: Davis-Poynter, 1977), p. 54; "Co-ordinator of Information, Psychology Division, Memorandum No. 11" (February 2, 1942); *Donovan*, box 82A, vol. 11.1, document 408.

30. Hugh Dalton, *The Fateful Years* (London: Frederick Muller, 1957), p. 367; David Stafford, *Britain and European Resistance 1940–1945* (London: The Macmillan Press, 1980), pp. 29–30; Stafford, "Britain Looks at Europe, 1940: Some Origins of SOE," pp. 238–39.

31. "Memorandum of Establishment of Service of Strategic Information" (June 10, 1941), *FDR*, President's Secretaries Files, box 141.

32. Bradley F. Smith, *The Shadow Warriors* (New York: Basic Books, 1983), p. 53.

33. Smith, *The Shadow Warriors*, p. 52. This conclusion by Bradley F. Smith is probably somewhat overstated, as Dalton invited Donovan to return to London in July 1941. The invitation was extended through Harry Hopkins, see Ben Pimlott, ed., *The Second World War Diary of Hugh Dalton 1940–45* (London: Jonathon Cape, 1986), p. 259.

34. Speech carried by CBS, MBS, and NBC, March 26, 1941, printed in *Vital Speeches*, April 15, 1941, pp. 386–89. Other speeches and writings by Donovan on the situation in Europe include "Our Spiritual Defense," *Vital Speeches* July 15, 1941, pp. 589–90; and "Who Says We're Soft?" *Reader's Digest*, April 1941, pp. 66–67.

35. Troy, *Donovan and the CIA*, p. 57.

36. Quoted in Troy, *Donovan and the CIA*, p. 42; and Cave Brown, *Wild Bill Donovan, The Last Hero*, p. 159.

37. Troy, *Donovan and the CIA*, pp. 44–49.

38. "Memorandum of Establishment of Service of Strategic Information" (June 10, 1941), *FDR*, President's Secretaries Files, box 141.

39. Troy, *Donovan and the CIA*, p. 62.

40. "Designating a Co-ordinator of Information," reprinted in Ford, *Donovan of OSS*, p. 337.

41. Troy, *Donovan and the CIA*, p. 69.

42. Sherwood's best-known plays include *Abe Lincoln in Illinois* (New York: C. Scribner's Sons, 1939); *Petrified Forest* (New York: C. Scribner's Sons, 1935); *Reunion in Vienna* (New York: C. Scribner's Sons, 1932); *This is New York* (New York: C. Scribner's Sons, 1931); and *Waterloo Bridge* (New York: C. Scribner's Sons, 1930). He received the Pulitzer Prize in 1936 for *Idiot's Delight*.

43. His speeches and writings are reported in "Sherwood Assails Appeaser 'Apostles,' " *New York Times*, December 22, 1940, p. 27; "Sherwood Assails Ford, Lindbergh," *New York Times*, August 26, 1940, p. 9; "Sherwood Opposes Entering War Now," *New York Times*, October 17, 1940, p. 15; "Rush All Possible Aid to Britain!" *Reader's Digest*, September 1940, pp. 12–17.

44. "Memorandum from William Donovan to the President," (March 4, 1942), *FDR*, President's Secretaries' Files, box 165, folder 7.

45. "Letter from Bob (Sherwood) to Bill (Donovan)" (June 16, 1941), Exhibits Illustrating the History of OSS, *Donovan*, box 99B, vol. 3, tab B.

46. "Letter from Bob (Sherwood) to Bill (Donovan)" (July 31, 1941), Exhibits Illustrating the History of OSS, *Donovan*, box 99B, vol. 3, tab C.

47. Allan M. Winkler, *The Politics of Propaganda—The Office of War Information 1942–1945* (New Haven: Yale University Press, 1978), pp. 23–24; and Eric M. Hanin, *War on Our Minds: The American Mass Media in World War II* (University of Rochester: Unpublished Ph.D. Diss., 1976), p. 59.

48. James P. Baxter II wrote *The British Government and Neutral Rights* (Lancaster, Pa.: Macmillan Company, 1928) and *The Introduction of the Ironclad Warships* (Cambridge: Harvard University Press, 1933).

49. McKay was author of *The National Workshops: A Study of the French Revolution of 1848* (Cambridge: Harvard University Press, 1937), *The United States and France* (Cambridge: Harvard University Press, 1951), and translator of *The Dreyfus Case* (New Haven: Yale University Press, 1937).

50. Read's works included *England and America* (Chicago: University of Chicago Press, 1918), *Factions in the English Privy Council under Elizabeth* (Washington, D.C.: American Historical Association, 1913), *Mr. Secretary Walsingham and the Policy of Queen Elizabeth* (Oxford: Clarendon Press, 1925), *The Tudors: Personalities and Politics in Sixteenth Century England* (New York: H. Holt & Company, 1936), and *Social and Political Forces in the English Reformation* (Houston: Elsevier Press, 1953).

51. Joseph Ralston Hayden's research included *The Senate and the Treaties 1789–1817* (New York: The Macmillan Company, 1920), *Philippine Independence* (Chicago: University of Chicago Press, 1933), *Pacific Politics* (Minneapolis: University of Minnesota Press, 1937) *The Philippine Policy of the United States* (New York: Institute of Pacific Relations, 1939), and *The Philippines: A Study in National Development* (New York: The Macmillan Company, 1945).

52. Professor James coauthored and edited *Elementary College Geography* (Ann Arbor: Edwards Brothers, 1928), *An Outline of Geography* (Boston: Ginn & Company, 1935), *Latin America* (New York: Odyssey Press, 1942), and *A Geography of Man* (Boston: Ginn & Company, 1949).

53. Langer, an historian, wrote *The Franco-Russian Alliance* (Cambridge: Harvard University Press, 1929), *European Alliances and Alignments 1871–1890* (New York: Knopf, 1931), and *The Diplomacy of Imperialism, 1890–1902* (New York: Knopf, 1935).

54. Richard Harris Smith, *OSS* (Los Angeles: University of California Press, 1972), pp. 15–16.

55. Solberg was removed as head of SO upon his return from England. He was then sent to Portugal, from where he launched unauthorized intriques into North Africa. He was ousted from Donovan's organization for insubordination in June 1942.

56. Kermit Roosevelt, ed., *War Report of the OSS (Office of Strategic Services)*, vol. 1 (New York: Walker & Company, 1976), p. 32.

57. State Department officials believed that FIS created rather than followed Cordell Hull's foreign policy. This often-voiced complaint asserted that "propaganda created policy." See Smith, *The Shadow Warriors*, p. 70; "U.S. Broadcasts News to Europe." *New York Times*, October 6, 1941, p. 5.

58. Roosevelt, *War Report of the OSS*, p. 36.

59. Although commercial broadcasters opposed government control over international broadcasting, they were neither enthusiastic about shortwave broadcasting nor willing to spend money on it. While NBC was licensed to broadcast on shortwave in 1929, by 1934 it still had no foreign-language service. In 1936, CBS operated a one-kilowatt shortwave station without a directional antenna. This technology was incapable of reaching a sizable foreign audience. Government actions in 1938 stimulated the commercial broadcasters to enter the field—but only to preclude the government from entering. See Charles J. Rolo and R. Strausz-Hupé, "U.S. International Broadcasting," *Harper's*, August 1941, p. 304.

60. "The U.S. Shortwave," *Time*, November 3, 1941, pp. 54–56.

61. Roosevelt, ed. *War Report of the OSS*, p. 41.

62. Roosevelt, ed. *War Report of the OSS*.

63. "The U.S. Shortwave," *Time*, November 3, 1941, p. 55.

64. Troy, *Donovan and the CIA*, pp. 112–13.

65. Roosevelt, ed., *War Report of the OSS*, p. 41. The stations to which FIS sent scripts were CBS's WCBX in New York and WCAB in Philadelphia, NBC's WBCA and WNBI in New York, General Electric's WGEA, WGEO, and KGEI in Schenectady and San Francisco, Westinghouse's WBOS in Boston, and the World Broadcasting Foundation's Boston stations, WRUL and WBUW. The Worldwide Broadcasting Foundation was secretly controlled by Great Britain's Secret Intelligence Service.

66. "Government to Run Short-wave Radios," *New York Times*, February 19, 1942, p. 10.

67. Kermit Roosevelt, ed., *War Report of the OSS*, p. 37. Dunlop, *Donovan—America's Master Spy*, p. 345 reports that the first Voice of America broadcast occurred on February 11.

68. "Government to Run Short-wave Radios," p. 10.

69. "U.S. Takes Over Short Waves to Win Air Propaganda War," *Newsweek*, October 19, 1942, p. 31; Rolo and Strausz-Hupé, "U.S. International Broadcasting."

70. Donovan attended the June 1940 Republican convention in Philadelphia as New York delegate at the very time that he was preparing to travel to England as Roosevelt's emissary. After returning from England, Donovan campaigned for Wendell Willkie. Curiously, Donovan's biographer, Anthony Cave Brown, fails to mention either of these activities.

71. Winkler, *The Politics of Propaganda*, pp. 27–28; Ford, *Donovan of OSS*, p. 125.

72. Ford, *Donovan of OSS*, p. 113.

73. "Memorandum for the President from William J. Donovan" (January 24, 1942), no. 182, FDR, President's Secretaries' Files, box 141.

74. Edmond Taylor, *Awakening from History* (London: Chatto & Windus, 1971), p. 244.

75. Taylor, *Awakening from History*, p. 246.

76. Roosevelt, ed. *War Report of the OSS*, p. 19; Ford, *Donovan of OSS*, p. 126; Winkler, *The Politics of Propaganda*, pp. 86–89.

77. Troy, *Donovan and the CIA*, p. 126; Roosevelt, ed., *War Report of the OSS*, p. 25.

78. Troy, *Donovan and the CIA*, pp. 118–120.

79. Roosevelt, ed., *War Report of the OSS*, p. 23.

80. Of newspapers endorsing presidential candidates in 1940, only 23 percent endorsed FDR. In the 1944 presidential election, 22 percent endorsed Roosevelt. Sixty percent endorsed Thomas Dewey. See Edwin Emery and Michael Emery, *The Press and America* (Englewood Cliffs, N.J.: Prentice-Hall, 1984).

81. Troy, *Donovan and the CIA*, p. 124. An earlier proposal by Smith was made in February. See "Memorandum for the President" (February 19, 1943), *FDR*, Harold Smith Papers, container 17 (plus attachments). To create even more embarassment for the president, a Republican-dominated Senate appropriations subcommittee started an inquiry into the spending of government agencies on publicity and promotion, according to "Studies Publicity Cost," *New York Times*, February 17, 1942, p. 4.

82. "Minutes of Meeting" (March 2, 1942), *JCS*, P. 1: 1942–45, Meetings, reel 1, no. 0023.

83. Denebrink revised his report three months later, but reached the same conclusions that he did in March. "Memorandum for General Smith" (June 10, 1942), *JCS*, P. 1: 1942–45, Meetings, reel 1, no. 0255.

84. "Memo to General Marshall and Admiral King from General W. B. Smith" (March 14, 1942), *JCS*, p. 1: 1942–45, Strategic Issues, reel 11, no. 0244; "Letter from William Donovan to General Smith" (March 23, 1942), *JCS*, p. 1: 1942–45, Strategic Issues, reel 11, no. 0255; Troy, *Donovan and the CIA*, p. 136.

85. Unlike Sherwood and MacLeish, Lowell Mellett was a former journalist. He was the editor of the *Washington Daily News* before heading the OGR. Despite his background, he was subjected to media ridicule. His agency was referred to as "Mellett's Madhouse."

86. "Man of Sense," *Time*, June 22, 1942, p. 21; "Elmer Davis and the News," *Business Week*, June 20, 1942, p. 7. One of the media not endorsing Davis was *Newsweek*, which ridiculed his appointment and the new agency as just another FDR propaganda agency in "Here's Elmer," *Newsweek*, June 22, 1942, p. 30.

87. Kermit Roosevelt, ed., *War Report of the OSS*, pp. 26, 212.

88. "Functions of the Office of Strategic Service" (December 23, 1942), Directive 155/4/D, *JCS*, p. 1: 1942–45, Strategic Issues, reel 11, no. 0379; "Joint Chiefs of Staff 47th Meeting" (December 22, 1942), *JCS*, p. 1: 1942–45, Meetings, reel 1, no. 0474.

89. Kermit Roosevelt, ed. *War Report of the OSS*, pp. 212–13; "MO History," Wash. Hist. Office Op–26, *OSS*, entry 99, box 75, folder 33.

90. "Say Roosevelt Gets Donovan-Davis Fight," *New York Times*, January 19, 1943, p. 16; "Too Much Quarreling in Propaganda Services," *Newsweek*, January 25, 1943, p. 26; "Editorial: OSS Reaches Out," *Washington Post*, January 21, 1943, p. 10; "War Psychology Battle Carried to the White House," *Chicago Tribune*, January 19, 1943, p. 12.

91. Winkler, *The Politics of Propaganda*, pp. 86–89; Wallace Caroll, *Persuade or Perish* (Boston: Houghton Mifflin Company, 1948), pp. 26–55; "Full News of War Promised by Davis," *New York Times*, July 11, 1942, p. 7; "OWI Aids Kelly Election Drive, Brown Charges," *Chicago Tribune*, January 20, 1943, p. 12; "Congress Blast Against OWI Portends Assault on New Deal," *Newsweek*, February 22, 1943, pp. 25–26.

92. "OWI Plows under the Almanac Singers," *New York Times*, January 5, 1943, p. 21; "Barrage on OWI," *Newsweek*, May 3, 1943, p. 36.

93. Paul Sweezy became the most prolific Marxist writer after World War II and founded the Monthly Review Press and *Monthly Review*, an independent socialist magazine. His first books included *Monopoly and Competition in the English Coal Trade, 1550–1850* (Cambridge: Harvard University Press, 1938); *The Theory of Capitalist Development* (New York: Oxford University Press, 1942); and *Socialism* (New York: McGraw-Hill, 1949). Some of his later works, all published by Monthly Review Press, include *The Present as History* (1953), *The Theory of U.S. Foreign Policy* (1960) with Leo Huberman, *The Communist Manifesto After 100 Years* (1964) with Leo Huberman, *Monopoly Capital* (1966), *Modern Capitalism and Other Essays* (1972), and *The Dynamics of U.S. Capitalism* (1972) with Harry Magdoff.

94. Maurice Halperin emigrated from the United States after being accused of being a Soviet agent while in OSS. He moved to Mexico, Cuba, then Canada. He wrote *The Rise and Decline of Fidel Castro* (Berkeley: University of California Press, 1972) and *The Taming of Fidel Castro* (Berkeley: University of California Press, 1981).

95. Marcuse became the best-known Marxist in the United States and a hero of the New Left. His writings include *Reason and Revolution* (New York: Oxford University Press, 1941); *Eros and Civilization* (Boston: Beacon Press, 1955); *Soviet Marxism* (New York: Columbia University Press, 1958); *One Dimensional Man* (Boston: Beacon Press, 1964); *Studies in Critical Philosophy* (Boston: Beacon Press, 1973); *The Aesthetic Dimension* (Boston: Beacon Press, 1978); and *Counterrevolution and Revolt* (Boston: Beacon Press, 1978).

96. Cora Dubois, an anthropologist, wrote *Wintu Ethnography* (Berkeley: University of California Press, 1935); *The Feather Cult of the Middle Columbia* (Menasha, Wis.: George Banta Publishing, 1938); *The People of Alor* (Minneapolis: University of Minnesota Press, 1944); and *Social Forces in Southeast Asia* (Cambridge: Harvard University Press, 1959).

97. Before the war, Polonsky was a radio scriptwriter and novelist. Some of his novels include *The Enemy Sea* (Boston: Little, Brown & Company, 1943); *The World Above* (Boston: Little, Brown & Company, 1951); and *A Season of Fear* (New York: Cameron Associates, 1956). He was also coauthor with Mitchell Wilson of such mysteries as *The Goose Is Cooked* (New York: Simon & Schuster,

1940) using the pseudonym Emmett Hogarth. Before being blacklisted, Polonsky directed movies *Body and Soul* (1947) and *Force of Evil* (1948). His first film after being dropped from the blacklist was *Tell Them Willie Boy Is Here* (1968), starring Robert Redford.

98. Ford, *Donovan of OSS*, pp. 135–36.

99. "Memorandum for the President from Harold Smith" (February 19, 1943) *FDR*, Harold Smith Papers, container 17; "Minutes of J. C. S. 63rd Meeting" (February 23, 1943) *JCS*, p. 1: 1942–45, Meetings, reel 1, No. 0656.

100. "Executive Order Defining the Foreign Information Activities of the Office of War Information" (March 12, 1943), *JCS*, p. 1: 1942–45, Strategic Issues, reel 11, no. 04550.

101. OWI never formally delegated responsibility for clandestine broadcasting to OSS. Davis said, "OWI was not doing 'black,' might never do it, but would not relinquish the right to do it," according to the OSS "MO History," Wash. Hist. Office Op–23, *OSS*, Entry 99, box 75, folder 33. As late as mid–1944, jurisdictional disputes occasionally flared up and were clarified. For example, see "Letter to Elmer Davis from William Donovan" (May 5, 1944), *FDR*, President's Secretaries' Files, box 6.

102. "Directive-Functions of the Office of Strategic Services," October 27, 1943, *JCS*, p. 1: 1942–45, Strategic Issues, reel 11, no. 0549.

103. Smith, *The Shadow Warriors*, p. 174; Roosevelt, ed., *War Report of the OSS*, p. 216; *Morale Operations Field Manual* (Washington, D.C.: OSS, 1943) in *Donovan*, box 99B, vol. 1 (bound), tab B.

# 3

## THE EARLY
## SUBVERSIVE STATIONS
## OF THE UNITED STATES

General Donovan believed that radio broadcasting was a strategic weapon of war. When used strategically, radio sowed disaffection among citizens within the enemy country, undermined the confidence that enemy populations and troops had in their leaders, and persuaded listeners to dissent. These tasks were accomplished by operating "freedom stations," as the British Political Warfare Executive did. The British-operated station, "Gustav Siegfried Eins," claimed that German leaders were getting larger food rations than the average citizen or soldier, creating distrust and disaffection in Germany. "Radio Italia," also British-operated, claimed that Italian resources, including bread, coal, soap, and electricity, were diverted from Italy to Germany. Hoping to make Italian leader Benito Mussolini appear as a puppet of Hitler who had no regard for his countrymen, the station asserted that Germans received twice the rations of Italians, even before Italian goods were sent to the Third Reich. With morale undermined by such broadcasts, the enemy's "will to resist" eroded, Donovan believed.[1]

Donovan's view of psychwar radio differed from that of Gen. Dwight Eisenhower, who was named Allied commander of Operation Torch, the code-name for the Allied invasion of French North Africa. North Africa rather than Sicily, southern Italy, or France was selected as the first target of a joint Allied attack because it appeared that a much-needed Allied victory could be achieved in North Africa more easily than elsewhere, and because Field Marshal Erwin Rommel's Afrika Korps was threatening the British presence in strategically vital Egypt. Rommel drove the British from Libya to el-Alamein by June 1942. The Allies, based on intelligence supplied by Robert D. Murphy, a U.S. embassy representative in French North Africa, and Lt. Col. William Eddy, an OSS-Special Intelligence (SI) agent who was posing as a "control officer," believed that an expeditionary force of 100,000 troops could easily seize Morocco, Algeria, and Tunisia. Murphy and Eddy were in Africa as part of an agreement made by Murphy and French General Maxime Weygand, the delegate general to French Africa and governor of Algeria. The Murphy-Weygand Agreement, reached on February 26, 1941, established trade links between French Africa and the United States, but specified that all goods shipped from the United States were to be consumed in North Africa, not shipped elsewhere. To assure that the goods did not leave North Africa, twelve U.S. "control officers" were stationed at Vichy-controlled ports and railways. The control agents, dubbed "Murphy's twelve apostles," were actually there to collect intelligence that was sent back to Washington.[2]

The reports from Murphy and Eddy stressed that an Allied landing would encounter little or no resistance because Vichy-French troops in North Africa were pro-American, as was the anti-Vichy underground there. If a respectable French military leader such as Gen. Henri Giraud, who escaped from Germany to France in April 1942, ordered French troops to welcome rather than fight U.S. troops that landed in North Africa, bloodless occupation could be achieved. With friendly French forces administering Algeria and Morocco, keeping U.S. supply and communication routes open, the Allies would then be in position to invade Sicily and Italy.

Because plans for the North African invasion were based on the presumption that French troops were potential allies who would not fight the Allied landing if approached in the proper way, the Torch campaign was forced to rely more on psychological warfare than on conventional military tactics. Eisenhower, unlike Donovan, viewed psychwar techniques—including radio—as mere tactics to be employed in a military operation, rather than as a strategic weapon. Radio and other psychwar techniques were to be used to supplement and coordinate military actions. Radio was to provide information to resistance forces, provide cover or deception for military actions, and provide surrender information to enemy troops. When used tactically, as Eisenhower wanted to use it, radio was no different from any other weapon in the military arsenal. It needed to be under the control of the theater commander and, like guns or artillery, was an artifact without ideological content. Eisenhower differed in this respect from other military commanders like Gens. George Patton and Omar Bradley, who believed that psychwar techniques were a waste of time. War, in their view, was waged with weaponry, not words.[3]

Because the invading Allied troops could not come ashore with their guns pounding French forces, Eisenhower turned to psychological warfare. General Eisenhower's interest in using psychological warfare was therefore an outgrowth of his beliefs concerning French attitudes and responses in North Africa, not his convictions concerning the utility of psychwar tactics during battle. Psychwar had not yet proven itself. The British used it consistently but never won a major battle.

Eisenhower formalized the Torch plan in London. He created a political subcommittee to provide advice and plans for propaganda and psychological warfare. The subcommittee was headed by Harold Mack of the French section of the British Foreign Office, who supervised seven other people. They were drawn from the OSS, OWI, and PWE. The political subcommittee provided advice and direction to the Supreme Commander, but was subordinate to him. Eisenhower insisted that OWI, OSS, and PWE personnel report directly to him, rather than to their respective supervisors. Because the subcommittee members were privy to military secrets, Eisenhower insisted that they be under military jurisdiction.[4] This arrangement, for the first time since the United States entered the war, placed military leaders over the civilian propaganda and psychwar specialists. This chain of command, which was repeated in virtually all other theaters during the war, had a long-term impact on U.S. propaganda policy. It made propaganda strategies subordinate to military needs. When immediate military needs and long-term strategic propaganda interests of the United States came into conflict, military needs won out.

The plans for Torch were intricate, but they needed to be. Numerous deceptions and logistical and propaganda problems had to be addressed if the invasion were to succeed. To assure that Germany would not fortify its troop strength or occupy French North Africa before the invasion, Eisenhower had to be sure that German commanders believed that the invasion would occur elsewhere. To maintain the element of surprise, rumors that the Allies were planning an invasion of northern France, Norway, Malta, and Syria were spread by SOE and OSS agents. These rumors did not divert attention from the French African coast, as Germany was aware that the Allies were amassing supplies in Gibraltar. Ultra intercepts indicated that the Germans were expecting an invasion of Dakar in French West Africa, where the British had previously attempted an invasion. Germany deployed U-boats off Dakar, believing it to be the location of the planned invasion.[5]

The Torch invaders also needed to allay French fears that the Allies were attempting to annex their colonies. This could be done, Eisenhower hoped, by claiming that the invasion force included French patriots like General Giraud. General de Gaulle's Free French forces were excluded from the invasion, and planning for it, because they were closely identified with the British and considered by some Frenchmen to be a British creation. De Gaulle's men were involved in the unsuccessful Dakar invasion that resulted in Frenchmen killing Frenchmen. The planners also had to hide British participation in the Torch campaign. The intelligence of Murphy and Eddy indicated that French Anglophobia remained high, and that if the British were known to be involved in an invasion of French territory, French troops would bitterly fight the occupation attempt. French resentment of the British, while historically ubiquitous, reached a peak during the German attack on France during May 1940. Paul Ferdonnet, André Obrecht, and other Nazi-sponsored broadcasters ceaselessly claimed that Britain was using France to fight its war with Germany. The resentment increased after France capitulated, while Great Britain continued to fight. It remained intense after Britain's unsuccessful attempts to seize Dakar and Syria. When German intelligence indicated that an invasion of French Africa was imminent, its propaganda machine went on the offensive, attempting to keep French Anglophobia high. The German-controlled clandestine station, "Radio Revolution," which claimed to be operated by loyal Frenchmen, reported:

The concentration of men-of-war at Gibraltar . . . mean[s] England is preparing a surprise attack . . . in the Mediterranean, Tunisia being the most exposed country. Naturally, it is once again a French colony that the Anglo-Saxons are threatening. The contrary would have surprised us.[6]

Edmond Taylor was sent to London to represent General Donovan on the Torch political subcommittee. Taylor was selected because he had experience with psychwar techniques, having served in London with the PWE during 1941. Wallace Carroll was dispatched to head the OWI team in England, replacing James P. Warburg. Carroll was later joined by Percy Winner, a former journalist for CBS and the International News Service, who was fluent in French and Italian. Winner was a friend of FIS head Robert Sherwood, and joined COI at Sherwood's behest. When FIS became the Overseas Branch of OWI, Winner stayed with it, rather than joining OSS, as Taylor had done. Winner was an adamant New Deal liberal with an uncompromising attitude toward the Axis and their collaborators.[7]

Torch plans called for President Roosevelt to make a "live" broadcast in French to Europe and North Africa. Eisenhower was to make similar broadcasts, assuring the French that the U.S. had "no designs either on North Africa or any part of French Africa." The broadcasts were to be carried by the BBC, but relayed over the powerful Aspidistra transmitter. The Aspidistra transmitter was selected because its 600-kilowatt mediumwave signals would reach not only France but North Africa.[8] "Voice of America" was to carry the Roosevelt and Eisenhower speeches, and additional commentaries on shortwave from U.S.-based stations. On November 2, a week before the Torch invasion, all shortwave stations in the U.S. except WRUL were handed over to OWI and Rockefeller's CIAA, allowing the broadcasts to be carefully coordinated with military actions.[9] A transmitter was placed aboard a battleship, the USS Texas. This transmitter was to make broadcasts directed at Morocco. A broadcast directed to the Moroccan Riffs, a hill people known for their warlike qualities and fierce independence, was written with the assistance of eminent anthropologist Carlton Coon, an OSS Arab specialist who had written an ethnology entitled *The Tribes of the Rif* in 1931.[10] General Giraud, whom Murphy convinced to become leader of anti-Fascist pro-Allied French forces in North Africa, was to simultaneously broadcast an appeal to North African troops, urging them to follow his leaderhip. Murphy's intelligence indicated that Giraud was one of the few avowedly pro-Allied French generals who commanded the respect of French North African troops. As Allied troops waded ashore, North African resistance forces would arrest collaborationists, keeping them from rallying other pro-Axis forces to defend against the Allied invasion. The plans called for combat propaganda teams to accompany the troops that came ashore. The propaganda teams were charged with seizing and operating the radio stations in occupied North Africa. Broadcasts from the French transmitters were to announce the success of the invasion and report that no conflicts between French and U.S. troops occurred, even if they had.[11]

Because the strongest voices in the psychwar planning committees for Torch were members of OWI rather than OSS, clandestine broadcasting and related psychwar techniques such as snuggling—the laying of a transmission adjacent to an enemy broadcasting station's signal—were not included as part of the invasion plan. The PWE, however, developed a separate plan that included several clandestine tricks not included by the Torch planners. PWE initially planned to broadcast Roosevelt's invasion speech alongside the wavelengths used by Lyons and Toulouse stations. The purpose was to generate greater listenership than would be obtained if the BBC's French service wavelength were used. The plan to "snuggle" the broadcasts of the French stations was vetoed because the act could be interpreted as "an act hostile to Vichy." PWE also planned to use the Aspidistra transmitter to create confusion and distrust between Vichy and Berlin during the first hours of the Torch invasion. This was to be done by making counterfeit German broadcasts purporting to emanate from Reichssender stations. The fake German broadcasts would announce that Vichy leader Henry Pétain had fled to North Africa and that Germany would therefore occupy Vichy France. The plan was to be implemented when needed. It was never implemented, however, because the Torch plans went completely astray. Eisenhower found himself collaborating with rather than arresting Vichyists in North Africa.[12]

As the final touches were placed on the Torch psychological warfare plan in London, Robert Sherwood and James Warburg, who returned to the United States after Wallace Carroll arrived in England, combed the woods in the United States for OWI men who could implement the plan.

The men were to comprise combat propaganda teams that were to seize and operate the radio stations and newspapers in occupied North Africa. Sherwood and Warburg could find only 16 French-speaking OWI volunteers. Among them were George Rehm, a former European writer for the *New York Herald Tribune,* Peter Tompkins, another journalist, and Oliver H. P. Garrett, a playwright and screen writer who was manager of OWI English language broadcasts originating in New York. Garrett was appointed head of the propaganda team that landed with the assault force at Oran, Algeria.[13]

Having found only 16 qualified individuals, Sherwood and Warburg asked Robert Bruce Lockhart, head of PWE, to provide additional personnel. Lockhart located 41 French-speaking PWE men, who were assigned to the Torch campaign. This brought the total psychological warfare force to 57. As the 57 men assembled in London before leaving for Gibraltar, General Eisenhower discovered that the team had no commander or legal standing. Two days before the team left for the Mediterranean, Eisenhower asked Col. Charles B. Hazeltine, a cavalryman best known for his battles with gin bottles, to head a newly formed Psychological Warfare Service (PWS). After the Torch invasion, PWS was renamed the Psychological Warfare Branch, Allied Force Headquarters (PWB/AFHQ). PWB/AFHQ was made a branch of the Information and Censorship section, headed by Gen. Robert A. McClure. McClure eventually headed the Psychological Warfare Division of the Supreme Headquarters Allied Expeditionary Force, which invaded Normandy on June 6, 1944. Hazeltine, who had no idea what psychological warfare was and no experience with it, protested Eisenhower's assignment, saying: "Why not make me head of the Medical Corps?"[14]

After being assigned commander of PWS, Hazeltine spent two days studying OWI, OSS, and PWE reports on psychological warfare, and discussing them with Winner and Taylor. He thereafter flew to Gibraltar, where he met the assembled team of psychwarriors. There he found a group of both experienced and inexperienced men, including "American officers, British officers, American civilians, British civilians, American non-coms, British non-coms, American privates and British privates... [whose] qualifications had no relationship to their grade or pay."[15] Hazeltine discovered that the group had no plans, no directives, no organizational structure, and no equipment. All that the team had was a "sheaf of plans for the radio bombardment from America and Britain during the first few hours of the operation."[16] There were no plans stating who comprised the propaganda teams or how they were to seize and operate the newspapers and radio stations in the occupation zone. There were no radio receiving sets for monitoring Allied or Axis broadcasts, or printing equipment for producing leaflets. What they did have were American Express traveler's checks, which were useless in French Africa.[17]

The confusion surrounding the development of PWS mirrored the confusion that confronted every aspect of the Torch invasion. British intelligence received reports indicating that Murphy and Eddy were wrong in their assessments of French troop loyalty. Rather than greet the Allied landing force, the French were likely to fight it. Gen. Henri Giraud, who Eisenhower hoped could persuade French troops to lay down their arms, arrived in Gibraltar on November 7, 1942, a day later than expected. By the time Giraud arrived, the Allied invasion force had already sailed for North Africa. More important, but unknown to Eisenhower, was the presence in Algiers of Admiral Jean F. Darlan, commander of the French Armed Forces and Marshal Pétain's successor-designate. Darlan had been the champion of economic collaboration with Germany. He secretly traveled to French North Africa to visit his gravely ill son, who was stricken with infantile paralysis.

Instead of getting briefed and making arrangements for broadcasting to French troops in North Africa, as he had agreed to do, General Giraud insisted on having a conference with General Eisenhower. When Eisenhower met with Giraud, the French general issued a demand that he be named supreme commander of the Allied invasion force. He argued that his and France's pride were at stake. Eisenhower explained that Operation Torch had been planned for many months, and that it was too late to change the plans. Eisenhower offered General Giraud anything—the governorship of North Africa—except command of the Allied troops. Giraud stubbornly refused to accept anything less than being named supreme commander.

Eisenhower was correct in stating that it was too late to change the Torch plan. At 1:30 a.m. on November 8, the operation began. The task force arrived off the coasts of Algiers, Casablanca, and Oran, as scheduled. Anticipating the Allied landing, the French underground went into action, detaining known collaborationists and seizing the mass media and other strategic targets. At Oran, just under 30,000 Allied troops poured ashore. At 2:00 a.m. London time, following the playing of the "Marseillaise," the BBC and the Voice of America simultaneously broadcast an address by President Roosevelt in French, billed as live but actually recorded, that in part said:

My friends who suffer day and night under the crushing yoke of the Nazis, I speak to you as one who was with your army and navy in France in 1918 . . . We come among you to repulse the cruel invaders who would remove forever your rights of self-government . . . Do not obstruct, I beg of you, this great purpose.[18]

FDR's statement closed with *"Vive la France éternelle!"* His address never mentioned the invasion of North Africa. News of the invasion was broadcast by the BBC and Voice of America in French, German, Italian, and every other European language immediately after Roosevelt's address. The news was repeated every few minutes, as was FDR's speech. Between the news reports and FDR's speech, Eisenhower's proclamation was aired. The proclamation, like FDR's, was in French and addressed to troops in North Africa. Eisenhower proclaimed:

This is a military operation directed against the Italian-German military forces in North Africa. Our only objective is to defeat the enemy and to free France. I need not tell you that we have no designs either on North Africa or any part of the French Empire. We count on your friendship, and we ask your aid. I have given formal orders that no offensive action be undertaken against you on the condition that you for your part take the same attitude.[19]

The ten-kilowatt transmitter on the forward deck of the USS Texas, off the coast of Casablanca, also broadcast the speeches by Roosevelt and Eisenhower. The broadcasts, made on the wavelength of Radio Morocco, urged French troops not to fight the invasion force. Radio Morocco returned to the air and warned listeners about the existence of this "clandestine" station. It urged them not to listen to the clandestine implorations.[20]

The broadcasts from the USS Texas were not clandestine but were clearly identified as originating from the Allied invasion force. After repeating its entreaties to not resist, the shipboard station warned: "You are listening to 'The Voice of America' broadcasting from the forward deck of the American battleship Texas. The next voice you hear will be the 16-inch guns of the USS Texas."[21]

Another broadcast, weakly heard on the wavelength of Radio Algiers, was made at 7 a.m. on November 8. The broadcast, attributed to General Giraud, said:

We cannot neglect this opportunity of recovery. I resume among you my position as a combatant. I ask for your confidence. You have mine. . . . Remember that the African army holds in its hands the fate of France.[22]

During the early hours of November 8, Eisenhower convinced General Giraud to support the Allied landing and accept appointment as commander of French, rather than Allied, troops. Although supporting the invasion, Giraud did not make the broadcast attributed to him. It was probably made by Raphael Aboulker, a member of the French resistance, which had captured strategic points in Algiers.[23] Aboulker made the broadcast after it became apparent that Giraud would not make the announcement himself. Radio Brazzaville, the broadcasting station of General de Gaulle's Free French Forces that was established in French Equatorial Africa with William Donovan's assistance, also spoke in favor of the invasion, even though Free French troops were excluded from participation in Torch. A speech by General de Gaulle supporting the Allied action was broadcast by the BBC. "French commanders, soldiers, sailors, airmen, officials, colonists: Rise, every one of you! Help our allies," de Gaulle commanded. The general's call was repeated by "Radio Gaulle," the Free French clandestine station that claimed to originate in France, but actually transmitted from Woburn Abbey in England.[24]

Despite the appeals of Roosevelt, Eisenhower, Giraud, and de Gaulle, French troops did not welcome the Anglo-American invasion force. French forces at Casablanca shelled the USS Texas, knocking out its transmitter moments after it warned the French not to shoot. In the port of Oran, two Coast Guard cutters were sunk, killing many on board. The Oran landing force encountered heavy fighting and suffered many casualties. Heavy resistance was encountered elsewhere. The invasion force at Rabat was late in arriving. Members of the French underground in Rabat who had taken the offensive in anticipation of the Allied troop arrival were dispersed. Some were arrested. In Algiers, the Allied landing was scheduled to take place at 2:00 a.m. It occurred many hours later because the troops accidently came ashore five miles west of the city. During the many hours that it took the troops to make their way to Algiers, the French rebels who supported the invasion were engaged by Vichy troops and routed. Almost every aspect of the Torch invasion went wrong.

Giraud's support of the Allied invasion did little to end the fighting because, contrary to the intelligence reports of Robert Murphy and Colonel Eddy, the aging general had little support among French troops. There was virtually no response to the broadcast made in his name. French troops followed the orders of Marshal Pétain and his subordinate, Admiral Darlan.

Unaware that Admiral Darlan was in Algiers or that Allied troops would land several miles west of the city, Robert Murphy called on the home of General Alphonse Juin, commander of French land and air forces in North Africa, after midnight on November 8. This was about an hour-and-a-half before the scheduled 2 a.m. invasion. Murphy informed Juin of the impending Allied action and asked for his cooperation. Murphy wanted General Juin to issue a command to French troops, forbidding them to engage the Allied detachments. Juin informed Murphy of Admiral Darlan's presence in Algiers. Juin said that Darlan's presence made it impossible for him to make any decision concerning French actions, as he could be overruled by the Admiral.

Encouraged by Murphy, General Juin telephoned Darlan. Juin informed the admiral of Murphy's desire to meet with him. Kenneth Pendar, the U.S. vice-consul in North Africa, drove over and picked up Admiral Darlan, who was only a mile from General Juin's residence. Darlan arrived twenty minutes later. Murphy immediately informed Darlan of the planned Allied invasion. Murphy urged the admiral to issue an appeal to French soldiers, ordering them not to resist the Torch landing. Outside, French underground forces surrounded General Juin's villa, where Darlan and Murphy were meeting. Darlan and Juin were informed that they were under arrest. Murphy used the arrest and the planned Allied landing to pressure Darlan to accept a truce. Darlan, however, insisted that Marshal Pétain, not he, had authority to order French troops to cooperate with the Allies.

By 6:00 a.m., the anticipated Allied landing force in Algiers had not appeared. Darlan soon questioned whether an Allied troop landing was actually planned. The Allied landing west of, rather than in, the city of Algiers weakened Murphy's bargaining power and emboldened Darlan. At 6:30 a.m. a detachment of Vichy guards attacked the rebel forces that surrounded General Juin's house. The rebels were dispersed, Darlan and Juin freed, and Murphy and Pendar detained. In other areas of the city, the French underground was also attacked and forced into hiding. Radio Algiers, which had fallen into the hands of the underground, was taken back by the Vichyists.

By the afternoon, it was clear that General Eisenhower's troops had indeed landed in North Africa. Fighting had broken out throughout the French territory. Realizing that Murphy had not been bluffing, General Juin called Robert Murphy and told him that Admiral Darlan wanted to negotiate an agreement to stop the fighting. The negotiations that began during the afternoon of November 8 continued for several days, as did French resistance. The negotiations were protracted because Darlan would only issue a partial ceasefire. He claimed that Marshal Pétain's approval was needed for a formal armistice, but Pétain was unable to publicly approve one for fear that this would trigger a German invasion of Vichy France. The Marshal's fears were well-founded, as German troops entered Vichy France at midnight on November 10/11. Given these difficulties, Pétain publicly denounced Darlan's ceasefire with the Allies, but supported it in secret. After obtaining Pétain's secret endorsement of a U.S.-French ceasefire, Darlan negotiated a formal end to the fighting. The ceasefire accord—known as the Clark-Darlan Agreement—belatedly and officially ended hostilities between French and Allied troops. By the time the agreement was signed, however, 567 U.S. troops had been killed or were missing, and 837 wounded. The British, who were disguised as U.S. troops during the invasion, suffered 65 casualties. It is estimated that as many as 4,500 French troops were killed or wounded.[25]

Admiral Darlan was recognized as the head of French North Africa by the Clark-Darlan Agreement. General Giraud, who Eisenhower had promised this post, was instead named commander in chief of ground and air forces, a position previously held by General Juin. General Juin was made commander of the eastern sector. The agreement gave Darlan political control of North Africa, including control of its mass media. The broadcasting stations that were seized by Torch combat propaganda teams were returned to Darlan's men. The Allies received not only a ceasefire, but an agreement that French troops would participate in an offensive in Tunisia, which German and Italian troops had quickly occupied during the fighting in Morocco and Algeria. Darlan also promised to secure Allied supply and communication lines in French North Africa during the Tunisian campaign.

The agreement created a new Vichy government in Algiers. Darlan, anything but a democrat, enforced rather than revoked existing anti-Jewish laws, imposed strict censorship, and arrested Gaullists and other Vichy opponents. The underground forces that helped Eisenhower during the Torch invasion of November 8 were arrested for being traitors. The Algiers and Rabat stations, after being returned to French control, reverted to their preinvasion programming, praising Marshal Pétain and denouncing his detractors. The broadcasts created confusion as to whether the stations were actually pro-Fascist or pro-United Nations. General Eisenhower accepted these "problems" as a necessary condition for maintaining relations with Admiral Darlan. Eisenhower argued that the agreement with Darlan prohibited him from interfering in domestic matters.[26]

On November 12, Free French representatives in London informed the Political Warfare Executive (PWE) that they no longer considered General Giraud to be an anti-Vichy leader. Three days later, General de Gaulle sent a violently worded denunciation of the Clark-Darlan Agreement to U.S. representatives in London. The following day, Radio Brazzaville declared the agreement an insult to the French nation. The station urged French troops to desert, despite Eisenhower's attempts to persuade them to fight in Tunisia. The broadcasts from Radio Brazzaville chastised the "irresponsibility" of U.S. generals. On November 21, a scheduled BBC broadcast by de Gaulle, which contained an attack on U.S. policies, was banned. In response, de Gaulle ordered the personnel of Radio Gaulle, the British-based clandestine station, to leave their posts. This was the first silencing of the clandestine station since it appeared on August 25, 1941. Although discussions between British and Free French representatives were held in an attempt to resolve the dispute and put the clandestine station back on the air, the conflict could not be resolved. The British were reluctant to give Gaullists another voice that could be used to criticize the United States.[27]

The silencing of Radio Gaulle was not seen as a major blow to British psychwar efforts because several other stations were simultaneously making covert broadcasts to France: Radio Inconnue, which appeared first on February 3, 1941; La France Catholique, which signed on July

2, 1941; and Radio Patrie, which appeared on October 1, 1942. The latter station, like Radio Gaulle, was used to broadcast instructions to the French underground. Because they had Radio Patrie, the British believed that they did not need Radio Gaulle and therefore discouraged rather than encouraged its resurrection. This strategy backfired when Radio Brazzaville denounced Radio Patrie as a fake that was misleading loyal Frenchmen. This Gaullist action angered members of the PWE.[28]

Members of the OWI also raised their voices in opposition to the Clark-Darlan Agreement. James Warburg complained that the agreement, while militarily expedient, undermined the beliefs of peoples in Europe, China and Russia about "the sincerity of our war and peace aims." The action suggested that "when we 'liberate' a country, we . . . make a practice of putting our friends in jail and of turning the 'liberated' country over to the enemies of democracy. If this impression is allowed to get abroad, the result of the North African campaign will be a political defeat irrespective of any military success," Warburg warned. This and other warnings were brushed aside by Eisenhower. Percy Winner not only objected to the agreement but to Eisenhower's attempts to censor OWI reports originating in North Africa. Winner and other OWI members did whatever they could to circumvent Eisenhower's censorship. Winner raised so many objections to army policy in North Africa that General Walter Bedell Smith declared that "Europe and Africa together were too small to hold Winner and the United States Army." It was this opposition that eventually led the Joint Chiefs of Staff to brand OWI "a nuisance to theater commanders."[29]

James Warburg's predictions concerning the long-term damage of the agreement proved true. De Gaulle's criticisms of the United States were repeated by other wartime allies—mostly those supported by the Soviet Union. The criticisms undermined the stature of the United States and its friends. Broadcasts from "Radio Kościuszko," a Soviet-sponsored clandestine station, and by the Union of Polish Patriots, which were carried by Radio Moscow, convincingly branded Gen. Władysław Sikorski and Stanisław Mikołajczyk, premiers of the Polish government-in-exile in London, as Fascists like Darlan. Radio Free Yugoslavia, the clandestine station of Marshall Tito's Communist partisans, attached a "Fascist" label to Draža Mihajlović's Chetniks. The Chetniks had the support of Washington until very late in the war. The United States suffered long-term political setbacks elsewhere.[30]

The U.S. reputation for supporting antidemocratic forces for short-term military or defense gains grew rather than receded following the war. The reputation was enhanced when Eisenhower, the father of the Clark-Darlan Agreement, became president. Eisenhower, who had displayed little devotion to democratic principles during the war, displayed even less when president. Despite Gen. Francisco Franco's authoritarianism and pro-Axis stand during the war, President Eisenhower signed a pact with the Spanish dictator in 1953 that guaranteed the continued existence of the Francoist regime. The pact gave Franco badly needed money and recognition in return for U.S. use of Spanish army and naval bases. The U.S. orchestrated the overthrow of Iranian republican leader Moḥammad Mosaddeq the same year. Mosaddeq was replaced by the despotic Shah Moḥammad Reza Pahlavi, who occupied the peacock throne until the Iranian revolution of 1979. In 1954, Eisenhower's government executed a plan that overthrew the democratically elected Guatemalan president, Jacobo Arbenz. Arbenz was replaced with an unpopular military leader. Two years later, Eisenhower helped install Ngo Dinh Diem as ruler of South Vietnam, despite overwhelming popular support for Communist leader Ho Chi Minh. These actions bred hatred for the U.S. among democratic peoples the world over. The hatred was so intense that visits abroad by U.S. Vice-President Richard Nixon and presidential envoy Nelson Rockefeller triggered riots.

## AFTER TORCH

The "Race for Tunisia" began in mid-November 1942, after Eisenhower secured Admiral Darlan's agreement to assist the Allied attack on the German- and Italian-occupied French colony. The race began without the assistance of PWS, as PWS had neither the printing presses nor broadcasting stations for making appeals to Axis troops. It was not until mid January, about a month after Admiral Darlan's assassination by a young French anti-Fascist, that PWS obtained time from Radio Algiers for broadcasting its own programs, and it was not until many weeks later that it secured complete control of the Algiers and Rabat broadcasting stations. Personnel from PWS, which by this time was called the Psychological Warfare Branch, Allied Force Headquarters (PWB/AFHQ), were assigned to censorship, given the tasks of checking the backgrounds of Vichy authorities and securing contracts with movie theaters for the showing of U.S.-produced feature films, and asked to design posters and information displays to woo the Arab population in North Africa. They were not asked to participate in the Tunisian campaign. Not until new faces like Heber Blankenhorn and C. D. Jackson entered PWB/AFHQ did it become a participant in the Tunisian campaign.[31]

Heber Blankenhorn was a military officer assigned to OSS by the War Department at the request of General Donovan. Donovan wanted Blankenhorn in his outfit because he headed the psychological warfare subsection of G–2 during World War I. Blankenhorn had also written *Adventures in Propaganda*, a book about psychwar strategy during WWI. He was the only uniformed veteran of World War I psychological warfare involved in the Second World War, and for that reason was habitually referred to as "the Pioneer." With this background, Donovan reasoned, Blankenhorn—and therefore OSS—was bound to be given a position of leadership in Colonel Hazeltine's newly formed psychwar unit. In February 1943, Blankenhorn was sent to North Africa by William Donovan, where he was made head of the PWB/AFHQ leaflet section by Hazeltine. When Blankenhorn joined the PWB/AFHQ leaflet section, it had no printing press, no secretary, no typewriter, no desks, no chairs, and no office to work in. Under the guidance of the Pioneer, the leaflet section acquired equipment and skilled personnel. By the second week of May 1943, when the Germans in North Africa finally surrendered, the leaflet section had produced 65 different leaflets, of which 33 were in Italian and 32 in German. Less than ten million leaflets were actually dropped during the Tunisian campaign, which was a small fraction of the number produced. The leaflets that were distributed achieved some successes, particularly among Italian soldiers, whom the leaflets promised safe conduct and a comfortable internment.[32]

Charles Douglas (C. D.) Jackson was a former general manager of *Life* magazine and vice-president of Time, Inc. His work at Time was administrative rather than editorial. During a leave-of-absence from Time, Inc. he founded and headed the Council for Democracy, a nonprofit organization that combated isolationist sentiment in the United States. In 1942 Jackson worked covertly for the Board of Economic Warfare and in 1943 was appointed head of the Office of War Information for North Africa by Robert Sherwood, replacing Oliver H. P. Garrett. After Jackson's arrival, Garrett became head of the PWB radio section. In the administrative structure of North Africa, C. D. Jackson's appointment made him PWB deputy director. He had supreme authority over OWI and military personnel involved in PWB, except in areas of actual combat. One of his assignments was to cultivate relations with military leaders, with whom other OWI representatives like Warburg and Winner had clashed over policy. C. D. Jackson was an ideal choice for this job, having worked as a public relations man and administrator at Time, Inc. He had media credentials, which OWI personnel liked, but no journalistic experience. This background made him less dedicated to press freedom and more sensitive to administrative concerns than were other members of OWI. Jackson functioned effectively in his role as PWB deputy director and soon became the branch's liaison with Allied generals and North African political agencies. Because he was a civilian with contacts in Washington, Jackson had more influence with the generals than did Colonel Hazeltine.[33]

Between the Torch campaign and the invasion of Sicily in July 1943, PWB grew in size and stature. Its growth and stature were not the direct result of psychwar accomplishments during the North African campaigns, but such factors as psychwar successes in other theaters, an infusion of trained personnel from the newly formed Morale Operations (MO) branch of OSS, and better organization, structure, and discipline.

A successful and widely reported psychwar radio campaign that reached the ears of U.S. military leaders in North Africa was conducted against German U-boat personnel in the Atlantic. The campaign was conducted by the Special Warfare Branch (Op–16-W) of the Office of Naval Intelligence (ONI) and OWI. The idea for the operation came from Lt. Col. Ralph Albrecht, an OSS officer assigned to ONI. Albrecht, like many other OSS officers, was a prominent attorney before and after the war, and veteran of the First World War. By the second war's end, he was OSS assistant director. Following the Allied victory, Albrecht served on the prosecution team at the International War Crimes tribunal in Nuremberg. He was originally sent to Great Britain in 1942 to learn prisoner interrogation techniques for ONI. During his stay in England, Albrecht was introduced to a British Admiralty psychwar radio campaign codenamed NID 17-Zed. Because Albrecht spoke flawless German, he was asked to make several 17-Zed broadcasts.[34]

The broadcasts were part of the Admiralty campaign to reduce the number of volunteers entering U-boat service. When 17-Zed was started, a recruitment campaign was being conducted in Germany for the newly expanded U-boat fleet. The German campaign glorified the life of U-boatmen. To discourage recruitment, the British navy launched 17-Zed, which through broadcasts, leaflets, and rumors, described the hazards of U-boat duty, including the spread of diseases among personnel confined to life beneath the surface, and the high casualty rates of those who volunteered for duty in the "steel coffins." When the German recruitment campaign got fewer volunteers than had been hoped for, the British Admiralty declared their psychwar campaign a success.

When Albrecht returned to the United States, he described the campaign to Capt. Ellis Zacharias, the assistant director of ONI. The psychwar campaign interested Zacharias, who suggested to his superiors that ONI conduct a similar campaign. He also contacted OWI chief Elmer Davis, who endorsed the plan. Davis promised that OWI would assist in production, in addition to broadcasting the ONI-produced program. The proposal by Zacharias was skeptically approved by naval authorities and a Special Warfare Branch (Op–16-W) of ONI created. Lt. Col. Cecil Coggins, a physician who was Zacharias' friend, was selected to head Op–16-W. Captain John Riheldaffer of ONI's interrogation unit joined the team, as did Ralph Albrecht. Albrecht was selected as the program's announcer. Coggins, Zacharias, Riheldaffer, and Albrecht, who knew little about psychological warfare, recruited two experts to their unit: Curt Riess and Ladislas Farago. Riess had written *Total Espionage*.[35] Farago was author of *German Psychological Warfare*.[36]

Using intelligence gathered by Riheldaffer's interrogation unit, Op–16–W wrote and recorded several programs directed at the German U-boat fleet. The first of these aired on December 7, 1942. After a few broadcasts, Farago concluded that the most effective speaker would be a U.S. Naval officer of unmistakable German extraction. Farago believed that this speaker would have great appeal to U-boatmen, so a fictitious "Commander Robert Lee Norden" was created. Albrecht supplied the voice for the fictitious commander. The first Norden broadcast appeared on January 8, 1943, following an overture from Wagner's *Flying Dutchman*. The overture became Norden's signature tune. The program aired from OWI shortwave transmitters in the United States. When OWI acquired additional transmitters, including several in North Africa, the Norden broadcasts were carried on these.

The "Commander Norden" broadcasts were aboveground and clearly labeled as originating from the United States. Although a U.S. naval officer, Norden spoke with an aura of omniscience about German U-boat activities. Using information obtained from German newpaper and radio, POW interrogations, and classified naval documents, he broadcast tales of deficiencies in German U-boat design; described how U-boat commanders exaggerated their successes; and reported the promotions and decorations awarded to members of the fleet. The broadcasts noted, for example, that the highest decoration, the "Knight's Insignia of the Iron Cross," was always awarded to commissioned officers, never seamen. The broadcasts were not designed to induce surrenders, as this was considered an impossible task. Even if German U-boatmen could be persuaded to surrender, which POW interrogations indicated was unlikely, their confinement inside U-boats physically precluded their doing so. Instead, the broadcasts were designed to lower morale. The broadcast concerning the "Knight's Insignia of the Iron Cross" suggested to seamen that the German Admiralty, not they, benefited from the war. These broadcasts led to a change in German naval policy. Shortly after the Norden broadcasts, the German Admiralty announced that several seamen were awarded the "Knight's Insignia."[37]

The Norden broadcasts, like the broadcasts of the British clandestine stations, the Atlantiksender and Gustav Siegfried Eins, also carried gossip in order to attract listeners. The broadcasts carried reports on the family life of naval chief Karl Doenitz, "the sweethearts of German naval officers in France, and Admiral von Friedeburg's refusal to permit one of his officers to marry."[38] Although there is no evidence that such broadcasts affected German U-boat morale, there is evidence of listenership to the broadcasts. German U-boatmen who were rescued in the Atlantic reported listening to Norden's broadcasts. One asked to meet Commander Norden and another suggested that Norden's broadcasting times be changed, as they coincided with the change of watch on U-boats. This deprived Norden of some of his loyal listeners. German radio also responded to a number of Norden's allegations, suggesting that at least the German Admiralty believed that the broadcasts were effective.

Norden broadcasts eventually aired seven times each day, three days a week from OWI transmitters in the United States, Britain, and North Africa. Over the next three years, 309 Norden broadcasts were recorded and broadcast by OWI. In addition, Op–16–W prepared a program for OWI entitled "Prisoner of War Mail." It consisted of greetings and news sent to relatives and friends from German and Italian POWs. The program was designed to increase listenership to OWI broadcasts in Axis countries, and counteract German propaganda that described life in Allied POW camps in hair-raising terms.

On January 3, 1943, one month after the first ONI-produced radio program aired from OWI transmitters, William Donovan issued General Order No. 9. The order created the Morale Operations (MO) branch of OSS. MO was assigned the task of conducting "subversion other than physical," as "ordered" by Joint-Chiefs-of-Staff Directive 155/4/D. The J.C.S. directive authorized OSS to conduct "special operations not assigned to any other Government agencies or under the direct control of Theater or Area commanders." It did not specify what these operations were, but Donovan assumed them to include the dissemination of "secret ('black') propaganda . . . by radio, by word of mouth, as in rumors, from hand to hand, as by pamphlets, leaflets, photographs, etc."

Wild Bill Donovan appointed Frederick C. Oechsner head of his newly created MO branch. Oechsner, a journalist in Europe before the war who wrote *This Is the Enemy*, joined OSS in November 1942.[39] He became Donovan's Special Assistant. After appointment as MO chief, Oeschner established his headquarters in a windowless basement room of the administration building, with makeshift equipment and no secretary. Charles P. Healy, an attorney who was Donovan's colleague, was made assistant chief of MO.

Oechsner and Healy were assigned several men so that MO would have a few braves in addition to its chiefs. The braves included Heber Blankenhorn, John Whitaker, John Weaver, and Robert Knapp. Blankenhorn left for North Africa to head PWB's leaflet section immediately after being assigned to MO by Donovan. Whitaker, a veteran foreign-affairs reporter for the New York *Herald Tribune* and Chicago *Daily News*, was appointed MO chief for North African operations. Weaver was made Whitaker's assistant. Knapp was the former director of the propaganda and research division of the State of Massachusetts who was recruited to OSS by James Grafton Rogers, a conservative Yale law professor who was friends with Secretary of War Henry Stimson.

Whitaker was sent to North Africa a month after Blankenhorn with an order to establish a clandestine radio station directed at German troops in Tunisia. Weaver was sent to Algiers four weeks later to find out what had happened to Whitaker, with whom MO lost contact, and to give him assistance. Neither Whitaker nor Weaver succeeded in establishing the proposed radio station, as they were assigned to PWB/AFHQ immediately upon arrival. An order of February 7, 1943, issued by General Eisenhower, placed "within the area controlled by the Commander in Chief, Allied Force, all personnel and activities in the field of Psychological Warfare, including those of OWI, OSS, and PWE and FCC and MOI . . . under the control, coordination, and direction of the Psychological Warfare Branch, INC." Eisenhower's order made Colonel Hazeltine the commander of all OSS-MO personnel in North Africa. Accordingly, Hazeltine appointed Whitaker head of the PWB intelligence unit, replacing Edmond Taylor. Taylor left North Africa for London, and then the United States. In September, he went to Asia on another OSS assignment. Weaver was assigned to the Communications Branch and later made a PWB liaison officer. Neither Whitaker nor Weaver were allowed to operate independently, and were even prohibited from contacting OSS headquarters in Washington. For several months, MO-Washington lost contact with both men.[40]

The departure of Blankenhorn, Whitaker, and Weaver left MO-Washington virtually unmanned, except for Oechsner, Healy, Knapp, and a few secretaries. MO had few personnel, no field agents, no transmitters, and no clear directive. Donovan's directive to MO to disseminate "secret propaganda" was rescinded by Executive Order 9312 on March 9, 1943. The president's order modified JCS Directive 155/4/D so that it did not conflict with OWI's directive. It reaffirmed OWI's authority to conduct propaganda abroad. As Oechsner viewed it, the executive order left MO with the following functions:

contacts with underground movements . . . bribery and subsidies, blackmail, counterfeiting of currency, ration cards, passports, personal papers of enemy prisoners or dead, rumor, abduction, chain letters, poisoning (distribution of and instructions on how to use toy gadgets and tricks), assassination by suggestion or agents, illness and epidemics by suggestion or agents, and diverse manipulations such as black market in neutral countries, etc.[41]

Conspicuously absent from Oechsner's accounting was any mention of newspapers, leaflets, or radio.

Having no agents to carry out abductions or assassinations, and no printing presses or personnel to counterfeit currency, passports, or ration cards, MO was left to rumor development. In Washington, new MO recruits were given intelligence reports and, based on these, asked to fabricate rumors. Because MO lacked the staff or equipment to circulate rumors, the "sibs" that were developed were forwarded to PWB in North

Africa or the PWE in London, which were asked to circulate them. PWB had little use for the rumors until mid-1943, when the invasion of Sicily was launched, and PWE had its own rumor factory. Consequently, very few of the rumors that were dreamt up in Washington were ever circulated.[42]

Oechsner's belief that MO was prohibited from producing and distributing mass media messages was not shared by William Donovan. The executive order, Donovan believed, reiterated OWI's responsibility for propaganda but did not assign the propaganda agency responsibility for psychological warfare. If OWI were not given responsibility for psychological warfare, it remained the responsibility of OSS, which, according to JCS Directive 155/4/D, was charged with conducting "special operations not assigned to any other Government agencies." Psychological warfare included the production and distribution of clandestine messages—by radio, newspapers and leaflet, as well as word-of-mouth. Although this was Donovan's interpretation, he did not wholeheartedly explain the distinction to Elmer Davis when they met a few days after Executive Order 9312 was issued, as MO lacked the staff and equipment to distribute clandestine messages, even if Davis conceded Donovan's point.

In April, Patrick Dolan, a young advertising man, was recruited by Oechsner. Dolan was made director of personnel recruitment and head of MO for the European Theater (ETO). As head of personnel, Dolan developed a profile of individuals whom he wished OSS to recruit. The recruits were to be mirror images of Dolan:

All prospects should be practical, hard-headed fellows, able to get along with other people in all classes of society. . . . The preferred background is "advertising men". . . . We would prefer men who have been advertising directors—it is most important that any man be able to write creatively. Foreign experience is not absolutely necessary. . . . The more successful they have been in their business life and the more money they have made, the better the prospects they are for us.[43]

Dolan's profile was followed when hiring personnel. Rae Smith, a J. Walter Thompson advertising executive, was recruited to head MO's London office. George Dibert, a media director at J. Walter Thompson, was appointed Deputy Chief of MO-ETO. Ira Ashley was also recruited. Before the war, he worked as a program director for the same advertising agency.

The profile developed by Dolan assured that recruits were conservative and approached psychological warfare as though they were selling toothpaste. MO sought to build the largest audience possible for its "subversive" messages, just as advertisers in the United States did; never attacked the established values of the enemy, for fear of alienating the audience; and rarely developed ideological messages. In practice this meant that personal attacks on Hitler were shunned; rumors that were developed frequently centered on sexual misdeeds of German leaders, rather than their political and war crimes; and revolutions against the existing order were discouraged. The "subversive" radio projects that OSS-MO eventually executed, like "Pancake" and "Radio 1212," sounded very much like commercial radio stations, and were subversive only because they were declared by German authorities to be enemy-sponsored.[44]

OSS-MO's advertising-based approach to subversive warfare can be contrasted with that used by SO1 under Hugh Dalton's leadership. One of SO1's first clandestine stations was the "Radio of the European Revolution" (Sender der Europäischen Revolution). The station's scripts were written by members of the Marxist Neubeginn group. In mid–1942 the Neubeginn radio was replaced with another socialist station called the "German Workers' Station" that promised:

After Hitler, we shall come. After Hitlers' downfall will come the socialist Germany, which will bring peace to everybody.... For the building of a workers' Germany, we need all the infantrymen from the front. We must therefore save them from the death ordered by Hitler.... Hitler has already lost this war, but Hitler wants to win some time and is willing to see millions of other soldiers shot, frozen to death and crippled.... Infantrymen: do not die for Hitler. Fight with us revolutionaries against Hitler, against the enemy in the rear.[45]

SO1 and its successor, PWE operated revolutionary stations that broadcast to other nations, including France, Italy, and Austria. In many instances, as with "Giustizia e Libertà," the stations were operated with the assistance of anti-Fascist refugees.

On May 15, 1943 Fred Oechsner went to London to set up a field office. From London, he went to North Africa, taking with him several MO recruits. Oechsner did not return to Washington until December. He left a poorly organized and leaderless staff of twelve behind in the capital. Charles Healy, the Deputy Chief, became acting head of MO in Oechsner's absence. Healy had neither the background nor temperament to run MO and, as a result of "Washington heat and nervous strain," resigned in July 1943. By the time Healy resigned, MO had grown to 36 people, including ten secretaries. The recruits included Major Herbert Little, who was named head of MO for Asia. Patrick Dolan, who was with the branch for less than four months, was appointed acting chief after Healy's departure.[46]

MO grew slowly until October 1943, after which it rapidly expanded. The expansion was due to the issuance of JCS Directive 155/11/D, which assigned OSS responsibility for "the execution of all forms of morale subversion by diverse means including: False rumors, 'freedom stations,' false leaflets and false documents, the organization and support of fifth column activities by grants, trained personnel and supplies and use of agents."[47] The JCS directive affirmed what Donovan had previously argued: Propaganda and psychological warfare differed, and OWI had responsibility for propaganda, whereas OSS had responsibility for psychwar. When the Joint Chiefs issued the directive, OWI did little to oppose it because OWI had no interest in conducting "subversive" warfare and was severely weakened by internal and external clashes.

OWI was always plagued with internal disgreements and conflicts, over which Elmer Davis was able to exercise some control. The conflicts erupted into warfare when a reorganization of the Overseas Branch in September merged the seven regional divisions into three, giving the Overseas Editorial Board in New York additional powers at the expense of OWI head Elmer Davis. In November, James Warburg and Joseph Barnes of the Overseas Editorial Board, backed by Robert Sherwood and Edd Johnson, submitted proposals that, in effect, stripped Davis of authority over foreign propaganda. This infuriated the OWI chief and led to another widely publicized dispute involving OWI, a Davis-Sherwood showdown that Davis won, and the firing of Warburg, Barnes, and Johnson.[48]

The external conflict involved OWI, the State Department, FDR, the media, and conservative congressmen. The late–1943 conflict arose from a series of five English-language broadcasts made after Benito Mussolini's dismissal as Italian premier, following the successful Allied invasion of Sicily. The broadcasts referred to the Italian monarch as a "moronic little king" and to Mussolini's successor, Marshal Pietro Badoglio, as "a high-ranking Fascist." To OWI leaders, the broadcasts appeared consistent with Allied policy, even though not approved by FDR or State Department authorities. Unknown to OWI, administration leaders decided that they were willing to negotiate with King Victor Emmanuel and Marshal Badoglio, despite their two decades of collaboration with Mussolini.[49]

Conservative journalists, who had always disapproved of OWI, used the broadcasts as a club against the propaganda agency, which was accused of trying to make U.S. foreign policy. The furor resulted in FDR's publicly rebuking the agency for not following directives. Anti-OWI Republican congressmen used this controversy as an opportunity to resurrect their charge that OWI was issuing domestic "New Deal" propaganda. Their charges were aired during congressional hearings that examined the uses of paper by government agencies. These clashes drained OWI of its strength to confront the Joint Chiefs or OSS concerning jurisdiction over clandestine propaganda.[50]

By November 1943, OSS-MO had 75 personnel, most of whom were recruited by other MO members. The number increased to 150 by January 1944. Dolan, upon urging from Donovan, sent several of the recruits to

London for training by the PWE. When the trainees returned, they were ordered to set up similar training programs for MO in the United States. The most important training center developed by MO was code-named Marigold. It was established in New York City in February 1944. Marigold was a training center for Japanese-Americans, who were recruited by OSS to conduct subversive warfare in Asia. A similar center was established in Washington a short time later. In April, a MO workshop was established in the capital that trained recruits and printed black propaganda. The branch also purchased several transmitters from General Electric for making psychwar broadcasts. Although it grew rapidly and acquired equipment during the first months of 1944, MO did not become fully operational—producing forged stamps, ration cards and newspapers, and operating clandestine stations—until May 1944, when Colonel K. D. Mann became its head.[51]

## HUSKY VOICES

Fred Oechsner left Washington on May 15, 1943, two days after the last enemy troops in Tunisia surrendered. With Tunisia occupied, Allied troops were in position to land on Italian soil by crossing the narrow Strait of Sicily. Plans for this landing, code-named Operation Husky, were drafted and redrafted between February and July, when the invasion of Sicily was scheduled to begin. Changes, particularly in the psychological warfare portions of the plan, were necessary because of shifting estimates of potential Italian resistance and differing attitudes toward, and interpretations of, the policy of unconditional surrender adopted by FDR and Churchill at the Casablanca conference in January 1943.

Operation Husky relied heavily on psychological warfare tactics because evidence obtained during the Tunisian campaign demonstrated psychwar's effectiveness against Italian, as well as German, troops. POW interrogations revealed that Italian soldiers, much more often than German soldiers, read and kept Allied surrender leaflets that they found; that they were greatly influenced by U.S. slogans such as "many of your fathers, brothers and uncles are in America"; and that they would buy safe-conduct passes from native Arabs in the belief that the passes were needed to safely surrender. The phrase "Germany will fight to the last Italian," plagiarized from Nazi broadcaster Paul Ferdonnet, was effective in undermining Italian troop morale, as Italian distrust of Germany was even greater than French distrust of Britain.[52]

Intelligence also showed that while Italian soldiers were susceptible to such slogans, they were likely to offer greater resistance in defense of their homeland than in North Africa. Husky planners therefore wanted to emphasize that it was in the interest of the Italian people "and not incompatible with their honor to refrain from resisting a United Nations invasion." The usefulness of such slogans, and their meaning in the context of unconditional surrender, were debated throughout the first half of 1943 by psychological warfare strategists and their political superiors.[53]

General Eisenhower wanted Husky propaganda to suggest an Allied willingness to negotiate peace rather than demand unconditional surrender. He felt that the policy of unconditional surrender would force Italian soldiers to rally to, rather than abandon, the defense of the nation. General Eisenhower wanted propaganda to state that "peace with honor" was possible, provided Italy capitulated á la Darlan. Eisenhower favored a "soft" rather than "hard" propaganda line. The "soft" approach emphasized the mutual interests and friendship of the U.S. and Italian peoples—and the possibility of a peace with easy terms, whereas "hard" propaganda emphasized the destructive consequences of Italian resistance. The soft propaganda approach preferred by Eisenhower, however, suggested that the Allied nations were willing to negotiate with Fascist leaders, something that the unconditional surrender policy expressly denied. For this reason, explicit references to "negotiated peace" were eventually excluded in favor of announcements stating the Allies were not landing "as enemies of the Italian people, but as an inevitable part of the war to destroy German overlordship of Europe." Eisenhower's proclamation of D day stated that the Allied "aim is to deliver the people of Italy from the Fascist regime which led them into war, and when this has been accomplished, to restore Italy as a free nation."[54]

Allied strategists, after considerable debate, decided to emphasize a "hard" line prior to the invasion. The hard line emphasized the Allies' uncompromising intention of emerging victorious. Propaganda during the preinvasion period would seek to undermine morale by emphasizing Allied industrial and military superiority. When the invasion began, the Allied propaganda line would change to the "soft" line, hoping that the change would encourage Italian leaders to surrender "with dignity." The soft propaganda described the invading United Nations forces as liberators rather than occupiers.

Fearing that the hard line would harden Italian resistance during the critical first hours of the invasion, General Eisenhower dreamed up a second psychwar tactic that he hoped would weaken Italian resistance: He suggested making the clandestine broadcast on Radio Rome's frequency that claimed Italy asked for and received an armistice. This clandestine broadcast was referred to by the code-name "Helga." If Italian commanders believed the broadcast, even for a very short time, it could give the invaders a much-needed psychological edge. Sefton Delmer, the head of British black propaganda directed at Axis countries, enthusiastically endorsed the tactic. He went beyond Eisenhower's initial proposal by suggesting that news of the armistice "be put out not only by Helga [but] on as many different transmissions as we can counterfeit."[55] Delmer suggested using the 600-kilowatt Aspidistra transmitter for overlaying counterfeit transmissions on Axis frequencies.

At the end of June, the Combined Chiefs of Staff considered and endorsed Eisenhower's Helga proposal. The Combined Chiefs recommended that the plan be implemented by shortwave only, as the Aspidistra transmitter was "reserved for the broadcast of a joint declaration by the Prime Minister and President after the beginning of 'Husky.' " The one possible drawback to Helga, which the Combined Chiefs thought unlikely, was the bogus armistice might be monitored by the Allied press, thereby reaching British and U.S. ears. If this were to occur, it could have a boomerang effect, falsely raising and then dashing Allied, rather than Italian, hopes. The possibility of this occurring was remote, the Combined Chiefs believed, because the "press would ask for confirmation [from] the Foreign Office or State Department" before publicizing the rumor. The Allied leaders would deny the rumor, thereby keeping it out of the press.[56]

After endorsement by the Combined Chiefs, the proposal was forwarded to and discussed at a Staff Conference of July 2 attended by Churchill, British Foreign Secretary Anthony Eden, and Minister of Information Brendan Bracken. Bracken was not enthusiastic about the proposal, but his opposition to it was neither well-thought-out nor clearly articulated. He believed that the plan could discredit other British and U.S. broadcasts if news of the ruse became widespread. Bracken's opposition was so perfunctory that the Helga plan was initially approved by the ministers. After thinking about the ruse for several days, Churchill's lukewarm support turned to opposition. His opposition was based on the belief that the possible negative effects of Helga far outweighed the potential benefits. On the negative side, the bogus announcement could undermine the credibility of future British and U.S. broadcasts, and undermine Italian beliefs that the Allies were "honorable" people. On the positive side, it could "soften" opposition to Husky, but this, even if it were to occur, would only represent a short-term Allied benefit. The long-term consequences were all negative. Churchill cabled his reversal to Eisenhower on July 7, three days before Husky was launched. Churchill's opposition killed the plan.[57]

Although the counterfeit armistice broadcast was not made, other clandestine broadcasts were. These broadcasts were made from a one-kilowatt transmitter located at Cape Bon in Tunis. The black transmissions were the brainchild of Oliver H. P. Garrett, the former Hollywood scriptwriter who became head of PWB's radio section after OWI deputy C. D. Jackson arrived in North America. Garrett's film credits included *Moby Dick* (1930), *City Streets* (1931), *A Farewell to Arms* (1932), *If I Had a Million* (1932), *The Hurricane* (1937), and *The Man I Married* (1940).

He was a political activist before the war, known for authoring the anti-Nazi play, *Waltz in Goosestep*. He renounced Hollywood for its failure to combat Fascism, and joined OWI in 1942. Garrett was head of OWI English-language broadcasts in New York before going to North Africa.[58]

Garrett's Hollywood manners did little to promote harmony within PWB, for he became even better known for his table-pounding and shouting than his colossal ignorance of Germans and Italians. Heber Blankenhorn, head of PWB's leaflet section, concluded that Garrett's philosophy was that he "could only control talented people by 'breaking them first.' " Garrett's praxis consisted of picking quarrels with colleagues, and if they did not submit, requesting that Colonel Hazeltine "enforce discipline." His attitude toward propaganda was the same as his attitude toward colleagues—arrogant. In Garrett's view, there was no need for intelligence, prisoner interrogations, or monitoring services, just stenographers who could record Oliver H. P. Garrett's dictation, and language specialists who could translate the dictation into Italian or German. Garrett believed that German and Italian soldiers would respond to his words in the same way as U.S. theatergoers—with applause.[59]

The idea for the clandestine station did not originate from intelligence, but from a Hollywood film called *Underground* that Garrett had co-written. *Underground* was a fictitious story about anti-Nazis who operated the "German Freedom Station" (or "Freiheitssender"). Rather than being located in Spain or France, as the true Freiheitssender was, this illegal broadcasting station was located within Germany. It was operated by handsome, daring members of the underground, who moved the transmitter from place to place to avoid arrest. The head of the underground was a young chemist, whose brother was a resolute Nazi. During the last reel, the Nazi brother realizes the true brutality of Hitler and his villainous gang, and joins the underground. A published review of the film accurately observed that "it would be nice to believe that there are such things going on in Germany as *Underground* depicts . . . recent reports from Berlin, however, indicate the contrary. *Underground* is just as fictitious as anything that Hollywood has ever cooked up."[60]

"Radio Italo Balbo," as Garrett's clandestine station was called, claimed to be operated by followers of deceased Italian hero Italo Balbo. As with other U.S.-operated clandestine stations that followed Radio Italo Balbo, the organization purportedly operating it was fictitious. There was no gathering of Balbo followers in Sicily or Italy, although the namesake of the station was real. Italo Balbo was a World War I officer and prominent Fascist who helped bring Mussolini to power in 1922. He was given several cabinet positions in the Fascist government, including minister of aviation. In this post, which he held between 1929 and 1933, Balbo developed Italy's air transportation system. He gained a popular following in Italy after making several highly publicized flights, including ones from Rome to Rio de Janeiro, and from Rome to Chicago. It was said that his differences with Il Duce led to his appointment as Governor-General of Libya, where he was "banished" until his death in a plane crash in 1940. Rumors claimed that the plane crash was engineered by Mussolini, who wanted to rid himself of this popular opponent.[61]

Plans for Radio Italo Balbo were submitted in May to the PWB planning board, which MO chief Fred Oechsner joined upon his arrival in North America. The planning board approved the Balbo operation, and assigned it eight personnel and a one-kilowatt mobile transmitter. The eight-man staff consisted of one British naval and two U.S. army officers, one U.S. enlisted man, and four civilians. The British naval officer was George Martelli, who worked for PWE's Italian section between 1940 and 1942. He was the only one of the eight with prior experience with clandestine radio stations.[62] The station's principal announcer was Joseph Savalli, an unprincipled, renegade Fascist. Fred Oechsner was one of the four civilians that worked on the station. He joined the staff to get some experience with black operations, over which MO claimed responsibility.[63]

Radio Italo Balbo operated for four weeks. It started two weeks before the Sicilian invasion was launched, and signed off on July 25. Its objective was to spread rumors and news that undermined "Axis military capacity by driving wedges between Fascist groups, between Fascists and Italians, and between Fascists and Nazis." The station first appeared on Radio Rome's frequency, interrupting a newscast with coded messages. It subsequently appeared on other frequencies between 710 and 725 kilohertz, where it was constantly chased by jammers. The station's principal output consisted of speeches and dialogues that were rumor-filled, and calls for resistance against the Fascists, not the Allies. The rumors were fabricated by MO-Washington and cabled to the station.[64]

The existence of Radio Balbo was a closely kept secret, even within PWB. Only members its staff, the PWB planning board, military leaders in North Africa, and civilian leaders in London and Washington were informed of its existence. Rumors spread by the station were heard by intelligence officers when they arrived in Sicily. Their intelligence reports led Garrett to boast: "I like to think that we had almost more to do with the downfall of Mussolini than any other political influence and we have some collaboration from within Italy itself, but I don't dare believe that we're as good as we hear we are."[65]

Broadcasts of Radio Italo Balbo were not the only ones directed at Sicily or Italy during Operation Husky. After Allied troops secured Palermo, a one-kilowatt black station was established there. As with Italo Balbo, a large part of its output consisted of rumors.[66] OWI, BBC, and PWE broadcasting stations were also busy before and during the operation. The output and power of these stations dwarfed those of the two U.S.-operated clandestine stations.

For several weeks before the Allied landing in Sicily, OWI and BBC transmitters battered Italy with "hard" propaganda, warning that resistance to the overpowering Allied war machine would lead to the destruction of the country. When Pantelleria Island in the Strait of Sicily was occupied by the Allies in June, OWI carried a statement of FDR demanding that Italy oust Mussolini and the Fascist party. The president added some "soft" touches to his declaration by stating that Mussolini's "irresponsible" acts were "not committed by the Italian people." He promised that after the Fascist defeat, Italy would be free "to choose a non-Fascist, non-Nazi form of government." Such aboveground broadcasts were supplemented with British-sponsored clandestine stations originating in Egypt and England. "Radio Matteotti" was started by SOE a month before the invasion of Sicily began. It claimed to be operated by Italian army deserters in Greece, who addressed surrender appeals to their "comrades" and "brothers" in uniform. The station's transmitter was actually in Cairo. The PWE-sponsored clandestine station "Giustizia e Libertà" signed on a week before Husky was launched. The station, operated by members of the well-known anti-Fascist organization "Justice and Liberty," broadcast calls for slowdowns, sabotage, and resistance against German troops.[67]

These and other British clandestine stations were also overwhelmed by the Allied aboveground psychwar campaign. By mid-May 1943, two months before Allied troops landed in Sicily, twelve of OWI's fifteen U.S.-based shortwave transmitters were carrying Italian-language programs. Seven of the stations carried three or more hours in Italian daily, for a total of 32 Italian-language programs each day. The broadcasts included appeals by New York City mayor Fiorello LaGuardia, who was well-known and popular in Italy. One OWI program was instantaneously rebroadcast each day from London over eight transmitters. Four of the transmitters were shortwave, three mediumwave, and one longwave.[68]

The psychwar assault on Italy was also carried by transmitters in North Africa. With the exception of one transmitter that was shipped to North Africa from the United States, the transmitters used for the radio campaign were formerly Axis-controlled. The stations were taken over after Morocco, Algeria, and Tunisia were occupied. The purpose of the North African broadcasts was not only to undermine Italian morale, as were the U.S.- and London-originated transmissions but to deceive Italy as to the time and location of the impending Allied attack. This psychwar campaign began even before the victory in Tunisia was achieved.[69]

The broadcast assault on Italy from North Africa began using time borrowed on Radio France's shortwave Eucalyptus transmitter. PWB took control of the mediumwave Radio Algiers after Darlan's assassination, making it the first station in the United Nations network. Italian-language programming appeared on this station during the last months of the Tunisian campaign. The programs consisted of news, talk, and entertainment programs, which were directed at Italian troops fighting in North Africa. These Radio Algiers broadcasts were also carried on shortwave by the Eucalyptus transmitter.

The amount of Italian-language programming broadcast by the Allies increased rather than decreased following the Tunisian victory. In Tunis, PWB took possession of one shortwave and one mediumwave station. The mediumwave transmitter had a maximum power of 120 kilowatts, making it one of the most powerful in the Mediterranean. On June 14, 1943, a 50-kilowatt mediumwave transmitter shipped from the United States went on the air. It was called "United Nations Radio." The station functioned as the official voice of Eisenhower's Allied Force Headquarters. At 6 a.m. on July 10, the United Nations transmitter went on the air in a special broadcast in four languages. It announced that Allied forces under the command of General Eisenhower had landed on the southern coasts of Sicily. As planned, the Aspidistra transmitter broadcast the joint statement of Churchill and FDR, which began: "Italian People! At this fateful moment in your history we, the President of the United States and the British Prime Minister, bid you think and act. Your future and the future of Italy is at stake."[70] Concurrent with this, leaflets were dropped on Sicily that asked support for the "Armies which are landing as liberators."

The leaflet drop was not the first. Over 4,000,000 Italian-language leaflets were printed in North Africa by May 20, 1943. These leaflets were supplemented with those produced in London, which were dropped by Royal Air Force (RAF) flights over Italy and Italian-occupied territories in France. Between May 20 and June 15, another 5,580,000 leaflets were produced in North Africa. These were dropped over Italian and Sicilian towns. During the nights of June 13–16, over one million leaflets were dropped over southern Sardinia and another 1,500,000 dropped on Naples. Five different types of leaflets were dropped. The leaflets described the massive "air power of the Allies, warn[ed] Italian civilians and soldiers to keep away from the ports and other military targets, reproduce[d] the speeches of Allied leaders regarding Italy and detail[ed] the results of the Tunisian campaign."[71]

The seven Allied divisions that landed in Sicily pushed across the island. Planes simultaneously bombed cities on the Italian mainland. This campaign, unlike the one in North Africa, went according to plan. The Allied successes and Italian defeats caused King Victor Emmanuel to dismiss Mussolini as premier on July 25. Mussolini was also arrested. He was interned on Sardinia, and later at a mountaintop hotel from which he was dramatically rescued by a German glider force. Marshal Pietro Badoglio was appointed to the premiership. Badoglio's appointment was announced by Radio Rome. The broadcast caused a celebration in the Italian capital.

The announcement caught Allied leaders by surprise. Although they assumed that Italian defeats would lead to Mussolini's removal, the speed with which it occurred was not foreseen. OWI leaders believed that FDR's policy of not negotiating with Fascists included not negotiating with King Victor Emmanuel or Marshal Badoglio. While not Fascist party members, King Victor Emmanuel and Marshal Badoglio had been closely allied with Mussolini. The king appointed Mussolini premier, while Badoglio was a member of Il Duce's general staff until 1940. Based on this assumption, OWI broadcast its description of the new government as "fascist" and King Victor Emmanuel as "a moronic little king." As previously mentioned, the broadcast had more negative consequences for OWI than for the new Italian leaders.

The PWE responded to Mussolini's dismissal in a typically clandestine fashion. With the British Admiralty's Naval Intelligence Division (NID), which sponsored the 17-Zed broadcasts, the PWE inaugurated broadcasts targeted at the Italian navy. The broadcasts originated from a station called "Radio Livorno," which claimed to be operated by an Italian naval officer and wireless operator. The two claimed to be members of a secret, patriotic association within the Italian navy. The broadcasts of the station identified Germany as the real enemy and warned that Germans should not be permitted to board Italian vessels. Germany planned to seize the Italian fleet, the station warned.[72]

The first Allied military response to Mussolini's dismissal was a halt to the bombing of the Italian mainland. Eisenhower sought Combined Chiefs of Staff approval for broadcasting armistice terms to the new government over all North African broadcasting frequencies. General Eisenhower believed that the broadcasts would put pressure on the government to seek an immediate peace. The general's proposed broadcast message commended Italy for ousting Mussolini, assured the nation that an honorable peace was possible, and promised that Italy would have a voice in final peace agreements after Germany was defeated. The broadcasts, while suggesting the possibility of an honorable peace, threatened that the terms might change if a quick response from the Italian government were not forthcoming. Eisenhower also wanted to broadcast his terms for a peace, which included the immediate cessation of hostilities, the return of all Allied prisoners-of-war, Italian withdrawal from occupied territories, the expulsion of German troops from Italy, and the opening of Italian airfields and ports to Allied forces. Eisenhower's proposed broadcasts would not mention unconditional surrender.[73]

President Roosevelt opposed broadcasting specific terms for an armistice because the Allied powers had not reached agreement on them. While not knowing the specific terms he wished to impose, FDR wanted the terms to be "as close to unconditional surrender as possible." This included having Italy surrender Mussolini to the Allies. Churchill, too, wanted Mussolini and other Fascist leaders surrendered as war criminals. Unlike Eisenhower, Churchill wanted the armistice terms to include an Italian declaration of war on Germany. Eisenhower opposed Churchill's proposal because it would require Italy to dishonor previous promises, suggesting a dishonorable rather than honorable peace, and because a declaration of war would be militarily meaningless. The declaration might be used for propaganda purposes but would otherwise be without significance because Italian troops would be unable to effectively engage Germany. If Italian troops were not effective in defending their homeland, they could not be counted on to fight their former ally, Eisenhower believed.

After an exchange of cables, a compromise statement was written for broadcast over the United Nations Radio. The statement began with Eisenhower's commendation to Italy for removing Mussolini, but contained no surrender terms. The statement, broadcast to Italy beginning July 29, went:

We commend the Italian people and the House of Savoy on ridding themselves of Mussolini, the man who involved them in war as a tool of Hitler, and brought them to the verge of disaster. The greatest obstacle which divided the Italian people from the United Nations has been removed by the Italians themselves. The only remaining obstacle on the road to peace is the German aggressor who is still on Italian soil. You want peace. You can have peace immediately ... cease immediately any assistance to the German military forces in your country.[74]

The broadcasts were correct in stating that the German troops in Italy were the greatest obstacle to peace. It was not, however, the mere presence of the troops that constituted an impediment to peace, but the threat they posed to the new Italian government. Hitler and his associates correctly surmised that Mussolini's dismissal was a prelude to an Italian surrender. To prevent the surrender, German troops were ominously moved to the Italian frontier. Hitler's representatives in Rome pressured Badoglio to allow the troops to enter, ostensibly to reinforce German troops already there. The large German troop concentration, the Germans insisted, was needed to repel an Allied invasion of the mainland. The real purpose of the German troop concentration was to be in position to occupy Italy, should Badoglio's government capitulate to the Allies. Under pressure, Badoglio acceded to the German demand, even though he was aware of Hitler's darker motives. Badoglio feared that if he did not accede, it would send a message to Germany that Italy was contemplating a withdrawal from the war. If Germany got this message, it would ruthlessly occupy the country.

Because of the pressure that Germany was exerting on him, Badoglio did not respond to Eisenhower's broadcasts. On July 31, Eisenhower broadcast a message accusing the Italian government of stalling instead of suing for peace. He warned that Allied bombing of Italian cities would resume, if Badoglio's silence continued. A broadcast on August 2 again warned Italians about the consequences of the stalling. Having received no response from the Italian government, Eisenhower ordered the resumption of bombing. Allied bombers attacked Naples five times over the next few days.

Eisenhower's broadcasts and the resumption of bombing triggered riots in Florence, Rome, and Naples. Turin and Milan were the scenes of near-revolutions. Workers and soldiers poured into the streets in these cities, demanding that Marshal Badoglio either resign or make peace. An illegal radio station broadcasting from somewhere in the Leghorn announced that five previously banned left-wing parties supported a general strike by workers to force the government to make peace. The station called Badoglio a traitor.[75]

On August 3, a papal representative, acting on behalf of the Italian government, asked for a statement about Allied conditions for declaring Rome an open city. This initial contact led to the opening of secret negotiations between Italian and Allied representatives. The negotiations led to the signing of an unpublicized armistice on September 3. It was signed by General Giuseppe Castellano on behalf of Marshal Badoglio and General Walter Bedell Smith on behalf of General Eisenhower. The Italian government wanted the armistice to remain secret to forestall a German occupation of Rome, while the Allies wanted to keep the armistice secret until just before they landed at Salerno. General Eisenhower was to inform Italy of the disclosure date by secret radio code, and by confirming the secret radio message through a BBC broadcast of a half-hour of Vivaldi music followed by a discourse about Nazi activities in Argentina. According to their agreement, Eisenhower would broadcast an announcement of the armistice from Radio Algiers at 6:30 p.m. that night, after which Badoglio would make a similar, agreed-upon announcement from Radio Rome.

Between Mussolini's ouster and when the armistice was signed, Hitler sent about sixteen divisions into Italy, bringing his strength there to nineteen divisions. Not only were there more German than Italian troops in Italy, but German troops had far greater firepower and mobility. The Italian Motorized Corps barely had enough gasoline to start its engines. Realizing that Germany had strengthened itself to the point that it could overwhelm the Italian army at any time, Badoglio renounced the armistice. He feared that Eisenhower's announcement of the armistice would inspire an immediate German attack on Rome. Badoglio's renunciation reached the AFHQ base at the very moment that Eisenhower planned on making the armistice public. Eisenhower scheduled the armistice announcement for 6:30 p.m. on September 8, the evening preceding the Salerno landing.

Eisenhower cabled Badoglio immediately upon hearing of the renunciation. The cable informed the Marshal that the announcement would be broadcast despite his change of heart. The agreement was reached in good faith by the Allies, and plans were made believing the agreement to be in effect. It was too late to change the plans, Eisenhower retorted. He promised to make the announcement as scheduled, and to inform the world of Badoglio's bad faith. Eisenhower's announcements, Badoglio realized, would inform Germany that it had been double-crossed by Italy, probably lead to renewed anti-government rioting, and precipitate new attacks on Italy by the Allied powers. Upon receipt of the cable, Badoglio called a meeting that included the king and other Italian leaders.

At 6:30 p.m., while the Italian leaders were meeting, Radio Algiers interrupted its normal programming for a special announcement from the Allied commander-in-chief. The announcement stated:

The Italian government has surrendered its armed forces unconditionally. As Allied Commander-in-Chief, I have granted a military armistice. . . . The Italian government has bound itself by these terms without reservation. The armistice was signed by my representative and the representative of Marshal Badoglio and it becomes effective this instant. Hostilities between the armed forces of the United Nations and those of Italy terminate at once.[76]

Radio Algiers followed the announcement with a report explaining how the armistice was negotiated. Despite this announcement, Badoglio did not broadcast news of the armistice over Radio Rome, as he had agreed to do under terms of the Allied-Italian agreement. Instead, he and other Italian leaders quickly discussed their options.

After waiting ten minutes, Radio Algiers broadcast in English Badoglio's agreed-upon proclamation. News of the Radio Algiers broadcasts soon reached Badoglio and his counselors. Their choice was simple: to claim that Eisenhower's broadcast was a lie that attempted to divide the Axis alliance, or to admit that the announcement was true. If the government remained silent, Italy would have two enemies: Germany and the United Nations. Their best option, the leaders decided, was to broadcast affirmation of Eisenhower's statement. If Badoglio announced the armistice, at least the Italian people would be happy. There was also a chance, the leaders believed, that a sufficient number of Allied troops would land in Italy to keep the Germans from occupying Rome. The latter was a false hope. Hitler, upon hearing of Badoglio's armistice announcement, ordered German troops to occupy the capital, which they did with ease. King Victor Emmanuel, Marshal Badoglio, and other leaders escaped from Rome to Brindisi, where they established their headquarters. Hitler then installed Mussolini, whom he had rescued from internment, as head of of German-occupied Italy.[77]

As Eisenhower and Badoglio's announcements of the armistice were broadcast, PWB worked on a secret plan to order the Italian fleet to sail to Malta, keeping it out of German hands. Morris Pierce, an OWI radio engineer, modified a transmitter adjusted to 1226 kilohertz so that it would broadcast at 500 kilohertz. The reason for changing the transmitter's frequency was the Italian naval officers were forbidden to listen to any radio programs other than their own—and 500 kilohertz, which was reserved as the International Distress Signal frequency. Pierce and his aides modified the transmitter, and, using the 500 kilohertz frequency, sent a surrender order to the Italian fleet. The order instructed the Italian fleet to sail for Malta, as the armistice agreement specified. The Italian army indeed sailed to Malta and surrendered. OWI claimed responsibility for the surrender. What the U.S. psychwarriors did not realize was that the British-operated clandestine station, "Radio Livorno," broadcast the same orders to the Italian fleet. The surrender of the fleet was interpreted by PWE as their victory. What neither OWI nor PWE realized was that King Victor Emmanuel ordered the fleet to sail for Malta. It was these instructions that the naval officers followed, not any others. Follow-up interviews with Italian naval officers in Malta showed that they had never even heard of Radio Liverno.[78]

With German troops occupying the northern four-fifths of Italy, propping up the newly proclaimed Italian Social Republic, Eisenhower realized that the next battles would be fought with bullets, not words. Psychwar would be a minor weapon henceforth in Italy because Mussolini's government did not need to be discredited through broadcasting or leaflets, for it was completely discredited from the start. Most Italians realized that Il Duce was a mere puppet of Hitler. As the Italian army had been defeated by the Allies in Sicily and then demolished by German troops on the boot, there was little to be gained from urging Italian troop desertions or surrender. Thus, PWB conducted few psychwar operations in Italy after September. It operated a station that appeared on some nights at 2 a.m., just as Radio Rome signed off. Operating on Radio Rome's frequency, the clandestine station would make announcements such as: "One more item—it was learned today that Il Duce has taken another mistress." These broadcasts constituted little more than harassment of the Italian puppet government.[79]

The psychwar stalemate in Italy allowed General Donovan to reach an agreement with General Eisenhower that allowed MO to operate independently of PWB. In January 1944, a PWB/MO agreement was reached, giving MO autonomy to distribute black propaganda. The autonomy agreement was immediately implemented by MO, which started a clandestine radio-telegraph station that was code-named "Morse." The Morse broadcasts were started in mid-January and were transmitted to Greece, Romania, Bulgaria, and German troops garrisoned in the Balkans. The Greek, Rumanian, and Bulgarian transmissions claimed to originate from indigenous resistance groups. They were designed to bolster the morale of resistance groups in these countries. The German transmissions claimed to originate from a Nazi wireless operator stationed in the Balkans, who was providing "inside dope" to his colleagues. The dope consisted of real news amply mixed with rumors. The transmissions actually originated in Cairo, where MO had a base. MO-Cairo was forced to use morse rather than voice by British authorities in Egypt, who jealously protected their monopoly over radio broadcasting in that country. The Morse operation was discontinued in October 1944, after Germany withdrew its troops from Greece.[80]

MO operated a second clandestine station that broadcast to Greece. The station originated from an OSS base north of Izmir in Turkey. The base was code-named "Boston," as were broadcasts that originated from it. The Boston broadcasts began on August 21, 1944 and continued for six weeks. The station transmitted in Greek and German, and was operated by seven agents, including several Greeks. Overseeing the operation was MO Lt. Col. Charles Vanda. The station's chief announcer was Cpl. Anastassious Vatis of the OSS, who claimed to be a former collaborator. Having realized his mistakes, the station's speaker tried to convince other collaborators that they, too, should stop acting as traitors. This was done by providing news about German defeats, and by issuing warnings about what was in store for collaborators after an Allied victory. Overall, the station broadcast six short programs daily, of which four were news programs. The news that was broadcast was obtained by monitoring the BBC English-language program of 10 a.m., and translating it into Greek. The translation was transmitted at dictation speed beginning at 11:30 a.m., so that Greek underground editors could transcribe and circulate the news. Like the Morse station, it signed off in October.[81]

## NOTES

1. *FBIS*, February 11, 1942, p. H4, March 18, 1942, p. K1, March 26, 1942, p. K1; entry 134, PID Research Units: Underground Broadcasting Stations, Pt. 2, *PRO*, FO 898/52; "Memorandum of Establishment of Service of Strategic Information" (June 10, 1942), *FDR*, President's Secretaries Files, box 141.

2. William L. Langer, *Our Vichy Gamble* (New York: Alfred A. Knopf, 1947, pp. 179–80, 399–401; Anthony Cave Brown, ed. *Secret War Report of the OSS* (New York: Berkley Publishing, 1976), p. 135.

3. Fredrick Painton, "Fighting With Confetti," *American Legion Magazine*, December 1943, p. 42; Bradley F. Smith, *The Shadow Warriors* (New York: Basic Books, 1983), pp. 148–49. Edgar Jones, "Fighting With Words," *The Atlantic*, August 1945, p. 48, wrote that several U.S. generals believed that Japanese soldiers were too inhuman to be influenced by psychwar techniques. It is

doubtful that similar racist beliefs were responsible for the initially negative attitudes of some U.S. generals participating in Torch, as General Patton, after seeing the effectiveness of psychwar techniques, used them in areas under his command.

4. Wallace Carroll, *Persuade or Perish* (Boston: Houghton Mifflin Company, 1948), pp. 26–27; Charles Cruickshank, *The Fourth Arm* (London: Davis-Poynter, 1977), p. 136; George F. Howe, *United States Army in World War II, The Mediterranean Theater of Operations, Northwest Africa: Seizing the Initiative in the West* (Washington, D.C.: Department of the Army, 1957), pp. 54–55.

5. Frederick Sondern, Jr. and Donald A. Coster, "But We Expected You at Dakar!" *American Legion Magazine*, August 1946, pp. 25–26, 49–51; Smith, *The Shadow Warriors*, pp. 147–48.

6. *FBIS*, August 31, 1942, p. Y3. Radio Revolution differed from most clandestine stations operating during World War II in that it was located within France and operated by collaborationists with German consent and assistance. See "Clandestine Radio Stations," Foreign Broadcast Intelligence Service, Special Report #58 (March 22, 1943), *FCC*, RG262.

7. Edmond Taylor, *Awakening from History* (London: Chatto & Windus, 1971), p. 321; Carroll, *Persuade or Perish*, pp. 12, 27.

8. "Mr. Bruce Lockhart—Aspidistra" (November 1942), Aspidistra File, *PRO*, FO898/43; Carroll, *Persuade or Perish*, p. 37.

9. "Radio Stations Kept Busy by Attack," *New York Times*, November 9, 1942, p. 8.

10. Coon was author of other anthropological studies, including *Flesh of the Wild Ox* (New York: Morrow & Company, 1932), *The Origins of Races* (New York: Knopf, 1962) and *The Hunting Peoples* (Boston: Little, Brown & Company, 1971). The broadcast written for the Riffs can be found in Anthony Cave Brown, *Wild Bill Donovan, The Last Hero* (New York: Time Books, 1982), pp. 252–53.

11. The "official" report on Torch plans is presented in Howe, *United States Army in World War II*. pp. 15–85.

12. "The Use of Aspidistra for Subversive (Black) Operations," "Recommendations for the Black Use of 'Aspidistra' After the First 48 Hours of Operation 'Torch' " (November 3, 1942), Aspidistra File, *PRO*, FO898/43.

13. Carroll, *Persuade or Perish*, p. 30; "Torch Personnel' (October 25, 1942), *Hazeltine*.

14. "Psychological Warfare Service, Allied Field Headquarters" (January 22, 1943), "The Psychological Warfare Branch of A.F.H.Q. from its Inception to Nov. 1, 1943" (November 5, 1943), *Hazeltine;* Cruickshank, *The Fourth Arm*, pp. 139–40; Henry F. Pringle, "The 'Balony Barrage' Pays Off," *Saturday Evening Post* March 31, 1945, p. 19. "Torch Personnel" (October 25, 1942), *Hazeltine*, listed 54 rather than 57 men. Among those absent from the list was the PWE's Torch representative, Richard Crosslman.

15. "Letter from C. B. Hazeltine to Wallace Carroll" (January 23, 1943), Hazeltine.

16. Carroll, *Persuade or Perish*, p. 32.

17. "Letter from C. B. Hazeltine to Wallace Carroll" (January 23, 1943), *Hazeltine;* also reported in James M. Erdmann, *Leaflet Operations in the Second World War* (Denver: University of Denver, 1969), p. 84.

18. "We Herald Freedom, President Roosevelt Tells French in Broadcast,"

*Washington Post*, November 8, 1942, p. 1; "Appeals and Proclamations to the French People," *New York Times*, November 8, 1942, p. 8. Carroll, *Persuade or Perish*, p. 29 reported that when British engineers rerecorded FDR's speech for broadcast over the BBC, they transformed his very "rusty" French into a presentation with faultless pronunciation.

19. "General Eisenhower Reassures Invaded Area on U.S. Motive," *Washington Post*, November 8, 1942, p. 2; "Appeals and Proclamations to the French People," *New York Times*, November 8, 1942, p. 8.

20. Edward W. Barrett, *The Truth Is Our Weapon* (New York: Funk & Wagnalls Company, 1953), p. 35; Carroll, *Persuade or Perish*, p. 37; Allan Winkler, *The Politics of Propaganda—The Office of War Information 1942–1945* (New Haven: Yale University Press, 1978), p. 115.

21. Leo Margolin, *Paper Bullets* (New York: Froben Press, 1946), pp. 91–92. Margolin's report of actual words broadcast may not be absolutely correct, as the U.S.S. Texas's main guns were 14-inch, according to Howe, *United States Army in World War II*, p. 159.

22. "Giraud Believed in African Revolt," *Washington Post*, December 9, 1942, p. 7; "General Giraud Emerges to Urge French in Africa to Join Allies," *New York Times*, November 9, 1942, pp. 1, 12.

23. Carroll, *Persuade or Perish*, p. 37; Howe, *United States Army in World War II*, p. 249.

24. "U.S. Equips Radio Station for Free French in North Africa," *New York Times*, May 16, 1942, p. 2; "Fighting French Welcome Invasion," *Washington Post*, December 8, 1942, p. 2; "DeGaulle Calls North Africa to Arms," *New York Times*, December 9, 1942, p. 10; Memo and Report to Rex Leeper from Colonel Sutton (August 27, 1942), PWE Research Units, *PRO*, FO898/60.

25. Howe, *United States Army in World War II*, p. 173; Cave Brown, *Wild Bill Donovan, The Last Hero*, p. 259.

26. "The Psychological Warfare Branch of A.F.H.Q. from its Inception to November 1, 1943" (November 5, 1943), *Hazeltine;* Langer, *Our Vichy Gamble*, pp. 376–78; Carroll, *Persuade or Perish*, pp. 57–60; "Darlan's Status Held Unchanged," *New York Times*, December 3, 1942, p. 6; "Rabat Radio's News Held Untrustworthy," *New York Times*, December 22, 1942, p. 9.

27. Kenneth Pendar, *Adventure in Diplomacy* (London: Cassell & Company, 1966), pp. 124–25; Carroll, *Persuade or Perish*, p. 65–67; "Memo to Colonel Sutton from Mr. Paniguian" (November 14, 1942), "Memo to Mr. Leeper from Dr. Beck" (January 3, 1943), "Memo to Mr. Paniguian from Colonel Sutton" (February 4, 1943), PWE Research Units, *PRO*, FO898/60.

28. There are discrepancies concerning the sign-on dates of Radio Inconnue and Radio Gaulle, as well as the latter's sign-off date. "PID Research Units: Underground Broadcasting Stations, Part II," *PRO*, FO898/52 reports that Radio Inconnue appeared on February 3, 1941, whereas "R. U. Statistics" (September 9, 1943), *PRO*, FO898/51, p. 238 (hand-numbered), and Ellic Howe, *The Black Game* (London: Michael Joseph, 1982), p. 267 give the sign-on date as November 15, 1940. The sign-on and sign-off dates of Radio Gaulle are given as August 8, 1941 and November 17, 1942 by the first source, but August 25, 1941 and November 15, 1942 by the latter. The August 25 sign-on date is also reported in "Research Unit—F.4. Report No. 1" (October 11, 1941), PWE Research Units,

*PRO*, FO898/60. The Brazzaville denunciation is discussed in "Memo from Charles Stirling" (December 25, 1942), PWE Research Units, *PRO*, FO898/60. Radio Patrie eventually became the voice of the Carte organization in France, according to "Black Propaganda," Propaganda Meetings, *PRO*, FO898/61.

29. Warburg cited in Winkler, *The Politics of Propaganda*, p. 86; Carroll, *Persuade or Perish*, p. 27; "Minutes of the J.C.S. 63rd Meeting" (February 23, 1943) *JCS*, 2: 1942–45, Meetings, reel 1, no. 0656. Even Edmond Taylor, who was far from being a New Deal liberal, attempted to circumvent provisions of the Clark-Darlan Agreement. Taylor, *Awakening from History*, pp. 322–37.

30. See broadcast descriptions in "Weekly Propaganda Directive: Poland" dated September 21, 1944, October 5, 1944, and October 26, 1944, *OWI*, reel 6, nos. 00414, 00515, and 00683; "Sikorski Charges Plot by Russians," *New York Times*, February 22, 1943, p. 13; "PID Research Units: Underground Broadcasting Stations, Part II," *PRO*, FO898/52, entry 173.

31. "The Psychological Warfare Branch of A.F.H.Q. from Its Inception to November 1, 1943" (November 5, 1943), "Letter from C. B. Hazeltine to Wallace Carroll" (January 23, 1943), *Hazeltine;* also reported in Erdmann, *Leaflet Operations in the Second World War*, p. 88. PWB/AFHQ was placed under the Chief of the Information and Censorship section of AFHQ, who was Brig. Gen. Robert McClure. Gerneral McClure received this appointment on December 15, 1942. He was brought to Algiers from Great Britain by Eisenhower to straighten out problems that arose from the Clark-Darlan Agreement. In Great Britain, McClure had been the U.S. military attaché and maintained relations with the London-based governments-in-exile. Like Colonel Hazeltine, he had no previous experience with psychological warfare before his appointment.

32. "Psychological Warfare Report" (typescript), *Blankenhorn*, folder 1; "Report on PWB Activities, AFHQ, from November 42 to November 43" (10 pages), *Hazeltine;* Margolin, *Paper Bullets*, pp. 94–97; Moscrip Miller, "Talking Them Out of It," *Colliers*, August 1944, pp. 23, 72–73. Blankenhorn also authored "The War of Morale: How America 'Shelled' the German Lines with Paper," *Harper's*, September 1919, pp. 510–24 and "The Battle of Radio Armaments," *Harper's*, December 1931, pp. 83–91.

33. "Letter from Robert Sherwood to Robert McClure" (April 30, 1943), "Organization of Psychological Warfare in North African Theater" (undated, pre-December 1943), *Hazeltine;* "C. D. Jackson," *Current Biographies* (New York: H. W. Wilson Co., 1952), pp. 298–300; "Memorandum from Eugene Warner to MO Branch, OSS" (September 8, 1943), History of OSS, *Donovan*, box 99B, vol. 6.

34. Richard Harris Smith, *OSS* (Berkeley: University of California Press, 1972), p. 239; Editors of *Army Times*, *The Tangled Web* (Washington, D.C.: Robert B. Luce, Inc., 1963), p. 178; Maria Wilhelm, *The Man Who Watched the Rising Sun* (New York: Franklin Watts, Inc., 1967), p. 144. Neither *The Tangled Web* nor *The Man Who Watched the Rising Sun* mentions Albrecht's OSS affiliation.

35. Curt Riess also wrote *Underground Europe* (New York: Dial Press, 1942); *Invasion of Germany* (New York: G. P. Putnam's Sons, 1943); and *The Nazis Go Underground* (Garden City: Doubleday, Doran & Company, 1944); and other books.

36. Farago was a writer of popular histories on World War II espionage and intelligence during and after the war. His books include *The Axis Grand Strategy: Blueprints for Total War* (New York: Farrar and Rineholt, 1942); *War of Wits: The Anatomy of Espionage and Intelligence* (New York: Funk & Wagnalls, 1954); *Burn After Reading: The Espionage History of World War II* (New York: Walker, 1961); *The Broken Seal: The Story of Operation Magic and the Pearl Harbor Disaster* (New York: Random House, 1967) and *The Game of the Foxes* (New York: David McKay Company, 1972).

37. Ellis M. Zacharias, *Secret Missions* (New York: G. P. Putnam's Sons, 1946), pp. 302–10; Edward W. Barrett, *Truth Is Our Weapon* (New York: Funk & Wagnalls, 1953), pp. 8–10; Charles Rotter, *The Art of Psychological Warfare* (New York: Stein & Day, 1974), pp. 143–45; William E. Daugherty, "Commander Norden and the German Admirals," in W. E. Daugherty with Morris Janowitz, eds., *A Psychological Warfare Casebook* (Baltimore: Johns Hopkins University Press, 1958), pp. 494–96.

38. Zacharias, *Secret Missions*, p. 307.

39. *This Is the Enemy* was published in 1942 by Little, Brown & Company. It was written during Oechsner's internment in Germany with other journalists.

40. "Introduction" (to MO History), Wash. Hist. Office Op–23, *OSS*, entry 99, box 75, folder 33; "Letter from Fred Oechsner to Gen. Donovan and C. Healy" (August 24, 1943), MEDTO-MO-General, *OSS* entry 99, box 32, folder 158; "MO History, NATO," MEDTO-MO-North Africa, Jan. 43–Apr. 44, *OSS*, entry 99, box 37, folder 189.

41. Kermit Roosevelt, ed., *War Report of the OSS (Office of Strategic Services)*, vol. 1 (New York: Walker & Company, 1976), p. 213; Cave Brown, ed., *The Secret War Report of the OSS*, p. 106.

42. "Introduction" (to MO History), Wash. Hist. Office Op–23, *OSS*, entry 99, box 75, folder 33; Roosevelt, ed., *War Report of the OSS*, pp. 213–14.

43. "Introduction" (to MO History), Wash. Hist. Office Op–23, *OSS*, entry 99, box 75, folder 33.

44. Possible exceptions to this were the clandestine stations "Volkssender Drei" and "Capricorn." The Volkssender broadcasts were written by William Necker, an exiled German writer, and Abraham Polonsky, a leftist who joined OSS-MO. Polonsky was blacklisted after being investigated by the House Un-American Activities Committee for his political affiliations. See "Score in Hollywood Named by Writer as Former Reds," *New York Times*, April 13, 1951, p. 1; "Once a Communist, Dmytryk Reveals," *New York Times*, April 16, 1951, p. 17; "The Fall and Rise of Abraham Lincoln Polonsky," *Look*, June 16, 1970, p. 10T. Capricorn was designed and written by sociologist Howard Becker, not former advertising copywriters.

45. *FBIS*, January 18, 1943, p. Y1–2.

46. The report on Healy's resignation appears in "Introduction" (to MO History), Wash. Hist. Office Op–23, *OSS*, entry 99, box 75, folder 33. However, letters written in late July and late August suggest that Healy was still functioning as MO chief, despite the resignation. See "Letter from Fred Oechsner to C. Healy" (June 30, 1943), History of OSS, *Donovan*, vol. 6, box 99B; "Letter from Fred Oechsner to Gen. Donovan and C. Healy" (August 24, 1943), MEDTO-MO-General, *OSS*, entry 99, box 32, folder 158.

47. "Joint Chiefs of Staff Directive: Functions of the Office of Strategic Services" (October 27, 1943) *JCS*, p. 1: 1942–45, reel 11, Strategic Issues, nos. 549--55; also reproduced in Thomas Troy, *Donovan and the CIA* (Frederick, M.D.: University Publications of America, 1981), pp. 439–42.

48. Winkler, *The Politics of Propaganda*, pp. 104–9; "OWI Row Awaits President's Word," *New York Times*, January 30, 1944, p. 31; "OWI Dispute Ended with Davis Ousting 3 Sherwood Aides," *New York Times*, February 8, 1944, pp. 1, 34.

49. James P. Warburg, *Unwritten Treaty* (New York: Harcourt, Brace & Company, 1946), pp. 107–12; "OWI Says Fascists Remain in Power," *New York Times*, July 26, 1943, p. 3; "OWI Broadcast Excerpts," *New York Times*, July 28, 1943, p. 5.

50. "OWI Views Unchanged," *New York Times*, July 28, 1943, p. 5; "Paging Mr. Durfee—Boner on Italian Situation Lights New Fire Under OWI," *Newsweek*, August 9, 1943, pp. 42–43; "President Rebukes OWI for Broadast on Regime in Italy," *New York Times*, July 28, 1943, pp. 1, 5; "Urges OWI Be Abolished," *New York Times*, October 5, 1943, p. 10; " 'Smear' on Congress Issue Put Before OWI Head," *New York Times*, October 19, 1943, p. 16. A discussion of many of the unfounded accusations directed against OWI are reported in "The OWI and Its Critics," *New Republic*, December 13, 1943, pp. 844–46.

51. Roosevelt, ed., *War Report of the OSS*, pp. 216–17; "Memorandum from J. Withrow to K. D. Mann" (October 31, 1944), Wash-MO-Op–76, *OSS*, entry 139, box 166; "Draft Report" (undated), Wash-MO-Exhibits, vol. 1, *OSS*, entry 199, box 75, folder 32.

52. Report on "Combat Propaganda—Leaflet distribution to date" (June 15, 1943), *Hazeltine*; Moscrip Miller, "Talking Them Out of It," *Colliers* August 1944, p. 23; Margolin, *Paper Bullets*, pp. 94–96.

53. "J.C.S.—OWI Outline Plan for Propaganda to Italy" (May 21, 1943), J.C.S. 181/D, *JCS*, p. 1: 1942–45, The European Theater, reel 5, nos. 0474–9. Differing proposals for psychological warfare can be found in "Office of Strategic Services—Basic Plan for Psychological Warfare in Italy" (February 19, 1943), JCS 139/2, *JCS*, nos. 0446–56; and "Special Military Plan for Psychological Warfare in Sicily" (April 9, 1943), JCS 258, *JCS*, reel 4, nos. 0508–27. Daniel Lerner, *Sykewar: Psychological Warfare Against Nazi Germany* (Cambridge, Mass.: MIT Press, 1971 reprint), contains extensive discussion of the effects of the unconditional surrender policy on propaganda strategy.

54. "Sir Orme Sargent. Political Warfare Against Italy" (May 16, 1943), "Brig. L. C. Hollis. Political Warfare Against Italy" (May 11, 1943), "Edited Literal Text, transmitted to Combined Chiefs of Staff by Eisenhower" (July 5, 1943), *PRO*, FO 898/349; Cruikshank, *The Fourth Arm*, pp. 77, 141–43.

55. "Incoming Message from Algiers to Etousa, Ag war for action, signed Eisenhower" (June 29, 1943), "Memo to the Director General from Mr. Delmer" (July 3, 1943), *PRO*, FO 898/349.

56. "Unparaphrased Version of a Most Secret Cypher Telegram from J.S.M. Washington to W.C.O. London" (June 29, 1943), "Cipher Telegram from AFHQ Algiers to War Office" (June 29, 1943), "Report from H. L. Ismay" (June 30, 1943), "Cable From: Air Ministry To: Britman, Washington" (July 2, 1943), "Op-

eration 'Husky'—False Armistice Rumours" (p. 173, handwritten), *PRO*, FO 898/349.

57. "Most Secret Cypher Telegram from Air Ministry to Britman, Washington" (July 3, 1943), "Letter to Sir Robert Bruce Lockhart from Office of the War Cabinet" (July 3, 1943), "Cipher Telegram from AFHQ to the War Office" (July 3, 1943), *PRO*, FO898/349; Cruikshank, *The Fourth Arm*, pp. 146–48.

58. Elliot Harris, *The "Un-American" Weapon: Psychological Warfare* (New York: M. W. Lads Publishing, 1967), p. 149; Oliver H. P. Garrett, "Why Write an Anti-Nazi Play?" *New York Times*, October 30, 1938, p. X3; "Oliver H. P. Garrett on the Perils of Authorship," *New York Herald Tribune*, November 25, 1945, p. V3; Carroll, *Persuade or Perish*, p. 30.

59. "Psychological Warfare Report" (typescript), *Blankenhorn* folder 1, pp. 32–33.

60. Leo Miskin, "Globe Brings in Another Anti-Nazi Thriller in Warners' 'Underground,' " *Morning Telegraph*, p. 9; "Underground," *Baltimore Sun*, August 4, 1941, p. 6; "Underground, at Globe, a Grim, Anti-Nazi Film," *New York World-Telegram*, June 23, 1941, p. 8; " 'Underground,' a Film Dealing with Radio Anti-Nazi Activities, Seen at Globe," *New York Times*, June 23, 1941, p. 13.

61. Denis Mack Smith, *Mussolini's Roman Empire* (New York: Viking Press, 1976); Ivone Kirkpatrick, *Mussolini, A Study in Power* (New York: Hawthorn Books, 1964).

62. "Memorandum from Charles P. Healy to Frederick Oechsner" (July 12, 1943), *Donovan*, box 99B, vol. 1 (bound), tab U; "An MO Example of Black (Italian) 'Italo Balbo,' " General-MO, *OSS*, entry 99, box 69, folder 306; "Organization Chart by W. Stewart Roberts" (February 18, 1941), EH and SO1 Meetings, *PRO*, FO 898/9 (p. 134, handwritten); "Group 'E' Personnel" Roster, *Hazeltine*. Martelli wrote several letters to the *Times* (of London) that described British black propaganda as ineffective. For example, see "Propaganda during the War," *Times*, June 4, 1973, p. 15.

63. "Letter from Fred Oechsner to Gen. Donovan and C. Healy" (August 24, 1943), MEDTO-MO-General, *OSS*, entry 99, box 32, folder 158; Report from F. Oechsner (after July 1943), Psychological Warfare Operations Reports Summary, *OSS*, entry 99, box 83, file 3; Elizabeth McDonald, *Undercover Girl* (New York: Macmillan Company, 1947), p. 31.

64. "PID Research Units: Underground Broadcasting Stations, Part II," *PRO*, FO 898/52, entry 133; "Rome Wireless Incident," *Times* (of London) June 26, 1943, p. 4. For lisits of rumors developed by MO, see Project-ETO-Italian Plan, *OSS*, box 176 and Wash-Mo-Op–77, *OSS*, entry 139, box 166.

65. "Letter from F. Oechsner to C. P. Healy and Rae Smith" (July 22, 1943), History of OSS, *Donovan*, box 99B, vol. 6; "Comeback from Black Radio 'Italo Balbo' " (September 8, 1943), Wash.-Hist. Office Op–23, *OSS*, entry 99, box 16, folder 67.

66. "Memorandum from Eugene Warner to MO Branch, OSS" (September 8, 1943), History of OSS, *Donovan*, vol. 6, box 99B.

67. "President Warns Italians After Pantelleria Vicitory," *New York Times*, July 12, 1943, pp. 1,3; "PID Research Units: Underground Broadcasting Stations, Part II," *PRO*, FO 898/52, entries 131 and 143; Howe, *The Black Game*, p. 271. The Justice and Liberty organization helped found "Radio Milano Libertad," the

pro-Communist clandestine station that broadcast to Italy from Spain before World War II, according to Franco Monteleone, *La Radio Italiana nel Periodo Fascista* (Venice: Marsilio Editori, 1976). For background on Justice and Liberty, see Max Gallo, *Mussolini's Italy* (New York: Macmillan, 1973).

68. "J.C.S.—OWI Outline Plan for Propaganda to Italy" (May 21, 1943), JCS 181/D, *JCS*, pt. 1: 1942–45, The European Theater, reel 5, nos. 0474–9.

69. "The Psychological Warfare Branch of A.F.H.Q. from its Inception to Nov. 1, 1943," "Appraisal of Major PWB Techniques and Equipment" (October 30, 1943), "Report on PWB Activities, AFHQ, from November 42 to November 43," *Hazeltine*.

70. "Declaration," *PRO*, FO898/349.

71. "J.C.S.—OWI Outline Plan for Propaganda to Italy" (May 21, 1943), JCS 181/D, *JCS*, pt. 1: 1942–45, The European Theater, reel 5, nos. 0474–9; "Combat Propaganda—Leaflet distribution to date" (June 15, 1943), *Hazeltine*.

72. Sefton Delmer, *Black Boomerang* (London: Secker & Warburg, 1962), pp. 103–4; Howe, *The Black Game*, pp. 171–72.

73. Albert N. Garland and Howard M. Smith, *United States Army in World War II, The Mediterranean Theater of Operations, Sicily and the Surrender of Italy* (Washington, D.C.: Department of the Army, 1965), pp. 270–73.

74. Garland and Smith, *United States Army in World War II*, p. 273.

75. "Italians Ask Peace in Riots in North," *New York Times*, August 1, 1943, p. 5.

76. "Italy's Fall Told by Eisenhower," *Washington Post*, Septemer 9, 1943, p. 1; "General Eisenhower Announces Armistice," *New York Times*, September 9, 1943, p. 1.

77. "Text of Statement by Badoglio," *Washington Post*, September 9, 1943, p. 1; "Announcement of Surrender," *New York Times*, September 9, 1943, p. 1; Richard H. S. Crossman, "An Armistice Message to Badoglio," in W. E. Daugherty with Morris Janowitz, eds., *A Psychological Warfare Casebook* (Baltimore: Johns Hopkins University Press, 1958), pp. 410–11; Garland and Smith, *United States Army in World War II*, pp. 274–75; "Germany Hurriedly Set Up Fascist Rule in Italy," *Washington Post*, September 9, 1943, p. 1.

78. Edward M. Kirby and Jack W. Harris, "Surrender of the Italian Fleet," in Daugherty and Janowitz, eds., *A Psychological Warfare Casebook*, pp. 408–10; "Save Ships, Allies Warn Italian Navy," *Washington Post*, September 9, 1943, p. 1; Lord Ritchie-Calder, "Propaganda During the War," *Times* (of London), June 11, 1973, p. 15; Delmer, *Black Boomerang*, p. 104; George Martelli, "Wartime Propaganda," *Times* (of London), June 18, 1973, p. 15. Morris Pierce never took personal credit for, and didn't even mention, the surrender broadcasts in his review entitled "Radio's Part in Psychological Warfare," *Broadcasting*, October 25, 1943, pp. 11, 30.

79. "Psychological Warfare" (report), p. 12, *Hazeltine*. PWB did broadcast consistently from aboveground transmitters, informing Italian citizens of Allied successes and urging German soldiers to surrender. Transmitters at Bari and Palermo were used for these United Nations broadcasts.

80. Kermit Roosevelt, ed., *The Overseas Targets: The War Report of the OSS*, vol. 1 (New York: Walker & Company, 1976), pp. 97, 122; "MO History, NATO," MEDTO-MO-North Africa, *OSS*, entry 99, box 37, folder 189; "Black Radio

'Morse,' " General-MO, *OSS*, entry 99, box 69, folder 306; "Major MO Achievements in ETO-MEDTO-METO," Wash. Hist. Office Op–23, *OSS*, entry 99, box 16, folder 67.

81. "Report by Charles Vanda" (December 6, 1944), *OSS*, entry 99, box 45, folder 215b; "Black Radio 'Boston,' " General-MO, *OSS*, entry 99, box 69, folder 306; "Major MO Achievements in ETO-MEDTO-METO," Wash. Hist. Office Op–23, *OSS*, entry 99, box 16, folder 67.

# 4

## OSS PSYCHWAR
## STATIONS IN EUROPE

Sefton Delmer wrote that U.S. leaders learned of the "Gustav Siegfried Eins" radio operation in 1941 after an American foreign service attaché in London monitored its broadcasts. The attaché mistakenly believed the broadcasts to be of German origin and reported to Washington that they indicated a dramatic increase in hostility between Nazi party and army leaders. Fearing that the report would mislead their naïve American allies, Valentine Williams asked David Bowes-Lyon, head of the Political Warfare Executive (PWE) mission in Washington, to personally inform President Roosevelt of the attaché's mistake. When told that Gustav Siegfried Eins was a British-sponsored station, Roosevelt "chuckled and chortled." Roosevelt, who Delmer concluded did not believe in security as much as the British, "could not refrain from telling his friends" about Gustav Siegfried Eins. News about the station was soon all over Washington. Having thus learned of the operation, leaders of the Office of Strategic Services (OSS) besieged Rex Leeper with "demand[s] to be initiated into the arts and techniques" of black propaganda.[1]

Delmer's report, while colorful, contains little truth. Before Delmer joined the PWE and long before Gustav Siegfried Eins signed on, Wild Bill Donovan visited London on a mission for President Roosevelt and was told by British leaders of their techniques for "setting Europe ablaze." Donovan's first trip to London began July 14, 1940, one month after France capitulated. At this time, two clandestine stations were broadcasting from Woburn Abbey to Germany: the "Free German Station" and the "German Revolution Station." During his tour, Donovan was "shown everything there was to see about British secret intelligence as well as special operations."[2] This included Britain's "ingenious propaganda devices."[3] Six months later, Donovan again visited London and was given an update on British activities. These briefings convinced Donovan that Great Britain could resist Germany and eventually win the war. He informed Roosevelt of his conclusions. What he was shown also affected his thinking about the conduct of modern warfare. Donovan's thoughts on modern warfare and the role of radio in it, were being written and sent to the president at the very moment that plans for Gustav Seigfried Eins were being laid. On May 23, 1941, Gustav Siegfried Eins inaugurated broadcasts. On June 10, Donovan wrote FDR that a central agency was needed that could conduct psychological warfare and collect and co-ordinate intelligence. "Radio," he wrote the president, "was the most powerful weapon" in psychological warfare.[4]

While it is not true that U.S. leaders learned about Britain's black radio operations because of a U.S. attaché's naïveté, it is true that Donovan wanted OSS personnel assigned to Woburn Abbey and Milton Bryant, where they could learn the tactics of psychwar radio. Donovan was impressed by Britain's dedication to unconventional warfare, its facilities, and ingenuity. Britain offered to train the Americans because it wanted them to join its fight against Germany. When the United States entered the war, OSS did not have the facilities, equipment, or experience to train its own personnel, so it accepted the British offer of assistance. By then, Britain already had eighteen months experience conducting psychological warfare. After being trained by Delmer, Donovan wanted OSS personnel to develop their own black radio operations, not just serve as a manpower pool for Great Britain. Edmond Taylor, one of the Coordinator of Information's first recruits, worked with the British and brought his acquired knowledge into the Psychological Warfare Board, of which he was a member. Gordon Auchincloss and George Dibert were trained in London and then assigned to write scripts for black radio stations in Asia. Alfred Leach and Abraham Polonsky were trained by Delmer and later sent to France to operate "Volkssender Drei" (People's Station Three).[5]

OSS not only gained experience working at Milton Bryant, but contributed substantially to the British radio operations. OSS's independent contributions began in May 1944, when Morale Operations (MO) branch chief Rae Smith, responding to a request by Britain, assigned Ira Ashley the task of evaluating the programming of "Soldatensender Calais." Ashley worked as a radio director in New York before joining OSS. He was asked to make recommendations to improve the station's entertainment features so as to enlarge and sustain an audience. In June, Ashley submitted his critique and on July 1 submitted a recorded half-hour program that incorporated his recommendations. The recording was aired on July 3. It was called "Memories" and was developed with the assistance of Egon Lehrburger, a German who had worked as a broadcast journalist before the war. It included the song "Paper Doll," which was translated into German by Lehrburger and recorded by the Carroll Gibbons Orchestra. Ashley's program was well-received. Because of it, OSS was invited to develop a series of programs for the Soldatensender. The program series produced by OSS first appeared on July 30, 1944 and continued until the station signed off on May 1, 1945. The program production was code-named "Operation Musak." This name was later changed to "Operation Pancake."[6]

The operation was originally code-named "Musak" because most songs played during the American-produced segments were recorded at the New York facilities of the Musak Recording company, not in London. A total of 312 popular songs were translated and recorded at the facility between July 1944 and April 19, 1945, when production ceased. The songs were recorded to fill a void in the Soldatensender's programming, which until the participation of OSS, had little of entertainment value to attract an audience.

The New York recording operation began when a small group of operatives was sent to New York by OSS-Washington. Their assignment was to create a cover through which musicians, performers, and facilities could be obtained. To accomplish this, they contacted the J. Walter Thompson advertising agency, which had produced a number of OSS-Morale Operations (MO) personnel, including Rae Smith and George Dibert. The Thompson agency was asked to function as the "cover" for the MO operation, and it agreed. The advertising agency conducted the solicitations and negotiations for personnel and facilities. OSS established a dummy corporation that reimbursed J. Walter Thompson for OSS bills that it paid. J. Walter Thompson also donated the services of one of its radio directors, Lester O'Keefe, who helped with the recordings.[7]

J. Walter Thompson negotiated rates with the Musician's Union for OSS. It could not reveal the real purpose of the recordings, but at the same time sought to obtain lower rates because the work was part of the war effort. Although the union was told that the recordings were part of U.S. propaganda operations directed at Germany, it was not told that the songs would air on a station claiming to be of German origin. The negotiations were successful, and J. Walter Thompson hired NBC's house conductor, Irving Miller, who was charged with overseeing an orchestra that numbered between eight and fourteen musicians. On occasion, the agency secured the services of the NBC house band for free. Kurt Weill, the German-born composer who wrote "The Three Penny Opera" with Bertolt Brecht and the Broadway musicals "Lost in the Stars" and "Knickerbocker Holiday," helped arrange American compositions "to suit the German personality." Singers were recruited from among the German exiles living in the United States. Auditions were held almost daily. Auditions were required because perfect diction was a requirement of each singer, something lacking in many. Perfect diction was required because the lyrics to some songs were changed slightly to give them an antiwar theme. For listeners to hear the new lyrics, clear pronunciation was needed. Among those recruited were John Hendrik, a German baritone who had worked for Telefunken and the British Broadcasting Corporation (BBC); Desi Halban, a soprano who had given concerts throughout Europe; and Vilma Kurer, a cabaret-style singer. The singers were told that their recordings would air on the Voice of America.[8]

Current and past hits were selected for recording and airing on the Soldatensender. Current hits were selected from those ranked by *Variety*. Past hits were subdivided into ballads, rhythm numbers and novelty songs, based on mood and tempo. A mix of slow and fast tunes was selected so that the station would attract listeners of all musical tastes. The tunes were selected from different genres, including jazz, spirituals, and broadway tunes. Songs from shows by Rogers and Hart, Cole Porter, Irving Berlin, and the Gershwins were translated into German and recorded. Current hits that were recorded included "My Heart Stood Still," "I Told Every Little Star," and "Is You Is or Is You Ain't." The spiritual "Nobody Knows the Trouble I've Seen" was rewritten with serious propaganda lyrics. Other tunes rewritten with propaganda lyrics included "San Fernando Valley," "Pistol Packing Mama," and "The Daring Young Man on the Flying Trapeze." About ten percent of the translations contained overt propaganda. The remainder were simply German translations of American songs.

The translations and propaganda lyrics were supplied by one lyricist, known as "Metzyl." Metzyl had to translate eight songs a week. The translations were a tedious project, as it was not possible to do simple literal translations, for the German language did not easily fit American tunes. In addition to the problem of making the translations rhythmic and singable, some songs needed to be rewritten with either slanted or openly propagandistic content. Of the 312 songs recorded in New York, Metzyl translated or rewrote 210. The other 112 were jazz or big band instrumentals. Permission was never sought from the copyright holders before the songs were changed or recorded. OSS personnel were indifferent to copyright laws because the project was "classified" and therefore precluded obtaining permission. J. Walter Thompson was not convinced by OSS's arguments and this produced considerable discussion within the project.

After Operation Muzak was established, better-known singers were recruited. These included Grete Stueckgold, the famed Metropolitan Opera singer; Sig Arno, the comedian who appeared in the broadway hit, the "Song of Norway"; Herta Glatz, a former member of the Vienna Opera; Jarmila Novotna, a soprano and star of the Metropolitan Opera; Lotte Lenya, the famed German cabaret singer who was the wife of composer Kurt Weill; and Marlene Dietrich. Dietrich was the first well-known singer recruited, and as of August 24, 1944, the only one informed of the nature of the project. The others were told that the recordings were to be used for "Voice of America" broadcasts. Marlene Dietrich was also told that the songs were being recorded in violation of copyright laws and was cautioned to "be most discreet" when discussing the subject.[9]

From July 7 onward, recording sessions were held once, sometimes twice a week at the Muzak recording studio. Altogether, there were 48 sessions. Twenty of these were single sessions where four recordings by one artist were made. Twenty-eight were double sessions, during which two artists were recorded. Each double session produced eight recordings. The time available for each single session was about three hours. Because time and funds precluded any new arrangements, stock arrangements were typically used. Any "brightening up" of old material was done on the spot. This was done by Kurt Weill, Irving Miller, and Miller's successor, Allen Roth. Allen Roth was the director of radio station WEAF's "Shaefer Review." The recordings were made on 16-inch, 33 1/3-rpm vinolyte pressings, of which each side carried four songs. The records were shipped to London weekly. Overall, 60 percent of the airtime used for OSS programs on the Soldatensender comprised recordings made in the United States.[10]

The other program time was filled with materials produced at the Milton Bryant studios in England. The materials were produced by an OSS staff that initially numbered twelve. This number was reduced to six in September, when several of the MO staff were sent to Paris to operate "Volkssender Drei." The initial staff included Douglas Bagier, Charles Kebbe, Alfred Leach, Abraham Polonsky, Stephen Schnabel, Manuel Segal, and Barry Trivers, in addition to Ashley, Lehrburger, and Smith. Bagier was a motion picture sound editor before joining OSS and helped write scripts and edit programs for the Soldatensender. Kebbe worked as a radio director before his duty with OSS. He not only wrote and directed programs for the OSS radio segments but helped Sefton Delmer improve British-produced programming. Alfred Leach was a radio technician who became OSS's leading authority on technical aspects of black radio. With Abraham Polonsky, he went to Paris in September. In 1945, Leach went to the Pacific, where he helped establish the only black radio station that broadcast to Japan. Schnabel was a German-born actor who became a naturalized U.S. citizen. He worked as an actor on the Pancake project. Manuel Segal was a sound-effects expert before the war and worked in the same capacity on the Soldatensender programs. Barry Trivers worked as a scriptwriter before the war and during his days in OSS.[11]

The most popular program segment produced by OSS was a musical show called "Vicki." It was written by Charles Kebbe and appeared three times weekly for fifteen minutes. Vicki was played by Agnes Bernelle, the daughter of Rudolph Bernauer, a Berlin playwright and theater owner who fled the Nazi takeover of Germany. Rudolph Bernauer was hired by OSS to work as a consultant for the radio programs. He advised and coached his daughter on how to play "Vicki, the girl with the pin-up voice." Bernauer's wife worked as a chaperon at the OSS compound at Milton Bryant, known as the "Grange." Vicki functioned as her own disc jockey, playing a mix of sentimental, nostalgic, and jazz tunes. The songs were interspersed with short, sexy talks designed to contrast life before and after the war. Vicki began her broadcast with the announcement: "This is Vicki speaking, saying 'hello' to all her friends in the Wehrmacht." This was followed by a comment with heavy sexual innuendo such as: "Just imagine you and me at a table for two . . . a glass of Riesling—my eyes look into yours, and in the background . . . " This would serve as a lead-in to a nostalgic tune. When the record finished, she would say: "Now the music changes. You stand up, tall and handsome. 'Will you dance?' you say." A dance tune would then air. The program typically ended with a comment like: "You find me in your arms at the end of the evening. And I'm yours. Here's a goodnight kiss from your Vicki. Until later, goodnight."[12]

Vicki received fanmail at a drop in a neutral country. The fanmail was analyzed and read over the air when relevant to the program's objectives. At first, the mail was read as received, for there was little propaganda inserted into her programs during the first months that it was on. Propaganda was avoided so that listeners would relax rather than feel guarded during her program. After an audience was established, fabricated letters were read that were designed to lower listener morale. She sent kisses to a German U-boat captain, whose fiancée had married another man. The story wasn't true, but the captain reportedly became so upset and discouraged that he surrendered. In another instance, she read a letter from a mother who was trying to contact her son. The mother wanted to reassure her son that the Russians had not reached Berlin, despite rumors to the contrary. Like other programs carried on the Soldaten-sender, the names, places, and events reported by Vicki were all derived from Milton Bryant intelligence files, so they had an authentic flavor.[13]

Agnes Bernelle was only one of four women who worked on the Pancake project. Trudy Binar, a one-time Miss Czechoslovakia, recorded German songs "with a saucy Czech accent that Germans enjoyed." Elisabeth Carroca played "Lisel, the Moonlight Madonna." Hildy Palmer appeared in comedy segments. Before joining the OSS operation, she performed in the musical "Something for the Boys." Hildy was recruited by Charles Kebbe, whom she later married. The three women appeared in several series developed by OSS: a "music hall" program, a comedy series, a monthly special feature, a poetry reading, and "Memories." The music hall program was time-consuming to produce and appeared only once a month. It claimed to originate live from a different German city each time. Rudolph Bernauer would play host one week, Stephen Schnabel another. It consisted of comedy sketches, songs, and barbs directed at German leaders. The special feature would be such things as a memorial tribute to Maurice Chevalier, following rumors that he had died. "Memories" was the program developed by Ira Ashley that first aired on July 3. It was written by Ashley and Douglas Bagier, who left for Paris in September to work on Volkssender Drei. "Memories" appeared weekly for fifteen minutes and featured music recorded in England and New York.[14]

Approximately ten songs were recorded each month at Milton Bryant. The lyrics for the songs were translated from English by Lehrburger. They were arranged by Pat O'Neill, an Irish pop musician. He was assisted by a German violinist, who had been taken prisoner-of-war. The compositions were performed by a German band led by Harry Zeisel, who was captured while touring North Africa, and six musicians that OSS had on staff. Overall, 71 songs were recorded in Great Britain for the Pancake operation. These were usually aired on Sunday nights, when MO contributed more than half of the entertainment carried by the Soldatensender.[15]

## BROADCASTS FROM GERMANY IN REVOLT

Operation Overlord, the Allied invasion of continental Europe, began on June 6, 1944 at 12:15 a.m. when U.S. and British airborne troops were dropped behind the Atlantic Wall, Germany's coastal fortification. At daybreak, seaborne troops of the U.S. 1st Army and British 2d Army landed on the beaches of Normandy as bombers and naval guns pounded German coastal fortifications. The ground troops were commanded by British Field Marshal Bernard Montgomery. On the Cotentin peninsula, U.S. troops established beachheads at Utah beach and Omaha beach. These were the scenes of fierce fighting. British troops landed near Bayeux on three beaches called Gold, Juno, and Sword. They quickly advanced but were slowed before they reached Caen. On June 12, the U.S. and British beachheads met. On June 18, after meeting considerable resistance, Saint-Lo, a vital communication center, was captured. Although initially stalled by a massive German tank concentration, the British also advanced. They captured Falaise on August 16. This trapped the German 7th army in the "Falaise pocket," between the British and northward-marching U.S. troops. By August 23, the 7th army was obliterated.

On August 24, Major John Harris and Howard Baldwin of MO arrived at OSS's Saint Pire headquarters. They were sent to France to secure facilities for a black radio operation that OSS-MO proposed to Brig. Gen.

Robert McClure, head of the Psychological Warfare Division of the Supreme Headquarters, Allied Expeditionary Forces (PWD/SHAEF). After hearing that Paris was liberated, Harris and Baldwin traveled there. They arrived on August 27, the day after de Gaulle entered the city and established a provisional government. Through C. D. Jackson, the head of radio operations for PWD, they contacted Jean Guignebert, the newly appointed French Provisional Minister of Information. Guignebert agreed to let OSS use the facilities of a powerful mediumwave transmitter that was about to resume daytime services. It had 24 kilowatts of power. The station was located at Villebon, 32 miles southwest of Paris. All daytime hours, Guignebert said, were scheduled for domestic radio operations. After the domestic broadcasts ended for the night, however, the facilities could be used by OSS. Howard Baldwin obtained an option for three hours nightly on this station and returned to London. Louis-Élie Clainville was appointed OSS's liaison with the French Ministry of Information. Throughout the German occupation, Clainville was head of Radio Français during the day and a member of the French underground at night. He was already familiar with OSS because its Jedburgh teams worked closely with the maquis.[16]

The MO radio plan submitted to General McClure consisted of two phases. The first-phase station claimed to originate from a German military commander who refused to follow orders, while the second claimed to originate from civilian members of a nonexistent "freedom party." The first station was based on widely disseminated rumors that the German army intended to pursue a "scorched earth" policy of retreat from the advancing Allies. The rumored policy was that German commanders were ordered to burn everything between themselves and the allies, while forcing their troops to fight to the last man. The proposed black radio station claimed to originate from a German commander of a garrison who rebelled, seized a radio station, denounced the policy and claimed that the war was lost, but that Germany need not be completely destroyed. He urged surrender. The commander invited civilians to the microphone, who also denounced the policy. After several days, the commander deserted and went underground. One idea proposed for the second phase of operation was that the civilians heard during the first phase would take over and continue to operate the commander's station. The second-phase station would therefore operate on the same frequency as the first. An alternative was to have a "different group" of civilians operate a station that was unrelated to the first. This required the civilian station to operate on a different frequency than the first.[17]

On September 7, General McClure approved the project, despite its not being completely worked out. On September 11, he informed PWE representative Sir Robert Bruce Lockhart that the project was approved, thereby keeping PWE from making the same mistake that Delmer attributed to the U.S. service attaché in London.[18] After McClure's approval was given, Howard Baldwin returned to Paris with a small staff of individuals who worked in London on the Soldatensender: Douglas Bagier, Alfred Leach, Abraham Polonsky, and Stephen Schnabel. They were joined by John Reinhardt, Arthur Menken, William Burke Miller, William Necker, locally recruited civilians, and prisoners-of-war. Menken had worked as a newsreel cameraman and radio commentator before the war, while Miller had worked at NBC news for fourteen years.[19] Necker was a German-born writer.[20] One of the civilians hired was Erika Mann, the daughter of novelist Thomas Mann.[21] The POWs were recruited from French war camps and prisons. Douglas Bagier and John Reinhardt inspected the records of and interviewed over a hundred German and Austrian prisoners before finding fifteen acceptable men and women who agreed to work with OSS. The staff assembled for the black radio operation numbered thirty.[22]

The Paris-based MO staff established a monitoring station at a private residence in rue Rembrandt that formerly belonged to the Dreyfus family and was used by German officials during the occupation. Radio receivers used for the monitoring were powered by a gasoline-powered generator, as this part of Paris was temporarily without electricity. Production offices were set up at 79 Champs-Elysées, where the National *Zeitung* formerly had its office. A German record library abandoned by fleeing Germans was located and moved to the offices. Alfred Leach located a recording studio near the Post Parisien studios, not far from Champs-Elysées. Leach thought that the records could be carried to the recording studio when needed, and that the finished radio program could be sent from Poste Parisien to the transmitter at Villebon through Paris Téléphone wires.[23]

Before any tests of Leach's plan were conducted, information reached OSS that key personnel at Poste Parisien and Paris Téléphone were suspected Nazi collaborators. These individuals would have access to information about or the ability to eavesdrop on the project. To avoid either a confrontation with the collaborators or exposure of the operation, Leach searched for other facilities. He went to the radio station at Villebon, where he found a mixer and control panel and a two-table record player. Although there were no recording studios there, a vacant storeroom was available that could serve as a makeshift studio. By setting up a studio in the room, the programs could be sent directly to the transmitter, bypassing Poste Parisien and Paris Téléphone. Mr. Clainville approved the new arrangements, so Leach and William Burke Miller toured surrounding warehouses and storage depots to find wallboards, heavy draperies, and other acoustical materials to outfit the makeshift studio.

At the same time, Abraham Polonsky and William Necker worked on scripts for the broadcasts. They concluded that the second station should appear to be unrelated to the first, because the commander's station represented a military situation that could "logically exist for only a short period." The German high command would quickly send new troops and a commander to any town where there was a mutiny. The commander's station, if it were to appear real, would have to be silenced after just a few days of operation. Another reason for separating the two phases of operation was that a station claiming to originate from a different town would give the impression that a revolt against Hitler was spreading to different parts of Germany, possibly stimulating others to join the "growing rebellion." Although Polonsky and Necker agreed to create two unrelated black stations, the MO writers disagreed on what the civilian "freedom station" was to broadcast. One proposal called for the operation of a freedom station that would broadcast "wholly objective news . . . plus suitable musical entertainment." The musical entertainment would include "music, comedy and sketches of an escapist, nostalgic sort." This proposal suggested building an audience with the transmitter and waiting until the appropriate moment to use it to sow confusion to gain military advantage.[24] Another proposal was that the station keep entertainment to a minimum while transmitting left-wing messages and sabotage instructions in the hope of stimulating rebellions.[25] MO decided that the second-phase station would be built around "the personality of 'Comrade Hoffman,' 'son' of General Hoffman, who signed the treaty of Brest-Litovsk" in World War I. The character of an old trade unionist was also written into the scripts. His transmissions included sabotage instructions for ending Germany's war production. This was approved by PWD/SHAEF, as were all scripts tht were eventually aired.[26]

News was made a regular feature of this station, but entertainment features were kept to a minimum. It was hoped that the news reports would help attract an audience. The only news put out by the station, however, was what had already been aired by German stations, except when ordered otherwise by PWD. The station was also ordered by McClure not to deviate from the truth regarding military events or the Allied policy of unconditional surrender. False statements concerning conditions in Germany were permitted, however.[27]

Throughout the period when Alfred Leach was testing the equipment at the makeshift Villebon studio, he played only U.S. marching music. Every voice and transmission test was also in English. This was to assure that the project remained secret until it was time for the black broadcasts to begin. At no time was the French staff of the station informed about the nature of the broadcasts that OSS intended to make. Because the French employees at the Villebon station would learn of the nature of the operation when the black station took to the air, the French staff was eventually briefed, but only 15 minutes before the "Volkssender" went on the air. The briefing took place when William Burke Miller requested the station's chief engineer to assemble the entire radio staff. When the staff was assembled, Miller thanked them for their assistance. He told them that the broadcasts that MO was about to initiate would hopefully "hasten the end of the war by fomenting revolution in Germany." Miller said that anyone who talks about the broadcasts jeopardizes "his own life, our lives and the entire project." Miller reported that members of the staff "stiffen[ed] to attention and instinctively salute[d] following his announcement."[28]

At 10:45 p.m. on September 21, 1944 trumpet flourishes were heard on 1075 kilohertz and then a voice announced: "Attention! Attention! You are going to hear a most important announcement." Martial music followed. Finally, a second, older voice was heard at the microphone. This speaker said he was the commander of a garrison in a town in western Germany that was in the path of the Allied advance. The commander said that until the morning, he had respected all orders, even though his troops were poorly armed, hungry, and exhausted. At 10 a.m. he received orders that his garrison was to force retreating German troops back to the front, even if he had to use machine guns on them. The commander refused to obey this order, he said. The SS commanding officer, who had been sent to arrest him after the refusal, was arrested and shot. By nightfall, he and his rebelling troops had seized "every key point of the town and . . . arrested all Gestapo, SS men and Nazi administrators." The commander went on to say that he was no plotter and was not attempting to seize power. He acted impulsively, he said, but on the convictions of his conscience. The commander closed with the statement that he hoped this was the first stage of an anti-Nazi uprising that ended the useless slaughter and destruction of German troops and towns. He then relinquished the microphone to the first speaker, his adjutant, who read a decree for the defense of the town. The broadcast ended with trumpet fourishes at 11:15 p.m., 30 minutes after it began.[29]

Although Gen. George Strong, the Director of Military Intelligence, reluctantly approved the black radio operation and knew its sign-on date, he gave no advance notification to others. Because of this, army monitors who heard the broadcast accepted it as genuine and passed the information up through channels. The broadcast was considered to be sufficiently important that Gen. Omar Bradley was awakened and told of it. An Allied paratrooper regiment was also alerted for a possible drop into the garrison town. The European correspondent of the *New York Times* monitored the broadcast and wired reports of it to the newspaper, which carried a story on the broadcast the following morning. Reports were carried in other U.S. and European newspapers.[30]

On its third day of operation, the station referred to itself as the "Westdeutscher Volkssender Auf Welle 281" (West German People's Station on 281 Meters). Resolutions adopted by the city administration, civil servant's association, and other community groups in the garrison town were broadcast. The mayor appeared and denounced the Nazis. The voices heard on the station were those of Lieutenant Reinhardt and Stephen Schnabel, who were fluent in German. They supplied all of the voices because PWD did not approve the use of POWs until October 14, three weeks after the MO station signed on. When the use of POWs was finally approved, it was with the provision that they were not to appear live or use their own scripts. Westdeutscher Volkssender remained on the air until October 3, when the commander announced that he was going underground to escape from troops who were sent to arrest him.[31]

The commander's station was replaced by a civilian station on October 6. This station, called "Volkssender Drei," broadcast on 785 kilocycles, near the frequency of Radio Leipzig. It appeared without fanfare, trumpets, or music. It signed on simply, with news reports about the Allied advance into Aachen and east Hungary. The news report was followed by an address by "Comrade Hoffman," who spoke "not as the individual I was a few days ago, but as a man among millions of others." He explained why he and others first supported Hitler, but now opposed him. He was followed by "Comrade Karl," "Comrade Weber," and "Comrade Gertrude," whose voice was supplied by Erika Mann. The other voices were also supplied by civilians hired by OSS. As the station evolved over the following weeks, new voices were heard. They included voices of foreign workers and former prisoners, who denounced nazism and voiced support for the "German Freedom party."[32]

As the station continued to broadcast, it explained its origins and purpose. The transmitter was from a secret powerful station erected by the Nazis in a mountainous region where Nazi leaders intended to retreat when the Allies were victorious. (A rumor that Hitler had built a hideaway known as the "Alpine Fortress" was widespread.[33]) The transmitter was seized by partisans operating in the mountains and workers who built the station. This partisan group wanted to expand their German Freedom party using the station. Membership in the Freedom party, the station said, was attained through action: writing and distributing anti-Nazi leaflets, industrial sabotage, and the operation of other freedom stations. Volkssender Drei broadcast instructions on organizing political cells and combat units, dictated leaflets, and rebroadcast messages of other freedom stations that it claimed "were too weak for most listeners to pickup with their receivers." These broadcasts were intended to give the impression that an anti-Nazi rebellion was spreading across Germany. There is no evidence, however, that the station was successful in achieving its objectives. Rebellions did not occur, underground organizations didn't form, and antiwar leaflets bezring the dictated messages were never found. There is some evidence of listenership, but even this is limited. A Special Intelligence (SI) operative in Alsace-Lorraine reported that "many Alsatians, a few Russians, and some French" informed him of the station and accepted its programs as genuine. An agent operating near Aachen heard rumors that anti-Nazi partisans captured a city and a radio transmitter. A few other reports of listenership and rumors based on the broadcasts exist.[34]

Not only did Volkssender Drei fail to reach its objectives, but it became the object of British scorn. Siegfried Wagener, an émigré German who became a naturalized U.S. citizen and operative for OSS, complained to Major Dibert and Howard Baldwin that the first phase of the "Volkssender" broadcasts were being met with contempt in London, because the station's cover was poor and its stated objectives unattainable.[35] One member of the Milton Bryant staff, when asked about the broadcasts, refused to comment, saying "it [was] too painful." The broadcasts were viewed as an attempt to conduct psychological warfare using Hollywood theatrics. The most accurate criticism was that the broadcasts did not sound as if they were made by "desperate revolutionaries fighting for their bare existence."[36] Instead, they sounded like speakers in a biblical epic filmed by Cecil B. DeMille, as the following broadcast, where Comrade Hoffman explains how he slowly turned against the war, demonstrates:

We thought a new, invigorating wind was blowing through the land. The hopeless discouraging time of economic and political descent seemed ended ... we heard our hearts beat higher in the expectation that shortly the German name would be honored and appreciated among nations of the earth ... And so it happened in the stormy spring of the year 1933, so many of us were willing to work with and under the leadership of that new order.... We had to recognize that our march into Poland would finally necessitate an action against us by the overwhelming force of the American armadas and by the armies of millions. It was our unpardonable guilt that instead of sensibly anticipating these probabilities we rather nourished the hope that our initial successes of a Blitz in Poland would paralyze the rest of the world with terror and admiration.... Today I think it German and honorable to perish as a simple soldier fighting against a brainless tyrant rather than to prepare myself to flee in good time at the side of this tyrant.[37]

Despite these criticisms, the operators of the Volkssender believed the project to be proceeding almost without difficulty. The one difficulty was that the agreement reached between Baldwin and Guignebert, which permitted the use of the station by OSS, expired on November 1. By that day, the agreement stipulated, all OSS personnel and equipment were to be gone from the Villebon station. As early as September 19, MO-Paris was making inquiries about using Radio Luxemburg to continue its broadcasts. These inquiries were made with the knowledge and support of MO chief Fred Oechsner. OSS's inquiries were quickly rejected by William Paley, the CBS mogul who headed the radio section of PWD/ SHAEF, because he opposed black broadcasting "on principle."[38] PWD/ SHAEF chief McClure agreed with Paley concerning the use by OSS of Radio Luxemburg's facilities, not because he opposed black broadcasting, but because he was contemplating operating another black station from that site. The code-name for the contemplated project was "Operation Annie." Approval for Operation Annie was officially sought by the 12th Army group in November, at which time McClure authorized the project.[39]

MO-Paris also sought time from the British, who already agreed to give the United States two hours of time each night on Aspidistra. The two hours, however, were allocated to Operation Pancake and a second operation that was scheduled to start a day or two following the silencing of the Volkssender. Unable to get time on Aspidistra, MO-Paris sought time on another French station. On October 26, Mr. Guignebert agreed to give MO one hour of time nightly on the Limoges transmitter, provided that production was done in London, not France. He suggested that programs produced in London could be beamed to France by shortwave and then rebroadcast from the Limoges transmitter on mediumwave. OSS accepted the time, but had no way of getting the programs to France, so Volkssender Drei's broadcasts expired along with the original agreement between Baldwin and Guignebert.[40]

## A GHOST CALLED "JOKER"

The black operation scheduled to begin after the silencing of Volkssender Drei was proposed by Abraham Polonsky before he left for Paris.[41] It was code-named "Operation Joker" and consisted of infrequent broadcasts by a speaker claiming to be General Ludwig Beck, the respected career soldier who committed suicide after being implicated and arrested in an attempt to kill Hitler on July 20, 1944. During World War I, General Beck became a member of the General Staff and in 1935 became its head. He opposed Hitler's aggressive plans and resigned in protest against the German occupation of Czechoslovakia. Beck became an opponent of Hitler and after successive attempts to remove him from power failed, became involved in a plot with other generals to plant a bomb in Hitler's conference room. The plot failed. Beck was arrested and committed suicide, although a rumor spread through Germany that said he was still alive. One reason for the rumor was that Beck was reported dead on a previous occasion, only to resurface later. After Beck resigned in 1938, the Nazis started a rumor that he had committed suicide.

An OSS-MO staff of eight civilians, one commissioned and one noncommissioned officer developed and executed "Operation Joker." The staff included Ira Ashley and Egon Lehrburger, who worked on "Operation

Pancake." The project was supervised by Major Dibert, who returned to Europe from Washington, where he worked on black radio projects targeted at Asia. Joker's script was the collaborative effort of Bruno Heilig, Egon Jameson, and Lehrburger, who were journalists who emigrated from Germany after Hitler's seizure of power.[42] Unlike the Volkssender operation, substantial time was spent conducting research before the scripts were written. Prisoners-of-war interned at Brondsbury, England, were interviewed about the believability of rumors concerning General Beck's being alive. After determining that many POWs believed them, Lehrburger and John Frey, a civilian in MO, compiled a detailed biography of Beck using materials at the Wiener Library. The Wiener Library contained a collection of German documents compiled by its founder, Dr. Alfred Wiener. Reports on the July 20 putsch were obtained from the OSS-Special Intelligence branch. While no recording of General Beck's voice was available for study, recordings of Rommel, Keitel, and Döenitz were. These were studied to determine the pronunciations and speaking styles employed by high-ranking German generals.[43]

The voice of one prisoner-of-war, a major, was found to closely resemble the tone, delivery, and accent of General Keitel. The major served on the German General Staff for five years and had met General Beck. Although reluctant to participate in the project when first approached, he was persuaded by special treatment, rolls, cups of coffee, and American cigarettes. Four other POWs at Brondsbury were also persuaded to participate. They were convinced by MO personnel that it was their "patriotic duty" to participate in the broadcasts and end the destruction of Germany. These POWs were asked to "Nazify" the scripts that were drafted by the MO writing team. The best phrases and interpretations of the POWs were selected and incorporated into the final draft. One of the POWs had worked as a radio announcer in Germany before the war. He was selected as the lead-in announcer for the broadcast. The complete program was recorded during one session because it was feared that the POWs might change their minds. The fear was not unfounded, as the day following the broadcast, the major who played Beck suffered an emotional collapse and lost his voice.[44]

The recording consisted of a half-hour of teasers followed by a 26-minute, 30-second speech by "Beck." The recording aired at 5:30 p.m. and was repeated at 10:30 p.m. on October 31, 1944. It was made on 282 meters, a previously unoccupied frequency, using the Aspidistra transmitter. MO started its Joker broadcast with an announcement recorded by the POW who worked for the Reichsender: "Attention! Attention! Keeped tuned in on this wave length. In exactly one half hour you will hear an important broadcast, which is of great significance to the German nation." At 5:35, the same voice said: "Attention! Attention! In 25 minutes you can listen to an important broadcast on this frequency." This announcement and countdown continued until 6 p.m. when "Herr General Oberst" was invited to the microphone. In a measured, dignified voice, he said: "I'm calling the whole of Germany." "General Beck" explained how he escaped from Germany and why he participated in the attempt on Hitler's life. The speaker said that Germany had lost the war because "the so-called General Adolph Hitler intervened and tried to teach us experienced members of the General Staff how to" wage the war. He blamed Hitler for discarding the plan to invade England, the failed invasion of Russia, and the "catastrophe at Stalingrad." The speech closed with the invocation: "Remember the old adage: The individual may perish, but Germany must live. And Germany will live. If we all do our duty and put an end to the despised Nazi regime."[45] The first broadcast occurred without jamming. When the speech was replayed five hours later, it was jammed throughout.

The purpose of the Beck broadcast was to drive a wedge between the Wehrmacht and Nazi party, something that Gustav Siegfried Eins, the Soldatensender, and the gray newspaper *Nachrichten* also tried. Although there is no direct evidence that Operation Joker was widely heard in Germany, there is some evidence that Nazi leaders feared the broadcast. For two weeks following the operation, German transmitters continued to jam the 282 meter band in anticipation of Beck's return to the air. Reports on the broadcasts appeared in the neutral and Allied press.[46] The broadcast also redeemed OSS-MO in the eyes of British psychwarriors. Sefton Delmer called the broadcast a "beautifully written piece and beautifully spoken."[47] Despite these apparent successes, "Beck" never returned to the air.

## RADIO ANNIE

Two weeks after "Beck's" broadcast, a proposal to operate a black station using the Radio Luxemburg transmitter was sent to General McClure by the Psychological Warfare Branch of the 12th Army Group (PWB/12th AG). Radio Luxemburg, the second most powerful transmitter in Europe, was captured by the U.S. 1st Army on September 10. German troops withdrew from Luxemburg City so rapidly that they left the transmitter intact, although they blew up the main control room in the station's basement. The tubes for the station were also destroyed. German strategy was to destroy radio stations as they retreated to keep them from Allied hands. The German army destroyed transmitters in Tunis, Naples, and Rome. In the case of Radio Luxemburg, the destruction was circumvented by Luxemburg radio technician Metty Felton and OWI technician Morris Pierce, who was the chief engineer at WGAR in Cleveland before the war. Pierce was known in OSS and OWI for having modified the transmitter that broadcast the surrender orders to the Italian fleet in September 1943. Felton convinced the Germans to limit their destruction to tubes. He also led Pierce to the transmitter. Pierce was followed by a tank brigade that surrounded and defended the station.[48]

Before the war, Radio Luxemburg was a commercial station licensed by and paying royalties to the Luxemburg government. It operated with 150 kilowatts of power until being silenced by the Luxemburg government in September 1939. The station was ordered off the air in an effort to appease Hitler and avoid German charges that the station breached Luxemburg's neutrality. In May 1940, Germany occupied Luxemburg and seized the station. It was used for aboveground and clandestine radio broadcasts until Germany was forced to withdraw in September 1944. After the German withdrawal, Radio Luxemburg's owners, Compagnie Luxembourgeoise de Radiofusion, requested that the Allies return the station to them, but this was refused until the war's end. The station was too militarily important to give to civilians.

On September 17, PWB/12th AG finished repairs on the transmitter and broadcast from it for the first time. William Harlan Hale of OWI was appointed head of the station by General McClure.[49] On September 23, the station started broadcasting on a regular basis, carrying relays from London and New York. PWB/12th AG personnel recorded and transmitted four 15-minute programs beginning on September 24. Unlike the relayed programs, PWB/12th AG programs were "tactical." They were directed exclusively at German troops and civilians in the immediate combat area. On October 3, General McClure placed the station directly under his command because it was located in and broadcast to areas under his jurisdiction. Following McClure's order, the amount of time allocated to PWB/12th AG programming gradually increased, as personnel from Great Britain arrived to assist in the production of SHAEF programming. By November 15, Radio Luxemburg was on the air a total of 11 1/4 hours daily, including 7 relays from New York, 23 relays from the BBC, and 4 relays from the American Broadcasting Station in Europe (ABSIE). ABSIE was operated by the Overseas Bureau of OWI from London and had been broadcasting to Europe since prior to D day.[50]

The PWB/12th AG was composed of members of the military, OSS, and civilians from OWI and the British propaganda agency, the Political Warfare Executive (PWE). OSS personnel included Maj. Patrick Dolan and Lt. H. J. Reinhardt, who worked on Volkssender Drei in Paris. Dolan was an advertising copywriter in peacetime who became one of Donovan's favorites among young OSS men. OWI personnel included Alfred Toombs and Brewster Morgan. Between 1942 and 1944, Brewster Morgan organized OWI's relay system and helped found ABSIE. Before the war he worked as a radio director and producer for CBS. On November 15, the 12th Army Group submitted its plan for "Operation Annie." Operation Annie was a plan for operating a black station from Radio Luxemburg.

The proposed clandestine station would claim to originate from the Rhineland and be operated by loyal Rhinelanders. It would operate on a different frequency and with lower power than regular Radio Luxemburg broadcasts. The lower power would keep the signal from traveling outside the target area of the Rhineland. It would operate between 2 a.m. and 6 p.m. Radio Luxemburg signed off for the night at midnight and returned to the air at 7:00 a.m. The time between Radio Luxemburg's sign-off and the black station's sign-on provided ample time to change the transmitter's operating frequency, the proposal said. The clandestine station would call itself "Nachtsender 1212" (Night Station 1212) and commence its broadcast with the announcement "1212 calling . . . 1212 calling . . . 1212 calling with front news for the Rhineland." The station's name was based on the proposed frequency of operation—1212 meters. The plan was approved by General McClure on December 5, 1944, despite bitter opposition from members of the PWD/SHAEF planning board.[51]

McClure assigned the station a frequency of 30 kilohertz or 1214.5 meters, sufficiently near the requested frequency that the black station could announce that it operated on 1212 meters. To appease opponents on the PWD/SHAEF planning board, McClure's approval limited the station to broadcasting materials not aired on Radio Luxemburg. Radio 1212's authorization to operate stipulated that it was to "carry no musical program material or other entertainment; no set talks other than military commentary; no prisoner of war statements; [and] no explicitly opposition statements or arguments." With the exception of the ban on prisoner-of-war statements, all of these restrictions were lifted before 1212 signed on two weeks later. The time when the broadcasts ended was also changed from 6:00 a.m. to 6:30 a.m.

Radio 1212, like Radio Italo Balbo, was a cooperative effort of members of the army, OSS, and OWI. OSS Major Patrick Dolan was commander of the operation, Alfred Toombs was chief of intelligence, and Brewster Morgan was program director. All were housed in a large, well-guarded house that was formerly occupied by ranking members of the Gestapo. The Gestapo, like the German Army, withdrew from Luxemburg with considerable haste, leaving behind the Nazi insignia and posters that decorated the walls. These were left up by the staff of Radio 1212 as reminders that 1212 claimed to be a loyal Rhenish station. The 1212 staff was housed separately from the staff of Radio Luxemburg to maintain secrecy and because 1212's staff slept during the day. They arose around 7 p.m. every evening. Dolan, Toombs, and intelligence specialists assigned to the project met at 9 p.m. to examine secret intelligence reports on military actions of the previous day. A short conference on the content of the night's news was then held, based on the intelligence discussions. After decisions were reached on the content and slant of Radio 1212's programs for the night, radio writers, directors, and announcers were briefed. The writers were provided with materials by the intelligence staff. The intelligence staff assisted the writers in interpreting and clarifying the materials. Between 10 p.m. and 1 a.m. the programs for the night were written.

The programs consisted of distinct segments, tied together by the station's principal announcer, Lt. Benno Frank. Frank was a Rhinelander who became a U.S. citizen before the outbreak of the war. He had an unmistakable Rhenish accent. Radio 1212 signed on with a few bars from a well-known Rhenish song with the lyrics: "There lies a crown, deep down at the bottom of the Rhine..." followed by the announcement "1212 calling," repeated three times. An announcer would then give a brief "news round-up." This was followed by news from the western and eastern fronts. News from the western front was presented objectively, disclosing Allied setbacks and defeats. Sometimes the degree of setback dealt the Allies was exaggerated, so that German defeats, when eventually announced, seemed even more unexpected. Reports on the eastern front were always pessimistic, reporting that Soviet armies "hammered" or "smashed" through German defensive positions. This and other segments were usually recorded and repeated at regular intervals during the night. Following the news of the front, a record of Rhenish music was played. The records were captured and taken from the front lines or requisitioned from Belgian and Luxemburg civilians. The musical interlude was followed by air-raid news, which frequently consisted of eyewitness reports on the Allied bombing of German cities, as in this broadcast of January 20:

The Hauptgueter bahnhof was damaged. Many of the tall buildings were destroyed or severely damaged including the harbor master's office. Many of the tall cranes on the Rhine quays were bent and damaged. Many bombs fell in the industrial area between the Muehlau Hafen and the Rhine. Some warehouses in this sector were demolished... Windows, etc., shattered in the electric works on Verlangerte Jungbusch Strasse...[52]

The longer Radio 1212 remained on the air, the more detailed the reports on air raid damage became.

The air raid reports were presented with detail to give them the appearance of having been written by on-the-scene reporters, adding to the station's cover of being a truly indigenous operation. The air reports also provided news that was not available from official Reich stations. Reich stations remained silent about air raid damage to maintain morale along the front and to keep the Allies guessing about the damage they inflicted. Goebbels's Ministry of Propaganda also conducted campaigns in bombed towns telling relatives not to mention the attacks in letters sent to troops on the front. The result of this news blackout was that soldiers became distrustful of official stations and increasingly reliant on Radio 1212 for news. This helped the black station accomplish the first of its missions: to build an audience while simultaneously lowering troop morale.

The detailed air reports were prepared by studying aerial reconnaissance photos of bombed cities and cross-referencing these with street maps, telephone directories, and other material that provided the identity of damaged buildings. Death notices in German newspapers were examined to determine the names and numbers of casualties inflicted by the bombing. The intelligence staff was assigned the task of finding and filing potentially useful materials that were recovered from areas occupied by Allied troops. These materials allowed the station to identify the owners of damaged houses by name. Soldiers from bombed towns therefore heard about streets, individuals, and descriptions with which they were familiar. Great care was taken to see that such reports were accurate.

After the air-raid news was presented, another record was played. This was followed by a segment on "home news." Home news included information on the prices and availability of goods in Germany, rationing, and party affairs. Interviews with POWs who reported listening to Radio 1212 showed that reports from this segment were more likely remembered than news from any other segment. Among convinced Nazis, this segment more than any other exposed the station as an enemy product. An item linking Hermann Goering with an Institute for Fat Research convinced one dedicated Nazi that the station was antiparty, despite the station's claims to the contrary. One apolitical POW vividly recalled a report that said "Goering (the report was actually about Himmler) had distributed vast quantities of food to needy farmers when he removed his possessions from a farm in the East to safer areas." The POW was irritated at Goering's being exempt from the rationing system and owning so many possessions that he couldn't move them all.[53]

On Sunday nights, football scores were broadcast. This was a scoop because, while the games were played on Sunday, official German radio had a policy of not announcing the scores until they were published in the Monday newspapers. The scores were obtained from the German news agency Deutsche Nachrichten Büro (DNB), using a DNB wireless printer left behind at Radio Luxemburg by rapidly evacuating German personnel.[54] Following the home news, stories from the front were aired. Front news included regimental gossip, awards, decorations, mess reports, and "helpful hints to soldiers on matters of health, pay, and furloughs." Included in this segment was advice given to soldiers by Field Marshal Walter von Model. He was famous among German troops for his fatherly advice on how to do such things as wash woolen underwear without soap and make sawdust-and-potato sausages. His advice was aired without retouching, as it made the German High Command look ludicrous.[55]

During the first two months of its operation, Radio 1212 maintained the same format and delivered a package of generally truthful news. It developed an audience among the German army and civilians in the Rhine. Interviews with newly captured prisoners-of-war indicated "that approximately half of the Wehrmacht members listening to broadcasts are listening more or less regularly to 1212."[56] Radio 1212's popularity was due in no small part to its having a stronger signal than most of its competitors. Between 2 a.m. and 6:30 a.m. when "Annie" operated, most aboveground stations were closed down for the night. Among stations on the air, it was closest to and had the clearest signal along the front. This was not the only reason for its popularity. Radio 1212, while recognized by many listeners as being anti-Nazi, was believed to originate within Germany. A large percentage of interviewed POWs believed the station was operated by an underground in Germany. Two believed the station was operated by Otto Strasser's group, which years earlier operated an anti-Nazi clandestine station that broadcast to Germany from Czechoslovakia. These beliefs about Radio 1212 can be contrasted with those concerning the Soldatensender. Most listeners either were told, guessed, or otherwise knew that the Soldatensender was enemy-operated. Its programs were polished and professional compared to those of Radio 1212. Radio 1212's roughness contributed to its being perceived as an underground station. The final reason for Radio Annie's popularity was that, among stations on the air, it seemed to provide the most truthful news. The Soldatensender was filled with clearly untruthful assertions, as were official German stations. While the BBC and Radio Luxemburg were considered truthful, their news was dry and dignified and they were openly identified as enemy-operated. Anyone caught listening to either of these stations faced the death penalty.[57]

After the Moselle breakthrough, Eisenhower ordered Radio 1212 to begin faking news. The faked news placed some Allied armored columns miles ahead of where they actually were, others miles in back of where they were. Eisenhower correctly believed that German communications had been so seriously disrupted that many Wehrmacht commanders might believe the reports of station 1212. If they did, they would be looking for advancing columns where none were, and not be looking for Allied columns where they really were. German troops in the Eifel mountains were defeated by these deceptions. They moved into an area where they were surrounded by Allied troops, believing that none were there.[58] Radio 1212 also reported numerous but imaginary surrenders, and announced serious German defeats. Eisenhower ordered this faked news to panic German troops along the front, forcing them to retreat rather than defend their positions. The station advised civilians to remain in their homes rather than evacuate. Evacuating citizens, the station said, faced being shelled by both sides.

The Rhine crossing was followed by a succession of German defeats. As the German army faced successive defeats, Eisenhower ordered Radio 1212 to again change its programming. He wanted the station to broadcast that further resistance was suicidal, but differently than done by ABSIE, BBC, or Radio Luxemburg. Instead of calling for surrender as other Allied stations did, Eisenhower wanted Radio 1212 to stimulate revolts in Germany. To accomplish this, the black station announced the existence of a "New Germany" group, which it said had cells in every German city. At 2:30 a.m. on April 4, 1945, Annie's usual news broadcast was interrupted by a special announcement addressed to "New Germany" groups in Osnabrück, Hanover, Erfurt, and other cities. For the next two days, Radio 1212's broadcasts were consistently interrupted with instructions for the "New Germany" groups. To the group in Stuttgart, the station advised:

The SS has plans to destroy the last water and power installations. The Attack Division must prevent every piece of Party sabotage under any conditions. It must be explained to your fellow citizens that the enemy is not dependent upon our water systems and the Party sabotage only leads to damage to the Germans.[59]

On April 6, Radio 1212 issued its first call for revolt:

Germany, our fatherland, bleeds from a thousand wounds. In the long history of our people, a history full of fame and greatness but nonetheless a history of suffering and trials, there has never been a period when the foundations of the life of the German people were so seriously threatened as they are today. . . . For today, we know that the war is hopelessly lost. Our defense fronts are broken to pieces—pitiless and unopposed, the enemy air fleets are destroying our factories and homes. . . . The time for decision has definitely arrived, and nothing remains but the choice between complete destruction and immediate peace. But we must fight for this peace and we know that we can help Germnany only if we act and fight for peace. . . . Whoever stands in the way of this peace must be destroyed for the sake of Germany. The miserable Party, which we have served and for which we have made sacrifices for long, hard years and which has lied to us and deceived us as a reward, must be done away with.[60]

The call for revolt was read by a speaker previously unheard on Radio 1212. He was a German revolutionary known as "George," whose convictions made the speech one of the finest radio performances that Brewster Morgan, a long-time CBS radio producer, ever heard. After the speech, the announcer wept.

For three weeks Radio Annie issued instructions to "New Germany" groups during its broadcasts. The station said that members were to scratch out the second, fourth, and fifth letters of all signs bearing the Nazi party's initials. The Nazi party initials were NSDAP. After the letters were crossed out, all that remained was ND, the initials of Neues Deutschland. Occupation troops found posters in Germany that were altered in this manner, suggesting that some listeners obeyed the station's instructions. Radio 1212 also recommended that followers of the group issue leaflets calling for surrender. It reported faked incidents, where members of the group arrested or shot Nazi leaders. Some of the instructions were issued in a meaningless code to lend plausibility to the broadcasts. Five villages were successfully organized along the lines recommended by the station. The organization was so successful that the German army was unable to use them for rearguard actions. Interrogations after the war showed that the villages were organized by one "crackpot" insurance salesman. When interviewed, the salesman attributed his success to the fact that he could understand Annie's coded messages![61]

At the end of April, Eisenhower concluded that the station had outlived its usefulness, as Allied armies from the east and west were converging on Torgau in Saxony. After Eisenhower reached his decision, Radio 1212 started reporting that the Allied army was disturbingly close to its studio. On April 25, the date when the U.S. and Soviet armies met at Torgau, Radio 1212 signed off. Rather than simply disappearing or announcing that it was really an Allied station, a faked death was staged for Annie. After being on the air for a half-hour, the news broadcast was interrupted by shouting from English-speaking voices. Benno Frank called for someone to put on a record. There were sounds of wood cracking and splintering. Finally, Radio 1212's theme music was heard. In the middle of the record, the station fell silent. This was last time the station was heard. It died the same violent death as Gustav Siegfried Eins, but its death signaled the end of World War II in Europe.[62]

## ANOTHER SUCCESS?

Despite Radio 1212's contribution to the capture of German troops, reports of widespread listenership, and the existence of NSDAP posters altered according to the station's instructions, Sefton Delmer concluded that the station was an ineffective " 'black' soap opera." His critique was repeated by BBC employee Julian Hale in his book, *Radio Power*. According to Hale, Radio 1212 achieved some success as a "tactical station," but, like other U.S.-operated stations, was "crude" and easily identifiable as a fake.[63] Hale's report was undoubtedly based on Delmer's conclusion, as Delmer was one of the only sources that Hale cited on World War II clandestine stations. Basing the report on Delmer was a mistake, as Delmer confused Radio Annie with another U.S. operation. Delmer wrote:

Over one of the transmitters of Radio Luxemburg his men broadcast for a period of about a fortnight what was to all intents a 'black' soap opera—the drama of a Rhineland town which had revolted against Hitler and the SS and was now appealing over an army radio to the Americans to come in and rescue them. The Burgomaster of the town was the chief speaker.[64]

Radio 1212 broadcast for 127 successive nights, not two weeks as Delmer suggests. Although Annie broadcast to the Rhineland, it never featured the burgomaster of a town nor did it appeal for help from the U.S. army. What Delmer described as a soap opera was actually an indigenous clandestine station operated by the "Freedom and Reconstruction Movement of Bavaria"! This group led an anti-Nazi rebellion in Munich that was partially stimulated by a U.S.-operated clandestine station code-named "Operation Capricorn." Capricorn, while on the air only two months, was one of the most spectacular and successful operations of the war.

Unlike other Allied-operated clandestine stations, months of research went into the development of Operation Capricorn. The research team was headed by sociologist Howard Becker, who taught at the University of Wisconsin.[65] Delmer described Becker as "a tall, slow-spoken, Gary Cooperish" type.[66] Becker's OSS research team established that a revolutionary group composed of civilians and members of a specialized military unit existed in Munich, Bavaria. The group was anti-Communist, but democratic and socialist in orientation. OSS intelligence and German rumors also indicated that Hitler planned to withdraw to a Bavarian stronghold called the "Alpine Fortress" in the event of an Allied victory. From the fortress, Hitler intended to direct a guerrilla campaign against the occupation troops.[67] OSS decided to direct broadcasts to the Bavarian revolutionaries, urging them to revolt "at the right time." The right time was when Hitler was evacuated to his Bavarian fortress.

The revolutionaries in Munich were members of the "Freedom and Reconstruction Movement of Bavaria," which was headed by a Captain Gerngross. Members of the group who were well-known anti-Nazis were underground. Others circulated freely in Munich. Although intensely anti-Nazi, the Freedom and Reconstruction Movement did not participate in previous attempts such as the July 20th putsch to overthrow Hitler. Participants in previous actions like General Beck were authoritarian German nationalists who sought Hitler's ouster in order to secure a more favorable peace with the Allies. The Gerngross group differed from them: It sought a complete change in the structure of German society and politics.

Based on the intelligence profile of Gerngross and the Freedom and

Reconstruction movement, a fictitious personality named "Hagadorn" was created. Hagadorn, like Gerngross, was "ideologically consistent and a man of integrity."[68] He represented the best of German liberal traditions. "Hagadorn" became the speaker on a black radio station that operated between February 26 and April 27, 1945. Hagadorn was played by Stephen Schnabel, who worked as an announcer for Volkssender Drei and Operation Pancake programs on the Soldatensender. One ten-minute speech by Hagadorn was recorded daily and repeated every hour between 8:15 a.m. and 8:15 p.m.[69] The same writer penned every Hagadorn speech to assure tht he remained ideologically consistent. The broadcasts were made on short and medium wave from PWE transmitters in London. A 100-kilowatt transmitter was used for the daytime transmissions and a 7.5-kilowatt transmitter was used for nighttime transmissions.[70] The broadcasts were made on a frequency that was previously used by Germany but had become vacant as a result of Allied bombing.

Hagadorn reminded listeners of their responsibilities as revolutionaries. He discussed Germany's socialist traditions and its experience as a democracy before Hitler's ascendancy. He called for revolution but stressed: "Do not act until the Allied armies are close enough to join with you; do not attempt a Warsaw or a July 20th." Germany responded to the station with broadcasts denouncing it for "false and deceitful broadcasts." "Do not listen to him," the Deutschlandsender implored. On March 12, despite a shortage of transmitters, Germany started jamming Hagadorn's speeches. OSS responded by increasing the power of the broadcasts.[71]

After 61 days of continuous operation, Hagadorn went off the air, claiming that it was about to be "seized by American Forces."[72] It disappeared with a call to revolution. The following morning, April 28, Captain Gerngross's forces inaugurated broadcasts on 405 meters from a station announcing itself as the "Freiheitsaktion Bayern."[73] This Bavarian Freedom Station signaled the beginning of a revolt by the Freedom and Reconstruction Movement. Members of the organization seized the offices of the Nazi newspaper and barricaded themselves inside. Others seized Radio Munich. During its 7:30 a.m. broadcast, Radio Munich suddenly announced that its program was being interrupted for "technical reasons." Five minutes later, it returned to the air with a proclamation from the "Freedom Movement of Bavaria," which said:

Bavarians, the hour of freedom has struck! The clique of ruling Nazis has been arrested. People of Munich! Descend into the streets and spread this news to everyone you meet. Workers! Leave your factories. We appeal especially to Wehrmacht officers and soldiers to discontinue the slaughter....

After the proclamation, the station broadcast a statement attributed to the governor of Bavaria, Gen. Ritter von Epp, who was identified as the leader of the Bavarian Freedom Movement. Ritter von Epp was previously known as one of the staunchest supporters of the Nazi regime. The speaker quoted General von Epp as saying that others should rebel in "the name of humanity and common sense." In reality, von Epp was an opponent, not a supporter of the revolt. Gerngross arrested von Epp and brought him to the studio of Radio Munich. General von Epp was placed before the microphone, and with a gun at his head, told to broadcast a surrender statement to the Allies. He refused. The refusal was picked up by the microphone and broadcast over the station. Nazi listeners regained their courage after hearing von Epp and went on the offensive. At 11:45 a.m., Nazi loyalists stormed Radio Munich. The ensuing scuffle was picked up and broadcast by the station. Twenty-five minutes later, Paul Giesler, gauleiter of Bavaria, announced that the uprising had been crushed.[74]

Gerngross and members of his group who were not killed went into hiding. Gerngross surfaced after the Allies entered Munich and, along with other German officers, was interned. The Allied officers that arrested Gerngross incorrectly believed that he was "just another German" who now claimed to have opposed Hitler. While interned, he was interviewed by Howard Becker. When asked about the Hagadorn broadcasts, Gerngross said that he listened to them. He described the broadcasts as "marvelous" and suggested that Hagadorn might be an ideal leader for a new Germany. Gerngross added that his advice about waiting to revolt was heeded. He then complained about his captors, the blanket prohibitions against political organizing, and the presence of Nazi collaborators in the occupation administration. Gerngross pointed out that many of the administrators, while not Nazi party members, had been helpful and sympathetic to the Nazi cause. They were free, Gerngross lamented, but he was captive. A short time later, OSS secured his release.[75]

Operation Capricorn was only one of several clandestine stations that OSS hoped to operate in the beginning of 1945. The other stations were code-named "Woodland," "Rockpile," and "Patriot."[76] The proposed stations had poorly defined objectives and targets, and showed that members of OSS-MO had learned few if any lessons about clandestine radio despite several years of experience with the medium. Project Woodland was written in late fall 1944 by Howard Baldwin, who became Chief of Morale Operations for the European Theater after Rae Smith's resignation in September. Woodland proposed making daily 30-minute broadcasts to Austria. The broadcasts would feature three speakers: a Syrian school teacher who supported the partisan movement; a Catholic student who had joined the partisans; and the widow of a Wehrmacht officer who was disgusted by Nazi policies. Each speech would be separated by an Austrian folk song or Viennese tune. The station was to broadcast on shortwave three times a week from transmitters in Great Britain. The station's objectives were to encourage an independent Austrian state, support for a separate Austrian peace with the Allies, resistance against German troops, and support for partisan resistance.[77]

The Woodland plan was submitted to General McClure for approval in December. McClure endorsed the idea of a station directed at Austria, but wanted a more comprehensive plan. Woodland was targeted to all Austrians, not a narrowly defined and potentially vulnerable segment. It also featured three speakers whose presence on one station defied logic: a school teacher who supported but did not join the partisans, despite partisan activity in his area; a partisan who asked listeners but not the school teacher to join his movement; and a widow, who had no connection with the two other speakers. In February the plan was rewritten. The revised Woodland plan called for broadcasts of ten minutes duration, patterned after those of Hagadorn. Only one speaker was scheduled for each broadcast. Proposed speakers were anti-Nazi patriots, middle-class Catholics, and partisan supporters. No music would be aired by the station. The revised plan was submitted to McClure in March. The plan was approved with some reservations on March 23. Two weeks later, OSS abandoned the Woodland project because the Red Army entered Vienna and the complete occupation of Austria was imminent.[78]

Patriot and Rockpile were proposals that had as their objectives the heightening of hostility between the Wehrmacht and the SS. Patriot was a station ostensibly operated by a pro-Goering faction of the Nazi party. The proposed station claimed to be loyal to Hitler's principles but opposed to Heinrich Himmler, head of the SS. The station claimed that Himmler was seizing power from older, loyal National Socialists, whom Goering represented. What Hitler was doing during Himmler's seizure of power was never explained in the Patriot proposal. Rockpile claimed to be operated by a German army battalion in Yugoslavia that was abandoned by SS troops. The batalion successfully fought off an attack by Tito's partisans. It was without supplies and stranded. Despite repeated radio requests from the battalion, neither supplies nor reinforcements arrived. What did arrive were orders from Himmler to continue fighting despite unbeatable odds. Why Himmler rather than Hitler issued the instructions was never revealed by the proposal's author. These transmissions were targeted at the Wehrmacht. Patriot and Rockpile were submitted to General McClure on December 6, 1944. He rejected the Patriot broadcasts but approved Rockpile. OSS was ready to put Rockpile on the air at the end of January, but, by this time, Tito and the Red Army had virtually cleared Yugoslavia of German troops, rendering the broadcasts obsolete.[79] As a result of the failure to get these proposed stations on the air, OSS could list only four clandestine stations among its accomplishments in the European Theater: the Volkssender, "Beck," Radio 1212, and Hagadorn. While OSS-MO contributed programs to the Soldatensender, it was a British rather than OSS-sponsored station. The Volkssender was a failure and "Beck" made only one broadcast. Of the stations, only Radio 1212 and Hagadorn can be described as "successful."

## NOTES

1. Sefton Delmer, *Black Boomerang* (London: Secker & Warburg, 1962), pp. 75–76.

2. Richard Dunlop, *Donovan—America's Master Spy* (New York: Rand McNally & Company, 1982), p. 212.

3. Corey Ford, *Donovan of OSS* (Boston: Little, Brown & Company, 1970), p. 91.

4. "Memorandum of Establishment of Service of Strategic Information" (June 10, 1941), President's Secretary's File, *FDR*, box 141.

5. Edmond Taylor, *Awakening from History* (London: Chatto & Windus, 1971), p. 244; "ETO. MO War Diary," vol. 6, Basic Documents, *OSS*, entry 91, box 4; Delmer, *Black Boomerang*, pp. 214–15.

6. "ETO. MO War Diary," vol. 3, Radio, p. 12, *OSS*, entry 91, box 5, book 1; Kermit Roosevelt, ed., *War Report of the OSS (Office of Strategic Services)*, vol. 1 (New York: Walker & Company, 1976), p. 219; Anthony Cave Brown, ed., *The Secret War Report of the OSS* (New York: Berkley Publishing, 1976), pp. 109–10. The *War Report* uses the spelling "Muzac" rather than "Muzak." These are only two of several spellings.

7. "Muzak," History of OSS, vol. 6, *Donovan* box 99B, tab N.

8. Thomas O'Toole, " '44 Windfall Aided Allies in Battling Nazis," *Washington Post*, June 25, 1984, p. 9; "Muzak," History of OSS, vol. 6, *Donovan*, box 99B, tab N; "Pancake–Musak Project," General-MO-Europe, *OSS*, entry 99, box 69, folder 306.

9. "Musac Project," Wash. Hist. Office Op–23, *OSS*, entry 99, box 16, folder 67; Cave Brown, ed., *The Secret War Report of the OSS*, pp. 531–32; Kermit Roosevelt, ed., *The Overseas Targets: The War Report of the OSS*, vol. 2 (New York: Walker & Company, 1976), pp. 299–300. Delmer, *Black Boomerang*, pp. 84–85, reports the exact opposite of the OSS documents. Delmer reports that Marlene Dietrich was never informed of the purpose of the recordings.

10. "Muzak," History of OSS, *Donovan*, vol. 6, box 99B, tab N.

11. "ETO. MO War Diary," vol. 6, Basic Documents,*OSS*, entry 91, box 4; "Soldatensender," General-MO-Europe, *OSS*, entry 99, box 69, folder 306.

12. "ETO. MO War Diary," vol. 3, Radio, pp. 18–20, *OSS*, entry 91, box 5, book 2; Delmer, *Black Boomerang* pp. 89–90. Delmer (p. 90) reports that Agnes Bernelle "lost half her family in the gas chambers of Auschwitz."

13. Elizabeth P. MacDonald, *Undercover Girl* (New York: Macmillan Company, 1947), pp. 32–36.

14. "ETO. MO War Diary," vol. 3, Radio, p. 15, *OSS*, entry 91, box 5, book 1; "Report on MO/ETO—July 1944—January 1945" (February 3, 1945), ETO-MO-General, *OSS*, entry 99, box 16, folder 66.

15. Delmer, *Black Boomerang*, p. 84; Macdonald, *Undercover Girl*, p. 34.

16. "ETO. MO War Diary," vol. 3, Radio, pp. 27–57, *OSS*, entry 91, box 5, book 1.

17. "Letter from PWD/SHAEF to MO Branch/OSS" (September 11, 1944), War Diary, vol. 7, *OSS*, entry 91, box 4; "Radio Paris," Wash. Hist. Office Op–23, *OSS*, entry 99, box 16, folder 67. Although not mentioned by name in the broadcasts, the town selected for the "revolt" was Soest, thirty miles east of Dortman. William Necker, one of the station's operators, had an intimate knowledge of the town, according to "Letter from George Dibert to Rae Smith" (September 7, 1940), Radio, *OSS*, entry 148, box 81, folder 1180.

18. "Letter to Director, PWD/SHAEF" (September 7, 1944), General-MO-Europe, *OSS*, entry 99, box 69, folder 306; "ETO. MO War Diary," vol. 3, Radio, p. 31, *OSS*, entry 91, box 5, book 1.

19. "ETO. MO War Diary," vol. 6, Basic Documents, *OSS*, entry 91, box 4.

20. Necker was author of the following books: *Nazi Germany Can't Win* (London: L. Drummond, Ltd., 1939); *Hitler's War Machine and the Invasion of Britain* (London: L. Drummond, 1941); *The Germany Army of Today* (L. Drummond, 1943); and *Invasion Tactics Here and On the Continent* (London: Bernards, 1944). He also wrote "German Strategy," *Fortnightly*, August 1939, pp. 178–85.

21. As a result of his contacts with Erika Mann, Abraham Polonsky was introduced to her father. Polonsky discussed *Mario the Magician* with the famed novelist. It became Polonsky's life-long ambition to make the novel into a movie, according to Henry Ehrlich, "The Fall and Rise of Abraham Lincoln Polonsky," *Look*, June 16, 1970, p. 10T.

22. "ETO. MO War Diary," vol. 3, Radio, pp. 33, 41, *OSS*, entry 91, box 5, book 1.

23. "ETO. MO War Diary."

24. "Proposal for Black Broadcasting from the Continent," Radio, *OSS*, entry 148, box 81, folder 1180.

25. "Proposal for MO-OSS Radio Broadcasting Operation," Radio, *OSS*, entry 148, box 81, folder 1180.

26. Cave Brown, ed., *The Secret War Report of the OSS*, p. 536; "Radio Paris," General-MO-Europe, *OSS*, entry 99, box 69, folder 306.

27. "Letter to MO-OSS" (September 7, 1944), General-MO-Europe, entry 99, box 69, folder 306; "Letter from PWD/SHAEF to MO Branch/OSS" (September 11, 1944), War Diary, vol. 7, *OSS*, entry 91, box 4.

28. "ETO. MO War Diary," vol. 3, Radio, p. 35, *OSS*, entry 91, box 5, book 1.

29. "ETO. MO War Diary," vol. 3, Radio, p. 47, *OSS*, entry 99, box 6, book 2; " 'General' Defies Nazi Fight Order," *New York Times*, October 23, 1944, p. 3.

30. Cave Brown, ed., *The Secret War Report of the OSS*, p. 536; Roosevelt, ed., *The Overseas Targets*, p. 300; " 'General' Defies Nazi Fight Order," *New York Times*, ibid.; " 'General' Says He Leads Nazi Soldiers Home," *Chicago Tribune*, September 23, 1944, p. 2. Other newspaper reports are listed in "Comebacks," General-MO-Europe, *OSS*, entry 99, box 69, folder 306.

31. "ETO. MO War Diary," vol. 3, Radio, p. 41, *OSS*, entry 91, book 5, book 1; "PID Research Units," Part 2, *PRO*, FO898/52.

32. "ETO. MO War Diary," vol. 3, Radio, pp. 119–32, *OSS*, entry 91, box 6,

book 2; "Radio Paris," Wash. Hist. Office Op–23, *OSS*, entry 99, box 16, folder 67.

33. The Alpine Fortress rumor might have been started by the Uberkommando der Wehrmacht (High Command of the German Armed Forces) to make the Allies believe that a secret plan existed for continuing the war after an Allied occupation. If believed, the Allies might settle for a negotiated settlement rather than unconditional surrender.

34. "ETO. MO War Diary," vol. 3, Radio, pp. 44–45, *OSS*, entry 91, box 5, book 1; "More Comebacks from Major John Harris" (November 1, 1944), General-MO-Europe, *OSS*, entry 99, box 69, folder 306.

35. "Memo from Siegfried Wagener to Mr. Baldwin and Major Dibert" (October 7, 1944), Radio, *OSS*, entry 148, box 81, folder 1180.

36. Wagener's complaints probably fell on deaf ears, as Howard Baldwin and George Dibert were both former "ad men," whose livelihoods before the war depended on their ability to use "Hollywood theatrics." Smith worked as advertising manager for the *New Yorker*; Dibert worked for J. Walter Thompson, an advertising agency. Baldwin's "Woodland" proposal, discussed later in this chapter, provides evidence that his understanding of the purposes of black radio was, at best, superficial.

37. "ETO. MO War Diary," vol. 3, Radio, pp. 119–20, *OSS*, entry 91, box 6, book 1.

38. Paley was acting as chief spokesman for OWI on the PWD/SHAEF planning board because C. D. Jackson "refused to participate in the direction of daily policy toward Germany, because he felt he did not know enough," according to Daniel Lerner, *Sykewar: Psychological Warfare Against Germany* (Cambridge, Mass.: MIT Press, 1971 reprint), p. 89.

39. "Memo to: PWD/SHAEF from 12th Army Group" (November 15, 1944), "Proposed Covert Tactical Broadcasts to Troops and Civilians in the Rhineland," Radio, *OSS*, entry 99, box 15, folder 65b.

40. "ETO. War Diary," vol. 3, Radio, pp. 42–43, *OSS*, entry 91, box 5, book 1.

41. Delmer, *Black Boomerang*, p. 214, reports that Polonsky and Howard Becker not only proposed but operated this black station. The assertion is incorrect. Becker neither proposed nor worked on Operation Joker, for he did not join OSS until August 21, 1944, after the plan was developed. Becker worked on Operation Capricorn, which started broadcasting in February 1945.

42. Heilig was actually Austrian, not German. "ETO. MO War Diary," vol. 6, Basic Documents, *OSS*, entry 91, box 4.

43. "ETO. MO War Diary," vol. 3, Radio, pp. 203–05, *OSS*, entry 91, box 6, book 2.

44. "The General Beck Broadcast," General-MO-Europe, *OSS*, entry 99, box 69, folder 306.

45. "ETO. MO War Diary," vol. 3, Radio, pp. 189–90, *OSS*, entry 91, box 6, book 2.

46. Cave Brown, ed., *The Secret War Report of the OSS*, p. 537; "Anti-Nazi Black Broadcasts in German," Wash. Hist. Office Op–23, *OSS*, entry 99, box 16, folder 67; " 'Dead' Nazi Chief Fans Rebellion," *Detroit Free Press*, November 1, 1944, p. 1; " 'Gen. Beck' Urges Reich to Revolt Against Hitler," *Philadelphia*

*Inquirer,* November 1, 1944, p. 1; "Mystery of Broadcast by 'Gen. Beck,' " London *Evening Standard* (late edition) November 1, 1944, p. 1; "Reich Called to Revolt," *Daily Mail,* November 1, 1944, p. 1. *Nachrichten für die Truppe* was a grey newspaper published by the Allies. *Nachrichten* is discussed by Delmer, *Black Boomerang,* p. 146, 147, 162–64, 170; Cave Brown, ed., *The Secret War Report of the OSS,* pp. 538–39; Roosevelt, ed., *The Overseas Targets,* p. 301.

47. "Report on MO/ETO—July 1944—January 1945" (February 3, 1945, ETO-MO-General, OSS, entry 99, box 16, folder 66; Delmer, *Black Boomerang,* p. 215.

48. "Memo to: PWD/SHAEF from 12th Army Group" (November 15, 1944), "Proposed Covert Tactical Broadcasts to Troops and Civilians in the Rhineland," Radio, OSS, entry 99, box 15, folder 65b; The Psychological Warfare Division Supreme Headquarters Allied Expeditionary Force, *An Account of its Operations in the Western European Campaign 1944–1945* (Bad Homburg, Germany: SHAEF, October 1945), pp. 39–40; Edward M. Kirby and Jack W. Harris, "Surrender of the Italian Fleet—1943," in W. E. Daugherty with Morris Janowitz, eds., *A Psychological Warfare Casebook* (Baltimore: Johns Hopkins University Press, 1958), p. 385.

49. Hale's description of the operation of Radio Luxemburg can be found in "Big Noise in Little Luxemburg," *Harpers,* April 1945, pp. 377–84.

50. The Psychological Warfare Division Supreme Headquarters Allied Expeditionary Force, *An Account of its Operation in the Western European Campaign 1944–1945,* p. 41.

51. Anthony Cave Brown, *Wild Bill Donovan, The Last Hero* (New York: Times Books, 1982), p. 551; Roosevelt, ed., *The Overseas Targets,* p. 301; Cave Brown, ed., *The Secret War Report of the OSS,* pp. 537–38; "Covert Operation of Radio Luxemburg," Annex F, "Memo to the Chief, P & PW Division, 12 AG from Robert McClure" (December 5, 1944), Radio, OSS, entry 99, box 15, folder 65b; H. H. Burger, "Operation Annie: Now it Can be Told," *New York Times Magazine,* February 17, 1946, pp. 12–13, 48, 50.

52. "Annie Script" (January 20, 1945), Annex G, pp. 5–6, Radio, OSS, entry 99, box 15, folder 65b. Benno Frank served as announcer for other psychwar broadcasts, including the broadcasts discussed by David Hertz, "The Radio Siege of Lorient," in Daugherty with Janowitz, ed., *A Psychological Warfare Casebook,* pp. 386–87.

53. "First Reactions to 'Annie,' " Annex H, p. 3, Radio, OSS, entry 99, box 15, folder 65b.

54. The Atlantiksender team also had access to and used reports from the DNB wireless, according to Delmer, *Black Boomerang,* p. 90.

55. Brewster Morgan, "Operation Annie," *Saturday Evening Post,* March 9, 1946, pp. 18–19, 121–24.

56. "First Reactions to 'Annie,' " Annex H, p. 1, Radio, OSS, entry 99, box 15, folder 65b.

57. "First Reactions to 'Annie,' " p. 6. A survey conducted in the Rhine immediately after the occupation found that 57 of 160 (35.6 percent) Germans surveyed listened to Radio Annie, according to "Poll of Germans Finds War Guilt on Nazis, Blames Leaders for Prolonging Conflict," *New York Times,* March 15, 1945, p. 2.

58. Burger, "Operation Annie: Now it Can be Told," p. 50.

59. "Annie Script" (April 6, 1945), Annex I, p. 23, Radio, *OSS*, entry 99, box 15, folder 65b. OSS-MO and OWI, with assistance from PWE, published a newspaper, *Das Neue Deutschland*, that claimed to originate from the same group. See "Das Neue Deutschland," Wash-MO-Exhibits, *OSS*, entry 99, box 75, folder 32. The OWI representative on the New Germany planning board was Hans Speier, author of "Nazi Propaganda and its Decline," *Social Research* 10 (September 1943), pp. 337–57; "War Aims in Political Warfare," *Social Research* 12 (May 1945), pp. 157–80; "The Future of Psychological Warfare," *Public Opinion Quarterly* 12 (Spring 1948), pp. 5–18; "Goebbels' Diaries," *Public Opinion Quarterly* 12 (Fall 1948), pp. 500–5; *Social Order and the Risks of War: Papers in Political Sociology* (Cambridge, Mass.: MIT Press, 1964); and several other works on psychwar.

60. "Annie Script," Annex J, pp. 3–4, Radio, *OSS*, entry 99, box 15, folder 65b. Part of the script is reproduced in Morgan, "Operation Annie," p. 123.

61. Howard Becker, "The Nature and Consequences of Black Propaganda," *American Sociological Review* 14 (April 1949), p. 231. This article is reproduced in part in Daugherty with Janowitz, eds., *A Psychological Warfare Casebook*, pp. 672–77.

62. Burger, "Operation Annie: Now it Can be Told," p. 50; Morgan, "Operation Annie," p. 124.

63. Julian Hale, *Radio Power* (London: Paul Elek, 1975) p. 107.

64. Delmer, *Black Boomerang*, p. 215. There is a slight possibility that Delmer was not describing a real operation, but a plan developed by OSS in October 1944. The plan was called the "Officers' Revolt Campaign." This black station was to broadcast from Radio Paris, but claimed to be coming from somewhere in Bavaria. One of the station's speakers was to be "General von Epp." This station never operated, but its operational plan was very similar to the real clandestine station that broadcast from Munich, which was operated by the "Freedom and Reconstruction Movement of Bavaria." The Officers' Revolt Plan is discussed in "Uprising in Tyrol," Project ETO, *OSS*, entry 139, box 177. The similarity between this plan and the actual German broadcasts is absolutely astounding.

65. Becker was author, coauthor or editor of the following books: *Through Values to Social Interpretation* (Durham, N.C.: Duke University Press, 1950); *Social Thought from Lore to Science* (Washington, D.C.: Harren Press, 1952); *Contemporary Social Theory* (New York: Appleton-Century Company, 1940); *Family, Marriage and Parenthood* (Boston: D. C. Heath, 1948); and *German Youth: Bond or Free* (London: Kegan Paul, Trench, Trubner & Company, 1946).

66. Delmer, *Black Boomerang* p. 214, erroneously reported that Becker worked on Operation Joker. In addition, Delmer confused the Waffen SS Station (Kampfgruppe Yorck, Code "G10") with Operation Capricorn, whose speaker was Hagadorn. The Waffen SS station is mentioned in "Policy and Methods of Black Propaganda Against Germany" (November 10, 1944), Wash. Hist. Office Op–23, *OSS*, entry 99, box 17, folder 80; Cave Brown, ed., *The Secret War Report of the OSS*, p. 528; and Ellic Howe, *The Black Game* (London: Michael Joseph, 1982), p. 272. Hagadorn was given the designation "U1" by PWE. The "U" referred to "United States Operation." Delmer, pp. 187–90, described Hagadorn (sic) as a

genuine Waffen SS officer who deserted. This was the announcer on G10, not Operation Capricorn. Hagadorn was played by OSS-MO civilian Stephen Schnabel. Lt. John Reinhardt, who worked on Volkssender Drei and Radio 1212, was in charge of the Capricorn operation, according to "MO Branch—Progress Report" (April 16, 1945), Progress Reports, *OSS*, entry 148, box 81, folder 1168.

67. As mentioned in note 33, the Alpine Fortress was believed by some in OSS to be German disinformation. If the reports were not just rumor, but true, OSS was prepared to operate a black station purporting to emanate from Hitler's Bavarian retreat. The plan was code-named "Hannibal." The announcer of the proposed station was to be "Adolph Hitler"! See "Hannibal," Project ETO, *OSS*, entry 139, box 175.

68. Becker, "The Nature and Consequences of Black Propaganda," p. 231.

69. "MO Branch—Progress Report" (April 30, 1945), Progress Reports, *OSS*, entry 148, box 81, folder 1168.

70. The 100-kilowatt transmitter was not used for the Hagadorn broadcasts until mid-March. "MO Branch—Progress Report" (March 15, 1945, Progress Reports, *OSS*, entry 148, box 81, folder 1168; "Black Radio 'Capricorn,' " General-MO-Europe, *OSS*, entry 99, box 69, folder 306; "Capricorn," Wash. Hist. Office Op–23, *OSS*, entry 99, box 16, folder 67.

71. "PID Research Units," P. 2, *PRO*, FO898/52; "MO Branch—Progress Report" (March 15, 1945), Progress Reports, *OSS*, entry 148, box 81, folder 1168.

72. Becker, "The Nature and Consequences of Black Propaganda," p. 232 incorrectly reports that the station signed off on April 20, seven days before it really disappeared.

73. "PID Research Units," P. 2, *PRO*, FO 898/52.

74. "Reich Army Rebels," *New York Times*, April 29, 1945, pp. 1, 10.

75. Howard P. Becker, *German Youth: Bond or Free* (London: Kegan Paul, Trench, Trubner & Company, 1946), pp. 259–66; "MO Branch —Progress Report" (June 30, 1945), Progress Reports, *OSS*, entry 148, box 81, folder 1168; "Comeback on Radio 'Capricorn' (Hagadorn)," General-MO-Europe, *OSS*, entry 99, box 69, folder 306.

76. Several other plans were developed and approved, but not implemented. They include the "Hamilton" plan and "Matchbox." Matchbox was designed with the assistance of PWE, but was terminated when the Allies moved into Germany.

77. "Memo from Howard Baldwin to Director PWD/SHAEF" (undated), "Memo from PWD/SHAEF to Chief, MO Branch-OSS" (March 19, 1945), "Letter from Robert McClure to Chief, MO Branch-OSS" (March 23, 1945), Project Woodlands, *OSS*, entry 139, box 174; "MO Branch—Progress Report" (December 31, 1944), Progress reports, *OSS*, entry 148, box 81, folder 1168.

78. "MO Branch—Progress Report" (April 16, 1945), Progress reports, *OSS*, entry 148, box 81, folder 1168.

79. "MO Radio Project 'Patriot' " (December 6, 1944), "MO Radio Project 'Rockpile' " (December 6, 1944), Project-ETO-Patriot, *OSS*, entry 139, box 174; "MO Branch—Progress Report" (January 15, 1945), Progress reports, *OSS*, entry 148, box 81, folder 1168.

# 5

## OSS IN ASIA: PLANS AND OPERATIONS

It was Wild Bill Donovan's intention to have detachments of the Office of Strategic Services (OSS) in Asia early in the war, even though the primary attention of the Allies at the moment was Europe. A Coordinator of Information (COI) office was opened in Honolulu within a month of the bombing of Pearl Harbor. Two months later, Donovan dispatched professor Esson Gale to China, where he was instructed to "improvise an underground apparatus." Professor Gale had years earlier worked in China for the Salt Revenue Administration, a taxation agency of Chiang Kai-shek's government.[1] In July 1942, a team of guerrillas under Major Carl Eifler embarked for India. These guerrillas became known as Detachment 101 and organized the Kachins and other Burmese into effective guerrilla fighting units. The OSS planning group was also at work, developing programs for the Pacific and China.[2]

Two things, however, prohibited Donovan from placing more OSS personnel in Asia: one, a shortage of skilled personnel, and two, the refusal of both General MacArthur and Admiral Nimitz to allow OSS into their theaters. Donovan's answer to the first problem was to recruit people who already had the skills for which OSS was looking. For Morale Operations (MO), this meant finding people who had worked at advertising agencies, radio stations, or newspapers, or who were lawyers. Donovan believed that attorneys, particularly corporate attorneys, had the training and discipline to do almost any job. This method of recruiting personnel created problems, as attorneys were usually given the positions of command. With their conservatism and penchant for procedure, they usually stifled the creativity of the personnel they commanded.

The problems that mixing attorneys and copywriters created were small compared to the problems created by the decisions of MacArthur and Nimitz to keep OSS out of the Pacific. Although MacArthur had no personal animosity toward Donovan, he never believed that an intelligence organization outside the military was needed and he obsessively objected to any interference in his theater, even by the president. Nimitz' objections to OSS were different: he had little respect for the organization. Despite his antipathy for OSS, Nimitz allowed OSS onto Saipan during the waning months of the war where a clandestine station was established that broadcast to Japan.[3]

Barred from the Pacific theater, Donovan tried to place OSS personnel in the China-Burma-India theater and in Southeast Asia. In India, the British severely restricted OSS activities, accurately believing that many OSS personnel were hostile to British colonialism in the region. When Lord Mountbatten was selected as supreme allied commander for Southeast Asia, Donovan did his best to convince Mountbatten to accept OSS personnel. Donovan's technique for persuading Mountbatten included getting him the best tickets for a sold-out performance of *Oklahoma!*, taking him "on the town" in New York, and flattering him. Donovan sent Hollywood director John Ford to Southeast Asia to film Mountbatten's adventures, hoping this would warm Mountbatten toward OSS.[4]

Donovan made repeated attempts to place OSS in China. While General Joseph Stilwell did not bar OSS from operating in China, he did nothing to promote its presence in his theater, either. The military situation in China also limited Donovan's options. By mid–1942, the Japanese had taken the coastal areas of China and cut the Burmese land route from India, allowing entrance to unoccupied China only by flying over the Himalayas (or the "hump"). This route led to Chungking, where Chiang Kai-shek established his Kuomintang capital. Chungking posed a problem rather than a solution for Donovan and OSS, as Chiang and his warlord allies were less interested in fighting the Japanese than they were in stockpiling weapons for use in an eventual showdown with Mao Tse-tung's "bandit" army. Further, if OSS were allowed to operate freely in Kuomintang China, it might provoke the Japanese or, worse yet, expose the fact that Chiang had no interest in engaging Japan. None of these possibilities made Chiang favorable toward OSS.[5]

Professor Gale, who arrived in China in March 1942, aroused Chiang's suspicion not only because he represented an intelligence-gathering agency but because he was a boastful socializer. Gale often dined and drank with old friends and told them he was on a secret mission for the U.S. government. Not even the U.S. ambassador to China, Clarence Gauss, trusted Gale, although the professor was never aware of this. He believed that things were going well.[6] Donovan eventually realized that he had sent the wrong man to China. He then enlisted Alghan Lusey, a former UPI correspondent who was also in China representing Donovan, to do what Gale had failed to do—procure an agreement with Chiang that would allow OSS to operate in China.

Lusey developed a close friendship with Captain Milton "Mary" Miles. Miles arrived in China in March 1942 as head of Naval Group China. The purpose of the Naval Group was to collect maritime intelligence and weather information. Miles was assigned the task of establishing a coastal surveillance team that would report on the activities and locations of Japanese vessels. Before leaving for China, Miles learned that his chief contact there would be Tai Li, director of the Bureau of Intelligence and Statistics and Chiang's trusted subordinate. In preparation for his mission, Miles researched Tai Li and discovered that the Bureau of Intelligence and Statistics was really a secret police force engaged in terror, murder, and extortion. Tai Li was known as the "Chinese Himmler" and his bureau as the "Chinese Gestapo." While initially repulsed by the revelations, Miles was later fascinated. After meeting Tai Li, his fascination turned to friendship. Miles became convinced that Tai Li was not a cut-throat, but the victim of Communist character assassination.[7]

Miles suggested to Lusey that OSS's best chance of entering China would be by joining a "friendship organization" that he was proposing to Washington and Tai Li. Although he had reservations about the organization, Lusey nevertheless returned to Washington in July 1942 and communicated Miles's plan to the Navy Department and OSS. Lusey reported to Donovan that Tai Li's organization was composed of cut-throats, but that an alliance with it might be productive.[8]

When Miles proposed the friendship society to Lusey, he had no intention of doing so to bolster the OSS presence in China. His intention was to develop an organization that would benefit the Navy and the "Chinese Himmler," not OSS. OSS was included in the plan to make it more palatable to Washington, place more resources at Tai Li's disposal, and provide a structure that legitimized restrictions on OSS activities. Not realizing Miles's or Tai Li's intentions and fearing that a failure to sign the friendship agreement would preclude OSS from operating in China, Donovan endorsed the plan. In April 1943, a pact creating the Sino-American Cooperation Organization (SACO) was signed. The agreement made Tai Li director of SACO and Miles its deputy director. In addition, Miles was appointed Far Eastern chief of OSS. The agreement's provisions made SACO independent of the U.S. theater commander in China and arranged for supplies to be distributed to Tai Li through the Navy rather than lend-lease. In practice, it barred OSS from effectively operating in China.

Miles accepted the post of OSS area chief so that he could use the organization's contacts and supplies to enhance Tai Li's power while simultaneously restraining OSS personnel. Miles established a police training school with a staff of fifty instructors from the Federal Bureau of

Investigation, the Secret Service, the Narcotics Bureau, and the New York Bomb Squad to teach Tai Li's agents how to use modern investigative techniques such as police dogs and lie detectors. By the end of 1943, large shipments of supplies were being flown over the hump and placed at Tai Li's disposal. Tai Li and Miles also used SACO to keep OSS from making contact with China's real fighting force—Mao's guerrilla army. Finally, the SACO agreement required that all intelligence gathering and subversive warfare activities, including psychological operations, be arranged through Tai Li. While the United States supplied funds and equipment for such operations, it was Tai Li who controlled them and had veto power. This assured that only operations that enhanced Chiang's and Tai Li's positions were approved.[9]

Believing that the SACO agreement opened the door to OSS operations in Asia, OSS started developing plans for psychological warfare there. A group consisting of experienced media personnel and attorneys was formed. The group contained Lts. Gordon Auchincloss and James Withrow, who reported to the Far East area operations officer for MO, Major Herbert Little. Auchincloss had been a writer/director on "Your Hit Parade" and other radio programs with Lord & Thomas Advertising for six years. In April 1943, while an independent producer, he was recruited to OSS by J. Walter Thompson's chief copywriter, Bill Griffin. In July Auchincloss received his clearance. In August, he completed training and was assigned the task of developing strategies for black radio. His title was chief of black radio operations, Far East. In November 1943, he became acting head of MO, Chungking.

James Withrow was a young attorney in Donovan's law firm who was asked by Wild Bill to investigate the legality of President Roosevelt's transferral of war equipment to Great Britain in 1940 without certification. In three days, Withrow found sufficient precedents and unrepealed statutes that enabled Donovan to submit a report to the president recommending the transfer. The statutes that Withrow uncovered were the legal bases for the lend-lease program.[10] Withrow was recruited into OSS by Donovan and made a lieutenant and assistant Far East operations officer (morale operations), even though he had no prior Asia or media training. He eventually replaced Herb Little, also an attorney, as operations officer for MO-Far East and by the end of the war had been operations officer for three theaters in the Pacific and two on the mainland.

Others who joined the morale operations staff for the Asia theaters were William Morwood, John Zuckerman, George Dibert, and Bogart Carlaw. Morwood worked as a radio writer before the war and applied for duty in OSS in late 1942. By the time that Morwood was accepted in OSS, he had been drafted and completed basic training. Transferred to morale operations as a conscript rather than an officer, Morwood was assigned implementation duties and excluded from making policy decisions.[11] John Zuckerman was a former member of OSS's Communications branch who had worked for a summer at Chicago radio station WGN. He was recruited into MO in July 1944 by Auchincloss. Between April and August 1945, Zuckerman operated "Voice of the People," the clandestine station that broadcast to Japan from Saipan. George Dibert was a media director at J. Walter Thompson before joining OSS. He was assigned to MO's Far East branch in Washington after "Marigold" and "Collingwood" were established. In August 1944, he was appointed deputy chief of MO for the European theater, where he supervised the black "General Beck" broadcast that was code-named "Operation Joker." Bogart Carlaw had worked with Auchincloss at Lord & Thomas before the war. Carlaw became production chief-Central Pacific at Collingwood in August 1944 after Dibert's departure. Production chief was equivalent to being a radio station program director.[12]

Marigold was the code-name of a special unit for the preparation of written and recorded Japanese subversive materials. The unit was established in February 1944 and located just off Madison Avenue in a New York City loft. The unit was manned by Japanese personnel and operated under special security regulations. The productions at Marigold were prepared from monitored Japanese broadcasts, magazines and newspapers, and captured letters. A secondary purpose of this project was to train Japanese artists, translators, writers, and broadcasters for future overseas assignments. In June, a second unit was established at the Collingwood estate near Washington. Collingwood was used as a dormitory, MO print shop and black radio training center. The center's students were recruited from relocation centers by Bruce Rogers, who spoke Japanese. Mostly first-generation Japanese, or issei, were recruited, as the language abilities of nisei were not considered good enough for the projects. The Japanese were taught recording and broadcast skills by Bogart Carlaw at an imitation radio station at the unit. None of the black materials produced at these sites were ever aired, however, as they were very dated by the time that OSS finally got into action in the Far East. By the end of August, thirty Japanese were working at Marigold and Collingwood. In October, the Secret Service learned of the Collingwood operation and, for security reasons, did not want Japanese near Washington, so in December the unit was dissolved.[13]

## THE BEST LAID SCHEMES O' DONOVAN

The first radio project of MO-Far East was the "North Pacific Plan." By the time Auchincloss joined the MO group, the plan was already on Donovan's desk. It was designed by Herbert Hilscher, an Alaskan journalist in MO, and quickly forwarded to Donovan by Herb Little. The plan called for placing transmitters aboard fishing boats, and from the shipboard transmitters operating "freedom stations." The ships were to move to different locations within a range of one to three hundred miles of Attu, the westernmost of the Aleutian islands that Japan occupied until May 1943. The mediumwave broadcasts were to be directed at the "thousands of Japanese operating off the eastern coast of Kamchatka and the Kurile islands." Mediumwave rather than shortwave was selected for use because intelligence indicated that there were only about 500 shortwave receivers in all of Japan and these were in the hands of the elite, while there were around 5,500,000 mediumwave receivers. Mediumwave signals required that the transmitter be placed near the target population, which is why shipboard transmitters were selected for the project. Signals from the five-kilowatt transmitter that was available could not reach Japanese-held territory from Alaska or other parts of North America.[14]

The transmitters were to broadcast programs for three freedom stations. One station claimed to be operated by stranded fishermen, another by a group of marooned naval officers, and a third by spokesmen for political or religious groups who, as the war progressed, realized that only bankers and industrialists were benefiting from the war. The three stations were loosely patterned after what MO personnel knew about "Gustav Siegfried Eins." The stations were to represent themselves as "pro-Japanese, sincerely professing loyalty to the Emperor with sufficient criticism of the United States to insure receptivity to Japanese listeners." The broadcasts were to be supplemented with messages placed in bottles and released in ocean currents that would take them into waters frequented by Japanese fishermen where, it was hoped, the bottles would get caught in fishing nets, brought aboard and read, or washed ashore on a Japanese beach, where an unsuspecting civilian would find the bottle, remove the note, read it, believe it, and spread the note's message as a rumor![15]

The plan was neither thought out nor fleshed out before it was submitted to Donovan for approval. Scripts for the broadcasts had not even been written. When Auchincloss joined the MO group, his first assignment was to write scripts for two stations: the one purporting to originate with stranded fishermen and the other from marooned officers. This he did. The fishermen script called for the station to appear on a frequency used by a Japanese radio station that signed off for the night. Seconds after the Japanese station signed off, a voice would faintly say, "Don't go away!" As the volume increased, the voice would continue: "We want to talk to you. Listen to us. We're lost." When the volume reached its full strength, a speaker would commence: "We've been sitting on this island for more than two months waiting for something to happen—and still no navy." The stranded Japanese speaker, while failing to see any of his fellow countrymen in uniform, reported seeing five American planes in two weeks. From this he concluded that the Japanese were running the war improperly. If current leaders continued to direct Japan's war effort, it would surely lose the war, he said.[16]

Even with a script, there wasn't much that could be done with the plan. The premise that Japanese fishermen were found by the thousands near Kamchatka was unfounded; purse seiners were too small to accommodate a transmitter, power generator, and other needed equipment, and were too slow to escape from a pursuing Japanese ship; and the ships could be too easily located by the Japanese using triangulation techniques and then attacked. The plan also failed to take into consideration that the broadcasting vessels would need protection. The portion dealing with notes in bottles was simply far-fetched. All of these objections led to the scrapping of the plan and the conclusion that some method other than ship-based transmitters would have to be used for making broadcasts to the Japanese.[17] The idea of placing messages in bottles was completely discarded. Nonetheless, Hilscher's general idea was the basis for all other north Pacific plans that were hatched.

The first radio plan of MO-Far East was so poorly developed that it was decided to send Gordon Auchincloss to Great Britain for training under Sefton Delmer. Auchincloss arrived in London in October, at which time "Gustav Siegfried Eins" and the "Atlantiksender" were operating. (Gustav Siegfried Eins was terminated on November 18, 1943, after Auchincloss arrived.) He joined several other members of OSS-MO, who came to London following the creation of MO's European theater branch in June. Also there were Fred Oechsner, head of MO, and Oliver H. P. Garrett, the Hollywood scriptwriter from PWB who worked a few months before on the north African-based clandestine station, "Radio Italo Balbo." In London, Auchincloss learned what effective freedom stations were and, most importantly, the role of research in developing plans and scripts. By the end of December, Auchincloss finished his training and returned to the United States.[18]

While Auchincloss was studying under Delmer in England, Donovan was making his way to Chungking. In August, Donovan decided that Miles's appointment as OSS China chief was a mistake. Miles was not only restricting the actions of OSS, but making sure that all intelligence sent to Washington came from Tai Li's men. Important intelligence was withheld, while distorted intelligence was sent. An agreement that was reached between Herb Little and Tai Li had also been abandoned. Little flew to Chungking a few months earlier than Donovan and signed an agreement with Tai Li, allowing for MO personnel to be sent to China, where they would work on projects, including black radio, with the

Chinese. Little extracted the agreement out of Tai Li after threatening that he would return to Washington and recommend that the "whole question of U.S. aid to China be reviewed."[19]

The agreement that Little worked out with Tai Li was very general, stipulating that "a joint Chinese-OSS Psychological Warfare organization should be established with . . . the Director to be appointed by the Chinese Government and the Deputy Director to be appointed by OSS." The objectives of the organization were to contribute "to the collapse of the puppet and Japanese regimes" and the "discrediting [of] Japan's co-prosperity sphere in China." The methods that were agreed upon to achieve these objectives included misleading leaflets, counterfeit newspapers, anonymous letters and "radio broadcasts pretending to emanate from Japan or Japanese controlled sources." After returning to the United States, Little decided that the agreement's lack of specificity gave Tai Li too many escape clauses. He asked Carl Hoffman, the Far Eastern theater officer who in 1944 became SO chief, to conduct additional negotiations in Chungking that would solidify MO's position in China. Little wanted Hoffman to negotiate another agreement that was "specific on all important points," including finances, material, media and personnel. Little even wanted terms like "freedom stations" and "morale subversion" to be clearly defined.[20] This agreement was never negotiated, as Donovan flew to China to do "negotiating" of his own.

Donovan was emboldened to challenge Tai Li and Miles after Lord Mountbatten was appointed supreme allied commander for Southeast Asia at the end of 1943. The new theater commander agreed to accept OSS personnel, which meant that OSS, even if evicted from China, would still have bases in Asia. After meeting in Cairo with Roosevelt before the Teheran conference, Donovan flew to India and then to China for a showdown with Miles and Tai Li. He arrived in Chungking on December 2. After a dinner party attended by U.S. Ambassador Patrick Hurley and General Albert Wedemeyer, Donovan informed Tai Li that OSS was going to operate in China with or without his help. When Tai Li smiled and responded that if this were to happen, OSS agents might be killed, Donovan responded that Tai Li's threats wouldn't deter him. Donovan reportedly added: "For every one of our agents you kill, we will kill one of your generals." That was language that Tai Li understood and respected. He agreed to let OSS operate in China. Donovan then took Miles to task. Donovan accused Miles of sabotaging OSS activities. Not denying the charge, Miles said that OSS had violated the SACO agreement. He added: "I quit." Donovan responded: "You can't quit. You're fired." Donovan appointed Colonel John Coughlin as Miles's replacement. Coughlin had previously served in Burma with Eifler's Detachment 101.[21]

Skeptical of Tai Li's willingness to implement the agreements that were reached, Donovan conferred with General Claire Chennault before leaving Chungking. Chennault commanded the only U.S. combat force in China, the Fourteenth USAAF. Chennault arrived in China as Chiang's air advisor before the United States entered the war. After Japan invaded the Chinese mainland, Chennault organized a volunteer force of American pilots that became known as the Flying Tigers. When the United States entered the war after Pearl Harbor, the Flying Tigers were incorporated into the U.S. Army as the Fourteenth Air Force.

Donovan proposed to Chennault that OSS work with his command, collecting intelligence and operating a propaganda unit to encourage Chinese peasants in occupied areas to rescue and return downed U.S. airmen. The proposed intelligence force would supply Chennault with information on strategic bombing targets. Chennault accepted Donovan's offer, which was made official four months later with the activation of a new unit called the 5329th Air and Ground Forces Resources and Technical Staff (AGFRTS), popularly known as "Ag-farts." AGFRTS became OSS's cover for collecting intelligence outside of SACO. After completing his discussions with Chennault, Donovan left China for Moscow, believing that the way had been cleared for OSS to swing into action.

Auchincloss worked on black radio projects, taught classes in subversive warfare, and experimented with "sonic warfare" after returning to Washington from England. The sonic warfare experiments were conducted with Bill Morwood, but they never got further than the experimental stage. Sonic warfare was the use of sound effects to demoralize the enemy. The first black radio project on which Auchincloss worked was called the "Vega project." Vega was a derivation of the original North Pacific plan. It proposed placing a 7.5-kilowatt shortwave transmitter on Kiska rather than using shipboard mediumwave transmitters. The targets of the proposed Vega broadcasts were Japanese occupation troops and fishermen. Although the number of shortwave receivers on Japan was too small to make black shortwave broadcasts to Japan worthwhile, it was believed that most Japanese fishing and naval vessels were equipped with shortwave receivers. Intelligence also indicated that Japanese troops in Korea, Manchukuo, and occupied China were given shortwave receivers so they could receive broadcasts over the 45 commercial shortwave frequencies used by Japan. The fishermen, it was hoped, would listen to the black broadcasts and when they returned home would spread the rumors that originated on the station.[22]

To give the proposal higher priority in Washington and among theater commanders, who had no previous experiences with psychwar radio techniques, Vega also proposed that the Kiska transmitter site be used as a listening post for monitoring Japanese broadcasts. Two other poorly thought-out proposals were tacked on to the Vega plan to make it even more attractive: broadcasting Japanese Morse code messages on the side-band of Japanese radio station signals, and sporadically bouncing black mediumwave signals into Japan on frequencies used by Japanese stations. The purpose of the Morse broadcasts was to reach amateur radio oper-ators, who would hopefully decode and spread the subversive messages. The mediumwave signals would be counterfeit versions of legitimate Jap-anese stations. The counterfeit broadcasts were to carry stories of Jap-anese military defeats to spread doubts and defeatism among the civilian population. These transmissions could be made only when atmospheric conditions permitted, as under most conditions mediumwave broadcasts could not reach Japan from Kiska. This idea evolved into other proposals, several of which were tested, but none of which was implemented.

One of the spin-offs was code-named the "Pluto plan." Pluto was de-veloped after Auchincloss, Zuckerman, and others left Washington. It consisted of two black operations, one leaflet and one radio, that rein-forced the other. Black leaflets were prepared that said either the Jap-anese army or navy had taken over the government from the emperor. These leaflets were to be dropped on Japanese cities by U.S. planes masquerading as those of the enemy. After the leaflets were dropped, a black radio station, operating on frequencies normally used in Japan, would announce "that whichever group has announced control over the government through the leaflets has not done so legally and therefore is not to be recognized, thus giving the subversive propaganda even wider currency."[23] The problems with the plan, which explain why it was never implemented, are obvious: it had no clearly defined objectives except to sow confusion; it was potentially dangerous to those on the leaflet-drop-ping mission; and it could not be implemented except by a mediumwave transmitter placed near Japan.

Auchincloss suggested that Vega be implemented as soon as the needed equipment—a speech amplifier, transmitter, antenna, power equipment, and recording studio—were obtained. Implementation at that time was not possible, however, as the necessary Japanese-language personnel were not available for the project. Bruce Rogers was at that moment searching for Japanese-language personnel to man the Marigold facilities. When the issei were found and Marigold established, this generated a need for an even larger MO staff. The larger staff included instructors, technicians, and researchers. MO-Far East began to grow even though it had no formally approved project on which to work. This growth im-pressed Donovan.

Formal approval for the Vega project needed to be obtained from a multiplicity of sources, including OSS superiors in Washington and thea-ter operations officers, the Office of War Information, Federal Commu-nications Commission, Alaskan Department, navy, and Joint Chiefs of Staff. Before formal approval could be granted, details of the project needed to be further explored. The possibility of using Kiska as a transmission site was proposed in Washington but needed to be investigated in the field. Herbert Hilscher, who wrote the first North Pacific Plan, was assigned the duty of going to Alaska and investigating OSS's choice of Aleutian Islands, as well as getting clearances for the project from commanders there. Before Hilscher could go to Alaska, however, OSS needed approval from the Joint Chiefs of Staff. It wasn't until March 10, 1944 that this permission was requested, some two months after the Vega project was submitted. The next day, Auchincloss formally complained that, while the MO group was growing rapidly, nothing had been accomplished and that the Vega plan was "lying with a dead stymie between it and activation." A week later, Hilscher's trip was approved.[24]

Vega was not the only plan on which Auchincloss worked. He worked on plans for the different theaters in Asia. For Burma-India, there was the Candy Plan. Under Candy, a 7.5-kilowatt transmitter would be placed in India or Ceylon for broadcasting shortwave programs to Burma, Thailand, Indochina, and Malaya. For mediumwave broadcasts, it was suggested that a transmitter be placed in the vicinity of Singapore. The plan also called for making counterfeit broadcasts on frequencies used by the Japanese in the region. Candy was never implemented, as the British jealously restricted OSS-MO operations in their colonies. Great Britain feared that OSS might make anti-imperialist broadcasts that promised independence after Japan's defeat. However, an improvised version of Candy was implemented by James Withrow after he became theater operations officer. The plan was code-named "JN–27." It consisted of feeding counterfeit versions of Domei news transmissions to Thailand, which were retransmitted by Thai authorities, who were puppets of the Japanese. The Thais believed that the transmissions were real Japanese news feeds. These counterfeit transmissions originated in Chittagong, Burma.[25]

The Five Star plan proposed making shortwave broadcasts to the Philippine Islands and Japanese troops in the southwest Pacific from transmitters on New Guinea. The transmitters would move closer to the front as the Allies pushed the enemy northward. This plan had little chance of approval, given General MacArthur's desire to maintain complete control over activities in his theater. By mid–1944, when the plan was submitted, it had no chance for approval. Colonel Courtney Whitney, an ultraconservative who believed in "the white man's burden" when it came to the Philippines, had become MacArthur's adviser on Filipino civilian affairs. Whitney had no claim to expertise on Filipino affairs, except for having been an attorney in Manila before being called to active duty from the reserves. Whitney barred OSS from the South Pacific because he feared that Donovan's men would aid Communist insurgents. He even excluded Joseph Ralston Hayden from participating in decisions concerning the

Philippines, even though Secretary of War Stimson appointed Hayden an adviser to MacArthur. Hayden was the former vice-governor at Manila and acting governor during the 1935 Sakdal revolt. He was recognized as the world's foremost authority on Philippine political affairs, but this didn't matter much to Whitney. Hayden was a member of OSS and therefore suspect.[26]

After learning that shortwave and coded broadcasts were being sent to Japan from members of the large emigrant Japanese population in South America, Auchincloss contacted the Federal Communications Commission to obtain more information about the transmissions.[27] FCC officials, who guarded their monitoring service (FBIS) from encroachments by OSS and OWI, first asked of Auchincloss where he heard about the Japanese transmissions and then informed him that the FCC would not supply the requested information because South America was out of OSS's sphere of operations. Undaunted, Auchincloss wrote the Tulip plan, which suggested that exact counterfeits of the South American "transmission characteristics and program content be produced" and relayed to Japan on the same frequencies as the originals. The counterfeits would contain falsified information that would be detrimental to Japan's war effort.[28]

The plan was submitted to Donovan, who indicated interest in it, but was also wary because the plan encroached on the turf of the Coordinator of Inter-American Affairs (CIAA), headed by Nelson Rockefeller, to whom Donovan had spoken little since the COI-CIAA conflict erupted in 1941. After receiving the Tulip proposal, Carl Hoffman, the Far Eastern theater officer, suggested that MO-Far East refine the plan and resubmit it to Colonel Otto Doering, another former law partner of Donovan who was given a command in OSS. He and Donovan would then decide whether to veto it or pass it up to the Joint Chiefs of Staff for consideration.[29]

The Tulip proposal was rewritten by James Withrow, who in civilian life had been a junior attorney to Doering. The proposal was submitted with the legalistic proviso that "such operations appear to be prohibited." If that weren't enough to kill Tulip, the proposal was revised so that most references to "black radio" were changed to "radio communications." Failing to make constant reference to black radio, which was the only type of radio broadcasting that OSS was permitted to conduct, helped doom the proposal, as did the recommendation that the transmitter be placed on Curaçao, "where the Dutch government itself has indicated a willingness to build a large station."[30] The plan might have been made palatable to Donovan, who was not looking for another fight with Rockefeller, by referring to Tulip as a black radio operation, and by suggesting that the transmitter be placed on Hawaii or somewhere else that lay in the region between South America and Japan. Even though the proposal was vetoed, Withrow's work on the plan paid off later. It gave him the idea for the black transmitter at Chittagong.

While the Candy, Five Star, and Tulip plans were not enthusiastically received by the Joint Chiefs, theater commanders, or Donovan, plans for Vega were forging ahead. Hilscher was in Alaska examining possible transmission sites. One of two 7.5-kilowatt transmitters that OSS ordered was earmarked for the project. Three other MO-Far East plans were also receiving positive reviews. They were code-named Orion, Agana, and Hump. The Orion plan was originated by Gordon Auchincloss and Paul Brown, a broadcast engineer in the Communications Branch of OSS. It consisted of mounting a 250-kilowatt mediumwave transmitter and trailing antenna in a B–29 bomber. The B–29 would accompany other bombers on raids over Japan. The transmitter would operate from 30,000 feet on frequencies normally used by Japanese radio stations and throw a signal into the areas below. It would broadcast prerecorded "one-time-shot freedom stations" over Japanese territory. At bombing sites the station would give false air raid instructions that would increase casualties, and warn factory workers to stay away from work and areas that "are officially closed due to delayed action bombs." The latter instructions were designed to slow Japan's war production.[31]

This was not the first proposal for using planes to disseminate verbal psychwar messages. Four PV–1 planes were equipped with loudspeakers in 1944 for use in North Africa and Europe. The operation called for the airplanes to make surrender announcements to Axis troops from 2,000 feet. At this altitude, however, the planes could be used only in situations where enemy ground defenses were weak, which made this proposal different from the Orion plan. Three of the loud-speaker equipped planes were sent to Europe. Two were damaged shortly after arrival and the other was never put into operation. The fourth plane was sent to the central Pacific command area for use against the Japanese. During tests, it was discovered that messages coming from the plane at 2,000 feet were inaudible, so the plane was mothballed. Several months later four larger planes were equipped with more powerful loudspeakers, but these never reached the theater before the war ended.

Despite its obvious failings, the loudspeaker plan was never completely scrapped. During the Korean war, a Navy veteran remembered the attempt to use plane-mounted loudspeakers in World War II. A call was made to air force headquarters in Washington on September 30, 1950 and in three days, a plane with technicians and equipment landed in Japan. On October 7, installation of the equipment was completed and the following day the C–47 transport flew to Korea. The plane's arrival in Korea was widely announced and this "brought a flood of requests from . . . several divisions" for its deployment in their sector. The plane was immediately put into operation. A second plane was put into operation in November. The planes were used until mid-March 1951 before any audibility tests were conducted. When the tests were done, they showed that the messages couldn't be heard. Even when more powerful speakers were remounted under the plane's fuselage, announcements remained inaudible. After these tests, the planes were retired.[32]

Orion had two problems that needed addressing before determining whether or not a clear broadcast signal could be transmitted from 30,000 feet. One problem was that an airborne transmitter might give away the location of the raiding planes when activated, and another was that the transmitter's heavy weight reduced payloads and, unlike bombs, represented a "return payload." Squadron commanders previously opposed dropping leaflets because this reduced payloads.[33] The leaflets were much lighter than a transmitter. As it turned out, these initial objections to the plan were easily addressed. Enemy radar was likely to spot the planes before the transmitter was activated, so worrying that the broadcast signal might be tracked wasn't worth the effort. Secondly, if the broadcasts enhanced the effectiveness of the bombing, then the transmitter's weight would more than compensate for the loss in payload. The Joint Chiefs accepted these explanations. Therefore, the plan's implementation rested first on whether a B–29 would be made available for test broadcasts and second, whether the tests produced positive results. A B–29 was made available for the tests, but not until Auchincloss left Washington for China.

Despite being in China, Auchincloss kept in touch with MO-Washington, concerning the outcome of the tests on his pet project. The first series of tests were conducted in late 1944 using 50-watt and 250-watt transmitters. The initial tests were positive. The tests continued into April 1945 at Wright and Bolling fields and indicated that a 250-watt transmitter was insufficient for the job; at least 25 kilowatts was required. The negative test results notwithstanding, the plan was not scrapped, but placed on a backburner. No final decision on it was ever reached, as the war ended four months later.[34]

The test results were not completely negative and the plan was revised for use in 1961, during the Bay of Pigs invasion. This derivation of the Orion plan called for the mounting of television rather than radio transmitters in planes. The planes were to fly around Cuba, breaking into regularly scheduled television programs, calling for an uprising against Fidel Castro. This and several other plans were never implemented during the invasion, but a clandestine station operated by the CIA from Swan Island, Honduras did broadcast coded messages and anti-Castro propaganda during the abortive invasion.[35]

The Agana plan proposed placing a 50-kilowatt transmitter on Guam after its liberation for broadcasts to the north, central, and southwest Pacific areas. The broadcasts would initially be in shortwave, but as the front moved closer to Japan, mediumwave would be substituted for broadcasts to that country. Auchincloss submitted the proposal for Agana and other plans on May 17, 1944, with Agana earmarked as a high-priority program. Even a time table for it had been worked out. The one problem with the plan was that there were still insufficient numbers of trained Japanese-language personnel to carry it off. Auchincloss suggested that Marigold be enlarged, but that other facilities were badly needed to give training for "duties in the field."[36]

Donovan gave the go-ahead to the plan and preparations were made for its execution, even though General MacArthur and Admiral Nimitz never gave it their approval. Donovan knew that Agana would have to be thoroughly worked out before the Pacific theater commanders would approve it. Facilities at Collingwood were made available to MO-Far East for training Japanese-language personnel. Recruits for the Collingwood facility included Takashi Ohta, folksinger Pete Seeger's father-in-law, and former newspaperman and Communist party activist Joe Koida, who helped Bruce Rogers recruit more personnel. Joe Koida wrote a book in Japanese entitled *Aru Zaibei Nihonjin no Kiroku* (The Chronicle of a Japanese in America) that recounted his OSS experiences. Collingwood was opened in June and in a short time, the facility was producing radio scripts. George Dibert was brought in from MO-European Theater to supervise the script writing. Dibert had not only written radio scripts professionally before the war, but worked in England with Sefton Delmer until sent to Washington. John Zuckerman was assigned the task of putting together a music library at Collingwood. He was assisted by Walter Gould, who went to Hollywood to acquire recordings and sheet music for the library. Gould spent his days in Hollywood acquiring musical scores that had been used in American feature films about Asia, such as *The Good Earth*, rather than authentic Asian musical compositions. Moreover, a 50-kilowatt transmitter was ordered for the project. In July, James Withrow assumed command of the project as area operations officer, MO-Pacific. In August, Bogart Carlaw replaced Dibert as production chief.

Three elaborate series of prototype scripts were written for Agana Collingwood. They were called the Toyama, Sayonara, and Voice of the People series. The Toyama series claimed that the radio station was operated from a secret location in South China by the Greater East Asia Peace League. The station's announcer was named Yasutaro Uejima, a member of the Peace League and devoted follower of Mitsuru Toyama, the recently deceased ultra-nationalist leader of the Genyosha organization who was known as the Japanese Robin Hood. Uejima advocated peace, but not the type of peace defined by Washington: his peace included "constant intrigue and countless tricks for the aggrandizement of Japan." The station appealed to members of other organizations in Japan that OSS believed formed an opposition. The station would attract listeners by "hitchhiking" on the frequency used by the Osaka central radio station after it signed off for the night.[37]

The Sayonara series was similar to a proposal for Vega—it consisted of broadcasts from supposedly marooned Japanese naval personnel. The announcer of the Sayonara series was the captain of the crippled destroyer Yamabuki, which the U.S. naval fleet had purportedly attacked and left to drift in the Pacific. Tsuzaki Shogo, the destroyer's captain, identified himself in the first script and explained how he and the 21 surviving members of his crew were engaged by the U.S. navy, nearly sunk, and left to drift to the island from where he broadcasts. Most of the seven Sayonara scripts that were written gave the names of surviving crewmen and relayed messages to their families. The messages were woven into the scripts to give the station an aura of believability and amateurishness. (Although the names mentioned in the Sayonara scripts were fictitious, OSS planned to substitute the name of a real vessel sunk by the U.S. Navy and the names of rescued crewmen for actual broadcasts.) These scripts, like the Toyama scripts, were discarded because they were "too pointed and specific." The Voice of the People series was finally selected as the model used in actual broadcasts because it was "more general." Voice of the People did not claim to originate from a specific organization, but an eclectic group of Japanese who opposed the war and favored peace. They favored peace because it was the only way to save Japan from complete annihilation.[38]

## OVER THE HUMP

The other MO project that met approval was called the Hump plan, named for the mountainous route between Calcutta, where OSS's Asia supply base was located, and Chungking. The Hump plan consisted of placing a 7.5-kilowatt transmitter in China for shortwave operation to Japanese occupied areas. The transmitter would broadcast from Chungking under the SACO-OSS agreements hammered out by Little and Donovan, or from elsewhere in China if Tai Li refused to cooperate. An alternative to Chungking was Kunming, where OSS had placed a small detachment beginning in February 1944 to work with Gen. Claire Chennault.[39]

The Hump plan met initial opposition from Donovan because he thought that the 7.5-kilowatt transmitter's heavy weight would make it too difficult to bring over the Himalayas, but his objection was withdrawn after Stilwell and Chennault approved the project. A series of actions were then taken to get the Hump plan from the planning stage into the field, something that MO had not yet succeeded in doing with any Asian plan. Colonel Charles Coughlin, who replaced Milton Miles as OSS chief in China, was asked to submit a list of needs to execute the project, which he did. The MO-China plan was then submitted to Col. Hsiao Hsin-ju, Tai Li's representative in Washington who had the title of assistant

Chinese military attaché. Colonel Hsiao gave it his approval. Gen. Hsioh Li Kung in Chungking was sent the plan in April, and it was approved there. General Hsioh was appointed the chief of SACO-MO. The plan called for MO to place three American scriptwriters, two American translators and one American "voice broadcaster" in China, in addition to five radio technicians who would be needed to operate the transmitter. The Kuomintang side of SACO was to provide Chinese translators for Japanese, Korean, and other languages that would be required, several scriptwriters, and a number of announcers with voices "suitable" for broadcasting. The exact number of personnel needed would be worked out later.[40]

Bill Morwood was sent to China in July to train the first group of Chinese who would function as field agents, sending back intelligence, spreading rumors, and distributing print propaganda. He arrived in July and trained three Chinese nationals, who were sent to Canton. Two did not reach Canton and after seven weeks were recalled to Chungking. The other disappeared entirely. The rest of the time, Morwood sat around the OSS base called "Happy Valley" that was outside of Chungking, where he idled away his time until Gordon Auchincloss arrived. Auchincloss was sent to China on a temporary basis on August 7, as OSS-Washington believed that he would be able to implement the Hump plan in about three weeks time.[41]

The details of the Hump plan had been worked out between Tai Li, Colonel Hsiao, and OSS. They called for the Chinese side of SACO to provide three Japanese-language personnel for black radio operations and five more for monitoring Japanese broadcasts. The Chinese were also to provide an additional twenty men who would be trained in intelligence gathering and sent into the field, and an additional ten men for training as black radio scriptwriters and announcers. The Chinese were to report for duty in mid-September 1944, two weeks after Auchincloss was scheduled to arrive in Chungking. Tai Li was informed of these details in several cables sent by Colonel Hsiao in July. Auchincloss would train the personnel with Morwood and then return to Washington for work on Vega and Agana, the Pacific plans. Morwood or someone else would then supervise the project.[42]

The day before leaving for China, Auchincloss met with Herb Little and John Zuckerman to work out the final details of OSS's equipment contribution to the China project. OSS-Calcutta had a 500-watt transmitter for voice broadcasting on shortwave that had been modified from a 600 watt C.W. unit. Calcutta also had acetate and wire recording equipment and several radios for monitoring Japanese broadcasts. Auchincloss was to pick up this equipment in Calcutta and take it to Chungking. The equipment would supplement the monitoring equipment already there. The 500-watt transmitter was to be used for pilot broadcasts until a 7.5-

kilowatt unit arrived. (The 7.5-kilowatt unit was eventually shipped from New York to Calcutta in November, for final shipment to Chungking.) Zuckerman promised to go through the Collingwood record library and find enough Chinese and Japanese music recordings for the project. These would be sent to Auchincloss after he established a base in Chungking.[43]

At the end of the second week in August, Auchincloss arrived in Calcutta. He was met there by Bill Morwood, who came over the hump to help move the equipment to Chungking. After wading through red tape for several days, Auchincloss located the recording and transmitting equipment, which was then sent to Chungking over the land route through the Himalayas. He and Morwood arrived in Chungking on the first of September, as scheduled, and met with Donald Monroe, the branch chief of OSS detachment 202 in Chungking. Monroe informed Auchincloss that General Hsioh, the Chinese head of SACO-MO, had been fired. No replacement for him had yet been named. Auchincloss also learned that several Chinese-Americans that OSS had trained in Washington for work in Chungking had not been approved by Tai Li for duty in China, leaving him with no trustworthy bilingual assistants—just those provided by SACO. At the meeting, Monroe told Auchincloss his conclusions about working with SACO, which had already been cabled to Washington: that no cooperation can be expected. Monroe suggested that MO's black radio plans, if they were to be implemented, would probably have to be done through AGFRTS, if permission for this could be obtained. Until such approval was obtained, Auchincloss was told to do the best he could in Chungking.[44]

In response to these problems, Washington decided not to submit the names of agents to Tai Li for approval, and asked Colonel Hsiao to again cable Tai Li, urging him to cooperate with OSS. Auchincloss decided to improvise by finding trustworthy, competent bilingual assistants from among the civilians in Chungking. He interviewed two candidates, Norman Li and Archibald Macmillan. Norman Li was a native Chinese who worked for RCA as a sales representative. Li agreed to work for OSS if it matched his RCA salary of $250 per month, paid in U.S. dollars, and provided him with quarters and rations or an allowance for these. Li also wanted a guarantee that if the Japanese overran the area where the station was located, he would be evacuated at the same time as the station's director. Li wanted only one more thing before he was willing to join the fight against Japan: two or three weeks off during every three months so that he could continue to work as the RCA sales representative. Li suggested that the last condition was necessary, so as not to leave RCA in a lurch. Auchincloss liked Norman Li but decided not to hire him until the problems with SACO had been resolved. The other candidate, Archibald Macmillan, was the son of missionary parents. Unlike Norman Li, he was willing to join the fight against Japan without pay, just a lieutenant's commission in the army. Like Li, Macmillan was considered to be competent but could not be hired or offered anything until the problems with SACO were resolved.[45]

Part of the resolution came in October when General Wang Ye Sun, who was nicknamed "General Wangler" because of his preoccupation with getting OSS supplies and money, was appointed General Hsioh's replacement. General Wang assigned a few Chinese to MO for training as field agents and asked to review the SACO-MO black radio proposal. Auchincloss supplied Wang with the project plans and with Morwood started teaching the new recruits. Enough were trained for intelligence-gathering stations in Foochow, Shanghai, Canton, Ningwo, and Amoy. When the agents were ready to be sent into the field, "General Wangler" informed OSS that no batteries were available in Chungking for their radio sets. (The batteries were to be supplied by the Chinese side, while the radio sets were supplied by the American side of SACO.) Without batteries, it was pointless to send out agents, as there would be no way for them to communicate with the Chungking base. Doubting General Wang's report, Auchincloss and Morwood went to the supply depot, where they got the names and addresses of Chinese battery companies, and proceeded to one on Main Street in downtown Chungking. The proprietor told the Americans that they needed a priority order from the Ministry of Priorities before he could sell them batteries. They went to the ministry, arrived during the lunch hour, waited, got a priority order, and went back for the batteries. Auchincloss and Morwood returned to the OSS base with twelve batteries within two hours of leaving. The batteries were paid for out of OSS funds. Auchincloss thought it worth the aggravation because he was able to present Wang with the bill and a complaint that the Chinese side was not meeting their obligations in SACO.[46]

On November 17, General Wang wrote Auchincloss that he approved the black radio plan and several assistants would soon report for training. Wang suggested that the transmitter of the proposed station be placed in Kunking, not far from where the Japanese were stationed. Auchincloss took General Wang's proposal to U.S. Army Headquarters in Chungking, where he was informed that Kunking was a poor choice of locations, as the Japanese "could occupy it within forty-eight hours anytime they decided to do so," which would probably be soon, because "it is in their indicated line of advance."[47] Auchincloss informed Wang of the army's report and scheduled a meeting to select a new location. At the meeting, Wang and Auchincloss agreed on a location between Ningwu and Chienou, preferably Shun-an.

Anticipating the arrival of the long-promised black radio trainees, Auchincloss and Morwood developed a rigorous one-week training course. The course covered the differences between black and white radio, tactical and strategic stations, and techniques such as snuggling, ghosting, and heckling. The course began with a history of black radio applications in Europe and ended with "hands on" production work, using the equipment brought from Calcutta. The syllabus was sent to General Wang for comments and approval.[48]

On November 20, Wang's hand-picked, seven-man team arrived. It included three Japanese language specialists, who were led by Lee Yen Ho. Lee was fluent in Chinese (Mandarin and Shanghai dialects), English (Boston and Texas dialects!), and Japanese. Although Auchincloss didn't meet any of the other men, he was delighted with Mr. Lee. Lee had every skill that Auchincloss was looking for. Just before the training classes were scheduled to begin, General Wang informed Auchincloss that Tai Li had reviewed their choice of transmitter locations and decided that Shun-an could not be used because of its "very complicated situation." Tai Li recommended that the transmitter be placed in Shanyou, Kiangsi Province. Auchincloss later learned that this location was also in the direct line of the Japanese advance. Wang also reported that Lee Yen Ho had "been transferred to a new position."[49]

Frustrated by Tai Li's actions, Auchincloss told Wang that the training course was cancelled until an acceptable location was chosen for the transmitter. General Wang was, in turn, irritated by Auchincloss's action and said that he needed to review the whole black radio proposal. As part of the review, "General Wangler" asked to see the budget and list of equipment that OSS was contributing to the project. Wang reviewed the list and noted that the contribution of the Chinese side was limited to providing housing for the Americans and salaries for the Chinese personnel. This meant that the Chinese side was supplying nothing but manpower. OSS was supplying transportation, a radio transmitter with accessories and spare parts, a power generator and fuel to run it, radio receivers, living costs of the American personnel, and even courier expenses, which Wang or Tai Li could pocket. Liking the arrangement, Wang encouraged Auchincloss to begin the black radio course, as an acceptable transmitter location would surely be found.[50]

In the first week of December 1944, Auchincloss and Morwood started the black radio training school. Of the three Japanese- language specialists assigned by Wang, only two showed up for the course. One of the two quit after two days. The third continued his training, but Auchincloss discovered that his Japanese language skills were confined to saying "hello," "good-bye," and "do you speak Japanese?" As Auchincloss reported it, he had the Japanese-language skills equivalent to "the average American's command of Sanskrit." The Chinese-language personnel were no better. One of the four reported for training before completing his "outside affairs" and left class for two days to wrap things up. Frustrated by the situation, Auchincloss canceled the classes until a team could be assembled that would make it through the program without constant interruption. Finally, Wang submitted another transmitter location selected by Tai Li. It, like the other two choices, was in the path of advancing Japanese troops. Thereafter, Auchincloss lost all hopes of working with SACO. He applied for permission to transfer the black radio operation from SACO in Chungking to Kunming, where OSS had its operational headquarters. Permission was granted at the end of January, when he and Morwood packed the equipment and left.[51]

During February, Auchincloss and Morwood looked for Chinese who could assist with future plans. They contacted a former professor from Wuhan University whom Herb Little had recommended. The professor had come to Kunming with two dozen former students. His students were fluent in English, some knew several Chinese dialects and Japanese, and all were willing to work for OSS. The students were interviewed and, based upon their backgrounds and abilities, were earmarked for work in voice, research, or monitoring.

With competent personnel finally available, Auchincloss and Morwood quickly wrote and submitted a plan called "Columbia," which suggested making black broadcasts to Canton, Shanghai, and other Japanese-occupied areas. They submitted a second plan called "Pegasus" that proposed transmitting sabotage instructions in easily broken code to nonexistent OSS commandos. The purpose of Pegasus was to make Japanese who monitored the instructions believe that commando units were operating in areas where they were not. If the messages were believed, it was hoped that the Japanese would send troops to these areas, thereby weakening their defenses in areas critical to the allies. The theater planning staff rejected Pegasus but approved Columbia. On March 3, Columbia was submitted to General Albert Wedemeyer, who had replaced Stilwell as theater commander. Wedemeyer gave it his approval.[52]

Several things transpired between December and February that allowed the Columbia plan to be moved rapidly forward. First, Wedemeyer demanded and received full command of all U.S. forces in China. Accordingly, he made OSS an independent agency that reported directly to him. Each OSS proposal was submitted directly to theater command for approval, not to SACO or Washington. Second, an OSS communications team including Joseph Matovich, Richard Marshak, and others arrived in Kunming from Cairo in December. Because their work in North Africa and the Mediterranean was completed, these OSS technicians were deployed in Asia. This enlarged OSS's communications team in Kunming and provided the expertise and manpower needed to operate the 500-watt transmitter that was brought from Calcutta. The team directed the antenna and changed the operating frequencies for the broadcasts directed to different Chinese cities. Third, a secluded facility was available for housing for the project. Because the project had a "secret" classification, seclusion was needed for it to operate. The available facility was eight miles outside of Kunming on the road to the Black Dragon pool. It was used by OSS to give Chinese commandos parachute training. The facility was originally built by a "wealthy Chinese who had succumbed to the lure of Western architecture."[53]

Auchincloss received word in mid-March that the Columbia plan had been approved. He told nine of the Chinese students to report for training on March 25. For the week and a half before the trainees reported, Auchincloss and Morwood transformed their Kunming compound into a work station. In one of the rooms, blankets were hung on the walls. This room was used as a recording studio and contained equipment brought from Calcutta. In this studio the black broadcasts were recorded for later airing.

The recordings were brought to the OSS communications center, some four miles away. The 500-watt transmitter was at the communications center, as was a mobile playback studio. The playback studio was in a British armored truck that Auchincloss had acquired through barter. He had traded two MO cameras for the vehicle. A cable ran from the playback studio to the transmitter, some 50 feet away. The communications personnel were neither allowed in the playback truck nor permitted to hear the recordings, as the recordings had a "secret" classification. Thus, while the technicians operated the transmitters for the broadcasts, they were never aware of the contents of the messages. Because Bill Morwood had the responsibility of bringing the "secret" messages to Chungking for theater headquarters clearances, he was promoted from sergeant to lieutenant. Commissioned but not noncommissioned OSS officers were permitted to travel with "secret" information. Auchincloss was simultaneously promoted to captain. When the 7.5-kilowatt transmitter arrived from Calcutta in March, it was stored at Auchincloss's compound. It was never placed into use at the communications center, because the center had no facilities capable of housing it. The transmitter was wrapped in canvas and placed behind the sleeping quarters of the Chinese students, where it sat until the war ended. The sleeping quarters were built to house the commandos who received parachute training there.[54]

(The transmitter was left behind when OSS left China. It is very likely that this 7.5-kilowatt transmitter was used by the Beijing government for making clandestine broadcasts to other countries in Asia. In 1962, the clandestine "Voice of the People of Thailand" started broadcasting from a "secret communications center" located near Kunming. This station broadcast until 1979. In 1971, another clandestine station called "Voice of the People of Burma" appeared. Like the Thai station, it originated from the transmitter in Kunming. Programs of both stations were written by Thai and Burmese communist exiles who lived in China. Voice of the People of Thailand and its Burmese sister station functioned as the voices of the Maoist Communist parties in these countries.)[55]

Other rooms in the compound were used as sleeping areas, offices and work rooms. Two rooms were used for monitoring Japanese broadcasts. From the first week in April, Japanese shortwave broadcasts were monitored by a multilingual team composed of Professor Pan's former students. The monitoring was conducted 24 hours per day, seven days per week. Morwood synopsized the transcripts made by the monitoring unit and wrote weekly reports from April through June. These reports were distributed to China Theater G–2, OWI, OSS, and other interested agencies.[56] Seymour Nadler, a former school teacher and radio writer, joined the black radio group in June and took over the writing of these reports. In August, they were written and issued daily. Nadler, Morwood, and Auchincloss had offices in other rooms, where they wrote scripts for the broadcasts. The scripts were translated by the Chinese personnel in another room. The Chinese-language scripts were brought to the studio, where the recordings were made. The recordings were afterward driven to the transmitter for final dispatch.

The Chinese recruits were trained and the facilities completed by April 16, but it was not until April 27 that clearances were given for the broadcast frequencies that were to be used. On April 28, 1945, almost two and a half years after the preparations for it began, OSS made its first clandestine broadcast to Japanese-occupied China. The broadcast occurred five days after OSS started broadcasting to Japan from Saipan and was therefore the second, not the first, clandestine freedom station that OSS operated in Asia. The Saipan-based "Voice of the People" went on the air April 23.[57]

The station that appeared on April 28 was code-named "Charlie." The broadcast was beamed to Canton, from where it claimed to originate. The station claimed to be operated by an underground, anti-Japanese resistance organization headed by Liang Ting Han, who explained his, the station's and the resistance group's existence thus:

My name is Liang Ting Han . . . at least that is the name I go under now. If you heard my real name you would immediately recognize me as an old friend and respected neighbor of yours in Canton. Not that I'm far from Canton now—in fact, I'll give you a hint of exactly where I am at this moment. If you've got good eyesight and can look toward the mountains, you can probably see the very hill under which I have this transmitter. . . . Do you hear that you shitty Jap gendarmes? Sometimes I have to laugh at how dumb you bastards are. That's right, friends in Canton, they've been trying now for some months to capture me and my band of guerrillas, but they've got nothing . . . to show for their pains. Yes, I'm a guerrilla and have been since . . . being forced out of Canton, after which my wife and child died. Only this broadcasting is a relatively new departure. I've only been at it for about six months. It came about accidentally when I had the opportunity to buy this radio transmitter from the shitty corrupt Japs. At first I used it to communicate with my men . . . but then I got the idea of a daily broadcast to tell my good friends in Canton all the news they never heard over the lying Jap radio.[58]

This and other scripts for "Charlie" were written by Gordon Auchincloss and then translated into Cantonese by Li Chi-wei, who also served as the voice of Liang Ting Han. Each broadcast lasted fifteen minutes and was repeated three times during the day. Between April 28 and August 17, when the station was silenced, 95 scripts were written and recorded. In addition to encouraging noncooperation and passive resistance rather than sabotage against Japan, the station pretended to communicate with agents in Canton, with messages such as: "Here is the special message for 85. Write it down. 9968 5014 7629 3184 0924. I repeat. . . . " Bill Morwood collaborated on some of the "Charlie" scripts with Auchincloss in addition to writing monitoring reports and scripts for the Pegasus operation, which was reactivated at the request of the theater command. In early May, shortly after the Canton freedom station signed on, the China theater planning staff asked MO to revise Pegasus. Morwood rewrote the plan, resubmitted it and, after its approval, was responsible for its implementation. The Pegasus operation consisted of transmitting texts in compromised or easily broken cipher to nonexistent agent teams in six different locations along China's coast. The texts were worded in such a way as to make them appear to be part of a two-way communication system. Some of the texts, for example, appeared to be responses to questions transmitted by agents. During the first phase of the operation, the texts provided information on supplies that were to be delivered, personal messages, and limited instructions. The purpose of this stage was to make Japanese monitors believe that agents were really operating in the coastal locations. The second stage, which began in July, was part of a larger deception scheme to make Japan think that the United States planned an invasion of North China, when in fact it was considering an invasion of the south. The planned invasion never occurred, as the United States ended the Pacific war a month later by dropping atomic bombs on Hiroshima and Nagasaki.[59]

To contribute to the deception, the one-way coded messages indicated that additional agents would be dropped in the north, as would explosives, munitions, and supplies. Agents in the south were told that no more supplies were being sent. The messages told these nonexistent agents to ration what supplies they had left. Morwood continued to write and send these messages until the war ended. Whether the Japanese ever monitored and decoded the messages isn't known.

In May, Lieutenant George Dail joined the MO unit and took over its administrative duties, freeing Auchincloss to continue work on "Charlie." In June, Lieutenant Nadler reported for duty. With the increased manpower, a second freedom station was established. The second station requiring the hiring of more Chinese employees, so their number was increased to 26. The new station, code-named "William," broadcast to the Wuhan cities of Hankow, Hanyang, and Wuchang. "William" appeared on June 6, claiming to have been on the air before this date by saying:

Businessmen of Hankow and the Wuhan cities. This is your business counselor, Wang Chu Mien, speaking. We are back on the air now, broadcasting regularly for all of you with advice on business conditions.[60]

Business conditions were bad, according to station operator Wang Chu Mien, because the so-called coprosperity sphere was really a Japanese prosperity sphere. The economy in occupied areas worked against honest Chinese businessmen. The only way to succeed, Wang Chu Mien advised, was to store goods until the Japanese left China. When U.S. troops arrived, the goods would be purchased with gold by the rich Americans, not with the worthless currency used by Japanese and their puppets. Synopses of several broadcasts in June were as follows:

| Date | Synopsis |
|------|----------|
| June 7 | Details on boom in Free China. Prepare for the coming of the Americans—hoard valuables. |
| June 10 | Japanese looting factories in Shanghai as they prepare to evacuate. Hide your valuables. |
| June 11 | Puppets are storing goods for eventual arrival of Americans. Honest businessmen should do so, too. |
| June 12 | Japanese-issued money no good. Only do barter business with Japanese. |
| June 14 | Yokohama Specie Bank increased capitalization from 10 to 30 million yen. This will produce run-away inflation. Tell everyone to be prepared. |

Wang Chu Mien, who called himself the "business counselor of Wuhan," not only dispensed advice, but advertised his services for sale. This was the explanation offered to listeners for the station's existence. It continued to broadcast until August 17. In all, 70 scripts for this station were written by Auchincloss and Morwood and translated and recorded by a Chinese national nicknamed "Franklin D. Woo." As with Charlie, the scripts were 15 minutes long and were repeated three times each day.

Seymour Nadler, also a former radio writer, was assigned the task of writing scripts for a third station dubbed "Hermit." It was beamed to Nanking from June 19 until August 17. Until its sign-off, "Hermit" operated twice daily for 11 minutes, as the first and last broadcast made by the 500-watt transmitter. The rotation of the broadcasts to Canton, Wuhan, and Nanking and their frequencies were as follows:

| Time | Frequency | Station |
|---|---|---|
| 3:55 | 9420 | Hermit |
| 4:15 | 6812 | Charlie |
| 4:40 | 7880 | William |
| 5:15 | 6812 | Charlie |
| 5:40 | 7880 | William |
| 6:15 | 6812 | Charlie |
| 6:40 | 7880 | William |
| 7:00 | 9420 | Hermit |

Nadler wrote 57 scripts for the Hermit. All were based on astrology, fortune-telling, palmistry, phrenology, and numerology. The station's purported operator was Wua Yan Chu-he, who called himself the "Hermit of the Clouds." Wua Yan Chu-he claimed to be a "latticintersticologist" or scientist who interprets the patterns of stars, numbers, and planets that govern peoples' lives. Each broadcast carried predictions based on Wua's pseudo-scientific investigations. Each prediction concerned future events facing Japan and its collaborators. According to Elizabeth McDonald, who for a brief period was assistant chief of MO for the China-India-Burma theater, Wua even predicted the dropping of an atomic bomb on Hiroshima. While she was visiting Auchincloss's compound outside Kunming in July, Nadler complained that his station wasn't doing much to frighten the Japanese. "Why don't you predict a combined earthquake and tidal wave?" McDonald asked. Nadler rejected her suggestion, saying that this was a common occurrence to the Japanese. Auchincloss suggested that Nadler predict that a catastrophe will occur in Japan during the first week of August. Auchincloss added, "don't tell them . . . what it will be." The next broadcast of Wau Yan Chu-he predicted that a disaster of monumental proportions would strike Japan in the beginning of August.[61]

While Hermit, Charlie, and William were directed at Chinese in Japanese-occupied cities, a plan and scripts were written for broadcasts to occupation troops. The "Jig plan" consisted of seven scripts that were written by Auchincloss, and translated into Japanese by the multilingual Chinese students. The scripts encouraged desertions during the period immediately prior to Japan's capitulation. The "Jig" scripts were never aired because the Japanese translations were less than perfect. Auchincloss decided to wait until Japanese personnel from Marigold and Collingwood arrived to assist in the production of "Jig." The war ended before any of the personnel arrived at the communications compound, but a number did arrive in other areas of China well before the war ended.[62]

## FROM THE SANDTRAP TO GREEN'S: THE VEGA AND AGANA PLANS

In April 1944, General Donovan visited Admiral Nimitz on Hawaii. Soon thereafter, naval officer R. Davis Halliwell was appointed OSS chief for the Pacific area and assigned to Nimitz's staff. Halliwell served as Donovan's contact man with Nimitz. In July, Nimitz asked Donovan to submit a detailed plan for OSS activities for the Pacific. A plan was drawn up that included Vega, which Herbert Hilscher had been working on in Alaska since March. While in Alaska, Hilscher obtained approval from Lt. Gen. Delos Emmons, the Alaskan department commanding general, and Vice Admiral F. J. Fletcher, the North Pacific naval commander, for placing the Vega transmitter on Amchitka rather than Kiska Island. Amchitka was larger, better protected, and about the same distance from Japan and Kiska. With the assistance of Stuart L. Seaton of the Department of Terrestrial Magnetism at the Carnegie Institute, Hilscher conducted tests that demonstrated that shortwave signals from a 7.5-kilowatt transmitter on the island would reach Japan. Under certain conditions, mediumwave signals would also reach there. Hilscher returned to Washington in late July, having accomplished his mission.[63]

Within days of Hilscher's return, Donovan gave approval for continuing the project. James Withrow, the newly appointed area operations chief for MO-Pacific, then reached an understanding with the Federal Communications Commission (FCC) that OSS would monitor Japanese broadcasts from Alaska, something that the FCC was not and had no intention of doing. On August 9, the Office of War Information (OWI) reported that the Vega project did not interfere with any plans or operations it had. This cleared the way for approval by Nimitz.[64]

OSS was so sure that the plan, and several others, would be approved, that implementation went ahead. A 7.5-kilowatt transmitter was sent to Seattle for future shipment to Alaska. Hilscher returned to Amchitka to make arrangements for the erection of the transmitter tower and to obtain accommodations for the station's personnel. Withrow tentatively assigned three Japanese from Collingwood—Takeda, Kurihara, and Yoshida—to the project. A day-by-day timetable for implementation was drawn up and by early November, the plans had been worked out to the point where it was determined that the station would operate about three hours nightly between nine and midnight.[65]

A detailed proposal consisting of OSS plans for the Pacific was submitted to Nimitz on November 13, 1944. The proposal included plans for the Research and Analysis (R & A) and Secret Intelligence (SI) branches, in addition to Morale Operations. The SI plan called for a landing and penetration of the Kurile Islands. The MO plans included Vega and Agana, which consisted of placing a 50-kilowatt mediumwave transmitter on Guam. At the last moment and without explanation, Nimitz vetoed all of the projects, a decision that almost guaranteed OSS's exclusion from the Pacific.[66]

The veto by Nimitz devastated MO-Pacific's morale, but it was not the only thing to do so. The Secret Service informed OSS that it wanted the Collingwood shop closed and all Japanese moved from Washington. As Marigold was too small to accommodate the larger Collingwood crew and too far from the Asian theaters, it was decided to merge the operations on the West Coast, provided facilities and permission could be obtained for the transfers. Special permission was needed for the move because persons of Japanese ancestry had been barred from the Coast since May 1942 by executive order. (This exclusion order was finally lifted on January 2, 1945.) Withrow assigned John Zuckerman the task of going to the OSS base on Catalina Island, off southern California's coast, to see whether housing for the Collingwood and Marigold staffs could be obtained there. This was one of Withrow's last orders in MO-Pacific, as he was soon thereafter named the operations officer for MO-Southeast Asia. Zuckerman went to the West Coast and obtained accommodations for the Collingwood personnel. Within days, permission for the transfer was obtained from Washington. By mid-December, the move to the OSS island base was completed and Collingwood and Marigold closed. The issei and nisei were virtually marooned on Catalina Island until March. The only contact they had with the outside world was through radio listening and by mail. They spent their days working and fishing and their nights watching the "lights of Newport Beach shimmer[ing] invitingly across 27 miles of the channel."[67]

The planned morale operations were also hurt by a manpower shortage. Auchincloss was in China, where he was later joined by Seymour Nadler and George Dail. Walter Gould had proven himself incompetent, Dibert had returned to Europe, Hilscher was in Alaska, and Withrow was assigned to southeast Asia. Bogart Carlaw remained with the unit until late-April 1945, but he was a civilian. This left Lieutenant Zuckerman in virtual command of the operation after having served in MO less than six months.

Donovan realized that Nimitz's veto of the Pacific plan excluded OSS from any meaningful operations in the war against Japan. While OSS was in China, Burma, and Indochina, these were secondary theaters that served only as diversions for the Pacific operations. These theaters tied up Japanese troops; they did not inflict major damage on Japan. Japan was being defeated on the Pacific islands and the U.S. military machine was moving steadily toward the enemy homeland. Saipan and Guam were taken in the summer of 1944; MacArthur landed in the Philippines in October; and bombing raids on Tokyo were launched from Saipan in November. If OSS did not enter the Pacific shortly, it would not enter at all. Donovan offered to share "secret intelligence information about Japan" with Nimitz if he would allow OSS operations in his theater. The offer was made through Commander Halliwell, OSS's representative with Nimitz, on January 29 by OSS deputy director Charles Cheston and OSS deputy director of intelligence John Magruder.[68] The intelligence, commonly known as the "Vessel Reports," purportedly originated from Vatican sources and concerned the attitudes and decisions of Japanese leaders. Halliwell was told that the reports were extremely valuable and were to be seen only "by Admiral Nimitz's staff intelligence officers." He was told that the reports originated from Vatican sources who had close contacts with Japanese officials in Rome. From the beginning, army intelligence analysts believed the reports were fraudulent and "planted" on OSS by Japanese agents. It was true that the Vessel Reports were forgeries, for they were produced by a former pornographer and journalist named Virgilio Scattolini, who sold the reports to newspapers and intelligence agencies to support his family. They were not planted on OSS by the Japanese. The documents were proved to be fakes at the end of February 1945, after Nimitz rejected Donovan's offer. Nimitz's rejection spared Donovan the embarrassment of having to explain OSS's mistake to the Pacific commander.[69]

Donovan returned to Washington from Europe on February 7, 1945 and learned of Nimitz's rejection. Three weeks later, he flew to Hawaii to confer with Nimitz. Donovan took the Agana plan with him and again tried to obtain approval for it. While Nimitz refused to allow OSS to have a base in Guam, as the Agana plan proposed, he agreed to let OSS operate a clandestine station from Saipan, where OWI was already operating. OWI established a 50-kilowatt mediumwave station on the island and was broadcasting directly to Japan. Nimitz suggested that OSS use this transmitter for making their broadcasts. The proposed black broadcasts were to be restricted to times when OWI was not transmitting, to a different frequency from that used by OWI, and with the proviso that persons of Japanese ancestry would be kept away from the island. On March 3, Donovan landed in Los Angeles, informed OSS personnel there that permission for Agana had been obtained, and then assigned the ranking commissioned officer of MO-Pacific, John Zuckerman, responsibility for the operation.[70]

Because Nimitz barred the use of Japanese personnel on Saipan, OSS established a production facility for the black programs in San Francisco. The production facility was code-named "Green's" and supervised by Bruce Rogers and managed by Bogart Carlaw. Rogers spoke Japanese, and Carlaw was a radio production expert. The assistant director was

Joe Koida. Green's was originally located in a dingy warehouse near the Embarcadero but moved to a second floor business office after the Japanese personnel complained about the first facility's shabbiness. The second location was above the United Airlines ticket agency, off Union Square, across the street from the grandam of San Francisco hotels, the St. Francis. It was hastily remodeled to provide dormitories and production facilities for its residents.[71]

San Francisco rather than Los Angeles was selected as the site for Green's because it was the gateway to the Pacific and because its large Chinese population allowed the Japanese to move about without fear of harassment. As the executive exclusion order was lifted on January 2, the Japanese were allowed on the California coast for the first time in almost three years. Thirteen of the personnel from Catalina Island were assigned to Green's. The remainder, primarily from the documents and arts squad, were sent to India.[72]

While Green's was being outfitted as a production facility, John Zuckerman was making arrangements to deliver the programs from San Francisco to Saipan. OWI had a relay facility in Delano, California, that was used to send its programs to Hawaii, which was then relayed to Saipan for rebroadcasting. Zuckerman contacted OWI headquarters in Washington and asked permission to relay the black programs using OWI facilities. He was told that the Delano relay station was already overtaxed, so it would be impossible for OWI to provide assistance. Zuckerman then contacted RCA, which had a low-power shortwave transmitter that broadcast to the Pacific. RCA agreed to relay the programs. Zuckerman then obtained speech scrambling and descrambling units that would mask the contents of the relayed programs. The programs were scrambled before being relayed so that monitors who intercepted the relays would not realize they were intended for and later broadcast by the Saipan-based station. However, when the shortwave relay signals were received and descrambled, they were found to be too distorted to rebroadcast. Even without scrambling, the signals were distorted. For this reason, the programs were recorded on 16-inch records at Green's and flown to Saipan by air-pouch.[73]

Before starting production at Green's, OSS asked the navy to make six Japanese prisoners-of-war available for interviewing and possible assignment to the "Operation Blossom" staff. (The Agana plan was called "Operation Blossom" after being approved and implemented.) Although initially reluctant, the navy made three POW's available for interviews on April 14. The prisoners-of-war were interviewed by Bruce Rogers and Joe Koida, who concluded that any would be "extremely useful" if available for just an hour a week or full time. The prisoners-of-war were needed to check the broadcasts for colloquial uses. Because most issei at Green's had not been in Japan for many years, it was possible that colloquial phrases had since changed. The use of dated colloquial expressions in broadcasts of "Voice of the People" would expose the station's foreign origins. One prisoner-of-war captured at Attu was finally selected and employed at Green's.[74]

Within four days of arrival in San Francisco, the Green's team completed their first script and recording. This, like all other broadcasts, was screened by a "panel of experts on far eastern policy and Japanese language." The panel consisted of experts from the State Department, navy, army, OWI, and OSS. The programs written and recorded at Green's claimed to originate from indigenous Japanese farmers, union members, and intellectuals who opposed the continuation of the war. The programs' theme was that "Resistance is Destruction"—a rephrasing of the Japanese military's slogan of "Resistance or Destruction." Programs consisted of nostalgic musical tunes, news broadcasts, and features. One of the features was presented in ten parts and consisted of unedited word-for-word readings from letters found on the body of a Lieutenant Yamagashi. The letters were addressed to his wife. The reading was done by a young nisei woman, who joined the Green's staff after it moved to San Francisco. Another feature directed at women was recorded by Mitsu Yashima, who escaped from Japan in 1939 after spending nearly nine years as a political prisoner. She was arrested for organizing a farm union and being a member of a Marxist study group. Her programs said that it was pointless for Japanese women to save money, as the currency was worthless; that women were prohibited from wearing pretty clothes and looking nice since the outbreak of the war; and criticized the lack of available food. Mitsu Yashima encouraged women to oppose the war and recommended that they leave the cities to escape the bombing. The latter recommendation was designed to lower Japan's war production, as women had replaced men on Japan's assembly lines.[75]

In mid-April, John Zuckerman arrived in Saipan with Alfred Leach, an OSS civilian who was an electrical engineer for RCA before the war. Before going to Saipan, Leach was in the European theater, where he helped operate the OSS-sponsored clandestine station "Volkssender Drei." On Saipan, Leach performed technical functions such as installing the recoding equipment and the descrambling devices that were eventually discarded. After two weeks, Leach returned to Washington, leaving Zuckerman to operate the black station. The first Voice of the People broadcast appeared on April 23, 1945 on 870 kilohertz, a frequency used by Osaka Radio. It broadcast for one-half hour daily until August 15 from 4:00 to 4:30 a.m. Each broadcast was a 30-minute recording prepared at Green's and shipped by airpouch to Saipan. The records were shipped seven at a time, once a week, and were accompanied by a romanized Japanese script. The script was provided so Zuckerman could follow the recording without knowing Japanese, and delete portions of the record that had become dated during the interim between recording and broadcast. Since Zuckerman could neither read nor speak Japanese and had a difficult time keying the romanized scripts to the records, he relied on two Japanese-speaking American officers to assist with the deletions. The method of deleting dated material consisted of turning off the transmitter during the time when the dated material appeared on the record.[76]

Believing that Voice of the People's sign-on represented just a first step in OSS's entry into the Pacific and that the war against Japan would continue for a long time, MO-Washington dusted off the Vega plan, made a few changes in it, and resubmitted it for approval. Vega originally proposed installing a shortwave transmitter on either Kiska or Amchitka. The revised plan suggested making mediumwave broadcasts from one of the Aleutian Islands using the 7.5-kilowatt transmitter that was purchased originally for shortwave broadcasting. The proposal also sought permission to move the Voice of the People operation from Saipan to Okinawa, where OWI operated a station. The revised proposal did not take into account the fact that 7.5-kilowatts was not enough power to send a mediumwave signal into Japan, except under certain atmospheric conditions, or that the navy, in conjunction with OWI, was sponsoring its own broadcasts to Japan. These were aboveground broadcasts, but contained suggestions that the policy of unconditional surrender did not mean permanent occupation by the allies. These broadcasts were made by Capt. Ellis Zacharias of naval intelligence. The revised Vega plan went nowhere.[77]

As "Voice of the People" was taking to the air from Saipan after over a year of planning, MO-Southeast Asia, under the new command of James Withrow, improvised its own clandestine radio operations from the field. These operations were code-named "JN–27" and "JN–28." JN–27 consisted of broadcasting fake Japanese, Malay, and Thai news adjacent to the frequency used by Radio JOAK, which carried information programs of Domei, the Japanese news agency. Domei provided news to all occupied countries. The black broadcasts originated from a 500-watt transmitter and began one-and-a-half minutes before the regular news broadcasts of Radio JOAK. Anyone trying to receive the Domei feeds could inadvertently pick up the black transmission, particularly if they were tuning in before the regular broadcast began, without knowing it was a counterfeit broadcast. Because Thai newspapers were required to carry Domei-originated news, the black materials made their way into Thai newspapers. Lt. Col. Alexander MacDonald of the OSS was in charge of the operation.[78]

JN–28 was a continuation of JN–27, using a more powerful transmitter. The operation was made possible "by the sudden appearance upon the scene of a five kilowatt radio station" in Chittagong, Burma. The station was built by the British, but all British radio personnel in the theater were moved to New Delhi to work at All-India Radio. All-India Radio, the regional voice of Great Britain, blanketed Southeast Asia in seven languages. The Chittagong transmitter was offered to OSS by Mountbatten, with the proviso that it would broadcast only black propaganda to countries outside the British commonwealth. The Chittagong transmitter counterfeited the Domei news feeds and occasionally beamed "freedom broadcasts" to Japanese troops garrisoned in Burma. The freedom station claimed to originate from a Burmese resistance movement. There is no evidence that the station ever had any clear objectives or that it was even heard by the enemy. The likelihood that the station was heard is small, because JN–28 operated only sporadically. It would have been due to chance alone that Japanese troops would have encountered and listened to the black broadcasts. Even if enemy troops did listen, the station could not have produced any effects because it had no objectives beyond "tricking" the enemy into thinking that Burmese partisans operated a transmitter when in fact they did not.[79]

## NOTES

1. Kermit Roosevelt, ed., *The Overseas Targets: War Report of the OSS*, vol. 2 (New York: Walker & Company, 1976), p. 365; Esson Gale, *Salt for the Dragon* (East Lansing, Mich.: Michigan State College Press, 1953), p. 215; Richard Harris Smith, *OSS* (Los Angeles: University of California Press, 1972), p. 243.

2. "Overall and Special Programs for Strategic Services Activities Based in China," By OSS Planning Group, *Donovan*, box 22B, pt. 1, vol. 2 (bound); "Basic Military Plan for Psychological Warfare in the Pacific Theater," by OSS Planning Group (June 12, 1943), *Donovan*, box 92A, vol. 23 (bound).

3. Bradley F. Smith, *The Shadow Warriors* (New York: Basic Books, 1983), pp. 310–12.

4. Richard Dunlop, *Donovan—America's Master Spy* (New York: Rand McNally & Company, 1982), pp. 413–14, 421.

5. William Morwood, *Duel for the Middle Kingdom* (New York: Everest House, 1980), pp. 304–05; Smith, *OSS*, pp. 259–60.

6. Smith, *The Shadow Warriors*, p. 132; Gale, *Salt for the Dragon*, p. 220.

7. Milton Miles, *A Different Kind of War* (Garden City, N.Y.: Doubleday, 1967), pp. 22–23; Michael Schaller, *The U.S. Crusade in China, 1938–45* (New York: Columbia University Press, 1979), pp. 234–35; Smith, *OSS*, pp. 245–46.

8. Smith, *OSS*, p. 246.

9. Roosevelt, ed., *The Overseas Targets*, pp. 419–22; Smith, *OSS*, pp. 253–54; Smith, *Shadow Warriors*, pp. 197–98.

10. Anthony Cave Brown, *Wild Bill Donovan, The Last Hero* (New York: Times Books, 1982), pp. 151–52.

11. After the war, Morwood wrote *Duel for the Middle Kingdom*, a history of the conflict between Mao Tse-tung and Chiang Kai-shek. He also wrote *Traveller in a Vanished Landscape: The Life and Times of David Douglas* (London: Gentry Books, 1973).

12. Smith, *OSS*, p. 278; "ETO. MO War Diaries", vol. 6, Basic Documents, *OSS*, entry 91, box 4; "Memorandum from J. Withrow to K. D. Mann" (October 31, 1944), Wash-MO-Op–76, *OSS*, entry 139, box 166.

13. "Memorandum from J. Withrow to K. D. Mann" (October 31, 1944); "Draft Report" (undated), Wash-MO-Exhibits, vol. 1, *OSS*, entry 199, box 75, folder 32. Elizabeth McDonald, *Undercover Girl* (New York: Macmillan Company, 1947), pp. 12–13, reports that Marigold was started by OSS Captain Max Kleiman, who moved to New York with seven Japanese assistants after being told that they could not stay in Washington. In Manhattan, he rented the seventh floor of an office building and established an MO print shop. This print shop became the Marigold Operation. Collingwood was established with the endorsement of Under Secretary of State Joseph Grew and Office of War Information director Elmer Davis. All Collingwood scripts and proposals were reviewed by a board of Far Eastern experts in addition to Donovan, the OSS planning board and section chiefs. The board of experts included Ambassador Joseph Grew, professors Serge Elisseeff of Harvard, Raymond Kennedy of Yale, Charles Nelson Spinks of the Office of Naval Intelligence, and Eugene Dooman of the State Department.

14. "North Pacific Plan," Project-Pac/FE Operation, *OSS*, entry 139, box 177; "Interoffice Memo to Morton Bodfish from G. Auchincloss" (March 11, 1944), Wash-MO-Pro–15, *OSS*, entry 139, box 180.

The ownership of shortwave receivers by civilians living in all but the outlying areas of Japan was illegal, according to Selden Menefee, "Japan's Psychological Warfare," *Social Forces* 21 (May) 1943, p. 433. This explains the small number of these receivers on Japan.

15. "North Pacific Plan," Project-Pac/FE Operation.

16. "North Pacific—Radio (?) Script," Project-Pac/FE Operation, *OSS*, entry 139, box 177; "Interoffice Memo to Herbert Little from G. Auchincloss" (October 23, 1943), Wash-MO-Pro–15, *OSS*, entry 139, box 179.

17. Letter to Herbert S. Little (September 30, 1943), Project-Pac/FE Operation, *OSS*, entry 139, box 177.

18. Sefton Delmer, *Black Boomerang* (London: Secker and Warburg, 1962), p. 76; "ETO. MO War Diaries", vol. 1, p. 1, Basic Documents, *OSS*, entry 91, box 4.

19. Smith, *OSS*, pp. 256–57.

20. "Suggested Proposals from OSS to the Chinese Government for Psychological Warfare Operations in Occupied China;" "Interoffice Memo to Maj. Hoffman from Maj. Herbert S. Little" (November 3, 1943) and attachments, Chungking-Reg-Op–2, *OSS*, entry 148, box 9, folder 133.

21. Dunlop, *Donovan—America's Master Spy*, p. 427; Edmond Taylor, *Awakening from History* (Boston: Gambit, 1969), pp. 346–47; Miles, *A Different Kind of War*, pp. 169–70; Corey Ford, *Donovan of OSS* (Boston: Little, Brown & Company, 1970), pp. 267–68.

22. "Brief of MO-SI Proposal for North Pacific" (January 12, 1944), Project Pac/FE, *OSS*, entry 139, box 178; "The Vega Plan," Wash-MO-Pro–15, *OSS*, entry 139, box 180. Sonic warfare was actually used during the "Husky" campaign, see "Sonic Warfare—Note by the Secretaries" (September 10, 1943), "Sonic Warfare—Report by the Joint Planners Staff" (October 28, 1943), *JCS*, Pt. 1: 1942–1945, Strategic Issues, reel 11, nos. 1046 and 1049.

23. "Pluto Plan," Project Pac/FE, *OSS*, entry 139, box 178.

24. "Memorandum for the Joint U.S. Chiefs of Staff" (September 12, 1944) and "Memo for the Joint Chiefs of Staff" (August 6, 1944) Project Pac/FE Operation, *OSS*, entry 139, box 177; "Interoffice Memo to Morton Bodfish from G. Auchincloss" (March 11, 1944), Wash-MO-Pro–15, *OSS*, entry 139, box 180.

25. "Candy Plan," Wash-MO-Pro–15, *OSS*, entry 139, box 180; Norman Moss, *Pleasures of Deception* (London: Chatto & Windus, 1977), p. 192; "MO Achievements in FE-IBTO-CTO and U.S.," Wash. Hist. Office, *OSS*, entry 99, folder 67, box 16. "Candy" was derived from the name of the Ceylonese city of Kandy, which OSS detachment 404 was headquartered near.

26. "Five Star Plan," Wash-MO-Pro–15, *OSS*, entry 139, box 180; James K. Eyre, Jr., *The Roosevelt-MacArthur Conflict* (Chambersburg, Pa.: Craft Press, 1950), pp. 168–70; William Manchester, *American Caesar, Douglas MacArthur 1880–1964* (New York: Dell Books, 1978), p. 439.

27. OSS estimated that there were large numbers of Japanese in Argentina, Brazil, and Peru. Between 300,000 and 500,000 Japanese were estimated to be in Brazil, but only 32,000 in Peru. The latter were considered a "special class" because they left Japan feeling that they were oppressed.

28. "Tulip Plan," Wash-MO-Pro–15, *OSS*, Entry 139, Box 180. A few reports on such Japanese activities appeared in the mass media (e.g., "Mexico Strikes Hard at Axis Operatives," *New York Times*, April 2, 1942, p. A12; "Ecuador Seizes Radio," *New York Times*, June 23, 1942, p. 7.

29. "Memo to James Withrow from Far East Theater Operations Officer" (March 3, 1944), Wash-MO-Op–76, *OSS*, entry 139, box 166.

30. "JCS Approval for MO Operations against Japan Based upon South America," Wash-MO-Op–76, *OSS*, entry 139, box 166.

31. "Memorandum for the Joint U.S. Chiefs of Staff" (September 12, 1944), Project-Pac/FE Operation, *OSS*, entry 139, box 177; "Memo from H. Little to D. Monroe" (August 7, 1944), Chungking-Reg-Op–2, *OSS*, entry 148, box 9, folder 133; "Letter from H. Little to Dr. Choukas and Mr. Gordon Smith" (July 4, 1945); "Memo from G. Auchincloss to H. Little" (August 23, 1944); "Orion Plan," Project-Pac/FE-Orion, *OSS*, entry 139, box 178.

32. W. E. D. (Daugherty), "Checking Operational Efficiency of Loudspeaker Equipment," in W. E. Daugherty with Morris Janowitz, eds., *A Psychological Warfare Casebook* (Baltimore: Johns Hopkins University Press, 1958), pp. 712–15.

33. Frederick Painton, "Fighting With Confetti," *American Legion Magazine*, December 1943, p. 24; Leo J. Margolin, *Paper Bullets* (New York: Froben Press, 1946), p. 94.

34. "Memo from R. Pratt to G. Auchincloss" (November 16, 1944), Chungking-Reg-Op–4, *OSS*, entry 148, box 18, folder 259; "Orion Operation" (August 11, 1944), "Memo from J. Zuckerman to H. Little" (undated copy), "Memo to H. Little from A. Pacatte" (April 24, 1945), Project-Pac/FE-Orion, *OSS*, entry 139, box 178.

35. U.S. Department of Defense, "Brief History of Radio Swan," in *Declassified Documents* (1985), 01562; David Atlee Phillips, *The Night Watch* (New York: Atheneum, 1977).

36. "Agana Plan," Wash-MO-Op–76, *OSS*, entry 139, box 166; "Agana Plan,"

"Special Timetable for Agana Plan" and "Recommendations," Project Pacific/FE, *OSS*, entry 139, box 180.

37. "Memo from MO Pacific Operations Officer" (June 1, 1944), Wash-MO-Op–76, *OSS*, entry 139, box 166; "Scripts and Synopsis of Toyama Program" (14 Broadcasts), Project-US/FE, *OSS*, entry 139, box 179.

38. "The Sayonara Broadcasts," Project-US/FE, *OSS*, entry 139, box 179. Another OSS plan was the "recording of a broadcast purporting to emanate from Osaka Central Broadcasting Station and delivered by Mr. Toshio Shiratori, former Japanese ambassador to Italy." Under the guise of "denouncing peace mongers" in Japan, Shiratori discloses many grim facts about which "the Japanese have been kept in ignorance." See "MO Morale Operations, OSS" (December 1944), *Donovan*, box 6A, files 2004–2005.

39. "The Hump Plan," Wash-MO-Pro–15, *OSS*, Entry 139, Box 180; Roosevelt ed., *The Overseas Targets* p. 428.

40. "Cable from WD [William Donovan] to 14th AF" (March 21, 1944); "Cable from Little through Chennault" (March 23, 1944); "Cable from Mann and Stevens to Coughlin" (April 16, 1944); "Cable from Mann, Stevens and McFadden" (May 2, 1944), Chungking-Reg-Op–4 Cables, *OSS*, entry 148, box 18, folder 256; "Letter to General Hsioh Li Kung" (April 20, 1944), "Outline of SACOMO Working Plans," Chungking-Reg-Op–4, *OSS*, entry 148, box 18, folder 260; "Memo from Major Little to Colonel Mann" (June 8, 1944), Project-Pac/FE-Orion, *OSS*, entry 139, box 178.

41. "Letter from H. Little to D. Monroe" (August 7, 1944), Wash-MO-Op–77; *OSS*, entry 139, box 166; "Letter to General Wang Yee Sum from Arden Dow" (December 18, 1944), Chungking-Reg-Op–2, *OSS*, entry 148, box 9, folder 133; "Letter from H. Little to J. Coughlin" (August 7, 1944), Project Pac/FE-Orion, *OSS*, entry 139, box 178.

42. "Memo from H. Little to G. Auchincloss" (November 18, 1944), Chungking-Reg-Op–4, *OSS*, entry 148, box 18, folder 259; "Letter to General Wang Yee Sum from Arden Dow" (December 18, 1944), Chungking-Reg-Op–2, *OSS*, entry 148, box 9, folder 133.

43. "Memo from H. Little to D. Monroe" (August 7, 1944), "Letter from R. Pratt to G. Auchincloss" (November 16, 1944), Chungking-Reg-Op–4, *OSS*, entry 148, box 18, folder 259; "Agenda of Points to be Discussed with Lt. Auchincloss, Lt. Zuckerman" (with notation by J. Zuckerman), Project Pac/FE-Orion, *OSS*, entry 139, box 178.

44. "Memo from D. Monroe to H. Little" (August 30, 1944), Chungking-Reg-Op–4, *OSS*, entry 148, box 18, folder 260; "Cable from D. Monroe to Kenneth Mann" (September 10, 1944), Chungking-Reg-Op–4, entry 148, box 18, folder 257.

45. "Memo to D. Monroe, Subject: Norman Li" (October 12, 1944), "Memo to Major Monroe, Subject: A. Macmillan" (October 12, 1944), Chungking-Reg-Op–4, *OSS*, entry 148, box 18, folder 259.

46. "Letter from G. Auchincloss to D. Monroe" (November 21, 1944), Chungking-Reg-Op–2, *OSS*, entry 148, box 9, folder 133.

47. "Letter from G. Auchincloss to Mr. Wang" (November 24, 1944), Chungking-Reg-Op–4, *OSS*, entry 148, box 18, folder 259.

48. "Letter from G. Auchincloss through General Wang" (November 26, 1944),

"Black Radio Training Schedule," Chungking-Reg-Op–4, *OSS*, entry 148, box 18, folder 259.

49. "Letter from G. Auchincloss to D. Monroe" (November 21, 1944), Chungking-Reg-Op–2, *OSS*, entry 148, box 9, folder 133; "Letter from Wang Yee Sum to G. Auchincloss" (November 27, 1944), Chungking Reg-Op–4, *OSS*, entry 148, box 18, folder 259.

50. "Letter from Lt. Auchincloss to General Wang" (November 27, 1944), "Letter from Lt. Auchincloss to General Wang Yee Sum" (November 28, 1944), Chungking-Reg-Op–4, *OSS*, entry 148, box 18, folder 259.

51. "Letter to General Wang Yee Sum from Arden Dow" (December 18, 1944), Chungking-Reg-Op–2, *OSS*, entry 148, box 9, folder 133; "Final Report—Black Radio, China Theater" (September 11, 1945), Kunming-MO-Pro–11, *OSS*, entry 148, box 59, folder 837.

52. "Columbia Plan" (February 25, 1945), "Memo from William Davis to Chief, OSS-China" (March 1, 1945), "Memo from R. Heppner to Commanding General, U.S. Forces" (March 3, 1945), Chungking-Reg-Op–3, entry 148, box 12, folder 87.

53. McDonald, *Undercover Girl*, p. 200.

54. "Final Report - Black Radio, China Theater", Kunming-MO-Pro–11, *OSS*, entry 148, box 59, folder 837. The Chinese employees were paid $100 per month plus room and board. By the time the war ended, they were receiving $125.

55. Kermit Roosevelt, ed., *The Overseas Targets*, p. 450, reports that MO operated the "7,500-watt radio transmitter" for the China broadcasts. The 7 1/2-kilowatt transmitter was never put into action during the period that OSS was there. For discussions of the Chinese-sponsored clandestine stations, see Lawrence Soley and Sheila O'Brien, "Clandestine Broadcasting in the Southeast Asian Peninsula," *International Communication Bulletin* 22 (Spring 1987), pp. 13–20; and Lawrence Soley and John Nichols, *Clandestine Radio Broadcasting* (New York: Praeger, 1987), pp. 297–301.

56. The China G–2 was Paul Linebarger, author of *Psychological Warfare* (Washington, D.C.: Infantry Journal Press, 1948); "STASM: Psychological Warfare and Literary Criticism," *South Atlantic Quarterly* 46 (July 1940), pp. 344–348; *The Handbook of Black* (manuscript); *A Syllabus of Psychological Warfare* (Washington, D.C.: The Pentagon, Propaganda Branch, October 1946); and "Psychological Warfare," *Information Services for Officers* 3 (March 1951), pp. 19–52. The latter three are available in *Linebarger*, Boxes 11 and 12.

57. Soley and O'Brien, "Clandestine Broadcasting in the Southeast Asian Peninsula," p. 13, incorrectly report that the Chinese stations were the first clandestine radio stations operated by OSS in Asia.

58. "Canton [Script] #29," Kunming-MO-Pro–1 Annex, *OSS*, entry 148, box 59, folder 852.

59. "Final Report—Black Radio, China Theater" (September 11, 1945), Kunming-MO-Pro–11, *OSS*, entry 148, box 59, folder 837; "Pegasus Scripts," Kunming-MO-Pro–1 Annex, *OSS*, entry 148, box 60. Pierre Lorain, *Clandestine Operations* (New York: Macmillan, 1983), pp. 70–76 contains a description of breakable ciphers.

60. "Wuhan [Script] #1" Kunming-MO-Pro–1 Annex, *OSS*, entry 148, box 60, folder 854.

61. McDonald, *Undercover Girl*, p. 201. According to G. Auchincloss, Mc-Donald's report was overly dramatic. Wau Yan Chu-he predicted a major disaster for the last week of July. When no disaster happened, Mr. Wau apologized to his listeners for having made an "arithmetic error." He calculated incorrectly and said that the disaster would be next week, which was the first week in August.

62. "Final Report—Black Radio, China Theater" reports that "Jig" made seven broadcasts between August 11 and 17. This is inaccurate, according to all other sources.

63. "Memorandum for the Joint Chiefs of Staffs" (August 6, 1944), Project-Pac/FE, *OSS*, entry 139, box 177. Stuart Seaton wrote a monograph for the Carnegie Institute entitled "Ionoscopic Research at College Alaska, July 1941-June 1946" based on his studies there.

64. "Letter to FCC from J. R. Withrow" (August 8, 1944), "Letter from OSS to OWI" (August 9, 1944), "Memorandum for the Joint U.S. Chiefs of Staff" (September 12, 1944), Project-Pac/FE, *OSS*, entry 139, box 177.

65. "North Pacific Schedule of Operations" (August 8, 1944), Project-Pac/FE, *OSS*, entry 139, box 177; "Memo from R. Pratt to G. Auchincloss" (November 16, 1944), Chungking-Reg-Op–4, *OSS*, entry 148, box 18, folder 259; "Memorandum from J. Withrow to K. D. Mann" (October 31, 1944), Wash-MO-Op–76, *OSS*, entry 139, box 166.

66. Kermit Roosevelt, ed., *The Overseas Targets*, pp. 365–66.

67. Jin Konomi, "Remembrances of Joe Koida, Pt. 2", *Pacific Citizen*, July 4–11, 1980, pp. 8–9. The report by Konomi may be a bit exaggerated because, according to John Zuckerman, the Catalina personnel were allowed to leave the island for visits to Los Angeles. Kermit Roosevelt, ed., *War Report of the OSS*, vol. 1 (New York: Walker & Company, 1976), p. 251, implies that Marigold continued to operate until "May 1945, when the entire focus of the war shifted to the Far East." This implication appears to be the result of sloppy editing or writing by the Strategic Services History Project.

68. Cave Brown, *Wild Bill Donovan*, p. 694. Cave Brown refers to Halliwell as a Lieutenant Colonel.

69. Smith, *The Shadow Warriors*, pp. 313–14; Cave Brown, *Wild Bill Donovan*, pp. 701–02.

70. There is some "mystery" concerning Donovan's movements between February 27 and March 5, 1945, according to Cave Brown, *Wild Bill Donovan*, pp. 733–34. Brown places Donovan in Europe during this period, despite there being no record of his arrival at Eisenhower's headquarters, and entries in his secretary's diaries reporting that Donovan left for Hawaii on February 26 and returned to Los Angeles on March 3.

71. "Black Radio—'Blossom' " (undated), Project-Pac/FE, *OSS*, entry 139, box 177. The shabby treatment accorded Japanese OSS personnel was also apparent in wage scales. The Japanese were paid substantially less than comparably qualified Caucasians, according to Jim Konomi, "Remembrances of Joe Koida, Pt. I," *Pacific Citizen* June 27–July 3, 1980, pp. 1, 8. To top off the indignities that he suffered during the war, Joe Koida became the target of anti-Communist hysteria during the 1950s and faced deportation under the McCarran Act. See "Letter to the Editor by Karl Yoneda," *Pacific Citizen*, October 24, 1980, p. 8.

72. Jin Konomi, "Remembrances of Joe Koida, Pt. II." The departure of the

Japanese for India was "interminably delayed" by Ruth Shipley, the vindictive director of State's passport division, who disliked OSS and its personnel, according to Smith, *OSS*, p. 24.

73. "Black Radio—'Blossom' " (undated), Project-Pac/FE, *OSS*, entry 139, box 177.

74. "To Assistant Chief of Staff, G–2 from Director of OSS" (April 2, 1945), "Memorandum for Director, Office of Strategic Services" (April 10, 1945), "Memo to B. Rogers, Lt. Little, Mr. Carlaw" (April 16, 1945), "File Memo by K. D. Mann" (April 17, 1945), Wash-Mo-Pro–15, *OSS*, entry 139, box 180.

75. "Proposed Black Radio Operation Based on Aleutian Islands" (after May 1945), Project-Pac/FE, *OSS*, entry 139, box 177; Jin Konomi, "Remembrances of Joe Koida, Part II," Judy Stone, "America's Tokyo Rose," *San Francisco Chronicle*, December 4, 1975, p. 11.

76. "ETO. Administration Biographies," Basic Documents, *OSS*, entry 91, box 4; Moss, *The Pleasures of Deception*, p. 192, incorrectly reports that "Voice of the People" inaugurated broadcasts in July, 1945. Roosevelt ed., *The Overseas Targets*, p. 367, confusing the original proposal with the actual operation, reports that the station was located on Guam and operated by a "small staff of specialists."

77. "Proposed Black Radio Operation Based on Aleutian Islands" (after May 1945), Project-Pac/FE, *OSS*, Entry 139, Box 177; M. J. (Morris Janowitz), "Captain Zacharias's Broadcasts to Japan," in W. E. Daugherty with Morris Janowitz, eds., *A Psychological Warfare Casebook* (Baltimore: Johns Hopkins University Press, 1958), pp. 279–91. That OSS leaders believed the Pacific war would continue for a long time is supported by their actions in July. During that month, the Green's studio was soundproofed and another thirty days worth of programs requested. See Jin Konomi, "Remembrances of Joe Koida, Pt. II."

78. Moss, *The Pleasures of Deception*, p. 192; "Major Achievements in FE-IBTO-CTO and U.S.," Wash. Hist. Office, *OSS*, entry 99, box 16, folder 67.

79. "Major Achievements in FE-IBTO-CTO and U.S."; McDonald, *Undercover Girl*, pp. 127, 144. Kermit Roosevelt, ed., *War Report of the OSS*, vol. 1, p. 221, contradicts McDonald by reporting that the scripts for JN–27 and JN–28 were written in Washington. The *War Report* is unclear about where these broadcasts originated. Although the *War Report* mentions Ceylon, they most certainly did not originate there, despite the existence of several plans that suggested making such broadcasts from Trincomalee. The plans for Ceylon are mentioned in "The Morale Operations Branch of OSS (speech)," (January 20, 1945), Wash-MO Exhibits, vol. 4, *OSS*, entry 99, box 75, folder 37.

# 6

## SOVIET PSYCHWAR AND THE START OF THE COLD WAR

The Soviet Union, like the United States and Great Britain, operated psychwar radio stations during World War II. The Soviet-sponsored stations differed from the Anglo-American stations in four respects: 1) the radios attacked the Nazi elite, their industrialist supporters, and the German military establishment as classes and as individuals: 2) the stations were often operated by exiled rather than ersatz opposition groups; 3) the stations admitted their pro-Soviet bias or their Soviet-sponsorship, and 4) the Soviet psychwar radio stations were operated independently of the other allies—there was no collaboration between Soviet psychwarriors and the Political Warfare Executive (PWE) or Office of Strategic Services (OSS).[1]

The Soviet-sponsored broadcasts directed at Germany and German troops frequently attacked Hitler as a gangster, a reactionary, or a lying psychopath, something that U.S. psychwar stations avoided doing. Because prisoner interrogations revealed that German troops were fiercely loyal to the Fuehrer, the Psychological Warfare Division (PWD) and OSS avoided personal attacks on him in their black propaganda. They approached psychwar as though it were advertising; they avoided making dissonance-arousing broadcasts. Instead of direct attacks on the German leader, the stations attempted to sow confusion, despair, and defeatism through subtle means. The United States-operated stations that broadcast to Germany claimed to be operated by Germans loyal to, or formerly loyal to, Hitler. While these stations oftentimes criticized Hitler's closest advisers, including Hermann Goering and Joseph Goebbels, the stations never personally attacked Hitler. The Soviet Union, which was undoubtedly also aware of the loyalty of German troops to Hitler, pursued a different strategy. Soviet psychwar stations disparaged Hitler and his followers, and called for revolution against the existing leadership.[2]

Many spokesmen on the Soviet-sponsored stations were well-known exiles who had taken refuge in the U.S.S.R. They also spoke for well-known leftist organizations. "Radio Milano Libertad" was operated by and spoke for the exiled Italian Communist party leadership. "Kossuth Radio" was the voice of the Hungarian Social Democratic party. "Radio España Independiente" claimed to speak for the defeated, exiled Spanish republican government. "Radio Free Yugoslavia" spoke for Marshal Josef Broz Tito's partisan guerrillas. These stations were unabashedly pro-Soviet. Upon receiving a shipment of grain from the U.S.S.R., Tito's partisans declared over Radio Free Yugoslavia that:

Brotherly help arrived by way of 500,000 tons of corn. Meetings were held in towns and villages from which expressions of gratitude were sent to the great Soviet Nation. The speakers stressed the fact that this help was all the more appreciated as we know that the U.S.S.R. itself had sustained ravages on a large scale in this war, more than any other country.[3]

Most Soviet-supported stations lavished similar praises on the USSR.

While Kossuth Radio, Radio Milano Libertad, and Radio España Independiente were clandestine, claiming to originate from Hungary, Italy, and Spain respectively, other Soviet-sponsored broadcasts were open about their Soviet origins. These included programs broadcast by Soviet aboveground transmitters for the Union of Polish Patriots, the Hungarian National Independence Front, and the Free Germany Committee and League of German Officers. These broadcasts differed greatly from those sponsored by the United States because they articulated the views of real rather than fictitious organizations, and because they represented a strategic rather than tactical approach to psychological warfare.

Soviet sponsorship of broadcasts by authentic anti-Fascist organizations, combined with U.S. ignorance concerning the method and purpose of Soviet psychwar operations, produced an intense distrust of the Soviets among conservative U.S. military and OSS leaders. The distrust was exacerbated when intelligence reports indicated that the Soviet operations were more effective than those of the United States. An analysis written by OSS conservative John C. Wiley, the former ambassador to Lithuania, claimed that Soviet propaganda successes produced the "dangerous paradox of having our political authority on the Continent of Europe diminish while our military strength is notably ascendent."[4] Memos by the OSS chief in Bern, Allen Dulles, echoed the same sentiments.[5] When these suspicions and fears reached the ears of reactionary anti-Soviet U.S. political leaders such as John Rankin, it provided them with an irresistible opportunity to resurrect their prewar investigations of

Communist subversion in the United States. Soviet critics like Congressmen Rankin, Karl Mundt, and J. Parnell Thomas were relatively restrained in their attacks on the Soviet Union between 1942 and 1945, for fear that loud denunciations of the United States' wartime ally would be viewed with suspicion, for prior to the entrance of the United States into the war these anti-Communist political leaders were known to be more sympathetic to Hitler than to the New Deal.

The distrust between the United States and the Soviet Union led to a breach in relations following the end of the war, despite Soviet attempts to demonstrate its support for the Allied agreements reached at the Teheran and Yalta conferences. Consistent with these agreements, no Soviet-sponsored psychwar stations broadcast to the Far East, the subcontinent, the Middle East, or Greece. The Soviets viewed Japanese-occupied areas in the Pacific as areas of U.S. interest. India, Burma, the Middle East, and Greece were viewed by the Soviets as areas of British influence, so no Soviet-sponsored stations broadcast to these regions. The Soviets also limited the amount of subversive propaganda directed at the low countries, France, and Italy, as these areas were considered to be in the Anglo-American sphere of influence. The one Soviet-sponsored station that broadcast to Italy, Radio Milano Libertad, started broadcasting in 1937, prior to the outbreak of the war.[6] Soviet psychwar broadcasts were instead directed at the countries of East-Central Europe, where the Soviets claimed a sphere of influence. Soviet-sponsored clandestine stations broadcast continuously to Germany, Bulgaria, Czechoslovakia, Hungary, Yugoslavia, Poland, and Rumania. For example, four clandestine stations broadcast from the Soviet Union to Czechoslovakia, while none broadcast to Luxemburg, Belgium, or the Netherlands.[7]

The psychwar broadcasts of the Soviet Union can be classified as "ghost" broadcasts, Christian stations, soldiers' stations, ersatz freedom stations, Comintern-originated stations, and the aboveground broadcasts of Soviet-sponsored anti-Fascist organizations. Unlike the United States and Great Britain, the Soviets did not sponsor any station that claimed to be operated by astrologers, dead generals, businessmen selling advice, foul-mouthed pro-Hitler officers, or "latticintersticologists." The Soviet broadcasts, including their ghost broadcasts, were straightforward anti-Hitler operations. The ghost broadcasts consisted of the interruption of German newscasts with anti-Hitler comments. Unlike the Intruder broadcasts used by the Anglo-Americans, the ghost broadcasters did not pretend to be authentic German announcers. The ghosts would instead break into aboveground broadcasts, heckling and degrading German government interpretations of events with comments such as:

Announcer: The positions of the German and enemy armies on the Eastern and Western fronts have remained unchanged. . . .

Ghost: That's not true! You are keeping silent about your new defeats.

Announcer: The V-weapons, which will result in German victory, are ready for deployment. . . .

Ghost: That's the greatest swindle! You are building castles in the air. Only Hitler monkeys believe in wonder weapons!

Announcer: Hitler Youth brigades have volunteered to fight on the Eastern front. . . .

Ghost: Cannon fodder! Hitler murders German youth. They'll rot in mass graves.

Announcer: The enemy is intent on destroying the German people. . . .

Ghost: That's a lie! Hitler invented that [lie]. He'll bring us to the grave if we don't get rid of him. Hitler destroys everything.[8]

The ghost voice would not only interrupt German newscasts, but also broadcasts of Hitler's speeches. When Hitler would pause between sentences, the ghost voice would interrupt with shouts of "liar" and "murderer."[9]

The Soviets started using ghost voices to interrupt German newscasts in the middle of 1941, and continued to make such broadcasts until the war ended. The USSR also used ghost voices to interrupt and degrade the broadcasts of other Axis broadcasting stations, including those in Hungary and Romania. The interruptions were widely discussed in the Allied press, and the ghost voices were given several nicknames, including "Der Snag," "Man of the Clouds," "Man of the People", and "Ivan the Terrible." *Time* magazine reported that the German-language ghost voice was that of Ernst Fischer, a Viennese journalist who had taken refuge in the USSR. Rather than fearing these broadcasts, most PWE and OSS agents looked upon them with a mixture of awe and admiration.[10]

The Christian stations that the Soviet Union sponsored were designed to counter Nazi allegations that the USSR was the bastion of "Jewish atheism." The Christian stations, which broadcast in Bulgarian, French, German, Hungarian, Polish, Slovak, and Spanish, depicted Hitler as the anti-Christ and claimed that Hitler, not Stalin, was the enemy of Christianity. The stations went so far as to describe the USSR as the chief "defender of Christianity" in Europe. These stations were similar in style and content to "France Catholique" and "Christus der König" ("Christ the King"), two clandestine stations operated by the PWE. For that reason, their operation did not unduly alarm conservatives in the U.S. military or OSS, except insofar as the stations generated goodwill for the Soviet Union in Europe.

The Soviet-operated soldiers' stations were primarily directed at German troops deployed along the Eastern front. One station called "Die Heimat Ruft die Front" ("Voice of the Front") described conditions inside Germany to soldiers. The station reported on the bombing of German cities, outbreaks of disease, and food shortages. Speaking in favor of family ties rather than loyalty to Hitler, the station urged soldiers to abandon their arms and return home. Another station was directed at German soldiers in the Caucasus. The station appeared on October 23, 1942 and was called "Sendung der Soldaten Wahrheit" (Soldiers' Transmission of Truth). Another station called "Der Soldatensender" appeared the same day. It used the same slogan as another soldiers' station called the "Polarsender Wahrheit" and a Comintern-operation station called the "Volkssender." The slogan of these stations was: "Hitler began the war and it will finish him in the end." The Polarsender was addressed to German troops in the "far north." Like Der Soldatensender, it was of unconcealed Soviet origin. In this respect, the stations differed from such Anglo-American stations as Soldatensender Calais, Wehrmachtsender Nord, and Radio 1212 that were also directed at German troops. By not openly admitting that they operated these stations, the Anglo-Americans appeared more duplicitous than the Soviets. The Anglo-Americans, who simultaneously emphasized unconditional surrender in their aboveground broadcasts, also gave the impression that they cared less about the plight and future of the average German than did the Soviets. As a consequence, the soldiers' stations of the Soviet Union produced greater goodwill for the USSR than did comparable stations operated by PWE and OSS.[11]

In addition to operating soldiers' stations, the Soviets also operated ersatz freedom stations. Like their British counterparts, these freedom stations claimed to, but did not, originate within the countries to which they broadcast. The USSR operated a clandestine station called "Radio France" that was similar in many respects to the British-operated "Radio Inconnue." The station advocated resistance and sabotage, but was not identifiably pro-de Gaulle. Two similar Soviet-operated stations broadcast to Czechoslovakia: "Radio of Czech Liberation" and "Radio of Slovak Liberation." Both were openly pro-Soviet, attacked collaborationists, and advocated sabotage. The British operated a similar station that broadcast to Czechoslovakia called "Radio Bradlo, Voice of the Slovak People." The Soviets operated another anti-Nazi station called the "Sudetendeutsche Freiheitssender," which broadcast anti-Hitler programs to the Sudetenland. A similar station, which held Norway up as an example of the correct method for defeating Nazism, was called "Finland's Free Radio." Except for being pro-Soviet, the station was similar in tone and content to the PWE-operated "Norwegian Freedom Station."[12]

The Soviet Union operated a clandestine station directed at Poland that not only differed in content from a British-sponsored Polish psychwar station, but attacked the British-sponsored station as a voice of the reactionary Polish aristocracy. The Soviet-sponsored station was called "Radio Kościusko"; the British-sponsored station was called "Radio Polska Świt." Both were anti-Nazi and broadcast from abroad—Radio Kościusko from Moscow and Radio Świt from Woburn Abbey. Radio Kościusko attacked the exiled government, for which Świt spoke, for doing nothing to expel the Germans from Poland. The Soviet station, unlike Świt, appealed to Poles to begin an uprising. The exiled government opposed an uprising on the grounds that it would lead to an unnecessary bloodbath. While Radio Kościusko criticized exiled Polish leader General Władysław Sikorsi during late 1942 and early 1943 for being pacific in the face of German atrocities, the criticism turned to vitriol in mid–1943 after Sikorski accused the USSR of murdering Polish officers in Katyn forest in 1940. The Soviets denied Sikorski's claim and said that the officers were killed by German troops. After this incident, Radio Kościusko attacked the Sikorski government for being a reactionary supporter of the Polish gentry and a collaborator with Hitler. Its major purpose became the discrediting of the exiled Polish government. The station gave the West its first warning that the USSR was unwilling to accept an unfriendly government in neighboring Poland. Soviet intentions became even more clear in July 1944, when the Union of Polish Patriots announced in a program broadcast by Radio Moscow that it was creating a Committee of National Liberation that would act as "provisional executive authority" in territories from which the Germans were expelled.[13]

Churchill and Roosevelt were aware of Soviet intentions before mid–1944, although neither were sure of the extent to which Stalin wanted to control the government of Poland. At Teheran Stalin made it clear that he would not accept an anti-Soviet government in Poland. Sikorski's actions together with Stalin's statements made it clear to Churchill and Roosevelt that the exiled government would not be returning to Poland after the German defeat. Although the Western leaders agreed that Poland was in the Soviet sphere of influence and that Stalin could install a pro-Soviet government there, this was never made public. Their silence regarding Poland's future allowed anti-Communists in the United States to claim that Soviet actions in Poland provided "clear evidence" of Stalin's nefarious intentions in all of Europe.

The Comintern-originated stations were continuations of stations that first appeared in the prewar era. The prewar stations broadcast against Hitler and Mussolini during the Popular Front period, but were silenced following the signing of the Ribbentrop-Molotov Non-Aggression Pact in 1939. The Comintern-originated stations returned to the air in mid–1941, following the German invasion of the USSR. These stations broadcast to Italy, Spain, Rumania, and Yugoslavia, and continued to broadcast after the dissolution of the Comintern on June 8, 1943. The Comintern was dissolved to dispel criticism from conservative U.S. and British politicians, who asserted that Stalin controlled a fifth column of Communist parties through the Comintern. By dissolving the Comintern, Stalin hoped to dispel such criticisms of the Soviet Union and its fraternal Communist parties.[14]

The operation of the Comintern-sponsored stations was supervised by Palmiro Togliatti, the fiercely independent leader of the Italian Communist party. Radio España Independiente was the first Comintern station to appear. It signed on July 22, 1941, one month after the outbreak of war between the Soviet Union and Germany. The station denounced Gen. Francisco Franco as a Nazi accomplice. Its manager was Dolores Ibarruri, better known as La Pasionaria during the Spanish civil war. The second station to take to the airwaves was Radio Milano Libertad. It appeared on August 1, 1941, breaking a two-year silence. The station's slogan was "Germans out of Italy." It reportedly had a very large audience in Italy. The large audience was generated by targeting specific groups in Italy. Radio Milano Libertad featured a special program for workers on Monday, for youths on Wednesday, for Fascists on Thursday, and for peasants on Saturday. On Sunday, the station broadcast a special program for Italians in North America.[15]

The third Comintern-sponsored station to appear was Romania Libera. This station's slogan was "Down with Hitlerism! Long Live Free Romania!" It shared a transmitter with Radio Free Yugoslavia, the station of the Yugoslav partisans. A fifth Comintern-controlled station broadcast from the Soviet Union to Germany: the "Deutsche Volkssender" ("German People's Radio"). This station was operated by the German Communist Party (KPD) and appeared on September 10, 1941. It claimed to be the successor of the Freiheitssender that broadcast during the prewar era. The station, in addition to publicizing KPD policy and providing news of the war, provided advice on methods of resistance. KPD members within Germany transcribed the broadcasts and clandestinely distributed the transcriptions. Several underground newspapers, including *Wahrheit* (Truth) and *Freiheit* (Freedom), were largely based on broadcasts of the Volkssender. The Volkssender was associated with a station that broadcast to German youths. The station, called "Sender der Deutsche Jugend," carried talks on the future, working conditions, and the number of young casualties produced by Hitler's war. It broadcast twice daily on two frequencies.[16]

## IN SOVIET PRISON CAMPS: THE "FREE GERMANS"

The continuation of broadcasts from the Volkssender, Radio Milano Libertad, and Radio España Independiente after the disbanding of the Comintern in mid–1943 went unnoticed by anti-Communists in the United States, for their attention quickly focused on the Free Germany Committee, an anti-Hitler organization established on Soviet soil on July 12/

13, 1943. The Free Germany Committee was composed of KPD exiles, well-known Communist sympathizers, German soldiers, and military officers. Until late 1944, the committee was the principal psychological warfare weapon in the arsenal of the Soviet Union. The Free Germans produced a program called "Radio Free Germany" that was aired by Radio Moscow four times, and later six times, daily; published a newspaper entitled *Freies Deutschland* that was widely circulated in prisoner-of-war camps and dropped behind enemy lines; and manned loudspeaker corps that shouted surrender orders to German troops along the Eastern front.[17]

The Free Germany Committee was the culmination of several attempts between 1941 and 1943 to organize anti-Nazi organizations among German POWs. In October 1941, four months after the German attack on the Soviet Union, exiled KPD leader Walter Ulbricht presented a manifesto at a compulsory conference held at Prisoner-of-War Camp No. 58 that called for a "free and independent" Germany. Ulbricht persuaded only 158 of over 1,000 prisoners-of-war to sign the prepared manifesto. The Marxist prose in the statement dissuaded all but a few privates and noncommissioned officers from signing it. Most that did sign were anti-Nazi before the war.[18]

Other conferences were held between December 1941 and mid–1942, but not surprisingly received only limited support from the internees. The KPD was unable to generate support for its organizations because most POWs, particularly officers, believed that joining anti-Hitler organizations was an act of treason, a violation of their loyalty oath, and an act contrary to their beliefs. The prisoners were both wary of the KPD and the Soviets, and difficult to persuade. A decade of exposure to Nazi propaganda made most German officers resistant to Soviets attempts at persuasion. Most officers also still believed in the possibility of a German victory, particularly after the German drive to the Volga and Caucasus in the spring of 1942.[19]

By the end of the year, these hopes of victory were dashed. In September, the Sixth and Fourth Panzer armies were tied down at Stalingrad. On November 19, Soviet armored divisions launched a drive that culminated in the encircling of the Sixth and half of the Fourth army. Caught in the encirclement were Gens. Friedrich von Paulus and Walther von Seydlitz. Paulus was one of Germany's most distinguished generals; von Seydlitz was distinguished not only for his leadership, but for being a descendant of the renowned eighteenth-century Prussian general, Friedrich Wilhelm von Seydlitz. Paulus and von Seydlitz sought permission from Hitler to fight their way out of the pocket, but were ordered to stay by Hitler. Hitler's mad hatred of Soviet leader Stalin, for whom Stalingrad was named, seemed to have undermined his ability to understand the dangers faced by the encircled armies. Instead of allowing the retreat,

Hitler ordered the generals to hold their ground. The Fuehrer promised air support and relief, but delivered little. Realizing that their position was quickly deteriorating, the generals again sought permission to break out in mid-December. Hitler refused to issue new orders. Three weeks later, the Soviets attacked the pocket on three sides. The encircled troops were able to hold out for just three weeks. After losing 200,000 of his troops, General Paulus surrendered on January 31, 1943.

The defeat at Stalingrad not only dashed hopes for a German victory, but provided a massive number of potential recruits for Soviet-backed anti-Nazi organizations. These POWs, unlike those taken earlier by the Soviets, proved to be a more receptive recruitment group because the loss at Stalingrad inspired soul-searching among the defeated commanders. Thousands and thousands of their troops died at Stalingrad because of Hitler's inability to grasp the gravity of the situation. How could Hitler so callously sacrifice the lives of 200,000 men? How could a competent military leader fail to order a withdrawal from the pocket? These questions were asked by the officers taken prisoner at Stalingrad. The answers to their questions pointed in one direction—to Hitler's incompetence. Their conclusions about Hitler, along with Soviet incentives, eventually led to the breaking of their loyalty oath and the creation of the League of German Officers. After its formation in September 1943, the league became part of the Free Germany Committee.

The Free Germany Committee and Officers' League were founded only after the KPD reevaluated its strategy. The reevaluation, and the subsequent strategy that it adopted, were undoubtedly inspired by Stalin, who exercised immense power over the German Communist leadership. At a series of meetings in Moscow during mid–1943, the KPD rejected its earlier line and reintroduced the concept of the popular front. The popular front strategy was used during the 1930s, but was abandoned after the outbreak of war. The KPD, like other Communist parties, declared the war to be an imperialist conflict and claimed that the only way it could be ended was by socialist revolution. The KPD, based upon this analysis, attempted to recruit POWs into pro-Communist, rather than purely anti-Hitler, organizations between 1941 and 1943. After resurrecting the popular front strategy, the primary focus of the KPD shifted to the building of a broad-based anti-Hitler organization among POWs— the Free Germany Committee. The Free Germany Committee never mentioned socialism, class conflict, or revolution in its propaganda.

By July 12, 1943, when the founding conference of the National Committee for a Free Germany was held at Krasnogorsk, the KPD had not only abandoned its revolutionary rhetoric but had adopted a strongly nationalist tone. The party's turn toward nationalism was endorsed by Soviet leaders, who went so far as to suggest that the Free Germany Committee adopt the colors of Imperial Germany. KPD leaders accepted the Soviet suggestion and chose red, black, and white—the Imperial colors—to adorn its printed propaganda. The slogan adopted by the committee was "Germany must never die!"[20]

The founding conference was attended by delegates from all prisoner-of-war camps, but officers above the rank of major were conspicuously absent. Although opposed to Hitler's policies, the officers had little incentive to join the new organization, as they were treated much differently than other POWs. They had better food, accommodations, and recreational facilities than regular soldiers. Soldiers were given additional food and other material incentives by the Soviets for joining the Free Germany Committee. The absence of high-ranking officers did not slow the formation of the Free Germany Committee, but did initially impair the effectiveness of its propaganda, for appeals from privates, corporals, and sergeants lacked the authority of those made by generals.

The Free Germany Committee chose leaders, developed a program, and issued a manifesto stating the committee's purpose at the founding conference. German poet Erich Weinert was elected chairman of the committee. Weinert was a Communist sympathizer, who escaped to France and then Spain after Hitler became chancellor of Germany. After the fall of the Spanish republic, he went to the Soviet Union. Major Karl Hertz, one of the highest ranking officers attending the conference, was elected vice-chairman. Lt. Count Heinrich von Einsiedel, the committee's best-known member, was elected second vice-chairman. Count von Einsiedel was a Luftwaffe pilot and grandson of German chancellor Otto von Bismarck. Because of his reputation, von Einsiedel was frequently quoted and depicted in Free Germany broadcasts and leaflets.

Prominent KPD leaders were not among those chosen to head the Free Germany Committee, although they were among thirty persons chosen for its steering committee. The steering committee consisted of nineteen soldiers and officers, and eleven civilians. Among the civilians elected to the committee were KPD leaders Wilhelm Pieck, Walter Ulbricht, Martha Arendsee, and Erwin Hoernle, who were identified in Free Germany communiqués as former Reichstag deputies, not KPD members.[21]

The manifesto issued at the end of the Free Germany Committee's founding conference reported that the organization was composed of "people with the most different political viewpoints who only a year ago would have considered such unification impossible." The aim of the committee, according to the manifesto, was the overthrow of Hitler and the "formation of a genuine national government . . . [that] will enjoy the confidence of the people and their former enemies." The government would:

[eliminate] laws based on national and racial hatred; of all orders of the Hitlerite regime which degrade our people; the annulment of all measures of the Hitlerite authorities directed against freedom and human dignity. It means the restoration and extension of the political rights and social gains of the working people; freedom of speech, press, assembly, conscience and religious beliefs. It means the freedom of the economy, trade and handicraft; the guaranteed right to labor and to lawfully acquire property.[22]

The committee promised that "if the German people . . . are determined to free Germany from Hitler, they would win the right to decide their fate themselves, and other nations will take them into consideration. This is the only way of saving the very existence, freedom and honor of the German nation." In effect, the document was a masterful weave of ambiguous promises.

The absence of high-ranking officers among the membership of the Free Germany Committee presented problems for the organization. It was German officers who had the most prestige and persuasive power over German troops. Without appeals from these officers, the Free Germany Committee would never be the effective propaganda weapon that the Soviets hoped to create. All attempts to persuade or offer material incentives to colonels, captains, and generals for joining the Free Germany Committee failed. The KPD and lower-ranking officers in the committee were unable to induce their leaders to join them in denouncing Hitler. When all of these efforts failed, Soviet NKVD leader, General Melnikov, intervened. General Melnikov persuaded General von Seydlitz and several other officers to create an anti-Hitler League of German Officers. He succeeded where others had failed by promising the officers that if they could inspire Hitler's overthrow and end the "war before it had to be fought on German soil," the Soviet Union would use its influence among the Allies to ensure a Germany with 1937 borders. The Soviet general promised that this Germany would have a liberal, democratic government that was allied with the USSR by friendship pacts. This promise induced General von Seydlitz to accept leadership of the League of German Officers. The organization was created on September 12, and soon thereafter joined the Free Germany Committee. Field Marshal von Paulus initially refused to join the League of German Officers, but did so after the abortive officers' putsch of July 20, 1944. Separate appeals were drafted by the league and addressed to members of the German army. The appeals were broadcast over Radio Free Germany and included in other Soviet psychwar broadcasts, including those of the Volkssender.[24]

During its first three months of operation, Radio Free Germany carried 179 talks addressed to German troops and civilians. As time went by, fewer talks were addressed to civilians and more addressed to the armed forces, suggesting that the Free Germany Committee's primary purpose was to undermine troop morale rather than lay the groundwork for a pro-Soviet, postwar Germany. Of the 179 talks, 101 were given by identified speakers: 47 by officers, 16 by soldiers, 17 by clergy, and 17 by civilians.

Few of the unidentified speakers appeared to be members of the KPD.[25] Most of the talks emphasized German defeats at the hands of the Allies, and stressed Germany's inability to win. The best thing that loyal Germans could do, the broadcasts said, was to overthrow the Hitlerite clique. Only by eliminating Hitler could Germany be saved, for the Allies would not negotiate with Nazis. Although the broadcasts never directly stated that the United Nations would negotiate surrender terms with a non-Nazi government, this was strongly implied by the broadcast, for an independent, democratic German government was promised to the German people if they overthrew Hitler.

The promises of the Free Germany Committee superficially appeared to contradict the Allied policy of unconditional surrender. The difference between the unconditional surrender policy and the Free Germans' promises was pointed out in Axis propaganda. Radio Rome announced that the committee's existence was proof of a "Disunited Nations." German radio described the committee as unerring evidence of Soviet determination to dominate "Europe by establishing a Soviet government in Germany." Tokyo voiced the same sentiments.[26] Although the Axis powers viewed the existence of the Free Germany Committee as evidence of a rift between the Soviets and its Western allies, the USSR did not see it in the same way. To the Soviets, the Free Germany Committee was consistent with past Allied activities. The United States negotiated with and accepted Admiral Darlan after the Torch invasion. The United States dealt with and later recognized King Victor Emmanuel and Marshal Badoglio, despite their associations with Mussolini. Moreover, Free German broadcasts warned Germany not to hope for a separate peace. This warning was broadcast with some regularity. However, the Soviet-sponsored broadcasts, unlike those originating from British and U.S. transmitters, never demanded or even mentioned unconditional surrender.

Another difference between Soviet- and U.S.-sponsored broadcasts was that the Free German broadcasts frequently disparaged Hitler. The Fuehrer was accused of betraying his officers, of having plans to use poison gas on German soil, and defaulting on his promises. The purpose of the committee and the Allies' war, the broadcasts warned, was "the elimination of Hitler, of his system, of his ideology of conquest, and the extermination of racial arrogance and claims of domination."[27] Free German print propaganda was even more disparaging of Hitler. One leaflet pictured Hitler as a spiderlike creature being stepped on by Lt. Count von Einsiedel.[28] The committee contrasted its respectable history with the disreputable rule of the Nazis. The Free Germans described themselves as the spokesmen of traditional German values. Speakers on the Soviet-sponsored psychwar station noted that the Free Germany committee, unlike the Nazi party, included individuals of all classes, all walks of life, all religions, and all political parties. Clergy said that the Free

German Committee represented the voice of Christianity, while Hitler was the anti-Christ.[29]

The German propaganda machine responded by labeling the Free Germany Committee a fiction of the Bolshevist mind. The names attached to the manifesto were either forgeries, German radio contended, or those of Communists. The official line was that German soldiers would not dishonor themselves by joining a Soviet-inspired organization. When it became clear from Radio Free Germany broadcasts that committee spokesmen were authentic German soldiers, Nazi media attributed the soldiers' participation to hunger, drugs, and torture. When committee spokesmen denied these allegations, saying instead that they were well-treated, German media branded the Free Germans "a clique of traitors who had dishonorably sold themselves to the Soviets." A German radio broadcast reported:

This committee is directed by emigre German Jews and Communists who have been joined by von Seydlitz, a general who shamefully deserted his gallantly fighting troops and went over to the Bolsheviks. These henchmen of the Bolshevik mass murderers are nothing but wretched creatures of enemy propaganda.[30]

German propaganda minister Goebbels initially believed that Free Germany propaganda was extremely harmful to German morale, but later concluded that the German "people are not taking the smallest notice of it." Nonetheless, the minister decided to counteract Free German propaganda by launching a domestic propaganda campaign that emphasized Soviet atrocities.[31] While the Soviet-sponsored broadcasts called for German troops to surrender, German broadcasts claimed that Soviet troops shot captured Germans, instead of taking them prisoner. Because German troops murdered captured Soviet soldiers, it was easy for them to believe that Soviet troops were doing the same.[32]

## REACTIONS TO THE FREE GERMANY COMMITTEE

German exiles greeted the Free Germany Committee in two ways, depending upon their attitudes toward the Soviet Union. Social and Christian Democrats derided the committee as a creature of Moscow. Their position was that the committee failed to provide any basis for collaboration between the KPD and other organizations. Pro-Soviet exiles, on the other hand, expressed support for the committee. In England, Mexico, and the United States, they created similar Free Germany Committees.

On August 1, 1943 German exiles in New York gathered at the home of stage and film director Berthold Viertel, where they drafted a statement endorsing the Free Germany Committee's aims. The exiles included

Bertolt Brecht, and Thomas and Heinrich Mann. Several weeks later, members of the exile group asked Thomas Mann to head a provisional Free Germany group in the United States. After consulting with the U.S. State Department, which discouraged the group's formation, Thomas Mann rejected the invitation. The exiles then invited Protestant theologian Paul Tillich to be their leader. Tillich accepted their offer.[33]

The organization headed by Tillich was called the Council for a Democratic Germany. Like the Moscow committee, it supported the overthrow of Hitler and the establishment of a democratic German government. The council was officially founded on May 2, 1944 by former Reichstag members Paul Hertz and S. Aufhauser, publisher Henry Müller, Bertolt Brecht, and others. The council started a newspaper called *Freiheit* that received financial and ideological support from the U.S. Communist Party and other anti-Nazi organizations, including the Joint Anti-Fascist Refugee Committee. Although not at the council's founding meeting, Alfred Kantorowicz, novelist Heinrich Mann, and composer and Brecht-collaborator Hanns Eisler soon joined. These individuals, along with Brecht, were involved in the operation of the Spain-based Freiheitssender.[34]

The initial reaction of the U.S. press to the Free Germany Committee was positive. *Time* reported that the manifesto put the Soviet Union "on record for a democratic, capitalistic regime in postwar Germany." The magazine described the committee's formation and its broadcasts as "expert psychological warfare."[35] The *New York Herald Tribune* reported that the manifesto was consistent with Soviet declarations that the Nazi state and army must be destroyed, but that the German people are invincible.[36] A commentary in the *New York Times* stated:

An analysis of the character and scope of [Free Germany] broadcasts from their inception to date brings the overwhelming conclusion that . . . [they] are imminent and military and not post-war and political. The implication is clear. The Soviet authorities feel that the morale of Germany is ripe for an all-out propaganda offensive.[37]

Another *New York Times* article described the committee as a "tactical move to add to the mental confusion of the Germans and convince them of the uselessness of long and bloody resistance." The article was written by Alexander Werth. The Free Germany Committee, Werth added, had no legal standing within or commitments from the Soviet Union.[38] An editorial in the *Washington Post* described the committee as "a propaganda weapon to help the Red army's counter-offensive by weakening the German home front." The editorial, based on views leaked by Washington officials, cautioned that the "Moscow committee could also be a tentative nucleus for a pro-Soviet organization to take authority in Germany."[39]

The initially positive attitudes toward the Free Germans quickly turned negative after U.S. officials publicly expressed their beliefs that the Free Germany committee could be a Soviet attempt to lay the groundwork for a Communist government in postwar Germany. Although President Roosevelt refused to comment on the formation of the Free Germany Committee, other U.S. officials did. A *New York Times* article based on these officially expressed views described the manifesto as a "notice to Great Britain and the United States from Premier Joseph Stalin that the Soviet government intends to proceed independently of us in post-war adjustments." Stalin, the officials warned, "aims to establish a European order on his own concepts and under the aegis of Moscow."[40]

This interpretation of Soviet intentions was the same as in Axis propaganda. Reich broadcasts described the committee as a Soviet attempt to "gain a key position for the domination of Europe."[41] While claiming this publicly, Goebbels and other Nazi leaders really believed that the committee existed for one purpose only—psychological warfare. Goebbels concluded the committee's purpose was tactical because its broadcasts appeared whenever the Germany army scored victories, but disappeared when the Soviets scored victories.[42] The public pronouncements about the committee were made to stiffen German resistance and to encourage conflicts between the Soviet Union and its allies.

In nonpublic forums, U.S. political and military analysts expressed even greater alarm about the committee's formation than they did in public. An evaluation of the Free Germany Committee made by James Grafton Rogers, a conservative former law professor, OSS leader, and long-time friend of Secretary of War Henry Stimson, concluded that "the Free German Committee might become the nucleus of the future government of Germany." Rogers' report was circulated within OSS and the Joint Chiefs of Staff (JCS). In it, he warned that the Soviets had created other exile committees that, like the Free Germans, could quickly be turned into Soviet-recognized governments. The committees included the Hungarian National Independence Front and the Union of Polish Patriots.[43] The Polish Patriots, like the German committee, broadcast their radio program over Radio Moscow. In another memo, Rogers expressed even greater doubts about Soviet peacetime intentions. He claimed that the Soviet Union had plans "for every country on the continent of Europe." Rogers accused the Soviets of having replaced the Comintern, which supported worldwide revolution, with groups with limited revolutionary objectives. Their objectives were to be in position to seize power in the political vacuum of postwar Europe.[44] Rogers undoubtedly conveyed his suspicions to Secretary Stimson.

Rogers' report not only charged that the committee represented Soviet expansionism but concluded that favorable reports on it that appeared in the U.S. press originated with Soviet propagandists. He described

Alexander Werth as a reporter "friendly to the Soviet Union" whose articles "faithfully" followed the official Soviet line. Rogers contended that information in Werth's articles were of "official [Soviet] inspiration."[45]

James Grafton Rogers was not the only influential OSS leader who believed that the Free Germany Committee was the nucleus for a Soviet-dominated postwar government. John C. Wiley, the former minister to the Baltic states, warned FDR that the committee "was built around the German section of the Comintern." The Free Germans, Wiley charged, would be used by Stalin either for negotiating a separate peace or to assist Soviet expansionism.[46] Dewitt Poole, a consultant to the State Department on the USSR who headed the foreign nationalities branch of OSS, sent memos to General Donovan and members of the Joint Chiefs warning that the "real danger to our civilization is Soviet Russia." He concluded that the formation of the Free German Committee "put in jeopardy the whole outcome of the war."[47] After the war, Poole became president of the CIA-inspired and funded National Committee for a Free Europe, which operated Radio Free Europe. Radio Free Europe was the United States' cold war counterpart to the USSR's wartime station, Radio Free Germany.

Allen Dulles, the influential OSS representative in Bern who became deputy director of the CIA in 1951 and director in 1953, warned that the Free Germany Committee had undermined the United Nations' policy of unconditional surrender. Because the Soviet-backed Free Germany Committee promised an independent government, the average German was less afraid of the USSR than earlier, Dulles concluded. When added to the fact that millions in Germany had lost all their possessions, thus making the country a "fertile field" for Communist ideology, Dulles was forced to conclude that "Russia will be the dominating force in determining the future of Europe."[48] Like Rogers, Wiley, and Poole, Dulles believed that "Russia [had] already . . . laid her plans for the kind of Europe she wants."[49]

The fears expressed by these OSS leaders were given support when the Soviet-backed Union of Polish Patriots declared itself the "provisional executive authority" of Poland. The Union of Polish Patriots declared the Polish government in exile to be an illegal extension of the illegal 1935 constitution. The Soviet-backed committee claimed that its power originated from Poland's original 1921 constitution.[50]

Although Stalin repeatedly informed Roosevelt and Churchill that he intended to have a pro-Soviet government in Poland, the creation of the "provisional executive authority" was nonetheless greeted with horror and suspicion in the United States. The press, Joint Chiefs, and conservative congressmen concluded that the Free Germans would do the same in Germany, even though Stalin sent numerous messages to the West that the USSR viewed the Union of Polish Patriots differently than the Free Germany Committee. Immediately after the German committee's formation, German Communist spokesman Alfred Kantorowicz described German officers as joining the committee out of "patriotic opportunism" or the belief that Germany's future lay in close collaboration "with Russia—whether Russia is reactionary or socialist."[51] Kantorowicz suggested that such opportunists could be used, but not trusted, by the USSR. At the Yalta conference, Stalin assured the Allied leaders that he would not reinstate the captured German officers as heads of a new German army. Other signals to this effect were also communicated to the West.

During the end of 1944 and the beginning of 1945, U.S. press reports about the Free Germany Committee's activities were intensely hostile. *Time* asserted that, while the Free Germany Committee was originally intended for use in psychological warfare, it had moved into position "to rule Germany after the defeat."[52] Following other press attacks on the committee, the USSR struck back in its own media. The Soviet publication *War and the Working Class* attacked the *New York Times, Baltimore Sun,* and *New York World-Telegram* for spreading "poisoned rumors" that the Free Germans were the nucleus of a pro-Soviet government. The latter newspaper was accused of spreading the rumor because it was pro-Fascist.[53] The committee, the Soviets declared, was created and used "as a military expedient." The USSR reported that German military officers in the committee were "unregenerate," having no sense of guilt or shame for what they had done. Such individuals could not be trusted, the Soviets said.[54]

Soviet denials about their postwar intentions did little to silence skeptics in the West. The Soviet denials focused more rather than less attention on the Free Germany Committee. The *Armed Forces Journal,* the authoritative but unofficial publication of the U.S. armed forces, reported that the possibility of the committee's being recognized as a provisional government by Stalin "is not overlooked by Washington." The journal added that Soviet actions in Poland provided evidence that this was possible.[55]

The Free Germany Committee also attracted the attention of John Rankin, who saw the committee and its supporters as a Soviet fifth column. Rankin was displeased with all anti-Hitler exiles, but particularly critical of Jewish and Marxist exiles. The Mississippi congressman denounced Albert Einstein on the House floor as a "foreign-born agitator." He also accused Bertolt Brecht, Hanns Eisler, and the Joint Anti-Fascist Refugee Committee of being dangerous, subversive elements.[56] The latter were supporters of the Free Germany Committee.

## THE RED SCARE

Congressman Rankin was able to use U.S. doubts about Soviet postwar intentions to resuscitate the House's prewar investigation of Communist activities in the United States. Rankin resurrected the Un-American Activities Committee as a permanent committee after it died at the end of the 78th Congress. He did this by a combination of shrewd parliamentary maneuvering and red-baiting. When Representative Adolph Sabath offered the usual resolution at the first meeting of the 79th Congress asking that the rules of the 78th Congress remain in effect, Rankin quickly attached an amendment to the resolution. The amendment made the Un-American Activities Committee a standing committee. Because Congress had not adopted its rules of operation, the amendment could not be killed by steering it to a committee for further deliberation. Congress was therefore forced to vote on Sabath's resolution, as amended by Rankin. The House defeated the motion by a vote of 134 to 146. Rankin then called for a roll-call vote on the resolution, stating that only a "yes" vote would keep subversives from throwing the records of the Dies committee "into the Potomac River." Not wanting to go on record as favoring such subversive activities, many congressmen changed their vote. In the roll-call, Congress passed the amended resolution.[57]

Members of the permanent Un-American Activities Committee (HUAC) included former Dies committeemen J. Parnell Thomas and Karl Mundt in addition to John Rankin. Other members were Georgia representative John S. Wood and North Carolina congressman Herbert Bonner. Both were known for their antilabor and segregationist voting records. Whenever anti-poll-tax legislation was introduced into Congress, Wood and Bonner led fights against it. Wood was selected chairman of HUAC during its first session as a permanent committee. The little-known Georgia congressman was on record opposing investigations of the Ku Klux Klan because "the threats and intimidations of the Klan [we]re an old American custom."[58] These committeemen eventually investigated the activities of Hanns Eisler, Bertolt Brecht, Alfred Kantorowicz, the Joint Anti-Fascist Refugee Committee and other "subversive elements." California congressman Richard Nixon joined the committee during the 80th Congress and used it as a stepping stone to the vice presidency. Nixon's participation in the HUAC investigations was not completely opportunistic. Like other anti-New Dealers on the committee, he hoped to discredit liberals, the Democratic party, and Roosevelt's legacy for ideological, as well as personal, reasons.

After becoming a permanent committee, HUAC initiated an investigation of Communist activities in the United States. The investigation started because members feared that Communists had penetrated and subverted the U.S. Army and the War Department. The committee's evidence of subversion was a U.S. Army pamphlet that explained "native American fascism." Native Fascists, the pamphlet said, claimed to be "100 percent American" and were "anti-Jew, anti-Negro, anti-foreign born, and anti-Catholic." Because this description fit Rankin, Wood, Bonner, and their constituents, they concluded that it was written by their Communist opponents. The committee reasoned that if the pamphlet were written by Communists, it necessarily "recommended the Soviet form of government." After reaching this conclusion, the committee denounced the army and War Department for coddling the "anti-Gentile" subversives who wrote the "pro-Communist" pamphlet.[59] HUAC soon thereafter asserted that the War Department was riddled with Communists who were attempting to steal atomic secrets while on the federal payroll.

Rather than discrediting HUAC, which logically it should have, the investigation placed the War Department on the defensive. Twenty-four hours after HUAC asserted that Communist fifth columnists were stealing atomic secrets, the War Department issued an order barring Communists from holding sensitive positions. Within the army, this meant that Communists were prohibited from holding commissions or working in areas such as cryptography.[60] The order was interpreted by HUAC as proof that Communists had penetrated the War Department, even though the order's purpose was to derail the HUAC investigation. Rather than silencing HUAC, the order caused the investigating committee to widen its inquiry into Communist activities. Within a year, it began investigating Communist penetration of the State Department. HUAC asserted that Maurice Halperin, Carl Marzani, Irving Goldman, Leo Drozdoff, and other "subversives" entered the State Department through OSS.[61] The inquiry eventually led to the trials and convictions of Alger Hiss and Carl Marzani for perjury.

The HUAC investigations started in 1945, when the Soviet Union and the United States were still allied in the war against Germany. This was two-and-a-half years before the national legislature in Hungary was dissolved; three years before the Communists seized power in Czechoslovakia; and three years before the Berlin blockade. These Communist actions are frequently cited as causes of the cold war.[62] In reality, HUAC's investigations were a cause of, rather than a response to, the cold war. The investigations generated suspicion and criticism of Soviet actions. The Soviets responded to these attacks with attacks of their own. The United States then responded to the Soviet actions, producing an ever-escalating conflict. The primary winners in the conflict were reactionaries like Congressman John Rankin, who opposed the U.S.-Soviet anti-Axis alliance from the start.

HUAC's public inquiries began a month after V-J Day, when it subpoenaed former and then-current Communist party chairmen Earl Browder and William Z. Foster, and Dr. Edward Barsky, chairman of the

Joint Anti-Fascist Refugee Committee. The congressmen learned little from Browder, less from Foster, and nothing from Barsky, who refused to cooperate with the investigation. Although Barsky appeared before the congressional committee, he refused to surrender his organization's records, as HUAC had requested. Because of his refusal, Barsky was cited for contempt of Congress.[63]

While HUAC found its first witnesses to be uncooperative, it did find two that agreed to cooperate: Gerald L. K. Smith and Louis F. Budenz. Gerald L. K. Smith was the leader of a pro-Nazi organization called the Silver Shirts, which violently assailed U.S. war efforts. HUAC treated Smith as a friendly witness. The Fascist leader testified about Communist activities, about which he knew nothing, rather than about Fascist activities, about which he knew much. Louis Budenz, unlike Smith, was an informed witness. He was a former Communist and editor of the *Daily Worker* who had broken with the party. In his testimony, Budenz asserted that the Comintern still existed, that it gave orders to the U.S. Communist party, and was represented in the United States by German refugee Gerhart Eisler. Gerhart was the older brother of Hanns Eisler, a composer, Brecht collaborator, and member of the Council for a Democratic Germany.[64]

As a result of Budenz's testimony, Gerhart and Hanns Eisler were called to testify. Gerhart refused, but Hanns agreed to cooperate with the committee. Hanns was called because he was chairman of the International Music Bureau, which HUAC believed to be "a section of the Communist International," and because the committee believed, although wrongly, that Hanns entered the United States after Eleanor Roosevelt intervened in his behalf. The committee's purpose in mentioning Eleanor Roosevelt was to discredit her and the deceased president. HUAC members quizzed Eisler about his musical scores and poetry, and his work in Hollywood. The committee learned that Eisler had written musical scores for several Hollywood films, including *Scandal in Paris, Jealousy*, and *So Well Remembered*. Eisler's testimony led HUAC to inquire further about the employment of Communists in the film industry. HUAC's investigations focused on Bertolt Brecht, former OSS psychwarrior Abraham Polonsky, John Howard Lawton, Ring Lardner, Jr., Dalton Trumbo, and others, who were first subpoenaed and then blacklisted. During the investigation, Ronald Reagan testified about Communist activities in the Screen Actors Guild.[65]

HUAC's investigations did not focus on the Free Germany Committee or its fraternal organizations, for they disbanded before HUAC convened its public hearings. The Moscow committee was officially disbanded on November 2, 1945, although it disintegrated in practice months earlier. Right-wing officers refused to cooperate with the Soviets except by broadcasting desertion orders to German soldiers. After the Reich capitulated, they became increasingly uncooperative with, and critical of, Communist members of the Free Germany committee. When the Soviet Union allowed Communists and sympathizers to return to Soviet-occupied Germany, the right-wing officers were kept in POW camps. Some were even tried for war crimes. General von Seydlitz was tried, convicted, and sentenced to death for his crimes. His death sentence was reduced to twenty-five years in prison, but he was released after serving seven years. General Paulus was also kept in detention after the war ended. He was released in 1953.

The U.S. Office of Strategic Services was disbanded six weeks earlier than the Free Germany Committee. Executive Order 9621, signed by President Harry Truman on September 20, 1945, terminated OSS and dispersed its branches. The Research and Analysis (R & A) branch was transferred to the State Department; the other branches were transferred to the War Department. The termination order was signed despite attempts by General Donovan to keep his organization intact and functioning as a postwar agency. In December 1943, Donovan sent a proposal to the Joint Chiefs that suggested OSS be maintained after the war as a peacetime intelligence agency under JCS jurisdiction. In fall 1944, he sent a different proposal to President Roosevelt, the Joint Chiefs, and Joint Intelligence Committee. This proposal recommended that the postwar intelligence agency report directly to the president rather than the military. Donovan's proposal received a cold response from the Joint Chiefs and the Federal Bureau of Investigation, which got wind of it from Donovan's longtime foes in military intelligence. The Joint Chiefs and the FBI feared that Donovan's proposed intelligence agency would encroach upon their jurisdictions. In February 1945, Donovan's proposal was leaked to the press—probably by FBI director J. Edgar Hoover. Headlines in Republican newspapers like the *Chicago Tribune* denounced the proposed agency as a "peacetime New Deal Gestapo" and a "New Deal version of the OGPU." Criticism of Donovan's proposal was so intense that it was scrapped by President Roosevelt and his successor, Harry Truman.[66]

Before OSS was disbanded, it was slowly down-sized. After the capitulation of Germany, OSS personnel who were not given postwar administrative responsibilities or reassigned to the Asian theater were relieved of their duties. Creekmore Fath, a member of OSS and friend of Henry Wallace, former vice president and secretary of commerce, complained that the Wall Street attorneys who headed OSS were systematically relieving liberals of their duties, while keeping anti-New Dealers in the agency. Fath decried "the speed at which Colonel Donovan's outfit is growing reactionary."[67]

Although liberals and leftists were relieved of their duties in OSS's operational branches during summer 1945, leftists remained firmly entrenched in the Research and Analysis branch. Well-known leftists in the branch included Maurice Halperin, Paul Baran, Paul Sweezy, Cora Dubois, Herbert Marcuse, and Irving Goldman. When R & A was transferred to the State Department, many of the leftists went with it. Maurice Halperin became head of the Latin American research and analysis division of the State Department. Irving Goldman became his assistant. Cartographer Leo Drozdoff also went to the State Department, as did Carl Marzani and Leonard Mims. These leftists in the State Department attracted the attention of HUAC. The investigation that the House committee launched was ruthless. As a result of the investigation, Maurice Halperin went into exile, and Carl Marzani was sentenced to prison for lying under oath about his Communist affiliations. The committee's investigation suggested that OSS was the most "thoroughly infiltrated" of any wartime government agency.[68]

HUAC's investigations, in addition to ruining the lives of many innocent people, created an atmosphere of distrust in Washington. All government employees were required to sign loyalty oaths. Individuals with leftist leanings were either fired from or not hired by most agencies. Likewise, when the Central Intelligence Agency was created, only political conservatives and moderates were hired. The moderates in the agency became targets of Senator Joseph McCarthy in 1953. Anyone with outright or suspected leftist sympathies was kept out. This gave the CIA a very different complexion than its predecessor, the OSS.[69]

HUAC and later Senate investigations had some very dramatic and unfortunate consequences for U.S. policy making by distorting officials' abilities to objectively analyze world events and formulate effective policies. These investigations reinforced the myth that there existed a monolithic Communist movement directed by Moscow. This myth became so tenaciously held by officials and intelligence analysts that they failed to recognize and exploit the conflict that emerged between China and the USSR in the late–1950s. The Sino-Soviet conflict was ten years old before U.S. policymakers reached the conclusion that it was real. The HUAC investigations also promoted the myth that Communist movements came to power solely through the use of fifth-column tactics. This implied that Communist governments in China, Yugoslavia, Vietnam, and the Soviet Union lacked popular support and remained in power only because they employed terror against their people. Guided by this belief, U.S. policymakers concluded that Communist leaders such as Mao Tse-tung and Fidel Castro could be overthrown if "encouragement" were given to the oppressed populations. The encouragement included such things as anti-Castro broadcasts beamed to Cuba from Radio Swan, coupled with a landing at the Bay of Pigs. The Bay of Pigs invasion and other CIA adventures that were based on false premises were doomed from the start.

# THE CIA AND THE "PEACETIME" PSYCHWAR STATIONS

After transfer to the State Department, OSS's Research and Analysis branch became the Interim Research and Intelligence Service (IRIS). Its director was Alfred McCormack, an Ivy League graduate who had been a special assistant to the secretary of war while in G–2. Although U.S. military leaders hoped to exert influence on foreign policy decisions by becoming the major supplier of intelligence information after the war, the opposite happened. Military influence was diminished rather than enhanced after the dissolution of OSS because it allowed the State Department to provide the president with intelligence through IRIS, bypassing the military. This caused the Joint Chiefs to oppose a proposal by McCormack to increase the size and scope of IRIS activities.

Opposition to making McCormack's unit the principal intelligence-gathering agency of the United States was also voiced by professionals in the State Department. Until the creation of IRIS, intelligence-gathering and dissemination in the State Department was the responsibility of regional departments. The creation of IRIS threatened the authority of these departments and produced an outcry from long-time State Department employees. The employees viewed IRIS with suspicion, not only because it threatened their authority, but because many members of IRIS were suspected of being Communists or sympathizers. Their suspicions were not alleviated by McCormack's leadership of IRIS, for he was accused of being the head of a pro-Communist faction in G–2.[70]

As a result of pressure, innuendo, and the complicated structure that McCormack proposed for his intelligence-gathering department, President Truman accepted a JCS proposal to create a new intelligence unit called the Central Intelligence Group (CIG), which was under a director of Central Intelligence. CIG was created by executive order on January 22, 1946. The new group replaced IRIS as the principal intelligence agency of the United States, for it assigned CIG the responsibility of obtaining and synthesizing intelligence generated by State, the military, the War Department, and other government agencies such as the FBI, which still operated in Latin America. CIG was composed of individuals drawn from several government agencies, over whom the Director of Central Intelligence had no power in personnel matters, pay, or travel. The structure of the organization, while unworkable, was supported by the War Department, the military, and other agencies that wanted to avert being displaced by a central intelligence agency.[71]

CIG and its director reported to the National Intelligence Authority, which consisted of the secretaries of State, War, and Navy, and a personal representative of the president. As his personal representative, Truman chose Admiral William Leahy. Truman appointed Rear Admiral Sidney

Souers as CIG director. Souers was a Democratic party activist and businessman in Missouri, Truman's home state, before the war. Souers remained director of Central Intelligence for five months. He was replaced by Air Force General Hoyt Vandenberg, who was replaced after one year by Rear Admiral Roscoe Hillenkoetter.[72]

The intelligence agency was not the only defense-related agency with a high turnover rate among its leaders, or an unworkable organizational structure. There was little liaison between the army and navy, for they were under separate federal departments and secretaries. The JCS, like CIG, also suffered from a high turnover rate. Peace had the effect of undermining the wartime institutional structures that permitted information exchanges between the departments of War, Navy, and State. By 1947, there was no institution for the sole purpose of consultation or information-exchange on matters of national security.

These institutional problems were solved with the passage of Public Law 253 on July 26, 1947. This law, called the National Security Act of 1947, consolidated all branches of the armed forces into a National Military Establishment. Within this establishment, the army, navy, and air force had their own secretaries, but they reported to a single head. An amendment to the National Security Act was passed in 1949 that renamed the National Defense Establishment the Department of Defense, and elevated the secretary of defense to cabinet rank. Public Law 253 also created the National Security Council (NSC) and the Central Intelligence Agency.

The NSC is the institution charged with advising the president in matters relating to national security. Its members are the president, vice president, secretary of state, and secretary of defense. The chairman of the JCS and director of the CIA attend NSC meetings as advisers. Public Law 253 places the CIA under the NSC. In addition, the law specifies that the CIA is to "correlate and evaluate intelligence" but is permitted to "perform such other functions and duties related to the national security as the National Security Council may from time to time direct." It is the latter clause that allows the CIA to be involved in covert propaganda activities.

Portions of Public Law 253 dealing with the CIA were amended by the Central Intelligence Agency Act of 1949. The 1949 legislation gave the organization a structure, budget, and a cloak of secrecy. The CIA was masked in secrecy by sections 7 and 10 of the act. Section 7 exempted the agency from disclosing information about the "organization, functions, names, official titles, salaries, or number of personnel employed." Section 10 gave the CIA the ability to spend its funds "without regard to the provisions of law and regulations relating to the expenditure of Government funds."[73]

The newly created CIA had two divisions: the Office of Special Operations (OSO) and the Office of Policy Coordination (OPC). OSO was headed by former OSS counterintelligence agent James Angleton and ex-FBI agent William Harvey. The division's responsibilities were the collecting and synthesizing of intelligence information. Despite its name, OPC was charged with conducting paramilitary and psychological operations, not policy coordination. The OPC chief was Frank Wisner, a former OSS operative from John Rankin's home state of Mississippi. Wisner chose another former OSSer, Franklin Lindsay, as his deputy. Lindsay headed the OSS mission in Yugoslavia at the time when relations between the United States and Tito's partisans soured. Wisner and Lindsay recruited other former OSS comrades into OPC. Their recruits included Albert Seitz and Lyle Munson. Seitz was an OSS agent in Yugoslavia who sided with the Chetniks against Tito. He was delighted with HUAC's exposure of the "leftish Americans in our government" and the political shift to the right in the 1950s. Munson was a former OSS agent who supported Chiang Kai-shek against Mao. After resigning from the CIA, Munson testified before a Senate committee investigating the Institute of Pacific Relations. During testimony at the Senate hearing, he charged that State Department official John P. Davies, Jr. tried to get Communists into the Office of Policy Coordination as advisers on Chinese affairs. Among the "Communists" named by Munson was former OSS research officer and China expert, John K. Fairbank.[74]

One of Wisner's first actions was to implement a suggestion made by Secretary of State Dean Acheson. Acheson suggested to former OSS intelligence chief Allen Dulles and several former State Department officials that the United States sponsor a radio station for broadcasting anti-Communist programs to Eastern and Central Europe. The former officials were Joseph Grew and Dewitt Poole. Grew was a former ambassador and undersecretary of state who sat on the policy board for OSS's Collingwood and Green's operations. He was intimately familiar with OSS's clandestine radio operations in Asia. Dewitt Poole was the head of OSS's foreign nationalities branch. It was he who warned General Donovan and the Joint Chiefs that the formation of the Free Germany Committee represented a threat "to the whole outcome of the war." Grew and Poole contacted Dulles, and laid the groundwork for the National Committee for a Free Europe, Inc., an ostensibly private, anti-Communist organization. The National Committee for a Free Europe was similar to the Free Germany Committee established by Moscow during the war. The Free Germany and Free Europe committees claimed to operate without official sponsorship, included in their ranks exiles who alleged that they were free to speak only because they were in exile, and operated radio stations named for their organizations. The Free Germany

Committee operated Radio Free Germany; the Free Europe Committee operated Radio Free Europe. In reality, both the Free Germany and Free Europe committees were government-financed organizations. The Free Europe Committee received its funds through Frank Wisner's department at the CIA.[75]

Grew, Poole, and Dulles recruited other prominent citizens into the Free Europe Committee. Among them were Adolph Berle, who was assistant secretary of state between 1938 and 1944. During his tenure as assistant secretary, he constantly sided with the FBI and G–2 in their conflicts with OSS. The committee was officially founded on June 2, 1949 with Grew as chairman, Poole as executive secretary, and Dulles as president. Its members, in addition to exiled Europeans, corporate chieftains and former government officials, included former generals Dwight Eisenhower and Walter Bedell Smith. Bedell Smith was Eisenhower's Psychological Warfare Branch liaison during the Husky invasion. He became director of the CIA in 1950 and assistant secretary of state in 1953. C. D. Jackson, the vice-president of Time, Inc. who was the civilian leader of the Psychological Warfare Branch under General Eisenhower, was selected as president of the committee's radio station, Radio Free Europe. The station signed on July 4, 1950 from a shortwave transmitter in Lampertheim, Germany.[76]

The success of the covert plan to launch Radio Free Europe led directly to other campaigns. In 1950, the American Committee for Freedom for the Peoples of the USSR was founded. This committee sponsored broadcasts to the Soviet Union over Radio Liberty using Radio Free Europe facilities. Like the Free Europe committee, it was CIA-financed. In 1953, President Eisenhower created a psychological warfare committee to deal with the "threat" posed by Guatemalan president Jacobo Arbenz and other foreign opponents of U.S. policies. Because Arbenz appointed a few Communists to cabinet posts in his administration and sought the nationalization of the U.S.-owned United Fruit Company, President Eisenhower considered him to be a Communist. Eisenhower's view was consistent with the view promulgated by John Rankin and others in HUAC—that all leftists were Soviet agents. Members of Eisenhower's psychwar committee included Allen Dulles, who replaced Bedell Smith as CIA director; Bedell Smith, who was then-assistant secretary of state; John Foster Dulles, Allen's brother and secretary of state; C. D. Jackson; and John Moors Cabot, assistant secretary of state for inter-American affairs. The Dulles brothers, Bedell Smith, and Cabot had financial links to the United Fruit Company. Adolph Berle attended strategy meetings of Eisenhower's committee, although he was not formally a committee member. This group recommended Arbenz's ouster. A plan to overthrow the Guatemalan president was developed by Frank Wisner and his deputy, Richard Bissell. The plan consisted of sponsoring a guerrilla army that would use a clandestine radio station called "Voice of Liberation" as one of its weapons.[77]

Two CIA operatives chosen to implement the psychwar committee's recommendation were E. Howard Hunt and David Atlee Phillips. Hunt was a fanatical right-winger who served with OSS in China. In the early 1970s, he worked with the covert-action team that was caught bugging the Democratic party headquarters at the Watergate office complex in Washington. Phillips became a part-time CIA operative in 1950 while living in Chile. He learned black propaganda techniques from a CIA specialist who had been in the Morale Operations branch of OSS. Hunt and Phillips taught psychwar radio tactics to supporters of Col. Carlos Castillo Armas at a CIA base in Miami. The students broadcast from the Voice of Liberation under the watchful eye of their CIA instructors using transmitters in Nicaragua and on Swan Island. Like the covert plan to start and finance Radio Free Europe, this plan succeeded. On June 27, 1954 Arbenz resigned and was replaced by Col. Castillo Armas. The new president outlawed the Guatemalan Communist party and arrested its members. Although Castillo Armas was assassinated in 1957, a long line of military officers succeeded him as president. Like Castillo Armas, they used imprisonment and torture to suppress the political left.

The strategy employed in Guatemala was repeated in 1960–61 in an attempt to oust Fidel Castro as leader of Cuba. Under the direction of Allen Dulles and Richard Bissell, a CIA-controlled corporation called the Gibraltar Steamship Company was created. The president of the company was Thomas Dudley Cabot, a former president of the United Fruit Company and brother of Thomas Moors Cabot. The company operated an ostensibly commercial radio station located on Swan Island that broadcast anti-Castro programs to Cuba. The station was called "Radio Swan." Its broadcasts were supervised by E. Howard Hunt and David Atlee Phillips. As in Guatemala, the broadcasts were coordinated with a military campaign—the Bay of Pigs invasion. But unlike in Guatemala, the plan failed. The anti-Castro invasion force was routed. As a result of the plan's failure, Allen Dulles was forced to resign as Director of the CIA. He was replaced by John McCone, head of the Atomic Energy Commission. Richard Helms replaced Richard Bissell as head of the CIA's clandestine services. Helms was an OSS veteran. Theodore Shackley, the CIA station chief in Berlin who coordinated activities with Radio Free Europe, was brought in to head the CIA team that was formed to conduct subsequent covert actions against Castro's government. Shackley's assistant for these anti-Castro operations was Thomas Clines.[78]

In 1966, in the midst of the Vietnam war, Richard Helms was named Director of the CIA. His station chief in Laos was Theodore Shackley, who in addition to organizing the Laotian Armée Clandestine, supervised the CIA communication complex from which numerous clandestine radio stations, including the black version of the "Voice of the National United Front of Kampuchea," broadcast. Shackley brought Clines with him to Laos. There they met Richard V. Secord, an air force officer assigned to work with the CIA. After retiring from the CIA, Clines and Shackley worked as consultants for retired General Secord's Stanford Trading Company, which in addition to buying arms for the Nicaraguan contras with monies diverted from covert U.S. arms sales to Iran, purchased a ship and equipment for making clandestine radio broadcasts to Libya and Cuba. These actions were approved by then-CIA director William Casey, another OSS veteran.[79]

In addition to sharing some personnel and tactics, the OSS and CIA also shared a belief in the existence of a fifth column. In the case of OSS, it was a belief in the existence of an international Nazi fifth column directed from Berlin. OSS hoped to build its own fifth column that would combat that of the Nazis. The fifth column that OSS attempted to build was composed of democrats opposed to nazism and fascism. CIA leaders also believe that there is a fifth column, but that it is composed of Communists who are directed by Moscow. The CIA, like its predecessor, seeks to create its own fifth column to counter the Moscow-inspired one. However, the CIA's troops are invariably disgruntled military men or members of the elite who want to preserve the status quo. This was true in Guatemala, Cuba, Cambodia, and Nicaragua, where CIA-backed clandestine radio stations and armies operated. These CIA-supported troops are invariably opponents rather than supporters of democracy, for democracy would strip them of the privileges that they seek to retain.

There was, however, no Nazi fifth column undermining democracy in the United States, Great Britain, France, or elsewhere prior to World War II, just as there was no international Communist fifth column conspiring to seize power after World War II. Where the CIA sees agents of Moscow, there are only indigenous radicals who oppose the status quo. The CIA world view concerning the "international Communist enemy" is the outgrowth of the postwar hysteria brought about by congressional opponents of the New Deal, integration, and democracy, such as John Rankin. For this reason, the CIA's history and ideology are more closely related to that of the House Un-American Activities Committee than to its predecessor, the OSS.

## NOTES

1. "Memo on Soviet Psychological Warfare to Lt. Col. Kenneth D. Mann" (April 7, 1944), Project ETO Soviet Psychological Warfare, *OSS*, entry 139, box 176.

2. For a discussion of the shortcomings of U.S. propaganda strategy, see Donald V. McGranahan, "U.S. Psychological Warfare Policy," *Public Opinion Quarterly* (Fall 1946), pp. 446–50.

3. *FBIS*, October 12, 1944, p. E3.

4. "Letter and Memo from John C. Wiley to the President" (August 11, 1943), *FDR*, President's Secretaries Files, box 167.

5. "OSS Official Dispatch, Bern" (pre-October 28, 1943), OSS Numbered Bullentin 72, *FDR*, Map Room Files, Box 72.

6. "Red Station Broadcasts to Europe 'From Milan'," *New York Times*, April 15, 1937, p. 9.

7. "PID Research Units: Underground Broadcasting Stations, Part II," *PRO*, FO898/52.

8. *FBIS*, March 21, 1945, p. BB3. This ghosting technique was probably developed by the German Communist party, which used it first in 1932. See "Hindenburg on Radio Warns on Burdening Reich Too Heavily," *New York Times*, January 1, 1932, p. 1.

9. *FBIS*, January 31, 1944, p. AAA1–2.

10. "Goebbels Hits Der Snag," *Time*, September 8, 1941, pp. 19–20; " 'The Man from the Clouds,' "*Times* (of London), August 25, 1941, p. 4; Charles Rolo, *Radio Goes to War* (New York: G. P. Putnam's Sons, 1942), pp. 202–5; *BBC*, October 15, 1941, p. 1A (xviii); *FBIS*, February 7, 1944, p. AAA2.

11. "PID Research Units: Underground Broadcasting Stations, Part II," *PRO*, FO 898/52; McGranahan, "U.S. Psychological Warfare Policy"; "Germany: Reaction to Allied Psychological Warfare" (April 5, 1944), OSS Numbered Bulletin 115, *FDR*, Map Room Files, box 73.

12. The Norske Freedom Station was silenced at the end of 1942 when the exiled Norwegian government, after discovering that it originated in Great Britain, demanded control over its operation. See Charles Cruickshank, *The Fourth Arm* (London: Davis-Poynter, 1977), pp. 54–56. No discussion of the Bradlo station has yet appeared in print, but the PWE's Czech station, "Nazdar Radio," is described in René Kraus, *Europe in Revolt* (New York: Macmillan Company, 1942), pp. 265–68.

13. "Weekly Propaganda Directive" (July 28, 1944), *OWI*, reel 5, no. 01102; "Sikorski Charges Plot by Russians," *New York Times*, February 22, 1943, p. 13; Stefan Korbonski, *Fighting Warsaw* (London: George Allen & Unwin, Ltd., 1956), pp. 200–14.

14. For a unique interpretation of the Comintern's end, see "Davies Hails Coup in Comintern's End," *New York Times*, August 1, 1943, p. 15. Joseph Davies, the former ambassador to the USSR, described the Comintern's dissolution as a triumph of Stalin's "wise leadership" over Trotsky's legacy.

15. Franco Monteleone, *La radio Italiana nel periodo fascista* (Venice: Marsilio Editori, 1976), pp. 179–81; Marcel Plans, "Radio Espanya Independent," *Nous Horitzons* (Barcelona) 49/50 (December/January) 1978/79, pp. 101–8.

16. Allan Merson, *Communist Resistance in Nazi Germany* (London: Lawrence and Wisehart, 1985), p. 237; "PID Research Units: Underground Broadcasting Stations, Part II," *PRO*, FO 898/52.

17. Eric Boehm, "The 'Free Germans' in Soviet Psychological Warfare," *Public Opinion Quarterly* 14 (Summer 1950), pp. 285–95.

18. Bodo Scheurig, *Free Germany* (Middletown, Conn.: Wesleyan University Press, 1984), pp. 35–6; OSS Research and Analysis Branch, " 'Free Germany': An Experiment in Political Warfare," *Donovan*, box 101B, vol. 7, p. 10.

19. Scheurig, *Free Germany*.

20. Scheurig, *Free Germany*, pp. 42–43.

21. For example, see "Here Are Signers of German Manifesto," *Daily Worker*, July 22, 1943, pp. 1, 6. There are conflicting reports as to whether Erich Weinert, the Free Germany chairman, was a KPD member. The report of Alfred Kantorowicz, " 'Free Germany' " in Moscow," *Free World* 17 (February) 1944, pp. 149–56 suggests that Weinert was not a KPD member. Kantorowicz was a Communist who helped operate the original Freiheitssender that broadcast from Spain. The OSS Research and Analysis Branch, " 'Free Germany': An Experiment in Political Warfare," *Donovan*, box 101B, vol. 7, describes Weinert as a "fellow traveller," not a Communist. However, Ruth Fischer, *Stalin and German Communism* (Cambridge: Harvard University Press, 1948), reports that Weinert was a longtime Communist party member.

22. "Text of Manifesto Issued by Free Germany Committee in Moscow," *New York Times*, August 1, 1943, p. 17; "Full text of Manifesto," *Daily Worker*, July 22, 1943, pp. 1, 6.

23. Scheurig, *Free Germany*, pp. 60–1.

24. "Free Germans?" *Time*, October 30, 1944, p. 30. Radio Free Germany also carried reports that originated on the Volkssender. See *FBIS*, February 12, 1945, p. B4.

25. OSS Research and Analysis Branch, " 'Free Germany': An Experiment in Political Warfare," *Donovan*, box 101B, vol. 7.

26. *FBIS*, July 26, 1943, p. H5; July 24, 1943, pp. F2–3; July 27, 1943, p. D14.

27. "Free Germany Warns of Soviet Invasion," *New York Times*, April 2, 1944, p. 5; *FBIS*, December 2, 1943, pp. M1–2; December 13, 1943, p. J2.

28. The leaflet is depicted in Kantorowicz, " 'Free Germany' in Moscow," p. 150.

29. *FBIS*, March 29, 1944, p. M1; Eric Boehm, "The 'Free Germans' in Soviet Psychological Warfare," p. 293.

30. *FBIS*, February 12, 1945, pp. B3–4; August 29, 1944, pp. B1–2.

31. Hugh Trevor-Roper, ed., *Final Entries 1945: The Diaries of Joseph Goebbels* (New York: Avon Books, 1979), p. 174; Louis Lochner, ed., *The Goebbels Diaries* (New York: Award Books, 1971), pp. 578–79.

32. Another German response was to create a "Committee for the Liberation of the People of Russia" and a "Russian Liberation Army" under captured Russian General Vlasov. Broadcasts of Vlasov's committee were beamed to the Soviet Union, just as Radio Free Germany broadcast to the Reich. See "PWE: German Propaganda and the Germans" (October 9, November 20, December 27, 1944), *Lerner*, box 33, folders 9–11.

33. Klaus Volker, *Brecht Chronicle* (New York: Seabury Press, 1975), pp. 121–24; James K. Lyon, *Bertolt Brecht in America* (Princeton: Princeton University Press, 1980), pp. 275–80.

34. Martin Esslin, *Brecht: A Choice of Evils* (London: Eyre and Spottiswoode, 1974), pp. 59, 102; Representative in Great Britain of the Freedom Station, *Freedom Calling* (London: Frederick Muller, 1939).

35. "East Wind," *Time*, August 2, 1943, pp. 28–29.

36. "German Revolt Asked by Exile Group in Russia," *New York Herald Tribune*, June 22, 1943, p. 6.

37. Ensign Andrew Roth, " 'Free Germany' Aims at Nazi Morale," *New York Times*, September 5, 1943, p. E4.

38. Alexander Werth, "Free German Move Not a Soviet Plan," *New York Times*, July 24, 1943, p. 6.

39. "Postwar Germany," *Washington Post*, July 24, 1943, p. 5X.

40. "Warning by Stalin to Allies Is Seen," *New York Times*, July 29, 1943, p. 6.

41. *FBIS*, July 27, 1943, p. D14.

42. Trevor-Roper, *Final Entries: The Diaries of Joseph Goebbels*, p. 174.

43. "Memorandum for the Joint U.S. Chiefs of Staff. Subject: Manifesto to German People by Moscow National Committee of Free Germany" (August 6, 1943), *Donovan*, box 82A, vol. 26.

44. "Memorandum of Dr. James Grafton Rogers, July 26, 1943, Referring to the National Committee of Freies Deutschland," *FDR*, Map Room Files, box 78, folder 2.

45. "Memorandum for the Joint Chiefs of Staff. Subject: Manifesto to German People by Moscow National Committee of Free Germany."

46. "Letter and Memo from John Wiley to the President" (August 11, 1943), *FDR*, President's Secretaries Files, box 167.

47. "Memorandum to the Director of Strategic Services and Secretary of State" (July 23, 1943), *FDR*, Map Room Files, box 72, OSS Numbered Bulletins (R & A); "Memorandum to Director of Strategic Services and Secretary of State" (July 27, 1943), *FDR*, Map Room Files, box 78, folder 2.

48. "Germany: Suggestions of German Labor Leaders for Allied Psychological Warfare" (April 29, 1944), *FDR*, Map Room Files, box 73, OSS Numbered Bulletin 121.

49. "Central and Western Europe: Prospects of Russian Dominance" (January 11, 1944), *FDR*, Map Room files, box 73, OSS Numbered Bulletin 94.

50. "Weekly Propaganda Directive—Poland" (July 28, 1944), *OWI*, reel 5, no. 01102.

51. Kantorowicz, " 'Free Germany' in Moscow," pp. 151–52.

52. "Stalin's Germans," *Time*, February 12, 1945, p. 27.

53. "Russia—Misunderstanding," *Time*, March 5, 1945, p. 32.

54. " 'Free Germans' Seen Distrusted by Russia," *New York Times*, February 15, 1945, p. 4.

55. "U.S. Said to Be on Watch for Move by Soviet to Back Captive Generals," *New York Times*, January 28, 1945, p. 4.

56. 79th Congress, 1st Session, *Congressional Record*, vol. 91 (1945): 10049; "House Report Hits Red-Front Groups," *New York Times*, June 8, 1946, p. 2; U.S. House Committee on Un-American Activities, *Thirty Year of Treason* (New York: Viking Press, 1971), pp. 73–109; Jan Needle and Peter Thomson, *Brecht* (Oxford, England: Basil Blackwell, 1981), pp. 58–59.

57. 79th Congress, 1st Session, *Congressional Record*, vol. 91 (1945): 11–5.

58. Lawrence S. Wittner, *Cold War America* (New York: Holt, Rinehart and Winston, 1978), p. 90.

59. 79th Congress, 2nd Session, *House of Representatives Report No. 2233* (June 7, 1946), "Investigation of Un-American Activities and Propaganda," pp. 14–16; "House Report Hits Red-Front Groups," *New York Times*, June 8, 1946, p. 2.

60. "Rankin Condemns Stimson and Aides," *New York Times*, July 20, 1945, p. 9; "Army Bars 'Reds' from Many Duties," *New York Times*, March 9, 1946, p. 2.

61. U.S. Congressional Committee on Un-American Activities (80th Congress, 2nd Session), *Interim Report on Communist Espionage in the United States* (Washington, DC: U.S. Government Printing Office, 1948), pp. 5–7.

62. This traditional view of the cold war's start can be found in Arthur M. Schlesinger, Jr., "Origins of the Cold War," *Foreign Affairs*, 46 (October 1967): pp. 22–35, 42–50, 52; Adam Ulam, *Expansion and Coexistence* (New York: Praeger, 1968), pp. 405–55; and numerous other sources.

63. "Vote to Put Barsky in House Contempt," *New York Times*, March 29, 1946, p. 16; "17 Foes of Franco Voted in Contempt," *New York Times*, April 17, 1946, p. 29; "House Group Calls Browder," *New York Times*, September 20, 1945, p. 24.

64. Robert K. Carr, *The House Committee on Un-American Activities 1945– 1950* (Ithaca: Cornell University Press, 1952), pp. 306–7; Michael Sayer and Albert Kahn, *Sabotage! The Secret War Against America* (New York: Harper and Brothers, 1942), p. 249; "Calls Communists Here 'Soviet Spies,' " *New York Times*, April 4, 1946, p. 19; "Eisler Subpoena Ordered in House," *New York Times*, October 22, 1946, p. 18.

65. U.S. House Committee on Un-American Activities, *Thirty Years of Treason;* "Federal Jury Indicts 10 Film Men on Contempt of Congress Charges," *New York Times*, December 6, 1947, pp. 1, 13. Ronald Reagan's testimony is in U.S. Congressional Committee on Un-American Activities (80th Congress, 2nd session), *Hearings Regarding Communist Infiltration of the Motion Picture Industry* (Washington, DC: U.S. Government Printing Office, 1947), pp. 213–18.

66. Walter Trohan, "New Deal Plans Super Spy System," *Chicago Tribune*, February 9, 1945, pp. 1, 10 and "Super-Spy Idea Denounced as New Deal OGPU," *Chicago Tribune*, February 10, 1945, pp. 1, 16. These articles can be contrasted with an objective report entitled "Donovan Upheld on Peace Spy Plan," *New York Times*, February 13, 1945, p. 14.

67. Jonathon Morton Blum, ed., *The Price of Vision: The Diary of Henry A. Wallace* (Boston: Houghton Mifflin Co., 1973), p. 444.

68. James Burnham, *The Web of Subversion* (New York: John Day Co., 1954), pp. 72, 119; U.S. Congressional Committee on Un-American Activities (80th Congress, 2nd Session), *Interim Report on Communist Espionage in the United States Government*, pp. 5–7.

69. Richard Harris Smith, *OSS* (Berkeley: University of California Press, 1981), pp. 366–68, acknowledges the influx of conservative anti-Communists into the CIA during its first years of existence, but contends that Allen Dulles eventually brought liberals into the agency. To support his point, Smith mentions CIA support for non-Communist leftists in many areas of the world. Smith neglects to mention the CIA's support for rightists during the same period, and its numerous and sometimes successful attempts to oust non-Communist leftists such as Jacobo Arbenz of Guatemala, Mohammad Mosaddeg of Iran, and Patrice Lumumba of the Congo.

70. Thomas Troy, *Donovan and the CIA* (Frederick, Md.: University Publications of America, 1984), pp. 311, 313.

71. "Executive Order 9690," *Federal Register*, vol. 11, no. 25 (February 5, 1946): 1337, 1339.

72. Brief histories of the CIA's origins can be found in David Wise and Thomas Ross, *The Invisible Government* (New York: Vintage Books, 1974), pp. 91–128; John Prados, *President's Secret Wars* (New York: William Morrow & Co., 1986), pp. 19–44, and previously cited books about Donovan and OSS.

73. "Public Law 253: Central Intelligence Agency Act of 1949" (June 20, 1949), *United States Statutes at Large*, vol. 63, pt. 1 (U.S. Government Printing Office, 1950), pp. 209–12.

74. U.S. Senate Committee on the Judiciary (82nd Congress, 2nd session), *Institute of Pacific Relations*, Report No. 2050 (Washington, DC: U.S. Government Printing Office, 1952), pp. 218–22; Albert B. Seitz, *Mihailovic, Hoax or Hero* (Columbus: Leigh House, 1953), pp. 2, 139.

75. "Added Voice," *Newsweek* July 17, 1950, pp. 48–49; "U.S. Reviews Role in Anti-Red Radio," *New York Times*, March 7, 1971, p. 10; "Subject: Chronology of RL, RFE and May Commission Inquiry" (April 8, 1960), U.S. President's Committee on Information Activities Abroad, *Declassified Documents* (1986), No. 3110; Victor Marchetti and John D. Marks, *The CIA and the Cult of Intelligence* (New York: Dell Publishing, 1975), pp. 174–78.

76. Prados, *President's Secret Wars*, pp. 34–35; Robert T. Holt, *Radio Free Europe* (Minneapolis: University of Minnesota Press, 1958), pp. 9–16; "The Needle," *Time*, January 29, 1951, p. 19.

77. Stephen Schlesinger and Stephen Kinzer, *Bitter Fruit: The Untold Story of the American Coup in Guatemala* (Garden City, N.Y.: Anchor Books, 1983); David Atlee Phillips, *The Night Watch* (New York: Atheneum, 1977), pp. 30–54.

78. Phillips, *The Night Watch*, pp. 85–111; "Brief History of Radio Swan," Department of Defense Report (5), *Declassified Documents* (1985), No. 01562; Prados, *Presidents' Secret Wars*, pp. 210–13.

79. Prados, *Presidents' Secret Wars*, pp. 282–84; "Ex-General Provided Arms Channel," *New York Times*, December 6, 1986, p. 7; "Retired General Emerges as Central Figure in Secret Talks," *New York Times*, December 9, 1986, pp. 1, 16; "Ex-CIA Officer Clines Emerges as Figure in Covert Security Council Operations," *Wall Street Journal*, January 2, 1987, pp. 2, 6; "Private Spy Agency," *New York Times*, July 11, 1987, pp. 1, 8.

# SELECTED
# BIBLIOGRAPHY

## ARCHIVAL RECORDS AND PAPERS

BBC              British Broadcasting Corporation Monitoring Service
                 Reports, Library of Congress (microfilm)

CBS              Columbia Broadcasting System Monitoring Reports,
                 Library of Congress (microfilm)

Donovan          William Donovan Papers, U.S. Army Military History
                 Institute, Carlisle Barracks, Pennsylvania

FBIS             The Federal Communications Commission's Foreign
                 Broadcast Intelligence Service Reports, Lehman
                 (Columbia University) and New York Public Libraries
                 (microfilm)

FCC              Radio Intelligence Division of Federal Communications
                 Commission archives, Record Group 173, National
                 Archives, Suitland, Maryland

FDR              Papers of President Franklin D. Roosevelt, FDR
                 Library, Hyde Park, New York

Hazeltine        Papers of Col. Charles Hazeltine, Psychological
                 Warfare Branch, Eisenhower Library, Abilene, Kansas

JCS              Records of the Joint Chiefs of Staff, Part 1: 1942–1945
                 (Frederick, Md.: University Publications of America
                 microfilm)

Lerner           Papers of Daniel Lerner, Hoover Institution, Stanford
                 University, Menlo Park, California

Linebarger       Paul Linebarger Papers, Hoover Institution, Stanford
                 University, Menlo Park, California

OSS             Record Group 226, Records of the Office of Strategic
                Services, The National Archives, Modern Military
                Branch, Washington, D.C.

OWI             Records of the Office of War Information, Pt. II:
                Overseas Programs (Frederick, Md.: University
                Publications of America microfilm)

PRO             British Public Records Office, Foreign Office Records,
                Richmond, Surrey, England

## BOOKS

*Army Times* Editors. *The Tangled Web* (Washington, D.C.: Robert B. Luce, Inc., 1963).

Balfour, Michael. *Propaganda in War and Peace 1939–1945* (Boston: Routledge & Kegan Paul, 1979).

Barrett, Edward W. *Truth Is Our Weapon* (New York: Funk & Wagnalls, 1953).

Becker, Howard P. *German Youth: Bond or Free* (London: Kegan Paul, Trench, Trubner & Company, 1946).

Bennett, Jeremy. *British Broadcasting and the Danish Resistance Movement 1940–1945* (Cambridge: The University Press, 1966).

Boelcke, Willi A., ed. *The Secret Conferences of Dr. Goebbels* (New York: E. P. Dutton & Company, 1970).

Briggs, Asa. *The War of Words* (London: Oxford University Press, 1970).

Brown, Anthony Cave, ed. *The Secret War Report of the OSS* (New York: Berkley Publishing, 1976), declassified July 17, 1975.

Brown, Anthony Cave. *Wild Bill Donovan, The Last Hero* (New York: Times Books, 1982).

Burnham, James. *The Web of Subversion* (New York: John Day Company, 1954).

Carlson, John Roy. *Undercover* (New York: E. P. Dutton & Company, 1943).

Carroll, Wallace. *Persuade or Perish* (Boston: Houghton Mifflin Company, 1948).

Childs, Harwood L. and John B. Whitton, eds. *Propaganda by Shortwave* (Princeton: Princeton University Press, 1942).

Cole, J. A. *Lord Haw-Haw & William Joyce* (New York: Farrar, Straus & Giroux, 1965).

Cruickshank, Charles. *The Fourth Arm* (London: Davis-Poynter, 1977).

Dalton, Hugh. *The Fateful Years* (London: Frederick Muller, 1957).

Daugherty, W. E. with Morris Janowitz, eds. *A Psychological Warfare Casebook* (Baltimore: Johns Hopkins University Press, 1958).

Delmer, Sefton. *Black Boomerang* (London: Secker & Warburg, 1962).

Donovan, William J. and Edgar Ansel Mowrer. *Fifth Column Lessons for America* (Washington, D.C.: American Council on Public Affairs, 1941).

Dunlop, Richard. *Donovan—America's Master Spy* (New York: Rand McNally & Company, 1982).

Erdmann, James M. *Leaflet Operations in the Second World War* (Denver: University of Denver, 1969).

Ettlinger, Harold. *The Axis on the Air* (New York: Bobbs-Merrill Company, 1943).

Farago, Ladislas. *The Game of the Foxes* (New York: David McKay Company, 1971).

Ford, Corey. *Donovan of OSS* (Boston: Little, Brown & Company, 1970).

Gale, Esson. *Salt for the Dragon* (East Lansing, Mich.: Michigan State College Press, 1953).

Grandin, Thomas. *The Political Uses of Radio* (New York: Arno Press Reprint, 1971, c. 1939).

Hanin, Eric M. *War on Our Minds: The American Mass Media in World War II* (University of Rochester: Unpublished Ph.D. Dissertation, 1977).

Harris, Elliot. *The "Un-American" Weapon: Psychological Warfare* (New York: M. W. Lads Publishing, 1967).

Howe, Ellic. *The Black Game* (London: Michael Joseph, 1982).

Jong, Louis de. *The German Fifth Column in the Second World War* (New York: Howard Fertig, 1973 [reprint]).

Langer, William L. *Our Vichy Gamble* (New York: Alfred A. Knopf, 1947).

Lean, E. Tangye. *Voices in the Darkness* (London: Secker & Warburg, 1943).

Lerner, Daniel. *Sykewar: Psychological Warfare against Nazi Germany* (Cambridge, Mass.: MIT Press, 1971).

Linebarger, Paul. *Psychological Warfare* (Washington, D.C.: Infantry Journal Press, 1948).

Lochner, Louis, ed. *The Goebbels Diaries* (New York: Award Books, 1971).

Lockhart, R. H. Bruce. *Comes the Reckoning* (London: Putnam, 1947).

Margolin, Leo. *Paper Bullets* (New York: Forbin Press, 1946).

McDonald, Elizabeth. *Undercover Girl* (New York: Macmillan Company, 1947).

Miles, Milton E. *A Different Kind of War* (Garden City, N.Y.: Doubleday & Company, 1967).

Moss, Norman. *The Pleasures of Deception* (London: Chatto & Windus, 1977).

Paddock, Alfred H. *U.S. Army Special Warfare* (Washington, D.C.: U.S. Government Printing Office, 1982).

Panfilov, A. *Broadcasting Pirates* (Moscow: Progress Publishers, 1981).

Phillips, David Atlee. *The Night Watch* (New York: Atheneum, 1977).

Pimlott, Ben, ed. *The Second World War Diary of Hugh Dalton* (London: Jonathon Cape, 1986).

Prados, John. *Presidents' Secret Wars* (New York: William Morrow & Company, 1986).

Psychological Warfare Division Supreme Headquarters Allied Expeditionary Force. *An Account of its Operations in the Western European Campaign 1944–1945* (Bad Homburg, Germany: SHAEF, October 1945).

Roetter, Charles. *The Art of Psychological Warfare* (New York: Stein & Day, 1974).

Rolo, Charles. *Radio Goes to War* (New York: G. P. Putnam's Sons, 1942).

Roosevelt, Kermit, ed. *War Report of the OSS (Office of Strategic Services)*, vol. 1 (New York: Walker Press, 1976), declassified July 17, 1975.

Roosevelt, Kermit, ed. *The Overseas Targets: War Report of the OSS (Office of Strategic Services)*, vol. 2 (New York: Walker Press, 1976), declassified July 17, 1975.

Sayers, Michael and Albert Kahn. *Sabotage! The Secret War against America* (New York: Harper & Brothers, 1942).

Scheurig, Bodo. *Free Germany* (Middletown, Conn.: Wesleyan University Press, 1984).

Seth, Ronald. *The Truth Benders* (London: Leslie Frewin, 1969).

Smith, Bradley F. *The Shadow Warriors* (New York: Basic Books, 1983).

Smith, Richard Harris. *OSS* (Los Angeles: University of California Press, 1972).

Soley, Lawrence C. and John S. Nichols. *Clandestine Radio Broadcasting* (New York: Praeger, 1987).

Stafford, David. *Britain and European Resistance, 1940–1945* (Toronto: University of Toronto Press, 1980).

Stuart, Campbell. *Secrets of Crewe House: The Story of a Famous Campaign* (New York: Hodder & Stoughton, 1920).

Stuart, Campbell. *Opportunity Knocks Once* (London: Collins, 1952).

Sweet-Escott, Bickham. *Baker Street Irregulars* (London: Methuen & Company, 1965).

Taylor, Edmond. *Awakening from History* (London: Chatto & Windus, 1971).

Taylor, Edmond. *The Strategy of Terror* (Boston: Houghton Mifflin Company, 1940).

Taylor, Fred, ed. *The Goebbels Diaries 1939–1941* (New York: G. P. Putnam's Sons, 1983).

Trevor-Roper, Hugh, ed. *Final Entries 1945: The Diaries of Joseph Goebbels* (New York: Avon Books, 1979).

Troy, Thomas. *Donovan and the CIA* (Frederick, Md.: University Publications of America, 1981).

United States Congress House Committee on Un-American Activities. *Thirty Years of Treason* (New York: Viking Press, 1971).

Warburg, James P. *Unwritten Treaty* (New York: Harcourt, Brace & Company, 1946).

West, Nigel. *MI6* (New York: Random House, 1983).

Wilhelm, Maria. *The Man Who Watched the Rising Sun* (New York: Franklin Watts, 1967).

Winkler, Allan M. *The Politics of Propaganda—The Office of War Information 1942–1945* (New Haven: Yale University Press, 1978).

Wittner, Lawrence S. *Cold War America* (New York: Holt, Rinehart & Winston, 1978).

Zacharias, Ellis M. *Secret Missions* (New York: G. P. Putnam's Sons, 1946).

## SELECTED ARTICLES

"Barrage on OWI," *Newsweek*, May 3, 1943, p. 36.

Becker, Howard. "The Nature and Consequences of Black Propaganda," *American Sociological Review* 14 (April 1949), pp. 221–35.

"Beamed to Europe: OWI's Propaganda Paves Way for Military Advances," *Newsweek*, September 27, 1943, pp. 73–74.

Boehm, Eric H. "The 'Free German' in Soviet Psychological Warfare," *Public Opinion Quarterly* 14 (Summer 1950), pp. 285–95.

"British-German Radio War," *Infantry Journal*, May/June 1947, pp. 36–39, 41–46.

Burger, H. H. "Operation Annie: Now it Can Be Told," *New York Times Magazine*, February 17, 1946, pp. 12–13, 48, 50.

"Congress Blast Against OWI Portends Assault on New Deal," *Newsweek*, February 22, 1943, pp. 25–26.

Durant, Henry and Ruth. "Lord Haw-Haw of Hamburg: 2. His British Audience," *Public Opinion Quarterly* 4 (September 1940), pp. 443–50.

"Goebbels Hits Der Snag," *Time*, September 8, 1941, pp. 19–20.

Hale, William Harlan. "Big Noise in Little Luxembourg," *Harper's*, April 1946, pp. 377–84.

Graves, Harold N. "Propaganda by Shortwave: Berlin Calling America," *Public Opinion Quarterly* 4 (December 1940), pp. 601–19.

Herz, Martin F. "Some Psychological Lessons from Leaflet Propaganda in World War II," *Public Opinion Quarterly* 9 (Fall 1949), pp. 471–86.

Jones, Edgar L. "Fighting with Words," *Atlantic*, August 1945, pp. 47–51.

Kantorowicz, Alfred. " 'Free Germany' in Moscow," *Free World* 17 (February 1944), pp. 149–56.

McClure, Robert A. "Psychological Warfare," *Army Navy Air Force Journal*, January 13, 1951, pp. 517, 537.

McGranahan, Donald V. "U.S. Psychological Warfare Policy," *Public Opinion Quarterly* 10 (Fall 1946), pp. 446–50.

Menefee, Selden C. "Japan's Psychological Warfare," *Social Forces* 21 (May 1943), pp. 425–36.

Michie, Allan A. "War as Fought by Radio," *Reader's Digest*, June 1940, pp. 17–21.

Miller, Moscrip, "Talking Them Out of It," *Collier's*, August 19, 1944, pp. 23, 72–73.

Morgan, Brewster. "Operation Annie," *Saturday Evening Post*, March 9, 1946, pp. 18–19, 121–24.

Padover, Saul K. "Psychological Warfare," *Headline Series* 86 (March-April 1951), pp. 3–56.

"Paging Mr. Durfee," *Newsweek*, August 9, 1943, pp. 42–43.

Painton, Frederick C. "Fighting With Confetti," *American Legion Magazine*, December 1943, pp. 24, 40, 42.

Pierce, R. Morris. "Radio's Part in Psychological Warfare," *Broadcasting*, October 25, 1943, pp. 11, 30.

Pringle, Henry F. "The 'Baloney Barrage' Pays Off," *Saturday Evening Post*, March 31, 1945, pp. 19, 78–79.

Rolo, Charles J. "The Strategy of War by Radio," *Harper's*, November 1940, pp. 640–49.

Rundt, S. J. "Guerrillas of the Radio War," *Redbook*, October 1942, pp. 58–59, 85–86.

Schuyler, H. Jr. "The Official Propaganda of Great Britain," *Public Opinion Quarterly* 3 (April 1939), pp. 263–71.

Sondern, Frederick, Jr. and Donald A. Coster. "But We Expected You at Dakar!" *American Legion Magazine*, August 1946, pp. 25–26, 49–51.

Stafford, David. "Britain Looks at Europe, 1940: Some Origins of S.O.E." *Canadian Journal of History* 10 (August 1975), pp. 233–48.

Stafford, David. "The Detonator Concept: British Strategy, SOE and European

Resistance after the Fall of France," *Journal of Contemporary History* 10 (April 1975), pp. 185–217.

Taylor, Edmond. "Political Warfare: A Sword We Must Unsheath," *Reporter*, September 14, 1961, pp. 27–31.

"U.S. Takes Over Short Waves to Win Air Propaganda War," *Newsweek*, October 9, 1942, p. 31.

# INDEX

Sun Myung Moon, 7
Supreme Headquarters Allied Expe-
ditionary Force (SHAEF), 32, 86
Surinam, 4, 5, 6
Swan Island, 1, 2, 171, 218, 223
Świt, 201–2
Syria, 83, 84

Tai Li, 159–60, 163–64, 172–77
Tallents, Stephen, 23, 34
Taylor, Edmond, 12–13, 58, 60, 65,
84, 86, 98, 124
Teheran Conference, 164, 199, 202
Texas, U.S.S. *See* USS Texas
Thailand, 2, 167, 179, 188–89
*This Is the Enemy*, 97
Thomas, J. Parnell, 45, 199, 214
Thompson, J. Walter (ad agency), 99,
125–26, 160, 161
Tigre People's Liberation Front, 5
Tillich, Paul, 210
Tiso, Josef, 49
Tito, Josef Broz, 7–8, 92, 149, 198,
221
Togliatti, Palmiro, 203
Tomkins, Peter, 86
Toombs, Alfred, 139, 140
Torch. *See* Operation Torch
Torgler, Ernst, 15
*Total Espionage*, 95
Toyama, Mitsuru, 172
Traitors of Stuttgart, 13
*Tribes of the Rif*, 85
Trivers, Barry, 127
*Trojan Horse in America*, 48
Truman, Harry S., 219–20
Trumbo, Dalton, 216
*Truth*, 203
Tulip plan, 168–69
Tunisia, 82, 91, 93–94, 98, 102, 104,
107–8, 138
Turkey, 7, 114
208 Committee, 4

Ulbricht, Walter, 204, 206
Ultra project, 50, 53, 83
Uncle Boo-hoo, 20

unconditional surrender, 103, 109–10,
132, 208, 212
*Underground*, 105
underground (French), 87, 88–91, 130
Unification Church, 7
Union of British Fascists, 19
Union of Polish Patriots, 198, 202,
211, 212–13
UNITA.. *See* National Union for the
Total Independence of Angola
United Fruit Company, 222, 223
United Nations, 91, 107, 108, 110
"Unknown Radio," 29
USSR, 5, 6, 7–9, 12, 14–15, 16, 20,
49, 56, 92, 138, 141, 145, 149, 215–
17, 218, 224; psychwar stations of,
7–9, 92, 197–213, 221; relations with
Poland, 92, 202
USS Texas, 85, 88, 89

Vanda, Charles, 114
Vandenberg, Hoyt, 220
Vanderbilt, William, 60
Vatis, Anastassious, 114
Vega project, 165–67, 169, 173, 183–
84, 188
Vessel Reports, 185
"Vicki," 127–28
Victor, Emmanuel, King, 101, 108–13,
208
Viertel, Berthold, 209
Vietnam, 3, 93, 218, 223
Voice of America, 32, 63–64, 84, 87,
126, 127
Voice of Brittany, 18
Voice of Democratic Kampuchea, 4
Voice of Iranian Toilers, 7
Voice of Liberation (Guatemala), 1, 2,
222–23
*Voice of Terror*, 22–23
Voice of the Arab Nation, 10
Voice of the Front, 200–1
Voice of the Islamic Revolution in Af-
ghanistan, 4
Voice of the Joint Resistance, 5
Voice of the Khmers, 5, 6
Voice of the Libyan People, 5

## ABOUT THE AUTHOR

LAWRENCE C. SOLEY is an associate professor at the University of Minnesota's School of Journalism and Mass Communication. He is the author of over sixty research articles and papers published in scholarly and professional journals dealing with journalism, mass communication, and advertising. He has also written numerous commentaries and articles for the mass media, many of which deal with psychwar and propaganda broadcasting. Dr. Soley is coauthor of *Clandestine Radio Broadcasting* (Praeger, 1987).